HUGHES

AFTER

HOWARD

Dave,

Fascinating to hear of your and our current background project!

[signature]

Feb 20 13

D. Kenneth Richardson

HUGHES

AFTER

HOWARD

THE STORY OF HUGHES AIRCRAFT COMPANY

Sea Hill Press
Santa Barbara

Sea Hill Press Inc.
P.O. Box 60301
Santa Barbara, California 93160
www.seahillpress.com
Design and Layout: Walter Sharp

Secound Printing 2012

Library of Congress Control Number: 2011926749

ISBN 978-0-9708050-8-9

Printed in the United States of America

This story is dedicated to the many thousands of team members who propelled the Hughes Aircraft Company into becoming a "national treasure" and the premier military electronics firm in the world. It is a tribute to their skill and dedication in creating unique complex devices and leading-edge technologies to serve the free world's military capabilities and to improve civilian lifestyles.

CONTENTS

FOREWORD

T HERE HAVE BEEN very few truly "blue chip" technology companies in the United States that are characterized by wide-ranging diversity
and the ability to meet difficult equipment performance challenges, with
interactive complexities. Primary among these was the Hughes Aircraft
Company, which Dean Wooldridge and I, along with the wonderful
team we were fortunate to recruit, were able to redirect from its singular
and sporadic aircraft tinkering into the fast-moving markets of advanced
electronics and guided missiles. This book fully describes the evolution
of a relatively obscure firm in California into what many proclaimed
was the world leader in military electronics, and which later became the
dominant developer and operator of communication satellites. My impressions of this firm first told in my book, *The Business of Science* (Farrar,
Straus and Giroux, 1988), are still valid today.

What eventually grew to be an astounding high-technology research
and development center was founded in 1946 in Southern California. It
became home to the largest family of technical professionals, both college graduates and PhDs, in any industrial facility—in its boom years
even exceeding the staff at the notable Bell Telephone Laboratories. By
winning almost all competitions, the newly oriented firm achieved a virtual monopoly in many critical military electronics and guided missile
technologies. For decades, every aircraft with the mission of intercepting
enemy bombers entering North America was equipped with high performance radars, computers, and weapons developed and manufactured by
that one source.

No military R&D effort received a higher priority in those years than
the projects to defend against a nuclear air strike. No military weapon
systems called for greater advances of technology. No group of scientists
and engineers received stronger support of their efforts by the United
States government. The key organization involved was neither part of the
government nor a publicly held corporation. It was the property of one
eccentric man, who was uneducated, uninformed about high technology, and virtually out of communication with the world. He was never a

participant in conceiving what was needed or in managing it. He did not have a security clearance; hence, he was only superficially aware of the company's essential projects. He never visited the laboratories where the research was being done.

How did this unique situation come to pass? Perhaps there was some similarity to the highly unlikely result of repeatedly tossing a coin, expecting a succession of heads with no intervening tails. However, the creation and growth of this unusual weapons-systems firm was quite different from the game of flipping a coin. It was not a statistical anomaly but the result of a series of odd events and timely coincidences: a national military urgency due to the growing Soviet threat; the post-World War II tendency of existing electronics corporations to focus on commercial markets; the plentitude of technical talent in the United States; the removal of Howard Hughes and his irrationalities from the scene; and the emergence of dynamic leaders with creative and long-range vision.

In the years after I left the company in 1953 to form with Dean Wooldridge what became TRW Inc., the Hughes Aircraft Company enlarged its span into every facet of defense electronics and elsewhere. It increased its staff six-fold and its revenues more than a dozen times in size. This expansion took place under the leadership of Pat Hyland, whose hiring I had strongly recommended to Howard Hughes and Allen Puckett, whom I had recruited earlier. They were supported by an enthusiastically motivated family of technical professionals.

Hughes and TRW, physically close-by in Southern California, pursued critical needs of the United States government. Both functioned with the same management methods and technical innovation, operating with great resilience to setbacks as well as attempting unusual business thrusts. We competed only a bit, recognizing the vital role each played in ensuring the security of our country. Because of mutual respect for the other firm, no destructive or hostile competitive maneuvering occurred.

I encourage the reader to savor the descriptions in this book of the many technologies presented as well as the unique management style that stimulated a large team of scientists and engineers to reach beyond previously perceived boundaries in electronics. The evolution of Hughes Aircraft Company is a story worth absorbing.

Dr. Simon Ramo
November 2010

PREFACE

J UST ABOUT EVERYONE, in the English-speaking world at least, has heard of Howard Hughes, his wealth, secrecy, and eccentricities. Few know that an experimental radio department begun as part of his small aircraft company transformed itself into the leading defense electronics firm in the United States, with more than 80,000 employees and hundreds of diverse products. Without Howard's participation in leadership or financial support—and even sometimes hindered by him—a high-technology family devised a unique management philosophy and operating style to become one of the most innovative organizations in the world. Because of its significant contributions to our country, Hughes Aircraft Company was in 1985 publicly proclaimed a national treasure.

Technical excellence was fundamental. Additionally, the company nurtured the creativity of its talented staff by adopting the culture of a research laboratory, which emphasized individual responsibility, freedom to explore, and teamwork across organizational lines. In doing so, it advanced the state of the art in military and civilian-use electronics and launched a new commercial industry, that of worldwide communications by satellite.

The company's rise to eminence was aided by five harmonious circumstances. First was the legacy of Howard Hughes relating to aircraft design—his insistence on innovation and his striving for perfection above all. Second was the competition for survival between the United States and the Soviet Union that created a well-funded demand for rapid and dramatic advancements in the performance of military hardware. Third was the superb quality of the staff, who were attracted by the technical challenges the company offered and who relished the intellectual and professional freedom found throughout the organization. Fourth was the cocoon of private ownership that sheltered management from short-term or frivolous demands by investment brokers and public stockholders. And last was the unusual management style and structure that fostered and rewarded individual creativity, set technical achievement above short-term financial gain, and strongly encouraged the sharing of knowledge throughout all segments of the firm.

This family propelled the company beyond the perceived limits in many fields of technology. Over the years, thousands of employees joined together to achieve spectacular breakthroughs in all forms of electronic and physical designs that delivered amazing progress in the pursuit of the world's security, scientific knowledge, and human well-being.

The public view of Hughes Aircraft Company has always been shrouded in mystery: its unique products were usually veiled by military security, and business results were masked by its private ownership. As you, the reader, will see, after 1953 Mr. Hughes had nothing to do with the company's later recognition as the foremost military electronics center in the world and the largest private employer in both California and Arizona. Because the enormous growth and diversification took place after his separation from any direct involvement, this book is appropriately titled *Hughes After Howard*. An unparalleled success story of a highly motivated family, it is a tribute to all the members of that remarkable team.

The company's dismemberment that began in 1996 is a most regrettable loss for the nation, but the contributions and creative qualities of Hughes Aircraft Company should be studied and remembered. Some achievements not to be forgotten are helping ensure the military stability of the free world; perfecting many technology bases at the heart of space-age and information-age consumer products; and establishing comprehensive worldwide communications networks using satellites.

I have written the book from the perspective of one who joined the company in 1952, and who served there for the next forty years, beginning as a hardware designer and retiring as president. It was my good fortune to participate in the remarkable expansion of Hughes Aircraft Company and to work with and observe many of those who made it possible. Descriptions of my own involvement are here to communicate a sense of familiarity, of what it was like within such an extraordinary organization.

This history of a company that accomplished miracles but became undone by events beyond its control was assembled with the help of ninety former employees. It consists of nine Parts, loosely set in chronological order. Parts Five through Eight encompass the twenty years of business boom and are arranged by the special characteristics of the diverse technologies, not necessarily in time sequence. Key events over more than seventy years can be seen in Figure 9.1, at the end of the text. Each Part highlights, as appropriate, the international background and political circumstances of the particular period and the company's technical efforts during that time, as well as the evolution of the distinctive management style, tales of many interesting personalities, and my own observations and experiences. The final Part describes the unfortunate events of the 1990s that caused this national treasure to disappear. It also summarizes the achievements of a group of people who created numerous benefits enjoyed today all over the world.

D. Kenneth Richardson
Santa Barbara, California
March 2011

ACKNOWLEDGMENTS

JUST AS IN all significant Hughes ventures, the creation of this book would not have been possible without a well-motivated team effort of more than ninety Hughes retirees. Their willingness and enthusiasm were most rewarding to witness. Twenty former leaders of the firm graciously participated in prolonged interviews. Experts from the many sophisticated design fields helped ensure technical accuracy; others searched their memories and archives to aid in completeness of this important and unique historic saga. The author heartily thanks this informal editorial team, but certainly retains responsibility for any errors in content.

As stated in the Preface, this book is a tribute to many thousands who dedicated their careers to making Hughes a world leader in all types of electronic technology. Many thanks to my friend Marcia Bures for inspiring me to compose this book after she had read *The Fords* by Peter Collier and David Horowitz, saying, "You must tell the real Hughes Aircraft story." Continual encouragement from my wife, Charlotte, allowed me to commit many long hours at this imposing task.

The readability, phrase accuracy, color, and flow of the final text could not have been possible without the talent and long-term enthusiasm and dedication of Ellen Dent and Jim Uphold. Ellen had been an excellent professional editor at Hughes and in other private endeavors; Jim, with degrees from USC and UCLA, was a superb multi-faceted system engineering manager at the company. It is impossible to render enough thanks to them both! Ed Cobleigh, Bert Crowder, Dick Giacoletto, John Richardson, Jr., and Boris Subbottin, acting as a traditional "red team" of evaluators, were also most helpful in providing their reactions to the manuscript's content and reader interest.

Twenty enthusiastic professionals refined and smoothed the wording by intensive editing of selected segments. Thanks to them, the technical content, I hope, is correct: Vern Andrews, Jim Bradley, Art Chester, Ed Cobleigh, Steve Dorfman, Dave Ethington, Jeff Grant, Tony Iorillo, Hal Jensen, Lou Kurkjian, Dave Lynch, Ben McRee, John Milton, Ed

O'Brien, John Olsen, Bob Parke, Bob Roney, Dick Schleicher, Bob Sendall, and George Speake.

The texture of this written saga was considerably enhanced as a result of personal interviews with twenty-one individuals with long-range and deep understanding of the company's roots and phenomenal success. Some of them contributed noteworthy quotations, which are included in the text. The sharing of their wisdom was a vital ingredient in composing this story: Tom Carvey (VP Materiel), Bill Craven (VP EDSG), Mal Currie (CEO), Dale Donalson (VP Quality), Steve Dorfman (President S&CG), Lou Kurkjian (President GSG), Warren Matthews (Corporate VP R&D), Ben McRee (Assistant Division Manager MSG), John Mendel (President IEG), Ed O'Brien (Division Manager GSG), Milt Radant (Corporate VP Technology), Dr. Simon Ramo (founding father of the electronics dynamo of Hughes and co-founder of TRW Inc.), Tom Reed (Secretary of the Air Force), Bob Roney (VP S&CG), Hal Rosen (VP S&CG), Bob Sendall (Senior Staff MSG), Blaine Shull (President GSG), George Speake (VP EDSG), Charlie Strider (Assistant Division Manager RSG), Jim Uphold (Program Manager RSG), Bud Wheelon (CEO).

Throughout this book are quotations from eminent customers and company employees expressing their perspectives of the organization. Some of these quotes are extracts from publications; some are from those listed above whom I interviewed and from nine others who kindly responded to requests from the author. I am indebted to the following people: Paul St. Amand, MD, Vice Adm. Robert Baldwin (Deputy Chief of Naval Operations), John Cashem (VP Northrop-Grumman), Purnell Choppin (President Emeritus, Howard Hughes Medical Institute), Lt. Gen. Walter Dürig (Commander, Swiss Air Force), Eddy Hartenstein (Publisher, *Los Angeles Times*), Lt. Gen. Donald Lionetti (Director, Army Ballistic Missile Defense Agency), Peter Michel, (Director, Lied Library, University of Nevada, Las Vegas), Gen. Richard Myers (Chairman, Joint Chiefs of Staff), Virginia Norwood (Senior Scientist, S&CG).

Searching for the complete story and all the major events over forty years was most difficult. Capable individuals formerly at the company were so numerous that comprehensive acknowledgment in this book is impossible. My apologies to any contributors I may have inadvertently overlooked; certainly no offense is intended. In addition to those named above, forty other professionals kindly scoured their memories and files to enable adequacy of the book's content. Particularly helpful in recruiting participants from GSG was Lou Kurkjian. Some of those listed below helped more than others, but to all I owe many thanks: Gene Allen, Lee Anderson, Ed Arnn, Elliot Axelband, Harry Axlerod, Dick Brandes, Ed

Cobleigh, Jim Easton, Tony Ede, Jim Ferrero, Tom Gillman, Al Herman, Phil Joujon-Rouge, Joe Karcher, Paul Kennard, Kim Kerry, Jim Kvett, Mark Landau, Dave Margerum, George Marrett, Brock McCaman, Bob Muth, Freeman Nelson, Walt Ordway, Al Pena, Bob Phelps, Gerry Picus, Bob Puich, Betty Robey, Bill Sagey, Tom Sheffield, Nate Simmons, Bernie Skehan, Collin Smith, Chuck Sutherland, John Tomlinson, Nick Uros, Don White, Howard Wilson, Ted Wong.

In addition to the many people who helped guide this book, many organizations and publications were beneficial and are greatly appreciated. Figures were constructed by Sheila Dent, pixel-relish.com. Bits of information were garnered from some publications listed in the bibliography. Sources of photographs include the author's personal files; *Fortune* Magazine; Howard Hughes Medical Institute; iStockphoto; *Los Angeles Times*; National Museum of the US Air Force, Dayton, Ohio; National Naval Aviation Museum, Pensacola, Florida; Space and Airborne Systems, Raytheon Corporation; *Time* Magazine; *Times-Standard*, Eureka, California; University of Nevada, Las Vegas, Lied Library Special Collections; Wikipedia.

"...at the forefront of technology"

PART ONE

OUR ROOTS

How did the brainchild of the elusive and eccentric millionaire Howard Hughes grow, without his help, from a personal plaything to become the world's leading electronics giant in 1985? And why did it disappear? World events played a role, and a flood of bright, inventive engineers and scientists enabled it to conquer almost any technical challenge in the field of electronics. Enlightened management gave them freedom to explore new frontiers, but government concerns about its private ownership eventually led to its unfortunate demise.

The first act of this colorful drama began in 1932, while our nation was in the midst of a stifling economic depression caused by a false sense of prosperity, excessive stock market speculation, the collapse of foreign trade, and the farming dust-bowl catastrophe. Soup kitchens and alcohol bootleggers fighting prohibition were everywhere. Out of a total national population of 125 million people, more than 13 million were unemployed; banks were almost insolvent; and the Lindbergh baby was kidnapped. Newly elected President Roosevelt suspended bank operations and declared, "We have nothing to fear but fear itself."

1

BEGINNINGS

Despite this abysmally poor new business climate, Howard Hughes founded the Hughes Aircraft Company in California as a subsidiary of his privately owned Hughes Tool Company headquartered in Houston, Texas. As a nineteen-year-old only child, he had inherited control of the profitable oil-well drill bit manufacturing company from his father, and he later used it as a revenue source to feed a personal ambition in several business fields. One was in film producing, inspired in 1922 by his uncle Rupert who was already active in Hollywood. Howard's fame was firmly established by the 1927 film *Hell's Angels*, a colorful adventure about air combat in World War I starring Jean Harlow. He later purchased controlling interest in RKO Studios. Mr. Hughes also aggressively entered the budding passenger airline business, buying Trans World Airlines (TWA) and two smaller regional carriers. Finally, the new Hughes Aircraft Company satisfied his appetite for direct participation in aircraft development. These many activities well matched the US public's enthusiasm in that era for those who set new performance records, helped cure the economic depression through enterprise expansion, and created entertainment to distract them from unpleasant hardships.

The US public in the 1930s was also strongly isolationist, believing that the cost and risk of again being involved in European conflicts was unacceptable. They were dismayed by the loss of life in World War I, as well as by its expense, with no apparent benefit to our nation. When World War II finally struck us in 1941, we were poorly equipped. It took us two years to catch up. However, corporations that were equipped to respond were able to thrive in this time of need.

Creativity, innovation, and experimentation were the hallmarks of the legendary Howard Hughes. However, Dr. Simon "Si" Ramo—who joined the Aircraft Company in 1946 and teamed with Dr. Dean Wooldridge and other stalwarts to remold the company's future into one of electronics—feels that, based on his own interactions with Howard (most of which occurred after the latter's near-fatal XF-11 crash), the public view of Mr. Hughes's abilities was quite distorted: it was possible that Howard's reputed inventive genius for aircraft design really reflected the accomplishments of a knowledgeable staff. Or perhaps the irrational behavior perceived by Si stemmed from the debilitating medical effects of the crash. Nevertheless, although most of the companies Mr. Hughes began morphed into diverse enterprises without his direct participation, they were imbued with his apparent desire to do things differently, to not be bound by convention, and to always seek innovation.

The Hughes Aircraft Company was originally established to design and build unique high-performance aircraft, but its new thrust into airborne radars in 1946 enabled the company to become the most accomplished military electronics organization in the world. Many of the devices it created were key in bringing the forty-five-year-long Cold War between the United States and the Soviet Union to a conclusion, without actual combat occurring.

The company's early logo was used to identify corporate literature and was the model for award pins given employees for each five years of service. The design symbolized the round-the-world speed flight by Mr. Hughes as well as implying successful worldwide business ventures. The corporate logo was later changed to an austere rectangle to de-emphasize "Aircraft" Company, the author presumes, since the focus had changed to electronics.

In 1985, General Motors Chairman Roger Smith called the company a "national treasure" as he completed its purchase by GM (see Section 58, "Saluting General Motors"). At that time, it was the largest private employer in California and Arizona (more than 82,000 men and women on its staff) and the largest defense electronics firm in the United States, managing more than a thousand projects and producing well over a thousand different types of products. Hughes Aircraft Company was successful by every measure: integrity, financial stability, diverse and satisfied customers, continual business growth, product lines vital to the nation, and with most employees feeling part of a family with noble objectives. Superb talent was recruited from around the nation, and a management style evolved that became a model for other high-technology enterprises. Occasionally, of course, errors were made in leadership and business moves, but they were quickly corrected.

How did all this happen? An unusual group of professionals with deep technical roots and unique people skills created an agile organization driven to achieve vital national missions.

3

Company Logo, 1948
(courtesy of UNLV)

Company Logo, 1965
(courtesy of UNLV)

Company Logo, 1985
(courtesy of UNLV)

Early Days of Growth and Expansion

Setting aircraft world records was an exhilarating motivator for Howard Hughes, whose zeal for aviation had begun with his first flight when he was only fourteen. In 1932, at the age of twenty-seven, he established his new aircraft company in rented space in a corner of a Lockheed Corporation hangar in Glendale/Burbank, California. Glenn Odekirk, who had managed the eighty-seven World War I vintage aircraft used in the filming of the lavish *Hell's Angels*, was made general manager. (Allegedly, Odekirk originated the company's name, Hughes Aircraft Company, with no suggestions from his boss, because he had to invent something in order to sign purchasing payments; when Howard Hughes learned of the name, however, he did not object.) Gathered in the small space were the men who were to design and fabricate the famous H-1 *Racer* (which Mr. Hughes renamed the *Winged Bullet* during a redesign effort). In it, in 1935, Mr. Hughes set a world speed record, averaging 352 miles per hour.

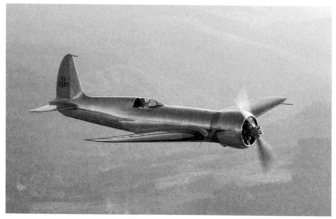

H-1 *Racer*, 1935
(courtesy of UNLV)

The H-1's unique design was mimicked by the Japanese in their Mitsubishi A6M *Zero*, one of the world's finest fighter aircraft in 1941. They copied the H-1's innovative cantilever wing form, leading edge air intake and bell shaped cowling for the engine, tail design, ailerons at the wing's rear, flush riveting, lightweight structure, and retractable landing gear. The Germans also used these ideas in creating the agile Focke-Wulf Fw 190. Peculiarly, the ponderous US military was slower to adopt these innovations; they were finally used in the P-47 *Thunderbolt*. The *Racer* is now a popular exhibit in the Smithsonian's National Air and Space Museum in Washington, D.C.

Noah Dietrich, Mr. Hughes's chief business advisor, and Howard Hall, his legal counsel, provided organizational and legal stability for the growing company while it designed and constructed aircraft subassemblies and specialized radio equipment for the government and other contractors. However, during a period of only a few years, the company had nine general managers! This instability at the top was usually caused by these leaders' inability to receive timely confirmation by Mr. Hughes of critical corporate decisions; a strict requirement for his approval was mandated in each executive's employment contract. They quit in frustration when they realized that they could not actively perform their leadership duties.

During this time, the national environment was also changing rapidly. The economy recovered after many difficult years, but the possibility

Howard in His Office
(courtesy of Raytheon)

of a new world war loomed darkly. The isolationist attitude of the public precluded modernizing and equipping the armed forces. Little federal funding was available for companies like Hughes to perform research and development to improve key military equipment. The war had to arrive before the nation was willing to invest to ensure its security.

In July 1941, the Hughes workforce relocated to 1,300 acres in Culver City, California, a few miles west of Los Angeles.

The staff quickly grew to 500 employees, including 100 engineers. Buildings were constructed of wood to avoid the use of strategic materials that might be needed if the war began. The strangely named "cargo building," completed in 1943, was the largest wooden structure in the world: 740 feet long and six stories high, spanning two large open bays. (During a visit to Japan, I was told that the Todai-ji Temple in Nara, built 1,200 years ago, was the largest; I am unsure which claim is correct. There are also assertions that the largest US building was the gaseous diffusion plant for separating uranium 235, constructed in 1944 at Oakridge, Tennessee. It's an interesting subject to debate.) The Hughes hangar-shaped building was later used for assembly of the H-4 *Hercules* flying boat (dubbed the *Spruce Goose*) and converted fifty years later to a movie studio after the company left the site and the surrounding land was sold to a developer.

For some reason known only to himself, Mr. Hughes required that all the buildings at the site be painted a pastel color called "sea mist green," which was quickly dubbed "Hughes green." He even specified the exact mixture of ingredients in the paint and how often repainting had to be done.

Entering the plant, employees passed several small tin-roofed buildings that had originally been part of a large farming area. One structure was delightfully called the "celery shed," even when it was later used for spray-painting subassembly parts. Staff members were especially fond of recalling this nickname, particularly after the shed was torn down.

Employee Event, 1945
(courtesy of Bob Roney)

2

THE WAR YEARS

T HE NATIONAL ISOLATIONIST attitude was quickly cured by the devastating Japanese strike on Pearl Harbor. Government funding priorities emphasized the buildup of new manufacturing facilities and their associated workforce to meet the large demand for military equipment.

Culver City Plant, 1943
(courtesy of Raytheon)

Hughes manufactured aircraft subassemblies for other firms, and invented a unique flexible transfer chute and electric booster drive method for machine-gun ammunition feeds in B-17, B-25, and B-26 bombers. Employment grew from the 400 of 1940 to 6,000 by 1944.

The World War II demand for production was limited only by workforce availability. Younger males were needed in the armed forces (more than 6 million were inducted during the four wartime years), and for the first time in the United States, women became a large and vital portion of the factory workforce. The popular "Rosie the Riveter" became their symbol. Companies frantically competed for employees.

Under contract to the US Army Air Corps, Hughes developed and assembled for flight testing two prototypes of a very advanced aircraft, the two-engine XF-11, constructed principally of plywood. Its mission was to fly over enemy territory and photograph their ground positions (photoreconnaissance). The photographs, developed after the aircraft's return to base, would help field commanders make tactical decisions.

XF-11 Reconnaissance Aircraft, 1946
(courtesy of UNLV)

It was an XF-11 test flight piloted by Mr. Hughes in 1946 that caused his lifetime physical injuries. The right-side propeller controller failed because of an oil leak. The leading counter-rotating propeller fanned flat and the rear one reversed. The resulting uncontrollable aircraft yaw caused a flat spin, precipitating a crash in Beverly Hills near the Los Angeles Country Club. Fate was kind, since Marine Sergeant William Durkin was nearby and managed to pull Mr. Hughes from the smashed wreckage.

Mr. Hughes survived despite suffering about a hundred bone breaks and internal bleeding. Drs. Mason and Chaffin saved him. When I met

Howard Visits President FDR, 1943
(courtesy of UNLV)

Dr. Chaffin around 1970, he said that Mr. Hughes's chest cavity was filled with blood, and his heart had actually been displaced to the opposite side of normal! Major medical efforts were needed. Many painkiller drugs had to be administered, and ever afterward he was addicted to morphine, replaced later by codeine and Valium.

Mr. Hughes apparently also had the innate malady called obsessive-compulsive disorder (OCD), a disease not understood at that time. Retrospective views showed two symptoms: inordinate attention to unimportant details and a persistent drive to fulfill them. This affliction, and his drug addiction, caused many of the legendary quirks in his later life. In the next year, he flew the second XF-11 prototype and the H-4 *Hercules* flying boat, and he greatly expanded his real estate holdings.

Jack Real became the full-time aide to Mr. Hughes as they traveled to hotels throughout the world seeking escape from taxation. Being his aide involved making all the arrangements for travel, daily living, and medical support. This was a big change for Mr. Real, the former head of the Helicopter Division of Hughes Tool Company! He told me in 2004 that Mr. Hughes had experienced many long periods of lucidity, allowing him to make sensible business transactions. At other times, Jack provided the essential continuity in the events of Mr. Hughes's life. Much of this story is revealed in his book, *The Asylum of Howard Hughes*.

During Mr. Hughes's recovery, development was under way at Culver City of the wooden-structured HK-4 *Hercules* flying boat. Henry Kaiser, who had established mass production as a way to build freighter and tanker ships, devised the idea of a flying boat using nonstrategic materials as a remedy for the stupendous Allied shipping losses in the Atlantic to the German submarine wolf packs. Mr. Kaiser invited Howard Hughes to design the vehicle, and their team was chosen for this program by the War Department, endorsed by President Roosevelt.

The government contract for the HK-4 *Hercules* (Mr. Kaiser removed his participation in this project after disputes with Mr. Hughes, so the designator was changed to H-4) stated that all the airframe structure and skin, as well as its fabrication facilities, must be of wood. Front-page stories broadcasting its giant size and development difficulties earned the *Hercules* the media nickname *Spruce Goose*. Although spruce and birch wood made into strong patented panels called Duramold had been selected for the structure and skin, that derisive moniker enraged Mr. Hughes, who thought it most demeaning. (It is notable that even after Hughes Aircraft Company products became exclusively electronics, the strongest union in our production organizations remained the Carpenters' Union!)

That eight-engine behemoth is still the largest aircraft ever built: 219 feet long and 79 feet tall, with a 320-foot wingspan and propellers 17 feet in diameter. Fully loaded, it would weigh 400,000 pounds, three times that of any aircraft to that date. Since then, two other aircraft have come close: 1988 saw the huge Antonov AN-225, which was 56 feet longer but had a wingspan 35 feet shorter. The giant Airbus A380 airliner, introduced in 2008, is 21 feet longer, but its wingspan is 42 feet shorter. The H-4 wings were so thick that a 6-foot-tall person could comfortably step from the fuselage into the wing. Sketches made at the time showed the cargo bay loaded with a dozen fighter aircraft ready for shipment.

Achieving strength and aerodynamic smoothness required many development and construction innovations. Design breakthroughs included electronic instrumentation, hydraulically powered activators for ailerons and tail controls, and electronic manipulation of control stick feel—so the pilot sensed a match between stick resistance and the desired aircraft reaction. Additionally, new solutions were devised for the difficult job of shaping and bonding the contoured Duramold plywood sections to the rib cage.

During a famous 1947 Senate investigative hearing, in a confrontation with US Senator Owen Brewster, Mr. Hughes mastered him in

Howard About to Fly the *Hercules*
(courtesy of UNLV)

H-4 *Hercules* in Long Beach, California, 1947
(courtesy of UNLV)

reasoning and speech and soundly rebuffed Congress's allegations of profiteering and duplicity. He had personally invested $7 million in the project, and he stated in the hearings that if the H-4 could not fly he would leave the country and never return! Mr. Hughes also publicly revealed several personal indiscretions of Senator Brewster in his home state of Maine; because of these revelations, state voters expelled him from office in 1952. But the $23 million claim by Mr. Hughes for meeting the contract specifications was not settled for the next twenty years. The government did not seem to like Mr. Hughes.

The only flight of the *Hercules* was for one mile at 80 feet altitude above Long Beach harbor on November 2, 1947. Howard Hughes was at the controls, and Dave Grant was in the right seat; sixteen mechanics, members of the press corps, and special guests made a total of thirty-two individuals aboard. Mr. Hughes was preparing data to rebut the lingering allegations about cost overruns and development delays.

Since World War II had ended, there was no need for the flying boat, and the contract was cancelled once development was complete. In later years, Mr. Hughes upgraded the *Hercules* engines twice to increase the power margins, but no one ever tried another flight, though Mr. Hughes expended another $50 million of his own funds. The bird—kept from public view until Mr. Hughes's death in 1976—became a popular exhibit in Long Beach in 1980; it was housed in a protective dome next to the famous *Queen Mary* ocean liner. In 1995, it was barged to McMinnville, Oregon, for display in a new aviation and space museum.

XF-17 *Sky Crane* Helicopter, 1952
(personal files)

The notable XH-17 *Sky Crane* helicopter was another warbird creation in the late 1940s. Its two-blade rotor was powered by jet nozzles at each tip. Hot gas distributed from an engine at the hub fed the nozzles; the gas passed through the rotor blades as they spun. The enormous bird was capable of lifting and transporting a large army tank. Watching the XH-17 in one of its test flights in 1952, I was sure it would never be chosen for combat use: it was so noisy it could be heard approaching from several miles away. There should have been a stronger priority on designing for audio stealth! The *Sky Crane* never was destined for quantity manufacture, perhaps because of that thunderous battlefield noise, or because the Korean War's conclusion eliminated its immediate need.

Another notable "Hughes" project in 1974, often erroneously attributed to be the work of Hughes Aircraft Company, was the creation of the famous *Glomar Explorer*. This vessel, disguised as a deep-sea mining ship looking to recover manganese nodules from the floor of the ocean, had a clandestine US mission to raise a sunken Soviet submarine to examine technically its nuclear missiles. That task was only partially successful, and soon became publicly known. This program was done under the auspices of Howard Hughes's Summa Corporation; Hughes Aircraft Company had no significant part in it.

Complete 1947 Telephone Book

3

LAYING THE FOUNDATION

IN 1944, THE growing need for capable electronic devices to provide many intricate functions in military aircraft prompted Mr. Hughes to form a Radio Department headed by Dave Evans, who had joined the company in 1937. Mr. Hughes had realized his dependence on communication radios and navigation electronics during his record 1938 around-the-world flight in a modified Lockheed L-18 *Lodestar*; he had also been active in amateur radio in his childhood. Evans had operated the ground stations that kept in touch with the aircraft during its global flight.

The department worked on radio, TV, and radar designs, and in 1947, demonstrated an airborne collision-avoidance radar. This venture into a different marketplace became a blessing for Hughes, whose 1944 employment level of 6,000 employees had dropped drastically to only 800 employees after the war-production demands ended. Its path was in the right direction, and the company became a major participant in a business arena that enjoyed rapid growth throughout the next fifty years.

Establishing a department with airborne electronics design capability was most timely since the world situation was changing drastically. The US involvement in World War II finally ended in 1945 after release of the world's first two atomic bombs on Hiroshima and Nagasaki. Thousands of returning veterans eager for work, combined with the innovative manufacturing discoveries in wartime production, fueled a rapidly growing US economy. Aerospace leapt ahead with the perfection of turbojet engines and, in 1947, the first sustained level flight of an aircraft at supersonic speeds.

Beginning in 1946, it became apparent that the Soviet Union intended permanent retention of Eastern Europe as an expansion of its empire. The USSR was also determined to persuade or pressure other nations to convert to the communist political system. This resolve is understandable as part of the USSR's self-protection philosophy. The Soviet

Union had lost about 26 million people in World War II, including over 14 million Russians. The siege of Leningrad (now called St. Petersburg as it had been before the 1917 revolution) had lasted nine hundred days, with combat, disease, and starvation causing massive losses. Would not any nation try to set up supportive geographic buffers to preclude a repeat of those disasters?

The United States regarded the USSR's position as a threat both economically and politically and, in 1947, created the secretive Central Intelligence Agency to gain adequate and current military and political data. Soviet attitudes were sharply highlighted by the sealing off of Berlin, provoking the Berlin airlift in 1948, followed by construction of the infamous Berlin Wall as part of the "Iron Curtain" separating the communist Warsaw Pact countries from the NATO assembly of Allied nations—in essence dividing East from West. Thus began the Cold War, which lasted forty-five years, fortunately with no direct combat between the two great powers. Highly emotional word-combat did occur along sharp political dividing lines.

Further world political and warfare turbulence came in 1948, as Israel, with much US support, became a new nation following its War of Independence, an event that relit the complex and long-standing disputes and violence in the Middle East.

One of the greatest US concerns in the emerging Cold War was the adequacy of its air combat capability. A principal worry was the possibility of Soviet strategic attacks using masses of long-range bombers delivering free-fall nuclear weapons. By this time, the Soviets were extremely competent in producing high-performance aircraft, including the soon-to-be-deployed Tupolev Tu-4 strategic bomber, which could reach US shores from Eastern Europe. Our capabilities for defense against these threats appeared to be minimal.

In 1946, Si Ramo, who had joined General Electric in radar development following his physics PhD award in 1936 from the California Institute of Technology (Caltech), became quite aware of this critical need, and the lack of interest or capability of existing US corporations to tackle this tough problem. Well-established companies—General Electric, Sperry, Martin, and Raytheon—had been somewhat active in radar programs, but their executives were giving higher priority to capturing a share of the lucrative post-war consumer market. The Navy had selected Westinghouse Electric for similar air intercept needs, but the Air Force desired a new approach and hoped that performance breakthroughs would come from a new creative team. Something very different was needed: an unconstrained aggregation of highly creative technical talent committed to inventing high performance electronic devices to achieve effective air intercept. Dr. Ramo's discussions with many of his government acquaintances revealed that if he could establish a credible plan and commit himself to its mission, the Air Force would fund the needed facilities and contract for unique sensors and weapon design work on a cost-reimbursement basis. The leadership efforts of Ramo and his teammate, Dr. Dean Wooldridge, in finally establishing this innovative organization at Hughes Aircraft Company in Culver City are aptly described in chapter two (intriguingly titled "Howard Hughes and National Security: the Odd Coupling") of Si's book, *The Business of Science*, published in 1988. What he initially intended as a small creative laboratory, with production of any resulting design to be performed by other companies, soon blossomed into a prominent design and manufacturing outfit with national stature.

The privately owned and innately secretive nature of the Hughes enterprises helped the newly formed Air Force to offer Hughes—with Ramo and Wooldridge inspiring the technical staff—a challenging set of tasks: design the necessary electronics and weapons for the self-defense of US long-range bombers and for fighter aircraft to intercept and destroy hostile aircraft attacking the continent.

Hughes Aircraft Company, with its existing Radio Department and the commitment of Dr. Ramo, was awarded several contracts for greatly improved radar systems that eventually equipped three Air Force fighters: the Lockheed F-94C *Starfighter*, North American F-86D *Sabre*, and Northrop F-89 *Scorpion*. Adaptations of these electronics were fitted to the Navy F3D *Skyknight* and F3H *Demon* and the Canadian CF-100 *Canuck*. (Government designators for these systems and their upgrades were E-1 through E-10 and APG-33, -36, -37, -40, and -51.)

Initial deployment began in 1951, and over a ten-year period Hughes delivered 5,718 of these radars. These large production contracts established at Hughes a capability and a stable base for manufacturing complex electronics. Concurrent with these radar programs, air-intercept guided missile design and production began at Hughes, described in Section 4, "Creating a Base of Technical Excellence; Weaponry."

Scientific, research, development, entrepreneurial, and business professionals were enticed to devote themselves to the breakthrough projects at this reconstituted Aircraft Company. One very important recruit was Dean Wooldridge, who was performing research in magnetism at Bell Laboratories; he had been Si's classmate at Caltech. The two partnered to lead the technical future of the rapidly growing cluster of talent at Hughes. Initial staff acquisition efforts identified excellent electronics and physics professionals at Bell Laboratories, General Electric, Westinghouse, Sperry, and other firms as well as at top universities. A management credo remembered for many years was, "If there are only 125 good engineers in this country, we are going to hire them all." Talented prospects flocked to California, excited by the company's vital national mission as well as by great improvements in their salaries and lifestyles.

Radar in Canadian CF-101 *Voodoo*, 1955
(courtesy of Raytheon)

The government remained dubious about its most critical programs being housed under the uncertain business purview of the erratic Howard Hughes. As Si relates, Mr. Hughes could not even be given a secret-level security clearance, since he vehemently refused to be fingerprinted. He would thus be uninformed about the most important details of these key Air Force programs, so how could he be effective as company president? To ease this concern, retired Gen. Ira Eaker, former World War II commander of the Eighth Air Force in Europe, was appointed vice president of Hughes Tool Company in 1947, to effect liaison with Hughes Aircraft Company; retired Lt. Gen. Harold George, who had headed the Air Transport Command during World War II, became vice president and general manager of the Aircraft Company in the same year. Both generals had some formal technical education, and their presence at Hughes gave the Air Force a degree of assurance that all would be well. Tex Thornton was also brought in as a means of improving business management practices.

Tex Thornton had been a colonel in the Army Air Corps, and led a group of ten officers, including the later-famous Robert McNamara, in applying statistical measurements to management of the air arm. They later joined Ford Motor Company as the "Whiz Kids," bringing the same discipline there. Disappointed at not becoming president of Ford, Tex moved to Hughes in 1948 and established mathematical management methods for administration of the enterprise.

The sensible application of numerical support for managing complexities, both in technical and business operations, as it became practiced at Hughes, was overdone elsewhere. The new statistical bookkeeping approach became a curse in future operations of the Department of Defense and the Air Force. The methods were beneficial in keeping complicated operations orderly, but excess devotion to the financial bottom line was very wasteful of staff time, debilitating to long-term goals, and a poor replacement for common sense. These flaws showed in the by-the-numbers Washington conduct of the Vietnam conflict; they also caused excessive costs in the performance of defense hardware contracts by US corporations. Dedication to statistical numbers often detracts seriously from getting the real jobs done, to the dismay of all participants.

Such overemphasis on the bookkeeper approach also plagued operations at Hughes from time to time. Long-term objectives were sometimes sacrificed for short-term fiscal results, most especially after the company became part of General Motors in 1985.

The principal operating location remained at Culver City. Since Mr. Hughes acquired the land years before, what had been prime farmland had been transformed during World War II into space devoted to aircraft design and development projects; then, after the switch to a new type of business, this expanded into a complex of buildings (all painted that infamous "Hughes green") for the design and manufacture of high-technology electronic equipment—even though Mr. Hughes greatly impeded the needed construction. The staff was required to obtain his approval to begin any new building, and when asked, he initially insisted that any expansion be done in Las Vegas, where he had already made significant real estate investments. When told that such geographical separation of the workforce would greatly hamper staff interactions and military security communications, he remained silent to any appeals. After frustrating delays, the leaders bravely assumed that silence implied no objection, and they began groundbreaking for the new facilities. Many other similar time and procedural obstructions to progress, coupled with the unclear definition of responsibility and authority throughout the upper management and between the company and its Texas-based owner, Hughes Tool Company, eventually festered into the leadership revolt described in Section 11, "Leadership Revolution."

Several of the new buildings had open-sided top floors, called roof houses, where radiation testing was performed on developmental radars by transmitting beams to safe airspace beyond the facilities and above

Missile Electronics Assembly
(courtesy of UNLV)

Radar Transmitter Assembly
(courtesy of UNLV)

Electronics Manufacturing
(courtesy of UNLV)

any residential communities. One building held manufacturing assembly lines for both radar equipment and guided missile electronic assemblies (ordnance additions were always done elsewhere).

The 9,300-foot-long grass airstrip, which Mr. Hughes used to fly in and out of Los Angeles as well as to test prototype aircraft, was the longest privately owned airstrip in the world. It was later paved to accommodate newer and heavier aircraft.

Unfortunately, many of the early buildings, including the enormous hangars, were constructed on former wetlands, the Ballona Creek (often jokingly referred to as "Baloney Creek") watershed. The story is that Mr. Hughes commissioned Noah Dietrich to buy a suitable parcel of land for the Aircraft Company because it had outgrown its Burbank quarters. Mr. Dietrich was fond of duck hunting, and when he saw multitudes of the birds landing on the Culver City site wetlands (it was a migratory flyway), he reckoned that he could combine his passion for sport with a good deal for the Aircraft Company!

What attracted the ducks and Mr. Dietrich, however, was not so good for the Aircraft Company. Flooding during heavy rains frequently caused management to order everyone to leave for home, so that their cars would not get bogged down in water or silt. A rumor once circulated that an employee driving a Volkswagen Beetle exited the parking lot and was quickly swept away in a flash flood; she perished when the floating car went down a curbside street drain. A fable, but scary!

4

CREATING A BASE OF
TECHNICAL EXCELLENCE

As MENTIONED EARLIER, a great concern of the Air Force was the growing difficulty of air combat caused by giant improvements in hostile aircraft performance. To understand the urgency of this concern, a quick look back in history is helpful.

Air combat began in World War I, when enemy aircraft caused great harm to ground forces with bomb drops and photographic spying on troop locations. Defensive fighters tried throwing grenades or shooting pistols. Deliberate aircraft ramming by a courageous (foolish?) pilot against an important adversary was very effective.

Both sides quickly added machine guns, either a swivel-mounted weapon fired by a backseat gunner or a fuselage-mounted gun fired forward. Forward-shooting guns were more accurate, but until the invention of a synchronizing device, the emerging bullets sometimes severed the wooden propeller blades, in effect the gun shot down its own aircraft. The French fighter pilot Roland Garros made the first attempt to remedy this severe problem by adding metal deflector plates to the propeller. After he shot down three German craft using this safer propeller, he was forced to land on the wrong side of the combat zone where the enemy closely examined his biplane. When made aware of the findings, Tony Fokker, a Dutchman working for the Kaiser, had a mental flash and quickly conceived a timing interrupter that synchronized shots from the gun's muzzle with open spaces between blades as the propeller spun. The Allies soon discovered that concept, and in a short time every fighter was properly equipped.

Effective target intercepts became feasible and frequent. The United States was in that war for only nineteen months, but its Air Service pilots managed to shoot down 1,472 German aircraft. Race car driver Eddie Rickenbacker became the top US ace with 26 victories. The Kaiser's Manfred von Richthofen scored a remarkable 80 official credits.

Fighters in World War II were faster, more maneuverable, and far better equipped with guns and cannon, helped by accurate aiming sights. Multiple weapons were mounted in the wings, with their trajectories set to converge from 100 to 400 yards ahead. Finding targets above bad weather was usually aided by sightings of large group formations of bombers and their escort fighters. Crude ground-based radar blips provided course direction, and distance also helped some positioning. At other times, ground observers, using their eyes and ears, could make out the direction and altitude of the incoming raid.

In the three-and-a-half-month Battle of Britain in 1940, the Royal Air Force (RAF) lost 1,546 aircraft, and the Luftwaffe lost 1,887. At first, the British *Hurricanes* and *Spitfires* took a meaningful toll on the Nazi *Heinkel* and *Stuka* bomber raids. But then the Messerschmitt 109 and Folke-Wulf 190 appeared. With their extended range, they were able to perform escort duty throughout the entire bomber missions. Loss of many RAF fighters and pilots caused extreme concern; replacement rates were most inadequate. Then Chancellor Adolph Hitler ordered Gen. Hermann Goering to change the bombing priority from RAF airfields and aircraft factories to raids on highly populated cities. Even though many city residents suffered cruelly, this decision enabled the RAF to regain control of the air. In spite of their horrendous losses, the British considered this a major triumph since the Nazis cancelled their planned invasion across the channel. At the end of the air battles, Prime Minister Winston Churchill again inspired the Allies by his tribute to the RAF: "Never in the field of human conflict was so much owed by so many to so few."

The United States, involved for three-and-a-half years, scored 27,526 victories against Axis forces, with Army Air Corps pilot Richard Bong scoring 40 victories. In the Marianas Islands "turkey shoot," a pivotal 1944 naval battle, US Navy pilots downed 243 Japanese aircraft in one day, with Alex Vraciu scoring 6 victories in eight minutes! In the European theater, the Luftwaffe's Erich Hartmann scored an incredible 352 kills. Another comrade of his performed 1,000 sorties and was shot down 16 times, but survived the war.

In both wars there was a critical need for excellent eyesight in addition to superb flying skills. The old Navy expression of reliance on the "Mark One Eyeball" was most appropriate. It was said by a P-51 Mustang squadron mate that the famous Chuck Yeager (who in 1947 became the first man to fly at supersonic speed in level flight) could spot enemy targets forty miles away. Reasonably clear weather was essential to find the hostiles, identify them as unfriendly, and maneuver to a useful firing position. Aircraft were fast and agile and able to operate up to 25,000 feet altitude. There was only an instant when one's shots could hit a vital spot in the enemy target. The intercept job was most challenging, with the outcome often determined by pure luck.

Radar to the Rescue

With the onset of turbojet power, aircraft became much faster and were able to operate at high altitudes and in all weather conditions, becoming far more difficult to intercept. Positioning a fighter in the right place so its gunfire would be effective required the pilot to have much earlier and more accurate information. Operation in all-weather or nighttime conditions required something other than the Mark One Eyeball to initially find the hostiles. The most apparent solution was to provide the interceptor with a radar.

✸

The term *radar* comes from the acronym RADAR created in 1940 for radio detection and ranging (ranging meaning the measurement of distances). Radar can operate at long distances to measure useful information about natural shapes and man-made objects. As the technology advanced, many types of radars emerged whose capability ranged from detecting tiny airborne targets to making finely detailed maps of Earth from space.

At the beginning of World War II, rudimentary radars were installed on ships and at many ground bases; they were large and very heavy. Combat demands, however, stimulated rapid advances in performance. The Battle of Britain fighter intercepts relied heavily on a crude radar net called Chain Home, set up on England's eastern beaches. Because the distances across the Channel were short, fighter scramble response time was hardly sufficient without the warning and vectoring provided by Chain Home.

Such vectoring enabled a single squadron of twelve fighters from bases near the target area to effectively break up massed groups of one hundred bombers by jumping them from "out of the Sun." An alternate defense strategy to even the numbers in intercepting each raid was to assemble many fighter squadrons before beginning the encounter, but there was never quite enough warning time. The Germans never really perceived the critical value of the Chain Home net, and they made little effort to nullify those radars.

The British were the first to deploy an airborne radar aboard a Bristol *Blenheim* (light bomber aircraft) in 1940 to attempt night intercept of Luftwaffe aircraft. Dubbed "Airborne Interception" (AI), it was marginally successful. Many other airborne intercept or ground-mapping radar equipments were fielded by both sides during the lengthy European conflict. The British projects carried colorful names: Ash, Boozer, H2S, Monica, Perfectos, and Village Inn. The German radars were named Berlin, Bremenanlafe, Hohentwiel, Lichtenstein, and Neptun. By 1945, all the opposing forces had airborne radars and jammers with significant capability in early warning, night intercept, ground targeting, passive electronic sniffing, and navigation.

Chain Home Radar, 1940
(courtesy of Wikipedia)

Shipborne radars and some airborne radars were somewhat successful in detecting submarines cruising on the surface; an attempted technical response by German scientists to such detection became the first radar stealth design (see Section 50, "The Evolution of Stealth"). Submarine hull surfaces protruding above the waterline were coated with a rubber film containing graphite fibers, an absorptive blend that would greatly reduce the echo power from incoming radar beams. The Germans used an amusing term for it: *schornsteinfeger*, meaning "chimney sweep." The design performed quite well when evaluated in dry-dock tests, but the coating became ineffective after exposure to seawater. Fortunately for the British, this Nazi stealth attempt did not work in combat operations.

The United States also had rudimentary ground radars for detecting incoming aircraft raids. One set was operating in 1941 on the north coast of Oahu; its two operators spotted the hundreds-strong Japanese raid heading to Pearl Harbor. Unfortunately, their superiors did not believe their telephone report, either thinking them too inexperienced or presuming that the radar blips were a group of US B-17 bombers known to be en route from California. Even if correct action had been taken, however, it is unlikely the outcome would have changed much: there was not enough time on that early Sunday morning to mount a meaningful defense.

As the war progressed, shipborne radars became effective for collision avoidance, gunfire direction, and early warning of air attacks. By 1944, the radar screen set to protect the US Okinawa invasion force from *kamikaze* raids provided excellent warning, enabling Navy ships within the warning screen to shoot down 2,000 of these suicide weapons. Even with this success, more than 34 Navy ships were sunk and 360 were severely damaged by *kamikaze* pilots who were able to penetrate the screen. The US casualties aboard the ships severely hit in those terrible few days of conflict were 4,900 killed and 4,800 wounded.

Radar Design and Operation

Radars consist of many hardware segments that have different functions; the segments are electrically linked together to operate as a single system. Figure 1.1 shows the major components of a post-1960 radar: the frequency source creates the radar signal required for the desired measurement; the transmitter amplifies the signal energy; the antenna projects a shaped beam of that energy into the area being examined and also catches its echoes reflected from objects ahead; and the receiver and signal processor interpret the echoes and provide target information. Not shown in the figure, but commonly included, are power supplies, a computer that manages system operations, and controls and displays. Radars of later eras featured a signal processor that enabled a far more sophisticated understanding of what was being seen (see Section 51, "Processing Signals Digitally").

In the late 1940s, airborne radar transmitters used a "cavity-magnetron" tube to provide the all-important function of signal generation. Their operating frequency was designated X band (a radio frequency of about 10 billion cycles per second). This frequency was good for penetrating clouds and air debris; it was chosen after tradeoffs among the desired transmitter power output, antenna beam width, and physical size. For example, internal passageways, "chutes," in the radar's aluminum waveguides transferred the power within the radar. The size of the passageways had to match the wavelength being moved. Higher frequencies—often desired because they improved the fineness or resolution of the target echoes received—meant shorter wavelengths and thus narrower chutes; therefore, how narrow the chutes could be and still be fabricated with precision imposed a limit on the power level achievable.

Figure 1.1. Radar Elements After 1960

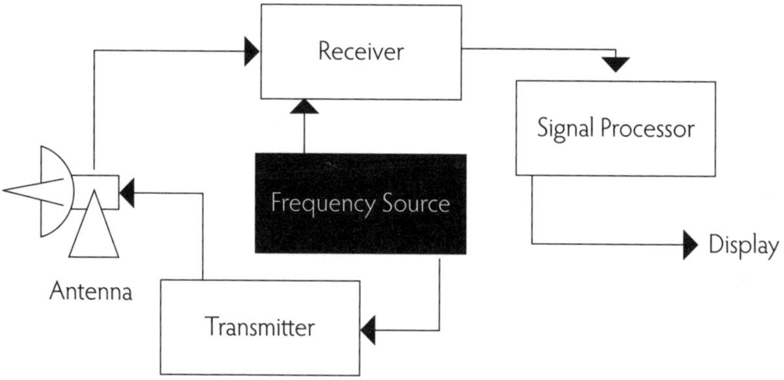

That era's "pulsed" radars formed a continual series of short power bursts at a repetitive rate called low PRF (pulse repetition frequency). Pulses were sent at about 250 to 2,000 times per second. The receiver was turned off while the outgoing power burst was sent; echoes reflected from targets arrived before the next transmitted pulse. Distance (range) of the reflection was equal to half the time since the pulse was transmitted. Because radio signals travel at the 186,000 miles per second speed of light, a pulse could make a round trip to targets up to fifty-miles distant in the quiet periods between power pulses. Attempts to see targets farther away were foiled by the next pulses.

These radars had sufficient power to produce a strong enough echo from fighter-sized targets up to thirty miles away. A display screen showed a blip for a target return. Two time-measurement circuits in the receiver were searched until the exact target echo range was found, by finding equal strengths in the "late" and "early" time gates. After the pilot designated that object as the one to be attacked, this mechanism stayed locked to the target echoes as the range changed.

An antenna is the radar's eyeball. The bigger it is, the better: more energy can be sent and captured. Fighter aircraft had enough interior space to allow a 30- to 36-inch diameter parabolic shape. The antenna was protected in the aircraft nose by a fiberglass cone called a radome; fiberglass caused little restriction of radar signals.

The parabolic dish formed a beam 2-1/2 degrees wide for X-band radars. The width of the beam of a parabolic antenna is affected by the frequency transmitted: higher frequencies mean narrower beams from the same dish shape. What is radiated can be visualized as a narrow flashlight beam with an oval shape at its farthest end. That shape means higher power at the center, falling away on the sides. To accurately find where an antenna was pointing, the energy pulses were sent from a horn placed at the antenna's focal center. The horn was rapidly rotated to form a narrow fan of these flashlight beams. The antenna's pointing center was always where a slight decrease in signal power occurred at the inner edge of the spinning beam. If the antenna was pointed slightly off that measured line, the power level would rise, giving an alert to reposition the pointing angle. That same technique was used to center the antenna on target echoes. This design was called a reflective conical scan antenna.

The antenna reflector was mounted on a gimbaled base, allowing horizontal sweeps parallel to the Earth's surface. Searches were 120 degrees wide and also moved up and down within the gimbal limits of 60 degrees. The gimbals were stabilized for fighter movements. With an aircraft roll, for example, the scan would still be parallel to the Earth's surface. Large sweeps were used to scan a wide area of forward airspace for possible target reflections (called the search mode).

Pointing the main beam to the ground resulted in much undesired background return, called ground clutter. Clutter power could be as much as one thousand times the echo strength from small objects and could totally obscure target reflections. In addition, interference came from the ground directly beneath even when the antenna pointed up; this is called sidelobe clutter. The receiver sensitivity was varied by elapsed time from the pulse sent; the purpose was to see target echoes, but to be blind to clutter returns when they were expected. Target echoes were strong enough not only to be seen with the beam pointing away from the ground, but also to be seen in lookdown conditions when targets were located at ranges between the fighter's distance above ground and the main beam ground-intercept distance.

When a target was spotted, the pilot switched the radar to a tracking mode. Scanning stopped and the antenna remained pointed at the designated target echoes regardless of maneuvers by either the fighter or the hostile aircraft. Tracking provided steering and timing information to the pilot to position the fighter for effective firing of its guns or rockets at the tracked hostile aircraft.

Squashing a high-performance radar into a lightweight combat aircraft posed many problems. Significant reductions in size and power demand and minimal weight were essential. All hardware units had to be physically shaped to match the different aircraft compartments. Metal structures were aluminum wherever possible, and moving parts were powered by electric motors. Since solid-state diodes and transistors had not yet been perfected, electronic circuits used miniature vacuum tubes and separate components mounted to plastic circuit boards with electrical interconnections etched on a copper laminate. Assembled boards were plugged into connectors and insulated wires to form a number of functional units (transmitter, receiver, power supply, display, etc.). The transmitters were about the size of half an automobile engine, and the other boxes looked much like today's larger stereo amplifier units. They all were supported by an aircraft installation frame, and they were interconnected with wire cable sets or waveguide strips to form the complete system. This hardware was configured for repetitive manufacturing and ease of disassembly in the field for repairing failed components.

Weaponry

Weaponry for fighter aircraft—machine guns and unguided rockets with a shooting range of as much as two-and-a-half miles—required the pilot to approach the opponent's tail to minimize speed and angle differences. Hostile combatants used agile maneuvering to escape an oncoming projectile, usually with great success. These armaments had no internal intelligence to cope with launch errors or evasive enemy moves. Inclement weather also limited many intercept opportunities.

A guided missile is a relatively lightweight weapon, usually propelled by a rocket motor that can be shot against a chosen target and has the sensor and brainpower to steer itself close enough for its warhead to demolish the target.

Sorely needed was an all-weather weapon that had longer range, a bigger destructive blast circle, the ability to compensate for rapid intercept dynamics, and imposed a minimal burden on its host aircraft. Friendly bombers had similar needs for their self-defense. The Germans tried several design ideas during World War II, including one weapon command-guided by a trailing wire, but there seem to be no records that any of these attempts resulted in a shoot-down of an Allied aircraft.

In 1945, Hughes began development of the Tiamat (JB-3) air-to-air missile to protect the Northrop JB-1 *Bat* bomber. The Tiamat was named after an evil and destructive Babylonian goddess who also was very aggressive and fat. The *Bat*'s radar illuminated the target; reflections seen by the weapon were used by its internal electronics for collision steering, the first attempt at what became semiactive radar guidance. The Tiamat used the first solid-propellant dual-thrust rocket motor, giving high boost for separation from its mother ship and a sustaining thrust for extended flight. Three missiles were assembled and tested with good results, but the weapon was too cumbersome for deployment (big and fat like its namesake goddess). The *Bat* aircraft was also cancelled as World War II ended.

Tiamat Radar Guided Missile
(courtesy of Wikipedia)

In 1946, Hughes was awarded another Air Force contract to develop a guided weapon for bomber self-defense. This missile was intended to be shot out of the aircraft's aft end and to use target illumination from the bomber's rear-facing radar. Such defensive weapons were never used in combat, and the design was soon adapted to use as fighter armament.

Initially designated the AAM A-2 (air-to-air missile), this new weapon was renamed the GAR-4 (guided aircraft rocket), then the AIM-4 (air intercept missile) Falcon in 1950. The project was veiled in secrecy until 1955, when it was revealed as the first air-to-air guided missile to be actively deployed. In contrast to the Tiamat, Falcon was small and lightweight, and had far more intelligence, sophisticated propelling power, ideal airfoils for sustained flight, and agile control surfaces for rapid maneuvering. Many of its unique design features were mimicked by other companies and nations as the ideal basis for guided missiles to satisfy almost any mission.

The Germans had successfully achieved inertial guidance in the V-1 buzz bomb, launched from the Continent toward British land targets: flying at fixed altitude, it could calculate its current position by time, speed, and course. A prelaunch setting of a geographic ground target location was remembered, and the terminal dive began when the weapon's internal measures matched the stored target coordinates. Many quantitative errors occurred, so accuracy was quite poor. Nonetheless, the drone weapons were quite effective as a civilian morale-buster. Dr. Hans Maurer, a brilliant scientist and a Hughes associate of mine in the 1980s, was the chief designer of the V-1 guidance system while at Peenemunde as part of Werner von Braun's engineering staff. When I asked him how he had invented such an advanced guidance system, his reply was, "It was very easy; London is a very big target!"

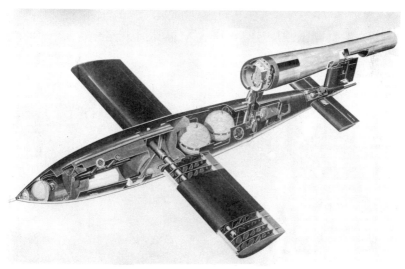

V-1 Buzz Bomb
(courtesy of the National Museum of the US Air Force)

The problem is much more difficult in air combat. Developing an intelligent, agile, and effective weapon to be carried into combat by a small fighter was extremely complex. Minimum demands on the aircraft were desired: small size and weight; little power and cooling; simple information transfer before launch; carriage safety; little added aerodynamic drag while being carried; and no damage to the aircraft during launch. The aerodynamic shape and surface texture of the missile fuselage, wings, and control fins determined its lift, drag, speed, and agility. It had to be sturdy to survive recurrent flight exposure and the rigors of its own high-speed intercept journey as well as enduring long-term storage and rough ground handling. The miniature electronics had to quickly accept complex information before launch, solve the dynamics of flight control, maintain a correct flight attitude, compute a correct intercept course, navigate accurately, and cope with signal interference from many sources, including enemy countermeasures.

Designing the airframe, wings, control surfaces, internal electrical power source, hydraulic systems for moving the control surfaces, and a lightweight rocket motor was most difficult. The mechanism to safely keep the weapon attached to the fighter under rigorous operating conditions also had to control launch separation and place the bird in an acceptable attitude for self-flight without damaging the friendly aircraft by collision or rocket motor plume debris. A lot to think about and test!

Figure 1.2 illustrates the essential elements of a guided missile. As the technology advanced, there were many design options to select from to produce the optimum result for the intended mission.

Figure 1.2. Guided Missile Elements

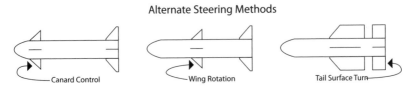

*Seeker types: Radar (shown), TV, IR, laser, sonar; if "none" then navigate by command, GPS or inertial
**Flipper Actuator

Alternate Steering Methods

Canard Control   Wing Rotation   Tail Surface Turn

The Falcon missile was 6-1/2 feet long and 6-1/2 inches in diameter, with a 20-inch wingspan. At launch, it weighed 119 pounds with an 8-pound warhead, or 150 pounds when equipped with a substantially larger explosive. Control surface "flippers" were located at the fuselage tail to ensure maximum terminal agility to hit a maneuvering target. In flight, the four wings and control surfaces formed an "X," with each wing 45 degrees from the fuselage lift plane. Many people credit Dr. Allen Puckett for the great success of this aerodynamic configuration. It proved far superior to the mid-fuselage control surfaces of Sparrow and the forward-mounted canards of Sidewinder missiles that the United States produced in later years. Although the X flying configuration is used on all these missiles, the higher steering-force Falcon tail control was made possible by the unique rocket motor shape that provided space for the control actuators, as described below.

Radar-Guided Falcon
(courtesy of the National Museum of the US Air Force)

There is a sharp contrast between guided missiles and aircraft in attitude control and steering: an agile missile needs a "time constant" five to ten times quicker than that for an airplane. Time constant (or reaction time) is the relationship between sensing and responding to a deviation from the desired travel condition. A long-standing historic problem in previous computations for attitude and steering commands was "buzz." Small flight deviations were detected; the system responded by applying too much correction, and thus over-steered. This caused another deviation followed by another overcorrection. The result was a continual and undesired fluttering. Effective new computational algorithms called proportional control were determined and refined at Hughes by Dr. Warren Mathews, a recent Caltech graduate, solving this crucial handicap for Falcon and future missile designs.

The Falcon's solid propellant rocket motor, which accelerated the weapon to Mach 4 speed (four times the speed of sound), had enough fuel to attain shooting ranges out to seven miles. It was an amazing engineering breakthrough in capability for its size and weight. A unique blast tube between the motor's burn chamber and the exit cone output nozzle (shown in Fig. 1.2) provided clearance inside the cylindrical fuselage for the rear-mounted control surface actuators. A high power pulse for launch separation followed by a half-second push for cruise was made possible by a molded propellant with an even-burning star-shaped interior surface running its length. Many competing rocket design companies were solicited to develop the motor; the second best offer to meet the required power was the size and weight planned for the entire Falcon missile! Hughes completed development of the new thruster itself, but decided to use two motor manufacturers to compete for the large production lots.

This motor material with long-term storage and safety characteristics was the first realistic application of experimental work done at Caltech's Jet Propulsion Laboratory (JPL) in Pasadena; it used polysulfide polymer as fuel with ammonium perchlorate as the oxidizer. Adaptations of this most successful configuration were later applied in ICBMs and stages of Apollo and Space Shuttle boosters. Hughes also pioneered the method of "deep draw" extrusion of steel to fabricate the motor's shell, resulting in a very strong but lightweight skin only fifty thousandths of an inch thick.

The Falcon guidance method used a semiactive radar seeker. (With semiactive guidance, a missile homes in on target-reflected radar energy that originated from someplace other than itself—in this case, from the aircraft's radar.) When the pilot selected a target and locked the fighter's radar to track and continuously illuminate it, the radar system prepared the Falcon's seeker by tuning it to the matching frequency and aligning it with the radar antenna's pointing angles. Given the launch signal, the rocket motor ignited, propelling the missile along a short retaining rail on the supporting launcher. In flight, the seeker continued to track the target radar echoes, providing information to its electronics to compute any flight path alterations needed to achieve collision. Command instructions were electrically sent to the four control system actuators.

Because Falcon guidance was so accurate that a direct hit on the target was always expected (enthusiastic design participants called it a hittle rather than a missile), there was no proximity fuse; impact sensors on the leading edges of the four wings triggered the warhead. As a result, the warhead was smaller and weighed less, greatly helping reduce total missile weight.

Tom Carvey (who later became a Hughes vice president) told me of participating in a most exciting early evaluation of a prototype Falcon at the Alamogordo, New Mexico, test facility. The bird was launched vertically at a tethered balloon illuminated by a ground-mounted radar. After successful intercept and propulsion burnout, the Falcon turned around and made a fall by gravity. Someone had forgotten to turn off the ground radar! Falcon's electrical battery still provided power for missile functions, so the test weapon came down straight through the radar antenna and smashed into the equipment bunker below. Luckily, there were no injuries; a thick concrete roof protected the test engineers, and the missile had no warhead. Some test! Even with human failure, there can be a top score in hardware evaluations.

The Hughes accomplishments by 1949 were truly astonishing. In winning the 1948 competition for the intercept weapon, the company had pledged a first flight in one year. Air Force urgency five months later spurred a new pledge to shorten that time to nine months and start production six months after that! Both of these promises were met. During that era, for the first time in world history, an intercept and destruction of a flying drone with a Falcon missile was done by a pilot who never saw the target. All these achievements assured an excellent future for Hughes.

Thomas C. Reed, former Secretary of the Air Force and Director, National Reconnaissance Organization, reflected this view in 2009 when he stated:

> "Howard Hughes and his brainchild, the Hughes Aircraft Company, laid the technological foundation for American success in prevailing in and ending the Cold War. During the post-World War II years, Hughes helped refocus industrial activity in Southern California from the simple assembly of aircraft to leadership in avionics and aviation innovation.
>
> "By 1948, Hughes had anticipated the critical importance of the embryonic fields of airborne electronics and guided missiles. He recruited brilliant talent and allocated significant resources to enable Hughes Aircraft Company to quickly attain technology leadership in electronic devices. This made Los Angeles the "Silicon Valley" of the aerospace golden age. After Hughes transferred the company's ownership to the Medical Institute, it broadly diversified; this core group soon became most active at the forefront of satellite intelligence collection.
>
> "During my years in the Pentagon, Hughes Aircraft became a preeminent supplier of airborne radar, air-to-air missiles and vital intelligence-collection systems.
>
> "It took decades for the Soviet Empire to collapse; the success of the West was based on its unmatched technological and industrial capability. The men and women of Hughes Aircraft helped put that foundation in place."

5

AVIATION DREAMS

WHILE HOWARD HUGHES was setting world records and his Aircraft Company began inventing new electronic devices, I was growing up in the Hawaiian paradise: surfing, playing the ukulele, and watching the rainbows over Diamond Head.

Waikiki Beach and Diamond Head, Oahu
(©iStockphoto/ssharick)

We young folks were allowed to be barefoot in schoolrooms until the sixth grade. And who could forget coming home from school and sliding down the steep, rain-slick, grassy hillside near home on your own bottom, or plunging into the cold and swift stream coursing below our house? Other fine memories are assembling my first bicycle using parts from several broken ones found in a junkyard, and listening to the crystal radio I had scraped together using spare parts from my father's radio repair shop in our basement.

My mother's ancestors Gerritt and Laura Judd, graduates of Yale University, arrived in 1828 from New England after a hazardous journey around Cape Horn. Gerritt was the doctor in the third group of Congregationalist missionaries to settle in Hawaii. He later became chief deputy to King Kamahameha III. My father, George Richardson, arrived in 1923 after traveling throughout the world as a radio operator aboard commercial ships. He settled in Honolulu rather than returning to his hometown in New Jersey because he met my mother Hester Pratt, graduate of Smith College and a teacher at Punahou School, which by 2008 was to be world-famous because President Barack Obama graduated there. (It's fascinating to me that President Obama also attended Occidental College, as did my son Bruce; surprising coincidences do occur.)

George and Hester married in 1927 and had three children, all boys; I was the youngest. Our mother instilled in us the deep-seated ethical and educational traditions of old New England, which had been faithfully transmitted through many generations of these Pacific isles immigrants. Our father generated in us a growing interest in mechanical things: how they worked, why they fail, how to repair them, and in what ways they could be improved. Both parents urged personal responsibility and that a good life requires hard work—a pretty good start for growing boys. This heritage provided a firm foundation for all three of us and helped us rise to the top of companies in different professions.

China Clipper, 1942
(courtesy of Wikipedia)

My aviation dream began at age five, when our family witnessed the landing approach of a Pan American *China Clipper*, a Martin M-130 flying boat. Three thousand visitors watched it land on the calm Honolulu harbor, marking the beginning leg of the first successful commercial attempt to cross the Pacific Ocean by air. The *Clipper* had departed from Alameda across the bay from San Francisco, with stops planned in Hawaii, Midway, Wake Island, Guam, and Manila. Piloted by Capt. Edwin Muslock, it carried US mail, other cargo, and a few passengers. Wow! What a thrill to witness a unique event in the history of commercial air travel! I imagined being way up in the sky, speeding from point to point, and viewing the landscapes from on high. I remember thinking what most young boys would: "I sure want to do that! It must be really exciting to take the controls and make that airplane strut its stuff!"

When I was six we visited my father's family home in New Jersey. During that time, the huge *Hindenburg* airship burned while approaching its linkup to the mooring mast at Lakehurst Naval Air Station. The vessel was enormous: more than two-and-a-half football fields long (804 feet), with a diameter bigger than a ten-story building (135 feet). This famous dirigible had just completed a two-day journey from Germany to the United States with ninety-seven people aboard. Unfortunately, its lifting element was an extremely combustible hydrogen gas. Theorists speculate that, in the presence of very bad weather with lightning, differential static electricity charges caused ignition before being discharged by ground contact through the mooring mast. Another credible theory was that an anti-Nazi group had secretly placed an incendiary device in the hull, with a timer set to explode after the *Hindenburg* was moored and empty of passengers. The late docking caused by bad weather resulted in what turned out to be a premature blast.

Our family was many miles away, but the alarming radio news, newspaper pictures, and movie newsreel clips made the disaster vivid to me, as if I had been at the scene. Although sixty people survived, this disaster was a dramatic lesson in my growing understanding of reality: not all flying can be safe.

Stories of heroism in air combat further kindled my youthful zeal, as the Battle of Britain raged in late 1940. As World War II began, the public illusion on the Allied side was of a resurgence of knighthood and chivalry in the air: noble men fighting for their strong beliefs. A foe was spared or even honored if he had performed well in a hand-to-hand struggle. Such chivalry among airmen was common during most of World War I, but quickly disappeared in the national struggle for survival in 1940. Combat brutality in air battle became far from noble. But little of this reality was obvious to this young boy in a remote Territory of the

United States. I was aware only of the images of those magnificent men in their flying machines.

Without much warning, on December 7, 1941, came the ingenious and surprise Japanese attack on Pearl Harbor. "A date which will live in infamy," according to President Roosevelt. It certainly was dramatic for us folks living in the Territory of Hawaii! A ten-year old, I awoke that morning hearing many thunderous explosions and saw huge smoke columns billowing skyward. It was fearsome to see Navy ships mortally damaged. We also noted many hostile "Rising Sun" aircraft marshalling over our home preparing to strafe Honolulu. It was obvious that—contrary to the Navy's belief espoused in the court-martial of Army Col. Billy Mitchell in 1925—aircraft can be extraordinarily effective in both air and surface combat. (Colonel Mitchell, opposed by the Navy, had conducted trials in 1921 and 1923 that sank a number of large combat ships with bombs dropped from aircraft.)

The Honolulu strafing was especially alarming to our family, since my father went downtown that morning on emergency duty to send commercial news stories by telegraph radio to San Francisco. He was one of the country's fastest Morse code operators—90 words per minute without error. I think he sent all the Pearl Harbor news that was published that day in the US mainland newspapers. After transmitting for twenty minutes, the station was shut down by the Navy Shore Patrol to ensure military security. During all this time, bullets were striking the building and nearby streets. Fortunately, his auto was not hit, and Pop arrived home safely.

Until war's end in 1945, I watched many types of military aircraft as they transitioned to battles in the South and Western Pacific. The PBY *Catalina* seaplanes were active in searching for hostile submarines. Seeing them land in Kaneohe Bay (when I was at Boy Scout camp) at night with their bright blue engine exhausts was another thrill for young observers like me. Even the engine noises evoked a sense of the exotic and mysterious—if only I could ride in a machine like that!

All these historic events engendered in me a lifetime fascination with aviation, a deep desire to learn how to pilot an airplane, and the determination to discover how I might qualify to participate in this challenging and creative industry.

PART TWO

BUILDING ON THE BASE

The period from 1949 through 1952 saw an upswing in the Cold War: in 1949 the USSR tested its first atomic bomb; the Western allies formed NATO (the North Atlantic Treaty Organization); and a few years later, the opposing Warsaw Pact was established by the Eastern bloc. Both the United States and the USSR began stockpiling nuclear weapons, including the newly created hydrogen bomb, first demonstrated by us in 1952, whose destructive force far exceeded that of "Little Boy" dropped on Hiroshima in 1945. Thus began the most extensive and expensive arms race in history.

Both sides made gigantic investments in defensive and offensive weapons to maintain a continuing balance of power, hoping that equal strength would assure each side that neither would risk a strike on the other for fear of massive retaliation. This philosophy was later called mutually assured destruction (MAD) or balance of terror.

Because of the frightful uncertainties during this period, US taxpayers were more than willing to increase military preparedness through increased defense spending, directly benefiting the industry devoted to this purpose, including Hughes.

No direct military confrontation between the two great powers occurred, but surrogate battles took place over contested borders between communist and noncommunist territories. The United States erred in endorsing a return to colonial empire concepts by supporting Great Britain in Malaysia and Burma, and France in Southeast Asia, setting the stage for Indonesian resentment and the future Vietnam War. Communism became the doctrine of the people in China in 1949, making it a natural ally of the Soviets. In 1950, the United States and its allies, under the aegis of the United Nations, became involved in countering North Korea's incursion into South Korea. To avoid asking Congress to declare war, the Truman administration called this the Korean Police Action. This conflict escalated into combat with the People's Republic of China, ending in a stalemate cease-fire three years later.

6

RECRUITING SUPERB TALENT

Although the Germans and British had each deployed jet fighters toward the end of World War II, the Korean "War" was the real proving ground for jet-fighter performance in protracted combat. North Korea and China flew USSR-supplied MiG-15 fighters (MiG is short for Mikoyan-i-Gurevich, the leading Russian fighter design bureau). The MiGs were countered mainly by US aircraft, principally F-86 *Sabres*. Compared to those in previous dogfight encounters, these aircraft were faster, flew at higher altitudes, and were more difficult to identify because of their swift closing rates. Most of these "simple" fighters were not equipped with radars. Moreover, there was little improvement in fighter weapons: still machine guns, cannon, and unguided rockets.

As Hughes Aircraft Company became essential to equipping Air Force fighter aircraft for continental air defense, a great increase in highly capable professional staff was mandatory. The work to be done was complex and at the outer edge of electronics technology. Recruiting possibilities were competitors, university graduates, and academic personnel. Talent from overseas usually could not be hired because of military security clearance requirements for defense-related programs.

Being centered in the Southern California cultural climate certainly helped. One mile from employees' offices were the Pacific beaches, a mile the other way was an RKO filming studio lot, two-hours distant were several winter skiing resorts. The magnificent Sierra Nevada range was ideal for backpacking; recreational boating marinas were nearby; magic Santa Catalina Island beckoned; three major universities were only a half-hour's drive; and the weather was close to perfect. Staff members could plan to watch the annual Rose Parade in Pasadena and afterwards cheer or boo the opponents at the celebrated Rose Bowl football game. They might even run into a famous movie star at a restaurant on the fabled Sunset Strip. Many apartment rentals and affordable homes were within a short commute. Who could ask for anything more? Recruitment from the eastern and central US states was usually a piece of cake.

Avalon, Catalina Island, California
(personal files)

In addition to Southern California's attractive ambience, the burgeoning aerospace electronics challenges and attractive compensation levels—even the aura of mystery that surrounded Howard Hughes—were powerful lures for potential staff members. Finally, the growing reputation for professional excellence at Hughes helped attract the best talent nationwide.

The national climate was also conducive to the development of new technologies. These years began what is now commonly referred to as "the golden era of aerospace." Government funding to support relevant research was evidenced by the teamwork, for example, between the Massachusetts Institute of Technology (MIT) and Lincoln Laboratories, Caltech, and the Jet Propulsion Laboratory (JPL), and the University of California and Lawrence Livermore Laboratory. Their programs focused on work directly related to the needs of aerospace contractors.

Universities expanded their programs in science and engineering in response to the eagerness of new college students to enter these expanding and challenging fields. This produced a surge of new professionals choosing aerospace engineering and graduates eager to be employees. Many PhD graduates opted to join industry rather than following their traditional academic pursuits. Thus, although recruiting the best talent was very competitive in the defense business, the growing supply usually met the demand.

Recruiting Brochure, 1951
(personal files)

Luxury Living in Southern California
(personal files)

Hughes fostered its connections with local science and engineering schools such as Caltech, the University of California, Los Angeles (UCLA), the University of Southern California (USC), and many more distant ones, by offering noted professors summer employment. When they returned to academia, enthusiasm about their company experience caused them to become recruiters for the firm, recommending their best students to consider Hughes. Some of these professors and many PhDs migrated to this exciting company with its healthy salary levels and rich opportunities for professional growth.

Hughes created a large fellowship program that became a magnet for top graduates of engineering schools. Selected new staff members worked part-time at the company as they attended UCLA or USC for two years to earn masters' degrees in their chosen fields. This program began in 1952 with 120 engineers. (I was one of this lucky bunch.) Each following year a similar group began the same process. In my forty years at Hughes, more than 4,000 engineers and scientists received master of science degrees, a great benefit to the firm and the two universities, as well as the nation. A yearly appointment of two PhD fellowships at Caltech also had begun a few years earlier, with excellent results throughout many years.

7

THE HOWARD
HUGHES LEGACY

ONCE JOINING THE company, employees quickly noticed that Hughes Aircraft Company embodied the aura and mystique of its founder, even though few personally met or even caught a glimpse of the famous man. Their creativity was stimulated by the reputation and break-the-precedent image of Mr. Hughes: it was rewarding to think outside the box, as he did, not inhibited by timeworn methods, and to be driven to do the task better and more efficiently. This spirit persisted long after Mr. Hughes was distant from the company's business and technical activities.

During his lucid years, Howard Hughes projected worldwide an image of a technical innovator who set new aviation records and was determined to do things in new ways. He can be credited for either inventing or enabling many unique airplane features: flush riveting of skins, retractable landing gear, lightweight wood-bonding, hydraulically powered control surfaces, electronic instrumentation, and electronic control stick operation. And don't forget the electrically powered hospital bed that the occupant can shape for comfort. Inventing that while recovering from his near fatal plane crash showed true grit!

Active involvement by Mr. Hughes in the diversities of aircraft design, setting world records, adding electronics to airplanes, overseeing an active portion of the movie business, sharing in the glamour of movie stars, owning three airlines, investing in real estate in Las Vegas, and controlling the primary oil-well drilling tool company provided plenty of fodder for story telling. Colorful tales about rambunctious Howard were added spice for Hughes employees. Some stories were probably true, others inflated by storytellers to beguile their listeners. Harmless humor about a legendary genius often eases the strain of intense and difficult work. Here are a few to enjoy.

Some Howard Hughes memorabilia were on-site at the Culver City facility. The H-1 *Racer* was safely kept in an old storage shed near the active flight test hangars. Seeing it, one could feel the excitement and visualize the events leading to the 1935 world speed record.

According to Noah Dietrich, this speed record flight had one unfortunate conclusion. Gen. O. P. Echols, head of the Army Air Corps, asked Mr. Hughes to bring the *Racer* to Dayton, Ohio, on his return to California following the cross-country speed run. Mr. Hughes agreed, but instead of landing, he overflew Dayton to refuel in Chicago on his way west. The gathered Air Corps senior brass were outraged, and General Echols reportedly declared, "He'll never get a dime's worth of business from me!" Mr. Dietrich's story has been questioned, since a different pilot actually returned the *Racer* on a different day, but the legend endures. In later years, many of us at Hughes perceived an on-going coolness in dealings with certain members of the Air Force, who perhaps had a lingering resentment of Mr. Hughes because of this incident, as well as his outspoken contempt for the federal government starting in the 1930s and continuing after the contentious 1947 Senate hearings on the *Spruce Goose* contracts.

Another colorful relic at Culver City was a World War II B-26 *Marauder* two-engine medium-range attack bomber that Mr. Hughes had reconfigured for recreational transportation. One side had a big picture window installed for sightseeing. A visitor walking beside the parked airplane could see a large well-carpeted suite with a luxurious swiveling seat, a very comfortable way to view the scenery as it passed beneath the touring B-26. Other comforts, apparently, were also available. Mal Currie, company CEO in 1989, told me that once, when he was invited to climb aboard, he spied a brassiere hanging from the flight control wheel. What a surprise!

John Black joined the company in the 1940s, and by the 1970s had become the senior vice president leading almost half of the 60,000-person Hughes staff. In 1943, he was in charge of designing the wing support structures for the *Spruce Goose*'s eight engines. He later led the assembly procedure for attaching the pre-molded plywood skin segments to the wooden fuselage using quick-dry glue. That glue cured in less than 1 minute. Precision woodwork and a lot of practice were required before the final assembly job. The assemblers got only one chance. Luckily, no errors were made—a misplaced skin piece would have required sawing it away along with its supporting rib structure.

During the design period, Mr. Hughes demanded frequent access to construction drawings and often directed very thoughtful improvement changes. His times for review were often late at night in his swank home overlooking the Bel Air Country Club. Once, John and three other engineers were told to arrive at midnight. A butler led them into the living room, where they enjoyed coffee while waiting more than an hour. Then two sets of high heels tripped lightly down the rear stairs, and a loud call came from Mr. Hughes to come on up. There he lounged in bed in his pajamas, and proceeded to roll out blueprints on his lap. During the next two hours, he directed several significant alterations to the design. An unusual way to operate!

Al McDaniel, a production acceptance test pilot from North American Aviation, joined Hughes in the late 1940s and eventually became manager of the company division that flew military test aircraft as well as corporate helicopters and passenger airplanes. During his early Hughes days, Al flew Mr. Hughes to many places and had to be on call twenty-four hours a day, seven days a week. Such a regimen was a real challenge to maintaining the mental alertness and stamina needed for safe piloting. Mr. Hughes once ordered Al to fly RKO starlets Rita Moreno and Terry Moore from Long Beach to Las Vegas. The evening before, the starlets were placed in a nearby hotel; Al was directed to stay at the same site, preparatory to driving them to the airport for early morning departure. Every half-hour during the entire night, Mr. Hughes telephoned both the hotel manager and Al to check on what the ladies were doing. In every case, their report was the same: fast asleep behind locked doors. Imagine the fatigue Al had to overcome to fly safely to Las Vegas the next morning.

Some time around 1950, Mr. Hughes scheduled a meeting in Sacramento with Governor Earl Warren to request rerouting of the planned new Marina del Rey freeway, which skirted the Hughes properties in Culver City. Mr. Hughes climbed aboard the transport aircraft at the company airstrip early in the morning; heavy fog completely obscured the runway. "Let's go!" Mr. Hughes commanded. McDaniel replied he could not see where to taxi to the takeoff position, upon which "Let's go!" was sharply repeated. Gingerly, Al gently powered the airplane to the end of the runway using the compass and relying on his memory. Readying for takeoff, he radioed the air traffic control center at nearby LAX (Los Angeles International Airport), requesting instrument takeoff. It was denied. Telling his passenger that news, he was curtly ordered to proceed anyway. Following orders, Al made the spooky blind takeoff with only compass direction, then stayed very low for a considerable distance, hoping to avoid LAX radar detection. If caught he would have to forfeit his pilot's license. They managed to get away safely, finally emerging above the fog bank and proceeding on visual course to Sacramento. Soon after they settled at cruise altitude, Mr. Hughes nonchalantly spent the remainder of the flight enjoying the comic strips in that morning's *Los Angeles Times*. The meeting with Governor Warren was a success, and the freeway was rerouted.

Airline flight planning at TWA was often not routine when Mr. Hughes was its majority owner. One of my friends, a senior TWA pilot, appeared at Chicago's Midway Airport one morning to pre-check an aircraft before a passenger flight to Memphis. Suddenly Mr. Hughes arrived in an old Chevrolet, strode up the entry stairs in his well-worn sneakers, and stated he was taking this aircraft to Canada! Much staff scurrying took place to find a replacement for the scheduled Memphis flight. Another airplane was found in the nick of time. The passengers were never told the reason for their delayed departure.

One day in 1949, Mr. Hughes appeared at Culver City in one of his ancient Chevrolets, complete with lunch sandwich and milk bottle. He had arranged to personally evaluate the new thrust-reversing propellers of a two-engine Consolidated Vultee Aircraft Company CV-240 passenger airplane. These devices, for decreasing landing runout distance on runways, had not yet been applied to public transport craft. At that time most pilots had an instinctive fear that a disastrous pitch reversal failure might occur in flight, as had happened to Mr. Hughes in his 1946 XF-11 crash. For his CV-240 testing, Mr. Hughes taxied out from one hangar of the cargo building, reversed propeller pitch, and taxied back in. He repeated this operation all afternoon.

In the XF-11 case, he had filed a lawsuit against Hamilton Standard, the designer of the reverse pitch mechanism. Because it was difficult to determine whether that failure had been caused by loss of oil pressure from plumbing leakage or a design error, the lawsuit came to naught. One person watching the repetitive CV-240 testing was Murray Beebe, leader of the Hughes rocket propulsion department. Murray previously had been manager of development engineering at Hamilton Standard during the XF-11 design. Ironically, Mr. Hughes was unaware that one of his current excellent performers had been the indirect target of that failed lawsuit.

Betty Robey was hired in 1949 as the secretary to the Service and Flight Department, and assigned to an office in the cargo building near the former assembly hangar of the H-4 flying boat. She had been quietly brought in as an applicant from the outside, since many secretaries in the front offices craved this assignment because of the opportunity to meet Howard Hughes and observe some of his exciting adventures. The office leader was somewhat concerned that none of them would be discreet and silent about what they would discover in this position. The job was with Joe Petrali, who had been part of the flight crew in the H-4's 1947 flight in Long Beach, and who accompanied Howard on many flights around the country. He now was in charge of all flight operations and maintenance. Betty did, indeed, get to observe many interesting incidents, as she related to me in 2010. In addition to many transport aircraft, a stable of old Chevrolets was housed in the hangar, many of which were often rescued from some remote parking lot after Mr. Hughes had abandoned them. Ava Gardner thought Howard had given one of these to her, and she became very upset when she found one day that he had driven it away to an unknown destination. There were also encounters with Katharine Hepburn, as she completed her flying lessons from instructor Howard, and Elizabeth Taylor, who had to be accompanied by her mother on a trip with Mr. Hughes to Las Vegas.

Betty also had many direct encounters with Howard Hughes, who usually arrived by the rear entrance of the Culver City facilities to avoid the front offices. For further privacy, he often used a small desk almost hidden in a rear corner of the cafeteria building. She always found him to be well dressed (seldom wore the oft-reported sneakers), and felt he was invariably kind and courteous. One amusing recurrent habit: if on his arrival he noticed she was in her office, he immediately dashed up to the ladies' room on the second floor to spruce up after a long trip. Knowing she was at her desk, he was sure the women's facility would be empty since there were no other females assigned to the cargo building. He could thus avoid undesired encounters with curious employees in the first-floor men's room! Everything about Howard required privacy and security. When he moved to Las Vegas, staff members from his Romaine Street office in Hollywood confiscated all of Betty's files, suspecting they contained information that should never be leaked to the public.

Several staff professionals, including Dr. John Mendel, who later headed our large Industrial Electronics Group, tell of mysterious nighttime visits by someone at the Culver City facility in the 1950s. Staff members would often work long hours to accelerate schedules on vital projects, their normal work hours followed by a quick dinner at a restaurant. Returning to the laboratory, they would see an old white Chevrolet with a single occupant parked some discreet distance from the security gate entrance. The anonymous visitor just sat there for hours, never approaching the entry gate. Everyone speculated that it was Howard himself, but none could gather enough courage to go out there and greet him. This peculiar event took place on many apparently random nights. No one ever knew for sure the occupant's purpose.

My actress friend Marcia Bures told me a story about the James Bond movie *Diamonds Are Forever*, starring Sean Connery and Jill St. John, which was filmed in Las Vegas in 1971. The producer, Albert "Cubby"

Broccoli, was a good friend of Howard Hughes, who at the time owned six hotels on the Strip: "Tell Cubby he can shoot anywhere at any time in all of the hotels I own." Cubby also got Mr. Hughes to arrange closing the main street for several days to shoot the exciting car chase. All the studio and acting principals were given complimentary hotel suites, free dining, and their choice of any entertainment performance. It's nice to have a good and hospitable friend who doesn't ask for reimbursement or movie residual fees!

In his later years, Mr. Hughes lived in Las Vegas, then tried avoiding national and local taxes by living less than six months at a time in many hotels in Europe, the Caribbean, Canada, and Mexico. According to Las Vegas service attendants, when he was in town, he would consume a pound of bacon each morning for breakfast! He apparently was also very fond of the film *Ice Station Zebra*, and watched it more than 150 times. (I personally am only up to twelve viewings of *Top Gun*.) He also delighted in banana-nut ice cream. In attempting to stock up plenty of that dessert, the hotel management found that Baskin-Robbins had discontinued the flavor, but they could make a special order of 350 gallons. After its receipt in Las Vegas, Mr. Hughes decided that he no longer liked banana-nut, so the hotel was stuck with a very excess inventory.

Hollywood Sign, Constructed in 1924
(©Massimo Catarinella)

Mr. Hughes strongly believed in real estate as the best way to invest and protect most financial resources. Visible to millions of people for almost ninety years has been a nostalgic remnant of his active participation in the movie business: the large "Hollywood" sign on a ridge overlooking Los Angeles. Made up of 45-foot-tall independent whitewashed letters, spanning 350 feet, it was constructed in 1924 for a real estate developer who hoped to snag excited buyers. Located on terrain known as Cahuenga Park, the site features a knoll with a 360-degree panoramic view of the main city, the San Fernando Valley, and the Pacific Ocean. Mr. Hughes bought the property in 1940, intending to build a mansion for his then-current girlfriend, Ginger Rogers.

They parted company soon after the purchase, so the house was never built. In 2002, the Hughes estate offered the parcel to other developers, sparking a very vocal public outcry to preserve the famous sign rather than suffering the blight of massive condominiums. Contributions from Hugh Hefner and others bought the site back for $12 million to forever preserve this old advertising marker that had become the symbol of a very popular industry.

Many public perceptions of Mr. Hughes stem from the spread of erroneous "facts" related to his contributions to aviation. A good example is found in the recent movie *Aviator*, a slick attempt at biography. The film concludes by saying it was his future vision that resulted in jet propulsion. Recognition for turbojet reality more properly must be given to the British and Germans in the 1930s. Mr. Hughes's best contribution to the world was his vision that electronics was the route to monumental aviation advances. Although he did not participate directly, that vision came to life through his creation of the Radio Department in Hughes Aircraft Company, which was always at the forefront of electronics technology.

The public is also not aware of the compassionate side of Mr. Hughes, who was quite sensitive to the well-being of his employees. In several cases, when he heard of illnesses of employees or their family members, he would give instructions to pay for the needed medical care. He did this in a way that the employee did not know the source of the funds. His doing good without credit was a virtue, usually cited by knowledgeable observers as a product of his innate shyness.

His fervent interest in new-product detailed design features persisted, regardless of his poor health. Dr. Albert (Bud) Wheelon, our CEO in 1988, told me that in Mexico only a week before Mr. Hughes's death in 1976, Howard demanded a full set of design drawings for the new Intelsat IV communication satellite. Surprisingly, he made no comment or criticism. He had not influenced designs at Hughes for more than twenty years, but his intense interest was unquenched. This interest had been well described by him years earlier "I am by nature a perfectionist, and I seem to have trouble allowing anything to go through in a half-perfect condition. So if I made any mistake it was in working too hard and in doing too much of it with my own hands." Such a prevailing characteristic was another reason for his reputation for endlessly procrastinating on important decisions needed by any of his subordinates.

An Abiding View

Despite the sometimes erratic and amusing anecdotes about Mr. Hughes, he maintained a very positive view of the future of Hughes Aircraft Company, as a 1949 publicly released letter to Gen. Harold L. George, the company's general manager, illustrates:

"I have observed with intense interest and great satisfaction the rapid rise of the Hughes Aircraft Company in the field of electronics to a position of leadership.

"Military applications of electronics are well recognized as of vital importance to the national security. The development of electronic devices of advanced design for military application has been a major factor in our rapid growth.

"However, our plans must envisage the research, development and production of electronic devices to fill a very obvious vacuum rapidly becoming apparent in our civilian and industrial economy. In fact, this program is already underway.

"Our national security requires the maintenance of worldwide leadership by this company, and I know you and I both feel a very definite responsibility to make even greater and more extensive contributions along the lines of research, development and production of electronic devices for both military and civilian purposes.

"Our responsibilities in military work, and our intention to develop civilian products, combine to make for this company a well-rounded program. Our objective must, therefore, be to pursue energetically a vigorous policy to establish this company as the foremost and most progressive electronics producer in this country."

The government thought in similar terms and actively urged the company to pursue advances in the use of infrared radiation to improve capabilities of many types of weapons.

Culver City Facility, 1956
(courtesy of UNLV)

8

TECHNOLOGY
ADVANCES: INFRARED

THE GERMANS GAINED another first, in addition to the robotic V-1 buzz bomb mentioned previously, when in 1944 they created a surface-to-air guided missile called Enzian. With an enormous 1,100-pound warhead, Enzian was made of wood for the same reason as the H-4 flying boat. Its guidance to the target area was by radio steering commands from a gunner on the ground. In the final stage of intercept, a telescope in the missile captured infrared (IR) emanations from the target and focused them on a movable mirror, which passed them to a single detector cell; four blades of a spinning fan interrupted the energy before it reached the cell. When the energy level was measured to be equal in the four samples that got through in one fan rotation, the mirror was known to be properly pointing at the target. That gave the missile enough information to steer to within its warhead's destructive zone. Nazi priorities changed rapidly in the latter days of the war, however, and the experimental Enzian project was abandoned.

In 1946, the Naval Ordnance Test Station at China Lake, California, began a ten-year development effort to perfect the AIM-9 Sidewinder, an air-to-air missile with an infrared guidance system. Although the program encountered many difficulties and failures in the first five years, it produced an extremely successful weapon that was deployed throughout the friendly nations of the world, with a fine combat record. Advanced versions are still in production today.

The early Sidewinder used a rather simple passive infrared guidance system—"passive" meaning it received thermal energy from wherever it was pointed but did not transmit IR energy to illuminate targets—that imposed little burden on the launch aircraft. The Raytheon Corporation and Ford Motor Company became the primary manufacturers of the weapon. Raytheon and Hughes were fierce competitors in missilery; "no holds barred" tactics were normal in this rivalry. My public speeches in the 1980s referred to that dreaded company as the "R-word," avoiding the use of its full name, to the delight of my Hughes associates.

⁂

The term *infrared* is used to define radiation in the form of heat. The word suggests that the thermal energy frequency is just below (infra) that of the visible color red. Sometimes objects show both IR and visible light at the same time, such as a candle flame. Figure 2.1 shows all parts of the electromagnetic spectrum, highlighting detailed sub-segments of radiations in the visible, infrared, radar, and radio frequency bands. The reader may wish to refer to this figure during discussions throughout the book.

Here's a quick overview of what IR is all about. As Figure 2.1 shows, electromagnetic energy radiation is observed in many distinct forms, identified by common names such as X-ray, visible, infrared, and radio. Each form differs from the others by its specific electromagnetic frequency, or number of oscillations per second. As mentioned earlier, frequency is the inverse of wavelength: the shorter the wavelength, the higher the frequency. The IR band is the region of thermal radiation. All physical things project some heat waves, unless they are maintained at absolute zero kelvin: -460ºF. Shaped inert objects, as well as living ones, radiate slightly differing temperatures (wavelengths) from each segment of their exteriors, so an IR image can appear with distinguishable characteristics, just as with reflected visible light. You can sense these differences by passing your hand from the tires to the sides and the hood when you step out of a car.

This phenomenon can be exploited for surveillance and targeting, and is described further in Part Five. In these beginning years, we were just trying to make a sensor see a hot spot like the exhaust nozzle of a jet engine.

By 1951, the Air Force had become aware of the Navy's progress in developing the Sidewinder, whose passive IR guidance gave the fighter freedom to operate without its radar locked on the selected target. Concerned about missing such an opportunity, the Air Force pressured Hughes to develop an IR version of the Falcon missile.

The company's infrared experience had begun in the late 1940s with the design of a star tracker for the Strategic Air Command's SM-62

Figure 2.1. Electromagnetic Spectrum Usage

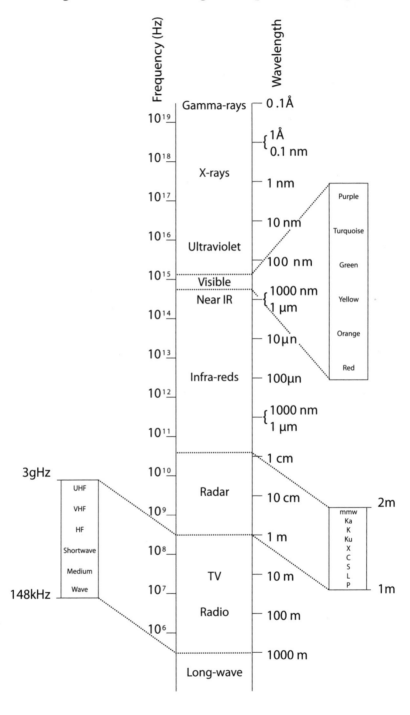

Snark, named after the beast in Lewis Carroll's amusing book *The Hunting of the Snark*. This weapon was a nuclear warhead cruise missile built by Northrop.

The tracker provided celestial corrections to keep the inertial reference guided weapon on course. Initial versions used visible light optics, but Hughes found that infrared sensing with an accurate stabilization system gave better performance. The sensor used a non-cooled lead-sulfide detector originally developed by the Germans during World War II. In addition to their efforts on the Enzian missile, the Germans produced IR devices that spotted incoming nighttime bomber raids and provided pointing information so that high power searchlights could visibly illuminate the area for their antiaircraft cannon gunners.

Snark Cruise Missile, 1953
(courtesy of the National Museum of the US Air Force)

After the war, one of their leaders, Dr. Kutcher, came to Lockheed, then to Hughes, along with several scientists from Poland, Belgium, and France. They formed a team of fifteen experts who made many rapid advances in IR technology. Special office arrangements were necessary, however, to preclude daily contact between the Poles and their new German boss because of the Poles' animosity stemming from bitter memories of atrocities perpetrated against their country by the Nazis.

In the Hughes star tracker design, incoming thermal energy from the selected star passed through a protective glass window and was focused by telescopic lenses through a spinning reticule onto the simple detector element. The reticule's rhythmic on-off switching of the starlight energy produced alternating current electrical signals. A gimbaled mechanism controlled by servomechanisms kept the telescope pointed at the star. Guidance corrections en route were determined from the star's geometric position relative to the desired flight plan to the target.

The IR Falcon Missile

The star tracker, although it performed well in flight testing, was not perceived by Hughes's senior management as a product line worth pursuing, especially as the *Snark* never entered full production. At Air Force insistence, however, Hughes completed an IR Falcon feasibility study and received development contracts for the missile in 1952. This push by the Air Force produced two results favorable to the future of Hughes Aircraft Company: an excellent missile to manufacture and the beginning of a large and diverse electrooptical product line (see Parts Five, Seven, and Eight). The nose of the IR Falcon, called an irdome, was a hemisphere sheltering the seeker. It was initially made of clear quartz that passed infrared energy at wavelengths matching the uncooled lead-sulfide detector. The gimbaled seeker mechanism, which supported and steered the detector, had a focusing telescope and spinning reticule similar to those of the star tracker.

Changing the detector material from lead-sulfide to lead-selenide, which responds at longer wavelengths (lower frequencies), provided two major performance improvements: (1) far better sensitivity (i.e., the ability to respond to far lower, or weaker, heat inputs, allowing detection at much longer ranges); and (2) far better discrimination between an engine nozzle and an exhaust gas plume. The protective irdome needed to pass energy at these longer wavelengths was made of a newly developed material, cast polycrystalline silicon, polished to an optical finish. Hughes also chose to process detector outputs by measuring wavelength (frequency) differences in the target scene. Sidewinder just looked for energy strength seen. This finer discrimination can be sensed when you listen to a radio tuned to an FM rather than an AM station. Far less distortion is evident.

The new detector design was made possible by giant leaps in the placement of thin films of exotic materials on ceramic substrates, the precursor to microelectronic devices. To operate properly, this detector had to be cooled to -321ºF. Falcon did this by dispensing liquid nitrogen from a container, achieving cooldown in four seconds and sustaining the sensor's low temperature for at least two minutes. The pilot had to command a start time prior to the intended weapon launch, which was no problem in bomber attacks but became a severe limitation in uncertain and rapidly changing dogfight situations, as occurred in Vietnam (see Part Six).

Seeker information for guidance was handled in a manner similar to the semiactive radar Falcon, with commands sent to control surfaces to correct deviations from the computed path to impact.

Tail attacks against an adversary began by pointing the Falcon's seeker to match the line of sight of the fighter's radar or by the pilot's visual aim. The pilot commanded IR seeker lockup upon hearing an audio confirmation signal in his headset. After the weapon separated, the fighter was immediately free to maneuver. The super-cooled detector allowed targets to be seen at ranges up to seven miles, permitting accurate intercepts at longer ranges than Sidewinder.

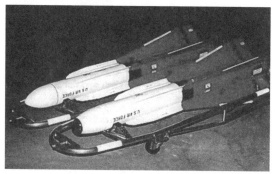

Radar and IR Guided Falcon Missiles
(courtesy of the National Museum of the US Air Force)

When both radar and IR Falcons were deployed, squadron commanders could choose a weapon type for each fighter: (1) semiactive radar guidance for longer intercept ranges and under conditions of poor visibility; and (2) IR for target tail shots and intercepts when radar was obscured by clutter or hostile countermeasures. A Falcon mixture could give great operational flexibility.

Hughes produced a total of 52,000 Falcons of both types for delivery to the Air Force. These missiles were matched to several fighter aircraft for more than thirty years, and the weapon was finally decommissioned in 1980. The final unique version was the AIM-4H with an IR sensor aided by an active laser and a four-laser-beam proximity fuse. Only twenty-five were made, and that project was aborted in 1971.

Although heavier, with less IR-detection sensitivity, and often performing with less accuracy, Sidewinder had overseas sales greatly exceeding Falcon's because it had several attractive features the Falcon lacked: it was normally carried outside rather than inside the fighter (Falcon later

employed protective dome covers for exposed mounts); it was less dependent on electronic integration with the mother aircraft; there was little
cooldown limitation; and its proximity fuse made a direct hit unnecessary.

Facility Expansion

In 1951, continuing government concerns about bomber attacks near
US borders prompted a search for a Hughes missile manufacturing site

Tucson Facility, 1951
(courtesy of Raytheon)

distant from California's Pacific shoreline. Safety considerations dictated
large acreage for remote storage and final assembly of products with rocket motors and warheads. An ideal site was found in the desert just south
of the airport in Tucson, Arizona. Hughes Tool Company purchased
the land and the Air Force paid for construction of the initial buildings.
Hughes Aircraft Company equipped and operated the plant, paying lease
fees to both Hughes Tool Company and the government. Selection of
this site was partially steered by Del Webb, a friend of Howard Hughes
who had developed most of the company's facilities at Culver City. Webb
predicted that desert land he already owned adjacent to the new plant
would gain immense value from a large demand for housing developments. He was right: a real bonanza!

More buildings were added in the 1980s, funded and owned by the
Aircraft Company.

An amusing incident occurred at this site one night in 1983: an invasion of the United States by boxcar! A spur rail line was used at the
Tucson facility for transporting incoming explosive devices and shipping

finished products to military storage locations. Security fences surrounded the final rail section, with armed guards at the gates. A set of "empty" boxcars, scheduled to pick up a large shipment the next day, arrived late one evening. Since all the rail paperwork was complete and apparently correct, there was no inspection inside the cars, and the guards let the car string into the fenced area. Next morning, the arriving day-shift guards were astonished to see a group of Mexicans cooking breakfast on small campfires in the secure area! The corralled group turned out to be illegal immigrants who had earlier boarded the empty boxcars at a remote siding. When they awoke they were very unhappy at finding themselves fenced in! Fortunately, the safety and security breach had no negative results for Hughes, and it had to be a no-cost benefit to the US Immigration and Naturalization Service.

Another story comes from Jim Uphold, one of our stalwarts in radar and program management. When he was a twelve-year-old boy living in Whittier, California, he noticed a neighbor working each day in his garage. Curious, Jim went in the garage one day and saw the man cutting many small square pieces from a thin fiberglass sheet. He asked what they were for, but received no answer. He also noticed that numerous stacks of these squares were trucked away each week. In later years, long after Falcon production had ended, Jim spotted an old shipping container for the missiles. On inquiry, he found that the protective inner lining of the container was fiberglass—made very tough by shaped molding of many laminated squares. Jim had finally solved the mystery of what his neighbor had been doing those many years earlier: he had been a garage-shop supplier who always practiced Hughes's trademark secrecy.

9

FROM PARADISE
TO ENTERPRISE

Aerospace was booming in 1952 when I began my forty years of personal experience with Hughes, its evolution, enormous growth, and worldwide acclaim. Like Howard Hughes, I fulfilled a dream of being part of aviation. Howard's genius and fame inspired many like me to want to join a team that was almost daily making technology breakthroughs in military defense and later in satellite and space exploration.

For me as a boy, however, the question was how I could realize my dreams. Much preparation was needed. Parental guidance gave me a solid foundation: education is of highest priority; ethical standards are vital; zeal and perseverance are essential to ensure meeting objectives; physical fitness and healthy lifestyle should always be of great importance. Friendliness, cooperation, and positive interaction with all varieties of people must be practiced constantly.

Education in the subtleties of life and the marvels of science took intense focus and hard work. In my case, planning on how to proceed was hampered by lack of funds. It was a tradition among Hawaiian missionary descendants to attend a New England college. I wanted to go to Yale, but could not swing the expense. Merit scholarships, part-time work at college, and summer jobs got me through my four undergraduate years at Tufts University in Massachusetts. My college study and work regimen, together with participation in competitive football and the swim team, demanded a lot of after-hours study with few social opportunities. The reward was a bachelor of science degree in engineering.

As if by magic, after I waited three months for a response to my application to Hughes, an offer finally arrived by mail in my fraternity dormitory. It included a fellowship at USC to earn a master's degree in engineering within two years.

I had already accepted an offer from the Chrysler Institute. The key interviewer there had asked how I would redesign the current Chrysler automatic transmission to improve its performance. I answered that I had no experience in this field, but I would begin by researching the transmission's current flaws, then try to invent and test remedies. "Perfect answer; you're hired!" he declared.

Imagine the difficulty of choice! Now it could be off to sunny Southern California instead of snowy and windy Detroit, coupled with the chance to sample the mysterious Hughes aura. I could also attend USC, the perennial national football winner. It was very embarrassing to notify Chrysler about changing my commitment, and revealing this to the Tufts career placement counselor was tough since I was the first graduate to be accepted at Chrysler Institute. My tremendous enthusiasm for a new life about to start pulled me through these difficulties.

Entering the Profession

At Hughes, I was assigned to the Airborne Systems Laboratories as a "packaging engineer." My first task was to design mechanical structures to house electronic circuits of airborne fighter radars for our Air Force contracts—particularly the design upgrades for the F-86D, F-89, and F-94C aircraft.

F-86, F-94, F-89 Interceptors
(courtesy of UNLV)

The job was not an easy one. Starting with a paper schematic drawing of the electronic circuit and a list of the resistors, capacitors, inductors, transformers, and miniature vacuum tubes, the packaging task was to design plastic boards to mount these components on and define the etching patterns of copper laminates on the boards to interconnect each electronic part. The next task was to create an aluminum support structure within which many of these cards interconnected to form a "black box" or "unit" that would perform a specific function. Connectors with many prongs electrically tied such subassemblies with other units comprising the complete radar.

Producibility and field accessibility called for configuring many easily separable subassemblies. Special attention was needed to ensure small size, light weight, adequate heat conductivity and circulating air-cooling, repairability, survival in the field, and low cost manufacturing. The ruggedness of any product for military use required a great deal of forethought: these items would be exposed to all possible environmental extremes, perhaps be soaked in saltwater, dropped into the mud, dragged over rough surfaces, bounced in a truck, and in this case, operated in the nose of an active combat fighter. Whenever possible, fastening devices, circuit cards, aluminum structures, and component types were selected from a standardized list to avoid unique purchasing demands or fabrication methods. Adherence to government requirements and standards was most important. All the many designed parts needed specific definition for purchasing, fabricating, and assembling. Production experts had to be continuously consulted to assure that the final design would be optimum for manufacturing in our facilities. With the assistance of a draftsman, the resulting hardware design would be finalized on a series of blueprints, purchasing lists, and fabrication instructions for use by the production team. Each black box had hundreds of parts and thousands of electrical connections, requiring precise definition and intensive care in construction.

I had no idea of how to do this work! I did know that garnering wisdom and visualizing the appropriate behavior in a new workplace was best done through observation of other staff members, and my seasoning took place among a most creative and colorful team. I was surrounded by office mates and associates whose life experiences were quite different from mine. They were quick to advise and correct in a diplomatic way my attempts as a team member at performing my design responsibilities.

Their many war stories helped expand my view of US culture, values, and shortcomings. One man had worked next to future movie star Robert Mitchum, both of them riveting wing skins on Lockheed's P-38 *Lightning* fighters. This man then enlisted as a transport pilot for the Army Air Corps and spent many months flying from Burma to China in a C-47 *Dakota* over the famous Himalayan "Hump," supplying wartime material to our Chinese allies. Another office mate survived the 1942 Bataan death march and was imprisoned by the Japanese for more than three years in a notorious Japanese concentration camp. He was a prime exemplar of the zealous work ethic, but he was a most inflexible and doctrinaire disciplinarian. His personality had likely been changed by his being subjected for years to a brutal and regimented camp lifestyle—a good case of a most likable person becoming a brainwashed camp survivor.

One of our fine marketing professionals had been a notable 1939 polo player in the US cavalry and was stationed in Luzon, Philippines, when the Japanese invaded. He led the last cavalry charge in US history, escaped capture, then organized and commanded the Filipino guerilla forces throughout Luzon until Gen. Douglas MacArthur made his "I shall return" invasion.

Other work associates included a P-47 *Thunderbolt* pilot who flew nine missions on June 6, 1944, supporting the Normandy beach landings; another who piloted a B-24 *Liberator* in two of the raids against the Ploesti, Rumania, oil fields in which more than half the US bombers were shot down; a man who performed many hazardous B-24 missions in the South Pacific; a noted fighter ace who scored fourteen victories against the Japanese; a Marine Corps private who survived the Iwo Jima combat after being buried under fallen palm trunks for three days with a broken back; an Army pilot who had flown Gen. Omar Bradley to order Gen. George Patton to delay the advance into southern France; a retired admiral who had commanded the destroyer flotilla protecting the Okinawa invasion fleet from innumerable *kamikaze* attacks; an officer who armed the A-bomb aboard the B-29 *Enola Gay* before it left Tinian for its Hiroshima target; and a Japanese-American Nisei who had suffered as a young boy in the atrocious and misguided World War II internment camps in the western United States. He was a close friend of mine, but I once made the grievous error of jokingly calling him James Cagney's frequent movie retort, "You dirty rat." I certainly never intended to insult him. In spite of my many apologies, he never forgave me for that rejoinder, since it was what the detention camp guards had called him. He never spoke to me again, much to my regret.

These associates and many others did a marvelous job of seasoning me for important work, imparting their personal wisdom, and expanding my comprehension of the many facets of the complexities of real life.

10

CAREERS IN WEAPONRY

AFTER MATURING IN this exciting profession, when giving speeches at many public gatherings, business conferences, universities, and high schools, I was often faced with the question, "How could you have spent your entire forty-year career making weapons that kill people?" Such a negative accusation was always difficult to answer in a way that could satisfy individuals who craved unchallenged peace with all disputes settled by sincere and good-faith negotiations. Most people in the academic audiences had a deep and sincere sense of moral values or perhaps religious beliefs and practices. They assumed I was somehow basically evil, so my responses were usually discounted.

Unfortunately, attaining the peaceful Nirvana envisioned by my questioners has not yet come to pass on this Earth. Maybe someday it will happen, but probably not in our lifetimes. Nations and segments of society always seem to differ on cultural values and comparative economic status or stability. Invariably, there are radical individuals and discontented groups wanting to control others by any means. These are usually described as extremists and can be found in any society, including the United States. Most religious groups espouse "peace and goodwill to all," but are very upset when others do not share religious beliefs exactly like their own. Many are eager to take physical action to force conversion or subjugation. Many of these zealots use the religious banner as a mask for gaining economic and political domination.

Certainly, national and representative groups should pursue diplomacy and diligent negotiation to the limit before resorting to force. If one nation is wealthy, like the United States, and another nation wants or needs major help, it's easy and morally right to share some assets. But suppose that nation is stronger and demands most of the richer country's resources? This would likely cause great hardship, so how far should one be willing to reach for compromise with this bully? An old saw among foreign-relations professionals is, "Diplomacy can fill the gaps, but only if the gaps are fillable." Surely, the Prussian Carl von Clausewitz in his 1832 treatise, *On War,* was correct in saying, "Force is the final step in diplomacy." Centuries of history have confirmed the truth of that simple phrase. It is too bad that human foibles are difficult to remedy by good faith and trust, even in current times.

My personal view on this issue was guided by my father's direct experience in four major wars, by personally witnessing the 1941 Japanese raid on Pearl Harbor, and by remembering several friends who perished in World War II and the Korean combat.

Surprise Attack on Pearl Harbor, 1941
(©iStockphoto/raciro)

Perhaps these twentieth-century wars could have been avoided by negotiation, but rulers like Hitler, Mussolini, Tojo, Stalin, and Khrushchev did not respond to many appeasement efforts made across the negotiation tables. The US peace-loving, isolationist, and cost-saving attitudes in the 1920s and 1930s actually encouraged aggressive moves by the Axis powers, perceiving little risk of US opposition. We apparently had forgotten the well-founded belief of President George Washington: "There is nothing so likely to produce peace as to be well prepared to meet an enemy." When we finally entered World War II, we were miserably unprepared, with only a small inventory of very obsolete weapons. I personally witnessed this during the attack on Pearl Harbor: a neighbor was killed in her home by a US antiaircraft shell that had failed to fuse aloft. The US manufacturing base was entirely consumer oriented, and it took more than two years to adapt to wartime needs. This lack of military readiness resulted in the loss of many thousands of US and Allied lives, and it probably delayed closure of that very destructive conflict by at least two years.

A piece of ancient history that happened on the Island of Milos in the sixth century BC is illuminating. As told to me by a PhD historian and tour guide there (as well as recounted by the famous Thucydides), Athenian city-state emissaries approached the island's leaders and asked them to ally with Athens in the coming war with Sparta. The people of Milos were innately peace-loving and believed that nurturing friendly trade was the best means to preserve harmony and gain wealth. No inhabitants used or owned combat weapons. After the Milos leaders refused the invitation to team with the Athenians, they were told to reconsider, and the representatives sailed away. Returning sometime later, and hearing another polite "no," the Athenians commanded their troops to slaughter every man, woman, and child on the island! So much for the effectiveness of deeply felt commitment to peaceful negotiations.

In my own lifetime, there was the notorious case of Great Britain's Prime Minister Neville Chamberlain. For more than a year, he personally negotiated with Hitler in an attempt to allay the German Chancellor's outspoken demands and forestall the obvious Nazi plan to overrun and control all of Europe. Chamberlain also set the government policy to curtail any buildup of British military equipment or personnel. This was a perfect example of selecting negotiation as the only method of averting conflict. Although the Prime Minister may have been as well motivated as the current "peaceniks," the results were catastrophic. It took the 1939 Nazi *blitzkrieg* of Poland for the English to finally oust Chamberlain from office and begin a frenzied rearmament policy. What a prolonged folly was that idealistic negotiation effort, especially when the negative outcome of these discussions was obvious to almost everyone.

As related in *Einstein, His Life and Universe* by Walter Isaacson, Albert Einstein was an ardent and leading pacifist until 1933 when Hitler came to power. A good scientist can change his or her viewpoint in the light of new evidence. Stating that absolute pacifism was for the moment not warranted, he left Germany and switched to a "no disarm without adequate security" policy, which antagonized the War Resistors International, for which he had been an ideal and active model. In 1939, Einstein, Leo Szilard, and Edward Teller recommended to President Roosevelt that intensive work begin to develop energy from atomic fission. They knew that Germany had already begun development, and they feared the Nazis would win that potentially deadly military race. Einstein was still very concerned about this radical change in his pacifist belief, but he finally felt rewarded when atomic developments enabled the end to World War II.

An illustration of poor technology preparation was the inability of the French to counter the rapid advance of the Nazis in 1940. Their defense plan relied on the "impregnable" Maginot Line of trenches, redoubts, walls, tank traps, and bunkers intended to resist and discourage

any invasion similar to those of World War I. The French did not antici-
pate, or technically prepare for, an end-around maneuver using tanks and
motorized transport. The Nazis, however, did not attempt to storm the
Line. Nazi combat equipment was so superior to that of the French, that
they suffered minimal losses in the assault.

French technology in World War I had been among the best possible, especially in fighter aircraft. But during subsequent years, the French
government could only think of waging any new war just like that in
1915 and made little investment in continual combat-equipment modernization. Even though they had a great advantage in numbers of troops
in the field, they didn't stand a chance against the blitzkrieg.

During my many years in aerospace, the United States faced a real
threat from the Soviet Union. There was a genuine worry that the "evil
empire" (colorful words of President Reagan) would use any military
advantage to dominate politically and economically all of Europe and
eventually the entire world. The Soviets had demonstrated the force of
arms very clearly in overpowering the nations of Eastern Europe. Both
national and individual safety were at risk throughout the western allied
countries. Indeed, this threat became a strong and urgent motivator for
these allies to invest for survival. The reaction of the United States to the
perceived threat was to create a defense force adequate to counter any
aggression, as well as to engage in an economic competition that could
influence the ultimate outcome. It took almost fifty years to finally feel
safe from attack by that hostile empire. Much of the success was due to
the significantly better performance of US military equipment and to the
stockpiling of adequate arms inventories among the friendly nations. The
superior training and demonstrated effectiveness of US military personnel were likewise major factors.

Unfortunately, when viewed in retrospect, some countermoves during that period were very wrong and counterproductive, particularly the
Vietnam War, which was based on faulty assumptions and ignorance of
the cultures involved, as well as having been ineptly managed. A dominant fallacy was a foreign policy based on the "domino theory," expressed
in 1954 by President Eisenhower: if one nation of southeast Asia became
communist, all others in the region would quickly succumb. Massive
intervention was undertaken in what was actually an internal Vietnam
revolution rather than a Soviet or Chinese attempt to seize control. Without engaging in combat, both those powers benefited from the prolonged
encounter: allied Western nations were distracted from the real threat.

The United States had enough manpower and sophisticated equipment to have attained its military objectives. However, political leaders
thousands of miles distant from the combat action (apparently moti-

vated only by their public appearance) minutely directed the field forces. Citizen discontent became extreme and violent; many fled to Canada to avoid legal difficulties back home.

Another error in US participation in the conflict was the regime we supported: a political clone of the odious French colonial regime ejected in 1954. It was corrupt and extremely unpopular with the local population.

In the United States, the very vocal protesters frequently discredited themselves by practicing abuse of returning soldiers, destabilizing universities, advocating "free love," and using several kinds of narcotics. Although there were many responsible and eloquent anti-war spokesmen, it was hard to discuss deep issues with somebody smoking pot.

The US policy makers started down a trail of many blunders and took too long to rectify them. This was a meaningful and painful example of military might misused; intelligent diplomacy, expansion of trade treaties, or perhaps "looking the other way," would have been a far better and less costly way to foil the domino theory fantasy.

The good news is that the fiasco did not result in significantly turning away from the genuine USSR threat. Active investment in weapon improvements avoided a disastrous clash between the superpowers, hastened the end of the Cold War, and enabled an impressive and quick victory in the first Gulf War.

Of course, the Middle East is always simmering. Thousands of years of instability continue, even after countless efforts by world leaders to arrange cease-fires, achieve disarmament, foster peaceful negotiations, offer economic inducements, and cement new trade relationships. All these steps have had only a short-term benefit. As soon as things seem to settle, some small event upsets all parties and fosters new disputes about who was at fault. The complexities are enormous: incompatible religious practices, land control and usage, national citizenship, work rules, birth control, widely divergent views of the limits of human rights, tribal controversies, diverse languages, preservation of historical artifacts, individual and group pride, and economic balance. Most everyone outside the region wishes these perpetual problems could somehow be resolved or simply disappear, enabling a permanent peace. Alas, this has not been possible in tens of centuries. The only stability comes from a balance in armed strength among all sides, restraining attacks for fear of damaging reprisals. Even if a reasonable balance were maintained, however, the extremist zealots and terrorists would still wreak havoc since they are perfectly willing to sacrifice themselves in pursuit of extremist religious propaganda. The entire world is unable to stop these tragedies. Maybe someday the outspoken peace activists will find the right negotiation tools to do the tough job properly, and then lead the way to total disarmament. I doubt that this Nirvana will ever be found, but we all can hope it will.

Today's public does not seem aware of the positive benefits that have resulted from the evolution of high performance US weaponry in the last half-century. A comparison of the Allied incursions in Iraq in 1991 and 2003 with the terrible combat carnage of World War II is most revealing. To achieve the same results in Iraq using technologies of the 1940s would have required the leveling of Baghdad and destruction of its surroundings, with great loss of civilian lives as well as the historic treasures of early civilization. Even the losses of active combatants on both sides were significantly less compared to those during the campaigns in Okinawa or in southern Italy. Use of discriminating all-weather sensors, intelligent guided weapons, electronic countermeasures, and robust communication networks resulted in focused elimination of hostile forces with miniscule collateral damage to people or property. Allied force casualties were hundreds of times less than those that occurred in many equivalent engagements in 1944. One might argue that opposing the Japanese or Germans was more difficult, but the Iraqi forces were well trained and far more numerous than the ground combatants of the Allies. Iraq possessed what they thought were modern weapons, mostly obtained from the USSR. Differences in weapon performance was a large factor in rapidly overcoming opposition.

Since civilizations throughout the ages have not seemed to change much, I strongly believe that a nation such as the United States with all its enormous natural resources must be adequately armed to avoid plunder. I was deeply honored and most pleased to have helped put us ahead in the operational performance of virtually all military implements for "our side." It has long been said that the best defense is an excellent offense, but I prefer "The best defense is to remain more capable than any opponent if combat cannot be avoided." Or better yet, "The best defense is deterrence; no combat will result." The phrase stated above, attributed to George Washington, is worth repeating: "There is nothing so likely to produce peace as to be well prepared to meet an enemy."

Efforts by Hughes Aircraft Company in the defense and intelligence fields to ensure our nation's preparedness to meet possible enemies have also greatly benefited civilian survival and lifestyle. Our products enabled the avoidance of possible wars, ensured quick settlement of other conflicts, and helped complete many combat missions with little collateral damage. Perhaps more importantly, most of our technology discoveries have quickly migrated into numerous devices used to improve the lives and pleasures of people throughout the world.

PART THREE

CONFRONTING CHALLENGES

THE UNITED STATES defense business continued to grow as the Soviets relished the Chinese-US standoff in Korea, applied more political pressure in Europe, and began their attempts to bring communism to the Western Hemisphere in the Caribbean and Central America. They also demonstrated fearsome destructive capability, adding to their 1949 fission atomic warhead a 1953 test detonation of an enormous hydrogen or fusion explosion. Substantial success in ICBM design and production by both the USSR and the United States prompted internal and external debate about remedies to this alarming strategic threat. Both President Dwight Eisenhower and Premier Nikolai Bulganin were well versed in military matters and encouraged investment in their respective national defense budgets.

In 1956, Egyptian Prime Minister Gamal Abdel Nasser nationalized the Suez Canal, precipitating an invasion by Israel, Britain, and France in their attempt to regain control. When the United States did not endorse this effort, troops were withdrawn and the UN took over management of the canal, with a new toll arrangement with Egypt.

In 1957, the Soviets beat the United States into space by launching Sputnik 1, the world's first artificial satellite. (I saw that newborn planet the second evening of its life: it passed overhead as I was leaving the Culver City facility). Competition between the East and West for international prestige and military strength generated political enthusiasm for investing large resources. Staying ahead already required emphasis on technological innovation in every type of military equipment, and now the space race demanded solutions to physical problems never before tackled. To manage the planning and financing of our space efforts, the United States formed the National Aeronautics and Space Administration (NASA) in 1958. The bombastic Nikita Khrushchev came to Soviet power in that same year, and his blustering personality was clearly in evidence in 1960, as he performed his famous shoe-pounding-on-the-conference-table tirade at the United Nations Center in New York.

These dramatic events made this an uncertain though exciting time. The best news for the electronics business was the rapidly growing maturity of solid-state circuitry devices as a replacement for bulky vacuum tubes. Diodes, transistors, and the beginnings of ceramic plates with laminated active metallic layers enabled dramatic reductions in the volume, power, weight, and cost of electronic equipment. The new devices permitted conversion, mathematical analysis, and storage of all information types in a numerical format. The civilization-altering digital computer age was about to begin.

11

LEADERSHIP REVOLUTION

AT HUGHES, TURMOIL prevailed among the corporate executives, partially due to Noah Dietrich's suspending their 1952 bonuses, but mostly because of their continuing inability to obtain Mr. Hughes's approval of key decisions. In a confrontation with them, Mr. Hughes promised to restore the bonuses, use a substantial part of company profits to develop commercial products to be manufactured by a new company, and assign portions of that company's equity to Hughes Aircraft Company executives. He also said, "Be patient; I may have a hard time making up my mind, but once I do, I move fast." After a twenty-day wait, none of his pledges materialized, so the revolt began.

Dean Wooldridge briefly described frustrations with Mr. Hughes in an interview by Dr. Lillian Hoddeson on August 21, 1976 (as related in an oral history transcript in the American Institute of Physics' Neils Bohr Library and Archives). He said that Mr. Hughes ran the Aircraft Company the same way he did all of his other operations, without a true manager—someone had the title, but Howard never allowed him to really manage. Howard was smart enough to run the company and could have done so, or he could have authorized someone he trusted to do so, but he didn't. During the Korean War, Mr. Hughes became more and more engaged in company operations—the company was providing armament and electronics equipment for fighter aircraft—to the point that Wooldridge's own position and that of Simon Ramo became intolerable. They decided to leave and gave a year's notice (to get the company in as good a shape as possible). Howard didn't believe them until they actually left after that one-year wait.

By 1952, the staff had blossomed to 15,000, an enormous growth from the 1942 group of 500 employees. In 1953, however, most of the top three levels of technical bosses abandoned ship. Employees called this the "Management Revolt at Culver City." Key losses included Drs.

Simon Ramo and Dean Wooldridge, who then formed a new firm providing technical leadership for the development and deployment of the US intercontinental ballistic missile force. It later became the Thompson Ramo Wooldridge Corporation and then TRW Inc. Not surprisingly, this excellent corporation's practices mimicked the creative approaches its founders had established at Hughes. As it became very active in spacecraft design and manufacture, TRW came to be a most effective competitor, using neither hostile nor deceptive maneuvers to win contests.

Wooldridge and Ramo, 1957
(From *TIME* Magazine, April 29 ©1957
Time Inc. Used under license.)

Several other new corporations were established by Hughes "escapees," notably, the enormous Litton Industries conglomerate formed by Tex Thornton and another departee, financial manager Roy Ash. Mr. Ash later served as director of the Office of Management and Budget under Presidents Nixon and Ford. Litton, too, became an extensive competitor, although with considerably less technical ability than Hughes had.

Thankfully, many individuals at lower seniority levels who were part of the founding fathers remained on the staff and were instrumental in the recovery from turmoil. Many others who were new to the Hughes family eventually became major contributors to our becoming a national treasure by 1985.

The management instability at Hughes threatened the very survival of the company because of the government's concern about the matter.

The company had many vital defense contracts, some of which no other organization was technically qualified to perform. With no alternatives, the Air Force felt itself in a bind, and there was considerable unease in the Pentagon. In late 1953, Secretary of the Air Force Harold Talbot personally visited Culver City and told Mr. Hughes, "You've made a hell of a mess of a great property," (as quoted in an April 1968 *Fortune* Magazine article entitled, "Hughes Aircraft: The High-Flying Might-Have-Been." This book's author notes that the article's title soon became most inaccurate!)

Secretary Talbot then issued a ninety-day ultimatum to Howard Hughes: either be present daily to run the company operations or get an appropriate general manager with full authority to do so. "You can't direct me like that," Mr. Hughes declared. Talbot quickly countered that if this ultimatum was not followed, all contractual funding would end. That did it!

12

TOP MANAGEMENT
CHANGES

A SEARCH TEAM APPOINTED by Mr. Hughes successfully recruited
Mr. Lawrence "Pat" Hyland from the Bendix Corporation to serve as the
new general manager. Mr. Hyland had been recommended by Dr. Allen
Puckett, a key technical expert who had remained with Hughes, and by
Dr. Harold "Howdy" Koontz, Dean of UCLA's School of Business Administration (now the Anderson School of Management). Howdy supplemented his professorship by spotting good executive candidates for
many companies. (In 1959, he encouraged me to go to Purex Corporation after I completed my UCLA master's degree in business administration. I never regretted deciding to remain in high-technology electronics,
even though my path to the top took many years—and perhaps I would
not have done well at Purex, anyway).

As mentioned before, decision-making by Mr. Hughes was slow as
molasses and terribly frustrating. Mr. Hyland, as related in his autobiography, *Call Me Pat*, discovered this trait during his recruitment. Dr.
Koontz first arranged an interview for him with Noah Dietrich, business
manager for Mr. Hughes; Dietrich was quickly satisfied. This interview
was to be followed by one with Mr. Hughes.

After a fruitless ten-day wait, Mr. Hyland returned to Detroit, and
again went back to Los Angeles for another week's wait. He then called
Nadine Henley, Mr. Hughes's executive assistant, saying he could spare
only twenty-four more hours because of his Bendix obligations. She
pleaded for more time, so forty-eight hours later the interview took place
in Mr. Hughes's cottage at the Beverly Hills Hotel. After what seemed
to be a successful meeting of minds, Mr. Hyland returned to Detroit,
then waited three weeks for a signed contract. None appeared, so he
told Ms. Henley that unless it showed up before midnight Friday, he

would not be available for the job. Just thirty minutes before that deadline, a TWA pilot knocked on his front door and delivered the contract signed by Mr. Hughes. What an agonizing wait, with no assurances or promised schedule!

Ms. Henley later told Mr. Hyland that the interview had been delayed for so many days because she could not get Mr. Hughes to wear a business suit and tie. She said something like, "He knew you must be a dignified person, and he needed to look like one also so you would think the same of him."

Mr. Hyland, born in Nova Scotia and raised in Massachusetts, had been active in aircraft radio equipment since almost the beginning of aviation electronics. After service in the US Army in World War I, he worked for the Naval Research Laboratories, and then founded the Radio Research Company in 1932. That firm later merged with the Bendix Corporation, and he was appointed vice president for research and engineering. Howard Hughes brought him aboard for the then large annual salary of $100,000, plus an elegant house in Holmby Hills. Stock options were not included. Surprisingly, Mr. Hughes never increased that salary in the next twenty-two years, even though the company expanded six times in staff size and thirty times in sales volume!

Mr. Hyland's technical acumen, management expertise, and steady leadership finally gave the company its rock to stand on. Nationally known and respected, he retired as chairman in 1980, but returned each day, serving as mentor for all Hughes managers. He passed away in 1989 at the age of ninety-two. Throughout his years at Hughes, he was a pillar of inspiration, stability, and integrity for his employees. His life and enormous contributions to the company were well summarized in the *HughesNews*, the internal company newspaper, in an issue published December 1, 1989. Captioned "Hyland leaves us a heritage of strength, a legacy of the future," it begins with "There is not a Hughes Aircraft Company employee who has not benefited from the vastly diverse accomplishments, wisdom, and leadership of Pat Hyland . . . ."

According to the previously-mentioned *Fortune* Magazine article, when his appointment was announced, a predecessor in that general manager's position declared, "God pity the poor man."

To strengthen his authority as general manager, Mr. Hyland finally solved the perpetual dilemma with Mr. Hughes about the latter's slow confirmation of management decisions. When a significant change needed endorsement, he would describe the details in written form and then formally ask Nadine Henley to hand the document directly to Mr. Hughes as soon as possible. The last sentence in each missive said, "If I do not hear from you in three days, I will consider that you have approved this issue." That strategy worked every time! Mr. Hughes was kept well informed, and he never objected to the procedure. Pat Hyland later stated that this continuous flow of important facts combined with the "silence means acceptance" procedure formed an unorthodox but very productive partnership.

A second action by Mr. Hughes in response to the Air Force's ultimatum was to offer the Aircraft Company for sale. Some maneuverings by Mr. Hughes to ascertain the company's value had already taken place in 1952, when he had several meetings in the Nevada desert with Robert Gross, president of the Lockheed Corporation. Mr. Gross offered $26 million to lease the Culver City plant for ten years; Mr. Hughes raised this to $34 million, then $36 million, which resulted in a handshake. Subsequently, Mr. Hughes raised it again to $50 million, which Mr. Gross thought was excessive, so no deal took place. Following this, General Electric and Westinghouse were both quite interested. (I saw Mr. Hughes escorting their senior executives through the facilities one day.) I don't know if this was a genuine offer of sale or simply a means of determining the company's asset value, because preparations were already in progress for forming the Howard Hughes Medical Institute (HHMI) and assigning ownership of Hughes Aircraft Company to that charitable Institute.

The mission of HHMI was to engage in biomedical research and the invention of medical instruments, and to give monetary support to medical universities. It became the largest medical research organization in the world. Initially headquartered in Florida (currently in Chevy Chase, Maryland) and ingrained with traditional Howard Hughes secrecy, it has had little public attention or recognition. The Hughes Aircraft Company assets were totally donated to HHMI and became the Institute's principal source of income. Fifty-eight years of achievements of HHMI are well described in the Appendix.

This transfer of ownership, which further distanced Mr. Hughes from direct company involvement, and the appointment of Mr. Hyland as general manager, satisfied the Air Force's concern about the firm's ability to perform its contracts. Mr. Hughes was now effectively separated from daily decision-making. He was still president, but was no longer a roadblock to rapid progress. His attention also was distracted by his sale of RKO in 1955 for $25 million, the largest price obtained for any transfer of ownership in the movie business. It seems that Mr. Hughes was always involved in rearranging his holdings, as evidenced by his activities with respect to HHMI, RKO, several airlines, and numerous Nevada land and business ventures.

Pat Hyland set new operating standards for the company, beginning by demonstrating a no-frills approach. During a formal visit to his office in Building 1, a senior Air Force officer demanded that he expand the size of his office and add decorative magnificence, saying something like, "The general manager of this important firm must display his position by operating in prestigious surroundings." There was also great dismay that Mr. Hyland carried only the title of vice president; senior-level customers always expected to deal with someone with the imposing title of "president" or "chief executive officer." Pat Hyland simply did not believe in pomposity, although he ultimately did increase his office size to mollify the critics.

Hyland Discussing F-106 with an Air Force Officer
(courtesy of UNLV)

Hughes Aircraft Company quickly established a stable corporate base, led by Mr. Hyland and two other stalwarts who had not abandoned ship at this crucial time: Allen Puckett and John Richardson. This team of three had the skills and drive needed, not only to visualize the future, but also to make the correct decisions in guiding the complex enterprise to a preeminent position in the world of high technology.

Allen, with his 1941 Harvard MS and 1949 PhD in aerodynamics from Caltech, arrived at Hughes in 1949. After World War II, he was asked to visit Germany to help select scientists who would enhance the military weapon development capabilities of the United States—an enterprising project called Paper Clip. Allen was also active in advising the US government on optimum approaches to the coming era of guided missiles. (During the 1953 management revolt, one manager, Dr. Nate Hall, admirably persuaded almost all of the missile design managers to remain at Hughes. Dr. Robert Roney told me that at that time Nate had declared, "We need to do whatever is necessary to retain Allen Puckett with us.") Throughout Allen's professional career, he participated in just about every professional US technical society and was the recipient of numerous awards, including the French Legion of Merit. He led the way in guided missile design, inspired the staff, and demanded technical excellence within Hughes. He became CEO in 1980 and, following his 1987 retirement, was appointed chairman emeritus. He was an exceedingly impressive technical leader with worldwide credentials.

John Richardson (no relation to me, to my regret) was one of the best people-skilled leaders ever, perhaps inheriting his charm and talent from his father, who had been the official greeter of important people formally visiting New York City. John, a student at Princeton University in World War II, volunteered for the Army Air Corps and piloted B-29 *Super Fortress* bombers. After the war, he became a tennis professional on eastern Long Island and then was recruited by RKO Pictures as a marketing manager. Disgusted with the manner in which movie studios operated, he migrated to Hughes. He initially was positioned at Wright Patterson Air Force base, in Dayton, Ohio, where he established lifetime bonds with junior officers who later advanced to leadership positions in the Air Force and made key decisions in contractor selection for important projects. Those good and friendly communication links were always nurtured.

Because of his ability to "read" people, John was adept at selecting personnel for organizational advancement. He was also an important mentor, advising us more junior managers how we might improve our leadership skills. Unfortunately, after inspiring the company as president for several years, he passed away of lung cancer in 1983.

From the 1950s to the 1980s, this triumvirate enabled the Hughes staff to grow to more than 82,000 people, deliver products in all areas of military electronics, and achieve many firsts in space science and commercial ventures. There was virtually nothing in these fields that Hughes could not do, and it placed first in most competitions. These remarkable achievements were due to many individuals joining together to tackle very difficult problems. The three helmsmen provided a solid foundation of long-term vision, sound business practices, operational integrity, agility in coping with external changes, and outstanding marketing skills. They also exhibited and spread the Howard Hughes image of creativity and unconventional approaches to problem solving.

13

THE BLESSINGS OF PRIVATE OWNERSHIP

ALTHOUGH MR. HUGHES remained titular president of the Aircraft Company, its almost complete independence from his control (or more likely "interference") resulted from the management abilities and perseverance of the top leaders, the significant divergence of Hughes product lines from those he was directly interested in, and his own focus on his expanding real estate investments. That focus led to Mr. Hughes's acquisition of six casino hotels, numerous abandoned silver mines, and a television station in Las Vegas, Nevada—a far cry from the advanced electronics business.

Private ownership of the company between 1953 and 1985 was of great benefit, however, because it isolated us from the profit and dividend demands of public stockholders, allowing much greater operating flexibility and the pursuit of long-term objectives. Mr. Hughes and HHMI exercised little direct control and made no demands for excessive cash returns. In addition to rental fees for the use of buildings owned by HHMI, only a modest portion of after-tax earnings was negotiated yearly (about one-quarter of the company's actual post-tax profit). These annual amounts did cause difficulty with respect to government regulations defining charitable trusts. It was alleged that HHMI should expend amounts based on a percentage of the Aircraft Company's growing asset value, but HHMI stated that it was unable to spend in a responsible way any more than the annually negotiated Hughes payments.

For the company, the negotiated dividend stood in great contrast to the badgering of publicly held firms by securities traders eager for short-term results and by shareholders hungry for higher dividends. Instead, Hughes could plow the balance of post-tax earnings into further desirable research and development. (Speaking of post-tax earnings, there was a common public myth, extending even to government agencies who should have known better, that the Hughes Aircraft Company enjoyed a lower tax rate on earnings than its competitors, based on its ownership by a charitable organization. This was absolutely not true: Hughes was subject to the same standard tax rates as any other US corporation.)

The lack of outside pressure for dividends allowed senior executives to adopt a "big picture" philosophy. Decisions could be predicated on anticipated long-term results, on nurturing an unusually large number of science and engineering professionals, and on investing in new high-technology exploitation. The company could survive program cancellations and could diversify into many new product lines. Innovation, experimentation, use of novel methods, and toleration of error could easily be accommodated.

Fiscal and operational recriminations against Hughes from its owners were few, giving considerable opportunity for misdeeds, but the three corporate officers were men of high business integrity, who preached ethics and promoted ideal mission objectives. They always pointed the firm in the right direction. Cost-plus contracts for development allowed pursuit of the most desirable technology goals. Production contracts usually resulted in a profit of at least 6 percent, with significant engineering support costs also carried by the contract. In both development and production programs, profit was secondary to technical advancement. Reinvestment of retained earnings in large part made possible the giant growth of the company during these times.

In spite of the firm's isolation from the handicaps of public ownership, establishing financial stability was vital. Overspending on non-contract technology exploration had to be constrained. In 1953, Hughes had few capital assets: Hughes Tool Company owned all the facilities (except the Air Force-owned Tucson structures) and much of the operating equipment was leased from the government. There was little operating cash flexibility—none supplied by Mr. Hughes—very limited borrowing power, and significant lease expenses to pay. There was even an incorrect lien placed by the Air Force for the use or return of loaned equipment. The future growth of Hughes had to come from continuous contract success and a fruitful marketing approach to the government.

Despite these initial financial challenges, it took Hughes only a few years after its entry into the "radio" business to become the world's technological front runner in most forms of electronics.

14

A DIFFERENT KIND
OF ORGANIZATION

RECOVERY FROM THE Management Revolt required increasing and nurturing a set of creative professionals. Staff morale rebounded under Mr. Hyland's leadership. In 1954, with Mr. Hyland's successful bargain with Air Force Gen. Bernard Schriever and Si Ramo to defer for three months the leakage of talent to the Ramo-Wooldridge Corporation, retention was no longer a problem; the hiring strategies described in Section 6, "Recruiting Superb Talent" were vigorously and successfully pursued.

Seniority titles of technical experts matched those of managers, with parallel upward growth giving equal recognition and remuneration. This practice emulated the arrangements at Bell Laboratories. Salary levels were set slightly above those of competing companies on the West Coast; these levels kept rising as firms vied to attract professionals from any source.

After the staff erosion to Ramo-Wooldridge was stemmed, there was still a lot of traffic between companies as individuals tried to increase their incomes by job-hopping. Hughes had an advantage in this maneuvering because its engineers had "private" offices with only two or three desks, whereas many other outfits housed their professionals in large "bull-pens," with little privacy or separation from unwanted noise. A further attraction was the promise of a performance review every six months. Those meetings were interactive and promoted mutual understanding and better relationships. In many cases, these discussions resulted in improvements not only in the subordinate's performance, but also in the supervisor's work behavior. At this time, salaries were adjusted, taking into consideration the quality of the individual's performance, economic inflation factors, and the need to deter external pirating threats.

Mr. Hyland described in 1968 the company's ability to attract and retain brilliant personnel by fostering an atmosphere, an environment, and a deep understanding of the scientific and technological challenges throughout the company. "It is an atmosphere characterized by *élan vital*, something you can't put in an organization chart or into rules and procedures. It has to do with honesty and integrity in the way one pursues business. We try to nurture this elusive *élan vital* to ensure that innovation and motivation thrive." Dr. Malcolm Stitch, a senior scientist in the Hughes Research Laboratories, added that "high morale and low turnover in the company is because it is a solid place much like Bell Labs; there is a real incentive-reward and no civil-service type of atmosphere. Things here are on the up and up—the hidden agenda isn't too big here. The guy above you is not a schnook. Here you can respect the people you work for; there are very few of the awful kind who will use your best work and put their name first on the paper you wrote."

First-Time Property Ownership

By 1955, more space was needed for radar production. Hughes bought an abandoned Nash automobile factory in nearby El Segundo south of the Los Angeles Airport, stripped and refurbished the building, and equipped it for manufacturing the most advanced electronics hardware. To ensure that the price of the property was not artificially inflated because of the magical Hughes name, Howard Hall made the deal through agencies that apparently had no ties to any Howard Hughes enterprise. Mr. Hyland was able to obtain an adequate loan and the facility became the first to be directly owned by Hughes Aircraft Company. This relocation of radar manufacturing freed up sorely-needed space for offices and laboratories at the Culver City site.

15

A NEW
MANAGEMENT MODEL

HUGHES PROSPERED IN the next six years, participating in all areas of military electronics, and in later years dominated the communication satellite field. Although the inspiring creative image of its originator was always present in employees' minds, the company's achievements were done on its own. A new and unique style of management enabled excellent staff motivation, rapid diversification, and astonishing business growth. That's why this book is titled *Hughes After Howard*.

Here was a chance for glory!—a highly energized gathering of technical talent in an environment of national support and with skills found

Hyland, Puckett, and Richardson, 1965
(courtesy of UNLV)

nowhere else. A turbulent foundation had firmed, undesirable customer problems had been settled, and the private owner was distant from the action. Pat Hyland, Allen Puckett, and John Richardson embodied a new philosophy in leading this large and thriving corporation of high-IQ employees.

The full-grown personality of Hughes Aircraft Company took many years of trial and error, customer interaction, and a sustained sense of family by dedicated participants. Was every employee imbued with this special Camelot spirit? Of course not, but new staff members quickly adapted, and those who performed well did so with an innovative and mission-oriented spirit.

In contrast to most large industrial firms, the Hughes organizational structure was modeled after that of a research institute. Dominant was the concept of "laboratories" conducting experiments in science. At this time, many other well-known firms in various technology fields used the same laboratory concept, but theirs was restricted to their research organization, rather than spanning all corporate functions as at Hughes. Even our large manufacturing plants had a similar philosophical base. After Pat Hyland took the helm, a clear distinction was made between the organizations of "line" groups responsible for product operations, and "staff" groups responsible for guidelines, standards, and financial control (not to be confused with "staff" as in "professional staff"). The boundary lines between line laboratory organizations were very liquid, with engineers migrating to the project of greatest need. This process was fully endorsed and encouraged by senior leaders, so there were few promotional risks or resentments caused by these migrations. Even as the corporation reached more than 50,000 employees in the late 1970s, the feeling prevailed that we're "all in the same boat." This attitude worked miracles in ensuring optimum results for company efforts; the talent needed to solve any surprise problem was always available.

Top-down management direction was strong on overall goals and corporate ethical and business standards, but made very little demand on how to accomplish the project job. Objectives and contract end results were clearly stated and monitored. Employees were encouraged to find the best method of performing their tasks, although lessons of the past were made clear by idea interchanges with experienced staff members. Innovation in operational methods was encouraged as much as technical inventions. The management philosophy in this dynamic company was well described by an old Chinese proverb: "The person who says it cannot be done should not interrupt the person doing it."

An excellent illustration of poor management style is the historic fiasco of seven Navy destroyers going aground off Central California in

1923. Military command has always been regimented and stratified into distinct levels of rank, most appropriate in combat conditions. In this particular disaster, fourteen destroyers were proceeding in-line southward down the Pacific coast. Orders for the squadron commander in the lead ship were to remain in single file and to maintain equal spacing. Because of a navigation error, the lead ship, the USS *Delphy* (DD-261), went aground near Honda Point, close to present-day Vandenberg Air Force Base. The next six destroyers followed orders and hit the same hidden rocky shoals! They did as commanded, even as they saw what catastrophe would occur. Fortunately, the eighth destroyer's skipper took the initiative, changed course, and saved the other six vessels. I don't know if he received a medal or was court-martialed. Unfortunately, similar rigors are imposed in many large corporations even today. In these outfits, top-down orders must be carried out with no question or deviation.

During the Hughes growing years (we jumped from our 1953 place as number twenty-two in size of US defense contractors to eleventh in 1959, with 25,000 employees), the laboratory philosophy was uncomfortable for manufacturing personnel, who believed they were viewed only as second-rate support for engineering. When everyone finally perceived that production was the real source of large inflows of funding, attitudes changed and a better balance was achieved. Manufacturing, as a function, cannot operate in the free style of inventors: schedules, repetitive fabrication methods, and costs must be rigorously controlled. But the company's philosophical umbrella of a research institute always prevailed in other portions of the firm.

Freedom to try new things inspired the employees to reach out, and think outside the box of conventional wisdom. Individuals were stimulated to try where others had failed. A new product line usually was not the inspiration of a senior officer; it often came from an engineer who had individually made a unique device (for example, the first practical laser in 1960). A small team would explore the possible products that could use this device and would recommend it as a new Hughes product to senior management. If the product seemed feasible, an organization would be created to develop, test, market and manufacture it, and sustain it in the field.

The central philosophy that made this approach work so well, even though to some it sounded like chaos, was stated in a 1986 Hughes publication *At the Forefront of Technology*: "Personal and professional integrity is the one value that must govern all of our actions. Closely allied to high integrity of our products and actions is the concept of personal responsibility to our customers and to our coworkers. This cultural value, personal and professional integrity, underlies all of our company culture."

Leaders and Leadership

This corporate ideal enabled everyone to share an unusual set of attitudes on how Hughes should function. Motivations were very unlike those of the stereotypical driven executive obsessed with defeating competition to gain market share and maximize earnings. The Hughes drive was primarily focused on technical excellence and creativity: rewards came from doing things no one else could do.

Executives felt free to try new paths. Noninvolvement by a private owner allowed flexible choices of alternative product routes. The leaders could experiment with diversification, find market uses for new creations, and explore new customer possibilities. Little owner retribution resulted from erroneous moves if they were quickly remedied.

Howard Hughes and HHMI did not permit stockholder positions for any employees, so sharing earnings or gaining from growth in stock value—usually a large motivator for managers in publicly held firms—were not possible for our managers before 1985. Hughes executives gained professional stature by successfully spurring growth in product types and increasing total sales volume. Each felt well rewarded by leading Hughes to become the best performer in the business. Profit was viewed only as a means to further research and development and growth in sales volume. Plans and results were analyzed with a long-range view of future capabilities and business expansion. The curse of demands for ever-increasing quarterly earnings to satisfy the trading market did not stifle long-range planning.

In 2009, R. Paul St. Amand, MD, characterized the special type of senior managers who emerged in this environment:

> "As an examining physician for Hughes Aircraft Company, I was fortunate to meet many top executives. I did the same for two other large organizations. Obviously, this almost mandated that my staff and I make comparisons.
>
> "During the annual examinations, I was impressed with the caliber and demeanor of the men I encountered. During these hour-long visits, we reviewed and discussed many items other than medicine. It was always evident that I was not speaking with nerds who could only discuss work. These were bright, knowledge-seeking individuals who lived a full life that embellished the delight each found in his work. These were inquisitive minds that extracted facts from many disciplines that sometimes stimulated novel applications in their research. This mind-set was likely instrumental in modeling

Hughes Aircraft Company into the respected icon that led the USA for many years to such heights.

"It was a great Company that has not been replaced."

Hughes executives believed that the future would be assured through technical excellence and stimulation of innovation, which could only happen if talented professionals were free to use their abilities with few constraints. The best ideas would come from the energetic self-starting technical staff. The executives also strongly agreed that the optimum way to tackle difficult projects was through teamwork, and that management's priority was to solve individual conflicts to ensure the unity of the family team in achieving the project's objectives.

Executive posture is one of inspiration, not direct command. Executives must clearly define the mission and its objectives, and inspire the professional staff to find the best way to fulfill them. Constraints of ethics, government rules, limitations of resources, and overall operating efficiency must be known and followed, but they dwell in the background. Autocracy works only in times of imminent disaster.

Most directors of organizations thought that the hardest thing to do was to turn a project off. Their thinking went like this: persevering individuals must sense that something of great value will result from their efforts; prematurely turning the project off will de-motivate many on our team. With time, we will find that something and apply it to a fruitful product.

All responsible employees understood these deep-seated attitudes. The operating credo was well stated in the corporate objectives, framed copies of which could be found on many office walls:

"Our purpose is to serve our nation and the world at the forefront of technology. To be permitted to do this we must create superior products in performance, quality, and reliability at an affordable cost, and provide complete support of our delivered product. We must obtain substantial earnings that are necessary to provide investment for human resources, R&D, facilities, working capital and corporate obligations."

Note that this credo emphasized national service, and stated that earnings would be reinvested in continuing internal research and development. The focus on profit use was positive for the creative technology staff; each person could feel personally motivated to assure his or her future.

Getting a lively set of mustangs to go in the proper direction, however, demands excellent leadership agility and style. The Hughes devotion to individual creativity, freedom to try new ways, and the preeminence of technology made the management task most difficult. Those who did a superlative job of leadership embodied the Hughes laboratory teamwork philosophy, were accepted by those they led, were themselves inspired and dedicated to the mission, insisted on and practiced integrity, were well informed and quickly perceived potential problems, and were decisive but willing to adjust rapidly to project reversals. Effective managers did not need their power base delegated by corporate to exert firm authority. The better operating style was to lead by persuasion, although autocracy with charisma was needed in times of crisis. I found no examples of wimpy behavior being effective. Dealing with many professionals with an exceptionally high IQ was a continuous and most exciting challenge.

A few old clichés fit very well in guiding new heads of organizations: nobody's perfect; the sins of the leader will be copied by the followers; loyal behavior toward the team will be reflected by the team's loyalty to the leader; you are most right when you admit you were wrong; personal integrity provides longevity; damn the torpedoes, full speed ahead!; taking the wrong fork in the road can be altered, and if later found to be incorrect, probably 80 percent of the effort will be usable after switching to the right track; waiting to decide which fork to take results in no gain because your team will be idle with its direction unknown; don't be distracted by trivia; ignore the mosquitoes, but be sure to avoid the crocodiles; be calm, and show true grit in adversity.

There were, indeed, many mavericks in our collection of dynamic innovators. Many were very frustrated by being subject to fixed documentation procedures, imposed by either the company or the government, that seemed to hamper rapid progress. An amusing example is that of one of our eccentric inventors who created unique precision mechanical devices such as miniature gimbal assemblies and support frames for optical lenses, which could adapt the positioning of the lenses to compensate for heat expansion changes. In one experimental piece of hardware, the inventor used a wooden toothpick as an alignment wedge. The drafting department, assigned to convert the concept to drawings, asked him to define this wedge structure and give it an approved title, even though it was only a temporary test gimmick. They rejected his quick response, "It's a toothpick," so he revised the formal title to "pick, tooth," to no avail. In an irate telephone call, he demanded the draftsmen cease this nonsense and get on with their job by figuring out their own description. This toothpick story was often retold whenever anyone complained about unnecessarily hidebound procedures. It's a fine illustration of the saying by Yale professor Kingman Brewster: "There is a correlation between the creative and the screwball, so we must suffer the screwball gladly."

Although naming all the exemplary leaders at Hughes during the forty years I was there would be right and proper, unfortunately, I can only give examples from my personal experience of a few, along with mention of contributions they made to the success of Hughes and the help they gave me in my professional growth:

- Pat Hyland solved the dilemma of Mr. Hughes's indecisiveness and welded a strong top management to lead the company into a successful future. He encouraged the staff to practice operational freedom, focus on technology innovation, and to recognize the benefits of dedicated teamwork. Pat insisted that subordinates who approached him on any issue had to be thoroughly prepared and have alternative solutions well analyzed for risk. "Get your job done before you request action from my office." He spent time mentoring upcoming managers (such as I); the conversations usually encouraged them to visualize what they were doing based on its interrelations and side effects in the big picture, for both the company and the nation.

- Allen Puckett set the style for technical excellence as the foundation of good decision making. In meetings with him as CEO, I always made sure I was able to answer any questions about how things work, what technical alternatives could be tried, and the risk of design malfunctions. Similar preparation by all those who approached Allen deepened subordinates' understanding of technology difficulties in the areas of their organizations' responsibilities.

- John Richardson was the exemplar of a people person. He had the appearance and charisma of a movie star, and a magnetic personality that no one could resist. His continual insistence that the customer is first priority influenced the whole staff's personal orientation. John also insisted that employees perfect "people skills," assuring complete communication and rapport with team members at all position levels as they pursued their responsibilities. John was an important mentor to me and many others. Once, after a difficult meeting with a dissatisfied customer, I asked him, "What else should I try in order to do a better management job?" His response was, "You've learned all the big things, now we'll just work on the little ones." That was an enormous morale boost for me!

- John Black was with Hughes for many years. He had worked directly with Mr. Hughes on many occasions, as described in Section 7, "The Howard Hughes Legacy." His demeanor projected calm, wisdom, and good humor, even in times of high stress. Subordinates learned that panic solves nothing. One notable quote from John was, "Let's fix the problem, not the blame." Since adventurous and potentially risky advances cannot always succeed, this credo was most reassuring to the performers. Of course, repeated failure would usually lead to reassignment or even discharge, but John's approach allowed professionals to reach boldly to new boundaries.

- Meade Livesay came from West Virginia, and as a Navy lieutenant was present at the invasion of the Philippines' Leyte Gulf in World War II (and witnessed General McArthur in his famous "I shall return" wade ashore). Meade's appearance, demeanor, and mellow Southern accent caused his admirers to call him "The Senator." He exemplified the ideal leader of high-technology teams at Hughes: able to converse with the most creative genius, astute in business matters, smooth in settling disputes, outstanding at mentoring budding managers, and very friendly and persuasive with customers. I never heard of any employee who criticized Meade as director of the very successful Radar Systems Group. I owe him much for helping and guiding my progress in the company.

- Walt Maguire, born in Canada, began his professional employment at Collins Radio in Iowa. When he came to Hughes, he quickly became a design expert in advanced radars, and was later one of the few world pioneers creating airborne pulse-Doppler radars (see description in Section 17, under "Fighting Clutter"). As his Irish surname implies, he had the gift of the Blarney Stone, using humor to ease stress with anyone he encountered. This style resulted in happy team members and contented customers. Once, to remedy a significant missile test failure, the responsible design team came to Walt saying, "We're unsure whether we can do this fix in a year by spending one million dollars." His quick response was, "Why don't you be unsure of the fix in only six months, using half that amount?" They did the job perfectly within the shorter time and cost! By intuitive insight, Walt selected staff members very well, and delegated authority and responsibility to a noteworthy degree. Being an electronics design expert helped him in technically complex discussions about how to resolve device malfunctions. Walt made possible my own professional reorientation from detail design to systems engineering and program management; this change in turn made possible my promotional progress until my retirement.

The informal behavior practiced by most leaders in the company greatly improved the flow of information and fostered the best approaches to key decisions. An example occurred during the Paris Air Show in 1985. Allen Puckett was waiting alone in the company's marketing chalet, and took the opportunity to try out a new computer-printer device just then being publicly introduced by a Japanese supplier. A French Air Force wing commander entered the room unannounced, and not realizing who Allen was, asked about how the printer worked. Allen cordially described all the technical details he had so far observed. The wing commander was flabbergasted upon later hearing that he had been chatting with the CEO of the gigantic and notable Hughes outfit. He remarked that nothing like this could have happened in contacting a French company: rigid hierarchy, cultivated caste system, and formal protocols would never allow a senior manager to mingle with any unknowns.

What were the feelings of the general staff? Naturally, not all staff members felt the same loyalty and eager motivation, or had completely favorable opinions about Hughes and its officers. Some were skeptical or cynical about our mission, others were just happy to have a job. Overall, however, harmony and effective teamwork prevailed during our growing years, and almost everyone responded to the aura and behavior of this unique assembly of talents. We shared a positive mindset.

Employees relished being part of a professional family with an important mission to serve our nation. If something technical went wrong in an area of development or operations, there would be someone nearby to help figure out a workable solution. Although independent effort to solve problems was highly encouraged, help could soon be on the way. The buddy system worked.

Staffers knew that since new operating methods were vital for our future, the bosses would tolerate some degree of error in decisions. Job security stemmed from this, and the performer was motivated to correct any flaw in judgment and do better the next time.

Professionals were informed that credit for invention patents would not be financially rewarding, since Hughes, their employer, would own the patents. If the patent resulted from a project funded by the government, the right to use it might even be granted to competitors. Nonetheless, the company's reputation, expansion in sales, and product line variety would most likely increase with each new invention.

The individual's rewards were increased professional prestige and career advancement. The employee's boss usually understood the technology involved, so the design problem and the employee's achievement could easily be communicated between them. Virtually every staff member felt highly motivated by a sense of achievement when doing something important, doing it well, and knowing the managers above them understood and appreciated what had been accomplished. Promotions came in this manner, so the entire management chain was filled with knowledgeable technical achievers. This certainly, in turn, inspired subordinates.

Customers' Home Plate, the Pentagon. US Department of Defense, Washington, D.C. (courtesy of iStockphoto/mikadx)

16

CONTRACTING WITH
THE GOVERNMENT

CORPORATIONS DEALING WITH the government in most procurements usually prepare an offer in response to a request, and if selected to do the work, they negotiate the content of the contract and its price. Price is made up of the base cost of labor and material, overhead expenses, some provision for uncertainty, and profit. Overhead expenditures allow the company to provide operating facilities, security, legal and financial services, employee benefits, and other support items to enable sustained operations. Since these costs traditionally represent an addition of 150 percent to the base labor cost, minute details of these many cost items are not only negotiated prior to contract award, but are monitored continuously by on-site government auditors. Some costs can be disallowed, although such changes are not imposed unilaterally, but are subject to further negotiation.

In the 1950s, there was a nationally perceived urgency of military need and the belief that innovative technology advances would increase the capability gap between the United States and USSR. This prompted the use of cost-plus-fixed-fee (CPFF), or "cost-plus," contracting by the Department of Defense (DoD) for development contracts. The motivation at this time was similar to the sentiment in a song from Irving Berlin's *Annie Get Your Gun*: "Anything you can do I can do better; I can do anything better than you." Perhaps the Russians felt the same way.

Under CPFF, the government reimbursed the contractor for all expenses incurred as the project progressed to meet performance objectives, hopefully unencumbered by financial constraints. The fee, or profit, was usually a fixed amount set at the beginning, not a percentage of total cost at the end. Cost overruns were paid by the government, but not rewarded. Corporations undertaking projects that demanded new inventions could do so with little monetary risk. The contractor could remedy unexpected design troubles by switching to another technical approach, using a different internal team, or even subcontracting to an outside source that appeared capable. Such internal and external competitions spurred rapid advances in the state of the art.

Major competitions were usually won because the government procurement agency believed that the winner was either the only one who could solve the cutting-edge technology challenges, or the most adept one; price was secondary. For many difficult but critically important programs, the government agency would ask a particular company to undertake the project without competition. Because of its excellent track record in meeting tough technical hurdles, Hughes was often that designated company. Unfortunately, in a number of key competitions Hughes was selected by the knowledgeable contracting agency, but the award went to another corporation because of political pressure due to the competitor's geographic location. Contractor ineptness led to dismal technical failure in several of these programs. So much for political influence! A competitive loss in politically influenced cases was very hurtful to the firm not chosen, and often to the United States, since it was likely that an inferior product resulted or a costly restart was needed.

When two companies had radically different design approaches, both could be authorized to prepare a prototype model for a performance "fly-off." The better equipment then usually won the final development award. Most often sole-source contracts were the norm, since insufficient government budgets precluded a competitive prototype runoff through the entire development period. Forecasts of high initial factory implementation expenses plus far-too-low annual production quantities did not justify keeping two sources to compete each year for subsequent production lots.

Being sole-source under a cost-plus development contract and offering reasonable production prices was a dream come true for creative and eager technology corporations like Hughes. The negative effect of this government recognition of the company's ability regardless of initial cost, however, was the likelihood that our staff members would ignore cost as they did their work. This hazardous mindset required constant management attention.

All was not completely rosy with CPFF contracting. Government auditors often readjusted charges that did not appear to be in accord with accounting standards, some of which had been modified after contract award. Other expenses thought legitimate by the performers were disallowed as not matching the contract's stated purpose. In addition, a few subcontractor costs were judged as improperly negotiated by the prime contractor, so a portion of the subcontractor payment had to be borne by the prime. Many such adjustments were a matter of the auditor's opinion. Occasionally these disallowances were large enough to offset the fixed profit amount assigned to a development project. Many of our CPFF contracts resulted in a financial loss due to auditor disallowances; thank heaven for follow-on production contracts!

Although reasonably low in financial risk, cost-plus contracts were not handled in a careless manner. Significant or frequent overruns could lead to program cancellation as well as damage to the contractor's reputation. But the enthusiasm generated by the freedom to experiment and the chance to apply the best talents were unrestricted. This usually resulted in breakthroughs in concepts and excellence in hardware performance. The military had an insatiable appetite for technical advances, and this contracting method fostered extraordinary results.

Almost exclusively, production contracts were FFP (firm fixed price), with the price established at the beginning, so overruns were costly to the corporation. These contracts also experienced government audit adjustments, lowering potential earnings. Bidding was not very risky because usually only one outfit had the needed expertise; competitors were few in number in those days. However, prices had to be reasonable and supported with extensive and credible documented data, including negotiated prices of suppliers. Before award, there were detailed audits of the cost details and lengthy negotiations.

During the performance of both the development and production contracts, the government had constant access to financial data; any discrepancies had to be remedied immediately. So there was no free ride; contractor performance had to comply with rigorous government standards. Several layers of auditors kept a tight harness on fiscal matters.

The real beauty of government contracts was their inclusion of progress payments. The company submitted monthly accounts of expenditures and received prompt reimbursement, greatly alleviating the need for cash to continue operations. By contrast, most commercial customers required the company to carry all expenses until the product was delivered, usually meaning a higher borrowing level to provide the needed cash.

17

TECHNOLOGY ADVANCES

IN THE EARLY 1950s, two business roots were solidly planted at Hughes: airborne radars and air-to-air guided missiles. In the months that followed, the company's breadth and depth of technical expertise practically guaranteed spectacular growth and evolution of these systems. In addition, performance improvements were demanded because the United States recognized a rapidly expanding threat from the USSR. Soviet military prowess continued to exceed that of our fielded weapon systems. The number of capable engineers in the USSR involved in military hardware design far exceeded that in the United States: perhaps double ours. In several technical disciplines, they were superior: chemistry, metallurgy, aerodynamics, and propulsion methods of several types. The US was far ahead in electronics. In the air combat field, Hughes focused on adding self-contained computer intelligence, battle surveillance, target detection and selection in all engagement conditions, and precision in weapon delivery.

By 1955, the Hughes engineering workforce had reached 8,000 employees. The dedication to the job in all aspects and to continuing a longtime bond with the military is revealed by a 2009 quote from Air Force Gen. Richard Myers, former chairman of the Joint Chiefs of Staff:

> "I remember Hughes being very customer oriented, with great people. These people not only had great technical skills, but had a good grasp of how the equipment they were developing would be used by the men and women of our military. I always came away from discussions with Hughes folks believing they understood our needs and had great technical capability to produce what we needed.
>
> "Certainly Ted Wong (see Section 53, "Strategic Warfare; Intercepting and Destroying") epitomized the type of person

I'm describing above. He is a great American patriot and superb engineer, who worked tirelessly to make the United States military the very best."

Smarter Radar

In the late 1950s, the United States believed that sophisticated Soviet bombers could easily approach our continental borders bearing nuclear bombs. The urgent need to intercept such hostiles required a new ground radar network, faster fighter-interceptors with all-seeing radars, long-range guided weapons, and an intelligent fire control system to aid the pilot's decision making. In the early 1950s, the Air Force initiated the "MX-1179" project, the first fully integrated high performance aircraft with an electronic fire control system, guided missiles, and a complex ground-based control network. This new nationwide information linkage could command friendly intercept fighters with the transmitted data immune to reception by an approaching hostile raid. Convair won contracts for the F-102 *Delta Dagger* and its follow-on F-106 *Delta Dart*. Hughes was awarded contracts for development of the MA-1 fire control system with its MG-3 or MG-10 radar and for improved versions of the infrared and radar Falcon missiles.

MA-1 Fire Control System and Falcons with the F-106
(courtesy of Raytheon)

The MA-1 featured for the first time a radar-mapping display of the terrain beneath the fighter. It had a higher output power and greatly improved low-PRF (pulse repetition frequency) pulse radar compared to those in the F-86D, F-89, and F-94C fighters. Other firsts were the use of tiny solid-state transistors instead of vacuum tubes throughout its circuitry, and fire control "intelligence" made possible by an airborne digital computer. The computer's memory was stored in a rapidly spinning magnetic-coated cylinder; data strips were perused by a set of readheads floating along the cylinder's surface as it spun by. Access times and total memory content were puny compared to today's microelectronic computer random-access memory chips, but that speedy cylinder did its assigned job quite well. The packaged drum memory unit was about the size of two shoeboxes; today, the same function could be the size of a grain of rice!

The F-102 was introduced into service in the Air Force Air Defense Command in 1956; 975 fighter-interceptors were manufactured. The improved F-106 began deployment in 1959, and 385 were produced. Modified versions of the Hughes radars, the MG-12 and MG-13, were installed in the McDonnell F-101 *Voodoo* and the French *Mirage* fighter; 931 of these were delivered.

Fighting Clutter

The biggest unsolved problem with fighter radars of the early 1950s was that they lacked "look-down-shoot-down" capability. For an IR missile shot, tail intercepts could be done with a close visual approach. However, most long-range radar missile attacks using the low-PRF radars (described in Section 4, "Creating a Base of Technical Excellence; Radar Design and Operation") were quite limited when strong ground reflections overwhelmed the target echo—in other words, whenever the target was below the fighter.

The solution was to exploit the "Doppler effect." This phenomenon is a frequency shift of a returned signal compared to the transmitted pulse that is exactly proportional to the comparative speeds of the fighter and its target. Everyone has experienced this as a train passes by blowing its whistle: a higher pitch sound as the train approaches, then lower pitch as it speeds away. When heard from a fixed position, the sound wave is compressed (making the vibrations closer together, therefore, at a higher frequency) by the train's speed, and stretched to a lower frequency as it departs. This physical effect was formulated in 1842 by Christian Doppler, an Austrian doing research in Prague, Czechoslovakia.

An early attempt to measure target speed to differentiate it from ground reflections was called moving target indication (MTI). The idea was to use electronic range gates to filter out clutter returns at fighter altitude and at the range of ground contacted by the main beam. Accurately moving the gates to match the changing flight conditions was most difficult. Attempts to directly measure target Doppler shift were also unproductive. The frequency transmitted by the unstable magnetron was too erratic to yield a base point of measurement. Many experimenters thought that a crude target Doppler shift could be made by averaging several sample sequences, but this also was not accurate enough.

The exact "carrier" frequency of the transmitted pulse must be known for accurate comparison with the echo's frequency to determine the Doppler shift. As 1960 approached, a precisely controlled carrier frequency finally became possible. The Hughes breakthrough program was called MOPA (master oscillator power amplifier). Now the Doppler shift could easily separate targets from that awful ground noise. The concept had already been used in radio communication equipment, but not for high frequency microwave devices such as radars. The unstable cavity magnetrons in then-current radars supplied both the frequency source and its amplification. MOPA split the job into a very stable crystal oscillator, an electronic frequency multiplier, and a stable power amplifier. The key element was that final power amplification.

Figure 3.1. Traveling-Wave Tube Design

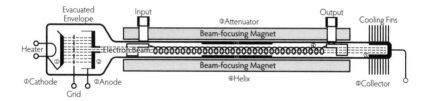

Drs. John Mendel, Bill Christoffers, and Mal Currie perfected a lightweight, highly stable power amplifier called a traveling-wave tube (TWT). This device, first constructed at a British Admiralty radar laboratory and later improved at Bell Laboratories, creates an electron beam in a long cylindrical vacuum tube to amplify a microwave signal. The original version used heavy magnets to focus the beam and a helical coil to guide the microwave signal so its course would match that of the electron beam. The Hughes design (Fig. 3.1) used a series of lightweight magnets to guide the electron beam, and coupled resonant cavities to guide the microwave signal. These design improvements permitted great increases in operating power and significant reductions in size and weight. For airborne radars, the mature Hughes device was a cylinder 3 to 4 inches in diameter and about 12 inches long. Pulses 1 microsecond in duration reached a peak power of 250 kilowatts, permitting long-range detection of small targets. The stable oscillator's frequency input to the TWT could quickly be changed so the radar could evade enemy countermeasure emanations or step away from interference from other friendly fighters.

The company's breakthroughs in TWT design led to formation of the Tube Laboratory in 1959, which later expanded to become the Electron Dynamics division, located on Lomita Boulevard in Los Angeles. This division became the world's leading supplier of these high performance devices for radars, missiles, electronic countermeasures, and spacecraft. It was a very lucrative endeavor, even though sales to competitors were avoided if the TWT was to be a key part of a large weapon system since that system could be a much bigger business opportunity for Hughes. In spite of our objections, sometimes the US government demanded that we sell TWTs to our competitors because our design was so superior to anything else available.

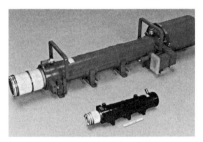

Traveling Wave Tubes
(courtesy of Raytheon)

As described earlier, low-PRF radars sent pulses separated with enough time to listen before the next transmission bursts. The new pulse-Doppler designs used a much closer spacing, or higher pulse repetition frequency (high PRF). Pulses were sent at about 250,000 per second, providing much higher average power radiated to achieve significantly longer range detections of small targets. Echoes could now be distinguished from clutter by their differing received frequencies.

Range measurement by elapsed time, as in low-PRF radars, was not possible: so many pulses occurred before the return echo that identifying the specific illumination pulse to count the elapsed time was not easy. Target returns filled many range bins with both real and ambiguous signals. The sorting was done by slightly changing the transmitted frequency while the beam was still on the target. This is called frequency modulation, or FM. Resulting Doppler shifts were unchanged for the real target echo, but all ambiguous range measurements were eliminated since their Doppler shift had changed.

Implementation in the F-108 *Rapier*

This design concept was successfully mechanized by Hughes in the ASG-18 fire control system slated for the North American Aviation supersonic F-108 *Rapier*.

Development began in 1957, and these new radar performance features were well demonstrated by 1959. The prototype system weighed 2,100 pounds, and extensive flight testing took place in a modified Convair B-58 *Hustler* bomber from the Hughes airstrip in Culver City. This was the world's first airborne pulse-Doppler radar making "look-down-shoot-down" possible.

F-108 *Rapier* Interceptor
(courtesy of the National Museum of the US Air Force)

The ASG-18 project also demonstrated the first fully integrated fire control system. The elegant radar was joined together with an infrared search and track system (see Section 30, "Exploiting Infrared"), a competent computer, a complex set of displays for the pilot or fire control crewman, system electrical and hydraulic power supplies, and electronics to prepare any weapon for launch. All data needed for a sophisticated intercept were stored, analyzed with forecasts of likely future dynamic changes, and disseminated to the aircrew to achieve maximum combat effectiveness. Functions carried out were providing target search and track information and fighter steering recommendations for the pilot, assessing and adapting to hostile electronic countermeasure attempts, and determining optimum launch position. The system then prepared a missile for the specific encounter, provided updated target status to the weapon while it was in flight, and suggested a proper escape route to the pilot. Displays, benefiting from ever-improving cathode ray tube technology, were now able to show the aircrew a full geographic battle planform in real time, as well as all the specific numerical data needed for a successful encounter with the hostile.

Intercepts Deadly Everywhere

Fundamental needs drove the evolution of air combat missile design: shoot at long range for early victory while keeping yourself from being shot down; carry a big enough warhead to effect destruction if there is a close guidance miss; use a fuse that triggers the warhead at the optimum time; and be able to compensate for launch errors in attitude or fighter movement. And there were even more: project minimal visible or electronic signature to the hostile; be immune to electronic countermeasures; and execute precise guidance to the designated target. And don't forget to have sufficient energy for quick terminal turns; perform agile aerodynamic steering to counter evasive maneuvering; be able to approach the target from any angle; and be useful in all weather conditions. Also, be rugged for carriage on a high performance fighter; make minimal demands on the mother aircraft in terms of weight, size, aerodynamic drag, power, and cooling; require minimal prelaunch instructions; be highly reliable; and survive long-term storage, crude transportation, and rough handling by munitions personnel. The weapon also must be inert for safety reasons until launch time. Lastly, the product had to be configured for high-rate and low cost manufacturing. An awesome array of demands upon any development team! I feel privileged to have participated in the exciting guided missile part of Hughes's business for more than half my career.

Hughes developed the GAR-9 (later AIM-47) Super Falcon missile as the F-108's primary weapon, married to the ASG-18 fire control system.

Internally carried, as were missiles in all Air Force fighters at that time (Navy weapons were externally mounted), Super Falcon was a bruiser: more than 12 feet long and 13-1/2 inches in diameter, with a 33-inch wingspan. Weighing 818 pounds at launch, it boasted a 100-pound blast-fragmentation warhead triggered by a radar proximity fuse. The bird's external planform was similar to that of its predecessor Falcon: four wings and aft control surfaces that flew in the "X" orientation; each wing at 45 degrees to vertical.

A sister version, GAR-11, had a small nuclear warhead. One can speculate about why such an anti-air weapon was thought to be needed. Missile guidance errors were expected to be small, so compensation for a near miss did not require such a huge fireball against a single target. The idea of multiple bomber kills with a single shot seems absurd, since the Soviet strategy surely was not to form mass formations like those "aluminum overcasts" of World War II. It must have been the desire to vaporize any nuclear bombs aboard an attacker. GAR-11 was fully developed and flight tested without its warhead, but fortunately never entered production.

AIM-47 Super Falcon Missile with YF-12
(courtesy of the National Museum of the US Air Force)

The Super Falcon found its assigned target by semiactive radar guidance, similar to the other radar Falcons; its gimbaled seeker, aligned and tuned to the radar's frequency before launch, locked on immediately during rocket boost, stayed alert to the Doppler echoes, and remained pointed and locked to those echoes until impact. The fire control radar beam continuously tracked the hostile to ensure target illumination; during the missile's midcourse flight, any necessary target updates were sent by another communication link to the bird's rear-mounted receiver.

Use of the Doppler effect ensured separation of the target from ground clutter, permitting intercept shots at all target altitudes. The combined missile/fire control weapon system gave the *Rapiers* the capability to detect and measure distant hostile bombers at any flight altitude and begin a lethal missile shoot one hundred miles away in all weather conditions.

18

A SHOCKING
FOUL BLOW

D ISASTER STRUCK IN 1959: the Air Force suddenly cancelled the *Rapier* interceptor program. Not only was the aircraft judged to be too costly, but also its need was negated because a large armada of ICBMs was rapidly replacing the threat of the Soviet bomber force.

The ASG-18 fire control system and Super Falcon missile represented 40 percent of Hughes's business that year. We were left hanging with no apparent application for our primary product lines. There was serious concern that the firm might not survive. Rather than precipitating the company's collapse, however, this disastrous event became the spark that ignited an extensive product line diversification and dramatic growth during the next decade.

19

PROFESSIONAL PROGRESS

For MANY YEARS, I imagined that I would continue my education through the doctorate level. After experiencing intensive engineering design work, obtaining my technical master's degree at USC, and getting a state professional engineering certificate, I felt inclined to modify my career goal. Focusing on a single technical area was not especially appealing when it was quite evident that I was not adept at inventive scientific tasks. Educational broadening seemed the better way to go. So, following five years of after-work classes, I received an MBA in 1959 from the highly regarded Anderson School of Management at UCLA. Somewhat later, I was also awarded an executive program certificate there. This more expansive training considerably improved my ability to do a credible managerial job and move up the management ladder at Hughes. UCLA later presented me with its 1991 Distinguished Leadership Award, a most meaningful honor, as were similar recognitions from Tufts and USC. I am most grateful to those educational institutions for what they taught me and for those honors.

In making the shift to big-picture work, I owe Walt Maguire a lifetime debt because he rescued me from the depths of mechanical design, encouraging me to focus instead on system engineering and program management. Walt's mentoring pushed me to eventually become involved in perfecting the tenets and practices of these tools of aerospace development (see Section 26, "Personal Progress"). The move to management assignments was the most important factor in my subsequent progress to the company's top echelons. By 1959, I had been appointed head of the physical design group of system engineering for the F-108 fire control system, managing an organization of about thirty professional engineers.

After seven years at Hughes, I was able to combine three weeks of accrued vacation time with one month of unpaid leave of absence, so my wife and I could take our long-desired dream journey. The plan was to drive a newly acquired Volkswagen Beetle four thousand miles throughout Western Europe. Connie also worked at Hughes and had majored in European history at Tufts, so she was very well informed about, and eager to finally see, the many places she had studied.

We reached Rome during our fourth week on the road without any communication with home. We happened to see a *Stars and Stripes* newspaper in an auto repair shop and read the startling headline "F-108 Cancelled!" What a shock! Nonetheless, we finished our journey using the last of our remaining cash and savings while envisioning that we would be unemployed when we returned to California. What unknowns lay ahead?

PART FOUR

CREATING A NEW BASE

T HE 1960S WERE frenetic times in the United States, with its younger generation rejecting the work ethic and moral values of their seniors. Also, the world political climate changed significantly. Both the United States and the USSR were switching from long-range bombers to ICBMs as their primary strategic weapon delivery vehicles. And it was alarming for us to read in October 1961 of the Soviets detonating the largest yield nuclear warhead in history. This nuclear weapon was equivalent to 50 megatons of TNT, or about four thousand times the power of the bomb that devastated Hiroshima, and with the apparent future capability of 100 megatons.

Dramatic confrontations between the two superpowers included Premier Khrushchev's continued verbal bluster and the construction of the Berlin Wall as a provocative part of the Iron Curtain. President Kennedy remarked, "A wall is better than a war." (In 1975, I saw the wall while at the Brandenburg Gate. As I pointed my camera at a Soviet watchtower, the guard swiveled a machine gun directly toward me! I took the photo anyway.) It was depressing for me to see in 2009 a similar wall installed in 2003 by the Israelis to separate the Palestinians in the West Bank. Will it be removed in thirty years as was the one dividing Berlin? Perhaps a wall is truly better than a war.

In 1962, the Soviets installed nuclear ballistic missile launch sites close to the United States, precipitating the Cuban Missile Crisis, which was finally settled by the Soviets withdrawing from the island. Some progress in good sense came from the 1963 test ban treaty prohibiting nuclear testing in the atmosphere. In 1967, the United States announced a policy of mutual deterrence for measuring strategic weapon inventories, which spurred more buildups by both sides. Middle East tensions increased again, culminating in the 1967 Israeli Six-Day War against allied Egypt, Syria, and Jordan, supported by most of the other Arab nations in the region. Israel scored a decisive military victory. The year 1968 saw the Soviet invasion of Czechoslovakia to quell the latter's attempted rebellion from the grip of the USSR. In a desire to limit Communist expansion, the United States greatly increased our military forces aiding South Vietnam in its conflict with North Vietnam. Fortunately, in 1969, Communist unity and composite strength were greatly weakened by the start of a long-lasting Sino-Soviet split. Previously cooperative relationships became poisoned by economic disputes, disagreements on the specifics of territorial borders, and arguments about methodologies in applying Communist doctrines. Prolonged armed conflict occurred along the very long boundary lines between those two countries.

In the space race, President Kennedy made a bold move in committing the nation to place a man on the Moon before the end of the decade. The public viewed that race with the USSR as a matter of prestige: which great nation could show its technical prowess by first achieving emotional (not necessarily useful) triumphs in space? The US goal was dramatically accomplished in 1969, as Neil Armstrong and Buzz Aldrin stepped onto the Moon's surface. (I had the pleasure of knowing many of the Grumman Aircraft Engineering Company designers who fashioned the incredible Moon-landing capsule.)

Political destabilization in the United States throughout the 1960s was inflamed by the 1963 assassination of President Kennedy, the escalating intensity of our combat in Southeast Asia, a great increase in use of hallucinogenic drugs, and antiwar and antigovernment activists stirring the younger generation almost to rebellion. This era's political turmoil, however, also spurred the world's appetite for the transfer of sound, video, and data streams from the newly proliferating digital computers. Discovery of far better communication methods had to be found to satisfy both military and civilian demands for international ties. To manage these national efforts, the new agencies of Comsat and Intelsat were formed in 1962 and 1965, respectively, and were well funded by the government.

For the aerospace industry, including Hughes, the rapid and unpredictable political changes made maintaining a stable base of product lines and operating facilities difficult. But at least it was still possible to attract government funding by offering innovative hardware concepts that might alleviate the perceived international problems.

Hughes was well positioned for diversification into new and unexplored domains. It had a proven record of technical achievements, a well-known heritage of innovation, private ownership with little demand for profit, and a physical location and lifestyle certain to attract talent of any type. With these assets, the company was able to establish a stable set of values, business principles, and standards of excellence. Moreover, Hughes could maintain high staff morale. New customers could be confident that choosing Hughes to tackle a tough job would bear minimal risk of failure.

20

CONTINUED AIR
INTERCEPT DOMINANCE

T HE MAINSTAY PRODUCT lines of airborne radar and air intercept missiles had begun with the F-84, F-86, and F-89 fighter series, followed by the F-102 and F-106 interceptor systems. Substantial design progress had been made in the next generation long-distance look-down-shoot-down pulse-Doppler capabilities of the breakthrough ASG-18 fire control system and Super Falcon missile destined for the F-108. After its cancellation, Hughes continued perfecting this weapon system without a known application, investing its own funds.

SR-71 *Blackbird*
(©iStockphoto/jondpatton)

Fortunately, in 1960 the Air Force chose Hughes to adapt these designs to fit its secret YF-12 interceptor, a reconfiguration of the Mach 3.2 SR-71 *Blackbird* surveillance aircraft operated by the CIA over Soviet territories (with the surprising code name OXCART).

The Hughes work was a "black" program, which is a need-to-know security classified project performed in a special manner, described later in this Part and in more detail in Part Eight. In only two years, the adaptation proved most successful. In test launches, six of seven Super Falcon missiles made target kills. One spectacular record set was a 1962 three-hour-long YF-12 round trip from California to Florida. While the aircraft was passing over New Mexico's White Sands Proving Ground on its return leg, a Super Falcon was launched from 74,000 feet altitude, 49 miles from a QB-47 *Stratojet* drone ground-skimming at 500 feet altitude. The missile scored a direct hit! This was a fabulous demonstration of look-down-shoot-down interception.

Unfortunately, like its *Rapier* predecessor, the YF-12 program was cancelled in 1965 because its forecasted production cost was too high. The government's strategic defense priority had shifted from bombers to ICBMs as the principal threat.

CORDS Difficulties

Although the priority had changed, the intercept job still had to be improved to ensure airspace control over battlefields in tactical situations and over Navy fleets. Because of Hughes's success in pulse-Doppler radar development, the Air Force chose the company to find a way to upgrade hundreds of F-4 *Phantom* fighters already deployed. The *Phantom* and its systems had been designed for the Navy, but the Air Force had purchased many squadrons of these fine aircraft. The *Phantom* had become their primary tactical fighters. The goal of the new project was to find a simple radar retrofit that would provide target visibility in spite of ground clutter—not at all a simple task. This ambitious program was called CORDS (coherent on-receive detection system).

These older F-4s had Westinghouse radars that used magnetron-powered transmitters with little frequency control, and were similar to Hughes radars from that production era (see Section 3, "Laying the Foundation" and Section 4, "Creating a Base of Technical Excellence"). The transmitted output signals were not stabilized enough in frequency or phase to make use of the Doppler shift that separates a moving target from the Earth's background. All devices operated in analog rather than digital format, complicating signal analysis and processing.

The retrofit technique chosen was to add a series of analog vacuum-tube storage elements to remember the transmitter frequency of each pulse long enough to allow comparison with the proper return echo. The remembered sample was used to reset the receiver frequency baseline for each transmitted pulse. A correct match between the received echo and the pulse that caused it would yield a measure of Doppler shift based on that target's speed, which would distinguish it from ground clutter.

To operate properly, the storage tubes needed to sense signal power levels as low as a weak target return to as high as a ground return, which could be a thousand times stronger. This energy awareness span is called dynamic range. Creating an actual vacuum tube to do this had inherent physical problems: the low-end response was limited by the tube's own electronic operating noise; the high end was bounded by the amount of power that would overload the tube, called power saturation. This is similar to what everyone knows: a one-quart milk bottle cannot be filled past its one-quart limit.

In testing the prototype, the low-end response level was set before each flight by an operator after measuring that day's internal radar noise. If set much higher than tube noise, the dynamic range window became too narrow to attain the needed performance. Such a preflight adjustment procedure was too impractical for a fielded military system. Two years of flight tests and attempts to make the adjustment automatically could not resolve frequency measurement uncertainties and signal contamination. The CORDS project was cancelled with the conclusion that electronic components had not matured enough to warrant production of this retro-fit design. The Hughes reputation for conquering any technical challenge was set back by this project's failure.

21

FROM *BLACKBIRD* TO *TOMCAT*

Particication by Hughes in the YF-12 *Blackbird* development perpetuated the company's virtual monopoly of the Air Force interceptor system business. The program's cancellation dismayed and frustrated the Air Force: their F-4 squadrons had an obvious performance inadequacy, and the service had to wait another five years to issue contracts for their replacement, the F-15 *Eagle*. The wait paid off, however, since the *Eagle's* requirement specifications benefited from great advances in the many needed technologies. A superb fighter resulted, one that enjoyed an operating lifespan of more than thirty-five years. Hughes competitively won responsibility for the radar, continuing its interceptor fire control dominance.

Hughes filled the gap in Air Force procurements and extended its reach into another service's interceptor business by winning the Navy's competition for arming the General Dynamics F-111B aircraft. The purpose of this interceptor was to achieve effective fleet air defense (FAD) against incoming waves of aircraft and cruise missiles intent on destroying Navy primary battle groups.

The Hughes system, the AWG-9 fire control system with its matching AIM-54 Phoenix missile, was required to find and continuously track up to twenty-four targets and simultaneously attack six of them. Development went very well and flight-testing proved the Hughes design concepts. However, as if continuing habitual government practice, the F-111B was scrubbed in 1968 because of underpowered engines and massive aircraft overweight. It was colorfully nicknamed the *Flying Edsel*, derisively comparing it to a disastrous Ford Motor Company automobile design. (In a Senate hearing, Vice Adm. Tom Connolly, Deputy Chief of Naval Operations for Air, declared, "There isn't enough power in Christendom to make that airplane what we want!") The Air Force's F-111A *Aardvark* strike-bomber

F-111B *"Flying Edsel"*
(courtesy of the National Naval Air Museum)

version continued and proceeded to full deployment. It should be noted that this two-service design requirement had been imposed on the Navy by Robert McNamara at DoD, and that service was never enthusiastic about the results.

To meet the Navy "wants," Grumman Aircraft Engineering Corporation won the competition for a new fleet air defense fighter, which became the world famous F-14 *Tomcat* (using the fighter pilot call sign of that delightful and crusty Vice Admiral Connolly). Hughes supplied a new version of the F-111B AWG-9 weapon control system and Phoenix missiles. In only two years, the F-14 went into production and two squadrons were deployed on the USS *Enterprise* aircraft carrier in 1973. The aircraft served the fleet for thirty years, and became a folk legend as the key player in the thrilling 1988 movie *Top Gun*, starring Tom Cruise.

The prolonged series of cancellations and revivals was an astonishing evolution of our primary product line. It took twelve years, but with every aircraft cancellation followed by a new application, the development yielded great performance advances and finally resulted in a fighter with astonishing capability.

This program established a long-term amicable Hughes relationship with the "Air Navy," as expressed in 2009 by Vice Adm. Robert Baldwin, former Deputy Chief of Naval Operations for Air:

"I remember several generations in the 'good old days' of working with various industry agents. My lasting impressions of the Hughes people were that in comparison with other aerospace reps the Hughes people were more focused on the product and not remembered for drinks and dinners! I do remember your people as being technically competent and responsive to performance questions."

The weapon control system hardware installed in the *Tomcat* weighed 1,300 pounds, occupied 28 cubic feet, and consisted of twenty-nine removable black boxes. The system provided the weapon control officer (WCO) in the rear seat of the aircraft with several displays and manual controls, including a 12-inch diameter panoramic scene display. The 36-inch diameter planar array antenna had two rows of small T-shaped antenna elements superimposed for receipt of identification messages. It could scan a wedge 170-degrees wide and 40 degrees in elevation. One feature I contributed was a fast narrow vertical scan of 50 degrees used for dogfight target acquisition while the *Tomcat* was in a sharp rolling turn. This operating mode was later added to all the world's fighters.

AWG-9 in F-14 *Tomcat* and a Phoenix Missile
(courtesy of Raytheon)

Unique features of the system—deployed in military use for the first time ever—were air battle observation and control using a search span covering 140 degrees; detection of hostiles 200 miles distant appearing from sea level to above 80,000 feet; continuous tracking of twenty-four targets; look-down-shoot-down capability against any hostile viewed from any aspect angle; launch of six Phoenix weapons to guide, simultaneously, to their separate targets starting at ranges up to 120 miles.

Making these operations possible were a pulse-Doppler radar with a high power TWT transmitter; an accurate, mechanically scanned flat-plate antenna with electronic beam shaping; complete digital rather than analog signal processing; a central computer managing all functions; time-shared updating to aid each missile's midcourse guidance; and an active radar seeker in the weapon for accurate terminal guidance.

The AWG-9 computer managed multiple target tracking by storing data on each target snapshot as the antenna continued its 2-second scan pattern. It then compiled a history file on each of twenty-four targets that it selected as the most likely threats and anticipated their future positions. The resulting tracks were displayed to the weapon control officer, who could then select and designate six hostiles to shoot. Each missile was assigned a specific viewing moment when its discrete target would be illuminated. This sampling technique enabled a single fighter to engage six separate targets at the same time.

Each Phoenix missile weighed 1,012 pounds at launch and was 13 feet long, with four 36-inch wings and control surfaces mounted on its 15-inch diameter airframe. For missile guidance during midcourse flight, the missile's seeker viewed AWG-9 radar's target reflections during its assigned viewing times, a snapshot appearing at two-second intervals. Since it "looked" only in its assigned time slot, each Phoenix was mute to echoes from other targets. With ten miles to go, active homing began—either to collision or close enough to trigger a proximity fuse—freeing the *Tomcat* for other mission operations. The 132-pound warhead exploded to form a 100-foot diameter expanding steel hoop that fatally sliced the target. It was difficult for any aircraft to survive a hit by hardened steel traveling at 6,000 feet per second. However, it was astonishing to read that a government damage-assessment analyst concluded that if that rod sliced off one wing and an engine from a Soviet Bison bomber, the injury would be insufficient to destroy that particular target; it could just continue speeding to its target! Surely, he would have changed his conclusion if he had watched one of these warheads detonating in a test arena. Perhaps because of this judgment, however, later models used a blast-fragmentation warhead whose pellets would shred anything in their path.

This missile development had a nostalgic tie to the famous *Spruce Goose* and Howard Hughes. Dave Grant was the engineer responsible for designing the hydraulic system that powered the activators to move the steering vanes of the Phoenix. Back in the 1940s, he had an identical duty of creating the hydraulic system for the H-4 *Hercules*. He had been selected by Mr. Hughes to be seated beside him on that exciting first flight. This method of powering aircraft flight control surfaces had never been done before, and the chief pilot wanted an expert nearby in case of operating difficulties. But the hydraulic system worked perfectly, and Dave's advice was not needed, and of course, he also did a fine job on our later missile.

All of the Phoenix capabilities were demonstrated in numerous flight tests conducted by Hughes and the Navy. One scored a direct hit on a target 120 miles away, and another was a spectacular 1973 six-on-six multishot test. The crew for the latter flight was Cmdr. John "Smoke" Wilson as pilot and Lt. Cmdr. Jack Hauver as WCO. It was astonishing to witness those six contrails heading to widely spaced targets, and hearing that there were five direct hits, with the sixth target barely escaping only because there was no warhead in this test!

Good Luck Rituals

Flight evaluation of weapons during their development stage is often surrounded by an aura of mysticism, omens, and symbols to generate good luck. One practice adopted by Ben McRee, at that time in charge of the Phoenix missile design, was to wear one green and one red sock on the day of a test shot. This ritual seemed to help, and was soon supplemented by The Great Chiquita Banana Sticker Missile Test Success Assurance gambit. Live test launches of this missile took place over the Navy's Pt. Mugu Pacific missile test range off the Southern California coast from F-14 *Tomcats* assigned to Hughes. For safety, and legal, reasons, the missiles were shipped from the assembly plant without rocket motors or warheads. The warhead compartment usually carried an instrumentation and telemetry unit. Rocket motors—and, for special tests, a warhead— were installed at the test site just prior to loading the missile onto the F-14.

Our engineers and technicians did the final assembly and ground testing at a remote shed at the Pt. Mugu airfield before the missiles' test flight. The process took about twenty-four hours, or two extended work shifts. One night, a technician brought a banana for a snack, and in jest, stuck the Chiquita banana logo sticker on the missile's exterior. The next day's launch was a phenomenal success in a very difficult mission, and the legend began that Chiquita always had to be aboard to assure us of good results. This good-luck symbol was added as a mandatory requirement on the Hughes and Navy final checklists that inspectors used to authorize the mission to proceed. We all believed the practice virtually assured our unbelievable record of test successes. It was not just mumbo-jumbo! The Chiquita International Corporation was pleased to be a part of this US defense effort.

Twenty years of Phoenix production yielded more than 5,000 weapons, with 600 going to Iran, the only overseas buyer. Navy combat use in the Balkans and the two Gulf Wars was very restricted because of visual identification rules: the pilot had to see the target with his own eyes before shooting, nullifying the missile's long range and multiple target advantages. Apparently unconstrained by such visual-ID rules, Iran claimed sixty to eighty Iraqi aircraft kills in their eight-year war that began in 1980, including two *Mirage* jets destroyed with a single Phoenix— a somewhat doubtful assertion because of the Iranian's history of poor F-14 maintenance and the usual exaggerations of combat results.

Phoenix Launched from an F-14 *Tomcat*
(courtesy of the National Naval Air Museum)

Culver City Plant with Paved Runway, 1965
(courtesy of UNLV)

22

OTHER FEET TO STAND ON

Relying on just one business base being unwise in this uncertain period, Hughes adopted a new strategy: invent and develop unique components where a known weakness or new need exists, use those devices to build new complex systems with superlative performance, and strive for major system-level breakthroughs beyond the efforts of all other firms in the competitive marketplace. Three examples of this strategy were (1) developing the lightweight traveling-wave tube amplifier that enabled frequency-stable amplification, which made possible our strength in pulse-Doppler radars; (2) perfecting the laser and becoming its highest volume producer, using lasers in many military devices; and (3) developing the mercury-cadmium-telluride detector, giving Hughes dominance in infrared sensors and imagers. More examples of this dynamic diversification during the next twenty-five years are described in the next four Parts.

This strategy was well summarized for me by Dr. John Mendel, former president of the Industrial Electronics group (also quoted in *The Tube Guys* by Norman Pond): "It seemed to me that in 1960 the Hughes culture was that the engineer was king, and technology was the focus. Fortunately, some guys became interested in using the technology to make products that solved real problems, and they created a production business that made money." Pond's book also quotes John about our team morale: "Hughes has been more insular than other major players, with [fewer staff] people [migrating between companies]; that's a real testament to the company and the management."

23

MANAGING GROWTH
AND DIVERSITY

T HE UNDERLYING MOTIVATION enabling the eventual Hughes triumph in this struggle for a rich future was well phrased by CEO Allen Puckett in 1985, re-emphasizing portions of the firm's mission statement (see Part Three) in the company newspaper, the *HughesNews*: "The objective of the Hughes Aircraft Company is to serve our nation and the world at the forefront of technology by creating and providing affordable products of superior quality, reliability, and performance."

Evolution of the
Organizational Structure

Companies attempting operations in creative technical design and manufacturing can go through three organizational stages: firstly, separate performers with similar abilities into clusters focused on specific technology disciplines (hydraulics, structures, aerodynamics, chemistry); secondly, group them into segments having all the needed skills to create a type of product (computer, radar, missile, field support); and lastly, assemble organizations that can respond to particular market segments (airborne, space, surface combat, artificial intelligence). Hughes progressed through these phases, as shown in the contrasting organization charts in Figure 4.1.

Figure 4.1a. Company Management (1949)

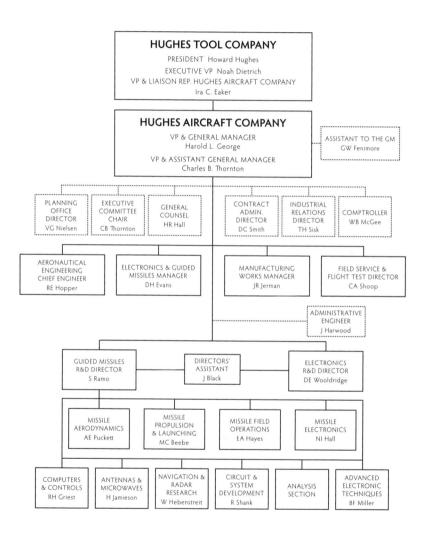

HUGHES TOOL COMPANY
PRESIDENT Howard Hughes
EXECUTIVE VP Noah Dietrich
VP & LIAISON REP. HUGHES AIRCRAFT COMPANY
Ira C. Eaker

HUGHES AIRCRAFT COMPANY
VP & GENERAL MANAGER
Harold L. George

VP & ASSISTANT GENERAL MANAGER
Charles B. Thornton

ASSISTANT TO THE GM
GW Fenimore

PLANNING OFFICE DIRECTOR
VG Nielsen

EXECUTIVE COMMITTEE CHAIR
CB Thornton

GENERAL COUNSEL
HR Hall

CONTRACT ADMIN. DIRECTOR
DC Smith

INDUSTRIAL RELATIONS DIRECTOR
TH Sisk

COMPTROLLER
WB McGee

AERONAUTICAL ENGINEERING CHIEF ENGINEER
RE Hopper

ELECTRONICS & GUIDED MISSILES MANAGER
DH Evans

MANUFACTURING WORKS MANAGER
JR Jerman

FIELD SERVICE & FLIGHT TEST DIRECTOR
CA Shoop

ADMINISTRATIVE ENGINEER
J Harwood

GUIDED MISSILES R&D DIRECTOR
S Ramo

DIRECTORS' ASSISTANT
J Black

ELECTRONICS R&D DIRECTOR
DE Wooldridge

MISSILE AERODYNAMICS
AE Puckett

MISSILE PROPULSION & LAUNCHING
MC Beebe

MISSILE FIELD OPERATIONS
EA Hayes

MISSILE ELECTRONICS
NI Hall

COMPUTERS & CONTROLS
RH Griest

ANTENNAS & MICROWAVES
H Jamieson

NAVIGATION & RADAR RESEARCH
W Hebenstreit

CIRCUIT & SYSTEM DEVELOPMENT
R Shank

ANALYSIS SECTION

ADVANCED ELECTRONIC TECHNIQUES
BF Miller

Figure 4.1b. Company Management (1954)

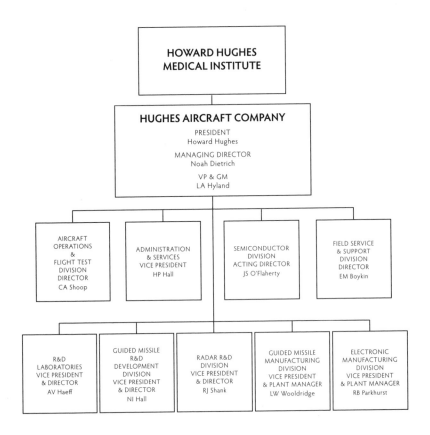

HOWARD HUGHES MEDICAL INSTITUTE

HUGHES AIRCRAFT COMPANY
PRESIDENT
Howard Hughes

MANAGING DIRECTOR
Noah Dietrich

VP & GM
LA Hyland

AIRCRAFT
OPERATIONS
&
FLIGHT TEST
DIVISION
DIRECTOR
CA Shoop

ADMINISTRATION
& SERVICES
VICE PRESIDENT
HP Hall

SEMICONDUCTOR
DIVISION
ACTING DIRECTOR
JS O'Flaherty

FIELD SERVICE
& SUPPORT
DIVISION
DIRECTOR
EM Boykin

R&D
LABORATORIES
VICE PRESIDENT
& DIRECTOR
AV Haeff

GUIDED MISSILE
R&D
DEVELOPMENT
DIVISION
VICE PRESIDENT
& DIRECTOR
NI Hall

RADAR R&D
DIVISION
VICE PRESIDENT
& DIRECTOR
RJ Shank

GUIDED MISSILE
MANUFACTURING
DIVISION
VICE PRESIDENT
& PLANT MANAGER
LW Wooldridge

ELECTRONIC
MANUFACTURING
DIVISION
VICE PRESIDENT
& PLANT MANAGER
RB Parkhurst

Figure 4.1c. Company Management (1990)

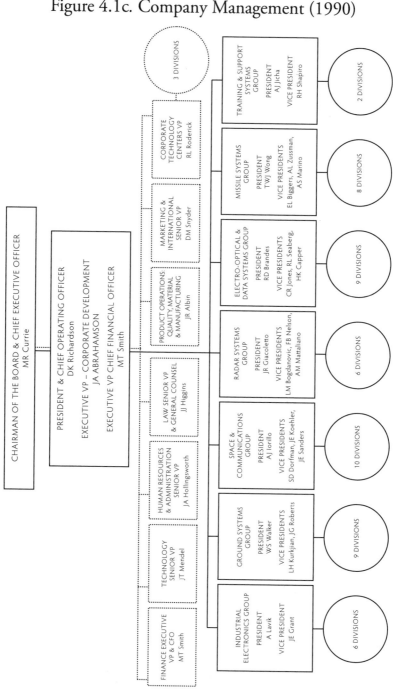

Organizational units are usually sized by limiting a supervisor's control to ten or fewer persons for technical work and thirty or fewer for repetitive manufacturing. This means that the larger the company is, the more layers there are in the total structure. During its period of peak employment, Hughes placed as many as 85,000 people into eight structural levels: corporate, system group, division, laboratory, department, section, group, and individual; the first opportunity for someone to achieve a title of vice president was the position of assistant system group manager.

Successful entry into major product line diversification generated rapid expansion and greater flexibility to compensate for occasional business downturns in some sectors. The unusual company management attitude and operating style that made this unfettered search possible had several noteworthy features.

As explained in Part Three, the Hughes structural concept was to form decentralized organizational "clusters" with minimal top-down steering. Supporting staff functions, such as financial and legal, were clearly differentiated from line organizations, which were defined as responsible for the creation and manufacturing of the product hardware. Support staff could only set formal ground rules, monitor progress, and advise improvements, but never attempt to issue operating commands.

Avoiding overlaps of responsibility between line segments was done by grouping product types according to their dominant technology (airborne radar, infrared systems, guided weapons, space endeavors, surface combat), and assigning professionals skilled in those disciplines. To create and build complex product lines, a fully equipped organization required adept management, a mix of the right engineering capabilities, an experienced manufacturing team, field support experts, and staff support from contracts, finance, legal, procurement, and marketing. As new product lines emerged through selective branching into previously untapped fields, a small cadre with the necessary skills would jump-start an independent segment, which then grew by transfers from other segments of the company and by recruiting from outside sources.

When a temporary need arose to solve a difficult problem, there was a free flow of borrowed experts between the already established product line organizations. This sharing of "family" members became the normal way of life in the growing years, balancing the workforce as programs waxed and waned, solving design and manufacturing difficulties, and stimulating the workforce to meet a variety of professional responsibilities. Sometimes the informal helping and sharing occurred without senior management's awareness. Prompt corrections were needed to ensure contract coverage, avoid mischarging, and avert customer concerns that talents assigned to their program were being distracted.

Corporate level overview and coordination of purchasing from outside suppliers (procurement) reduced costs and improved quality: key suppliers served several product lines, rather than only one, and virtually became part of the Hughes family team. Often they were asked to innovate and overcome a particular technical or manufacturing hurdle for us. The suppliers delighted in this growth of business for them as one of the few favored suppliers. These corporate efforts to share suppliers benefited all the participating product lines.

Family Style

One can be tempted to visualize this dedicated and motivated company as a rebirth of Camelot, with Sir Pat Hyland leading many knights of the Round Table toward a noble destiny. Nothing but good intentions, excellent capability to perform, and few political intrigues. Of course, this was not nearly true; there were many imperfections, especially in the later years of rapid expansion when the zeal and mission orientation of many new hires did not fit that legendary image. But a great part of the inspiring vision was there during the 1960s and 1970s. The growing successes of Hughes were in large part made possible by its stellar talent, recruited and nurtured as previously described, a continuing process that was a management priority. As the company increased in size, bonding all those independent-minded managers into a sharing family team was enhanced by an annual corporate offsite conference—three days at comfortable resorts in Santa Barbara, Palm Springs, or Rancho Bernardo. Spouses attended and participated in evening dinners and light entertainment. Often the theme of the gathering was that of the "Old West," with historic attire and country-western music. Morning conferences dealt with mission emphasis, mutual problem solving, and analysis of customer concerns and attitudes. Afternoons were casual, with golf, tennis, boating, riding, and other recreational enjoyments.

Some Hughes employees not on the attendee list and some government watchdogs criticized this offsite practice as a waste of company funds and an inappropriate lark for the bosses. However, the meetings were important in knitting together the Hughes family, imparting a true feeling of camaraderie, enabling future sharing of organizational assets in times of need (it's easier to ask for help from someone you know and trust than from a stranger), ensuring a better understanding of corporate objectives, and mellowing spousal concerns about each manager's operating stress—as well as helping point the enterprise in the optimum direction. (Senior management's intended direction was vigorously debated and frequently reformed in those offsite conferences). Strong family attitudes, starting at the top and demonstrated by middle managers' behavior, motivated the rest of the employees to emulate and practice the same spirit. The annual meeting also was an incentive to spur junior staff members to strive harder for promotion, so they could become eligible to attend.

The family feeling that existed among the teams was well described by George Speake, division manager in the Electrooptical and Data Systems Group:

> "Please don't credit me for a project's achievements. During five years of difficult development, several hundred people worked long and hard to make the program a success. Leading the effort involved much coordinating and persuading the customer to avoid canceling the program, and the project probably would never have succeeded without the team's superhuman efforts. But none of us managers did the 'real' work to get the job done under extremely tough conditions. The family team is who should be praised; that's far better to do than to name any individual."

The Integrators

Diversification was considerably aided by the demonstrated ability to create exceedingly complex weapon systems, and the company continually refined its management methods to do the job more swiftly and reliably. Three fine examples emerging from the late 1960s were the command and control networks managing air defense for all NATO nations; the high capacity synchronous communication satellite series beginning with *Early Bird*; and the unifying of lasers, IR sensors, optics, and computers into effective tank fire control systems. These systems involved designs and production outputs from several separate Hughes product line organizations, a number of major subcontractors, and several suppliers of government-furnished equipment linked into the overall system. Directing, controlling, and integrating into a harmonious whole the activities of these independent outfits, each of which had its own internal priorities, demanded great foresight, tactful diplomacy, and skillful communication. Such helmsmanship was performed by a small management and technology team, fully authorized with corporate power and assigned as a unit reporting to the product line organization that had the most relevant technology involved in the entire system. This function was called program management, which contained a strong technical arm called system engineering.

Program Management

The program management (PM) team was empowered with corporate level authority over all participants in its project, regardless of their organizational location. The team's many tasks included marketing, proposal preparation, contract negotiation and recording, financial budgeting and control, master scheduling, technology integration, motivating the entire workforce, maintaining customer contact and satisfaction, and reporting

❋

Contractor effort on a challenging defense program goes through many stages and involves many skills. A proposal team of perhaps fifty full-time people and many part-timers prepares a response to a customer's Request for Proposal (RFP); the proposal contains a detailed conceptual solution showing proof of feasibility, a master schedule, and plans for technical and schedule risk alleviation. A competitive price bid estimated by senior management is offered. After much discussion with the buying agency and a favorable selection, the firm negotiates detailed legal, financial, schedule, and technical requirements.

Upon contract award, a team is assembled within each specialty organization with skills needed for the design and development of the system. These separate segments are directed by an administrative and technical center, comprising about 10 percent of the entire program staff, that provides overall program direction; issues schedules and budgets; defines the system architecture and detailed technical requirements; and closely interacts with the customer. The program proceeds through design, development, rigorous testing of prototypes, and a manufacturing trial run, followed by full-scale production and field deployment. Ongoing efforts include logistical supply of repair spares, field operator training, other field support functions, and sustaining engineering to remedy faults and create performance improvements. Continual contact with and approval by the customer as well as several government monitoring agencies occurs throughout all program stages.

status and problems to senior management. It is important to separate this function from the performing organizations to preserve objectivity and wide vision. A project to develop a laser for several applications may need only a single person as the PM. Intermediate size programs such as the tank fire control system required a PM staff of up to ten. A giant system development like the F-14 weapon system required hundreds.

Hughes perfected the principles and practices of program management and its technical arm, system engineering. The company developed and documented detailed guidelines of how to operate successfully; those practices became a focus of management training. Successful program managers were enthusiastic about the program's mission, attentive to customer needs and relations, thorough in their understanding of technical realities, and adept with financial controls. They had comprehensive knowledge of the company's design and production assets, and practiced excellent public and private communication skills. An innate ability to forecast attainable schedules was most important.

I prepared a program manager's credo for use at Hughes. I personally taught these tenets in UCLA's corporate training program and as a consultant to several government agencies. (That is, until president John Richardson directed me to cease teaching outsiders, for fear of unnecessarily helping our competitors!) Nonetheless, these performance recommendations eventually became recognized throughout the aerospace industry. The following were some of those guidelines:

- It ain't easy to be a PM. But having full corporate authority to go with your responsibility helps immensely. Performing well requires training, seasoning, and lessons learned from other program successes and failures.
- Importance of the program manager. You are the general manager: controlling design, manufacturing, finance, marketing, contracts, and field support. (The F-14 *Tomcat* weapon system program management team of 300 had responsibility to integrate the efforts of 5,500 people within Hughes, and controlled an annual expenditure of $300 million.) A PM must project and inspire dedication to success and be a most enthusiastic advocate for the program's mission. He or she must thoroughly understand the customer's motivations, needs, and attitudes. When with the customer, the PM must represent the company; within Hughes, he or she must represent the customer. Program management teams must ensure the project's continuity spanning the times when customer and participating individuals change.

- Top management expectations. A PM can't be perfect since complex programs are always fraught with risks and uncertainty. You are expected to stay on top and always be well informed. Obtain teamwork by all the participants in your matrix of diverse performing organizations. Always have participants make a plan for your approval, and be sure they personally commit to its outcome. Keep us informed on critical issues, events, and forecasts; always alert us before telling the customer. Present to us alternate solutions, not just a definition of a problem. Be efficient in the use of our time.

- Providing for uncertainty must be continual. After all, this project may be trying to push beyond existing boundaries of performance, so trial and error will be expected. Ameliorate uncertainty by early risk analysis to forecast potential difficulties: setting schedules with some slack to allow for possible delays; forming budgets with reserve funds controlled by you so risky areas can be reinforced; negotiating with the customer a contract clause to counter dollar-inflation; setting technical levels for each program segment such that in the entire system assembly those segments whose final designs exceed their goals can offset weaker ones to meet total contract performance requirements; begin alternative developments for segments that look marginally risky; consider funding both internal and external sources to ensure needed results; keep abreast of skill pools throughout the company to muster help quickly when needed.

- Dealing with problems. Use the business tools provided, but do not be overly dependent; find the best method for the situation at hand. Hit problems hard, early, and with sufficient resources; quickly feel and absorb your lumps, and do not be distracted by them. Take seriously, but do not panic about schedule impact—there may be offsets to cure the delay caused by this setback. Try to get customer help, perhaps with a slight change of the technical specifications or by altering the contract budget. Do not wait long to drop poor performers, whether an individual or an organization; find apt substitutes quickly. Proper conduct with performing organizations is essential to ensure team rapport. Give them a good business deal with stability and sufficient budget; delegate full authority to match their responsibility; push back on the customer when requirements are found to be excessive; ensure program management direction is given through only one spokesperson to avoid confusion; insist on periodic formal design and status reviews; treat their engineering and manufacturing staffs with equal respect; discuss and promptly rectify customer concerns. By all means, enthusiastically credit and advertise performers' successful accomplishments to senior management and the entire corporation.

- Qualities of a great PM. Those selected must have adequate technical knowledge; think like a general manager; exhibit leadership by persuasion and influence; be an enthusiastic advocate of the customer and the project's mission; be comfortable and adaptive to rapid change; be quickly decisive; admit errors and rectify them immediately; communicate well with individuals and in public; demonstrate good understanding of people's attitudes and needs; and always practice and advocate high integrity. This large array of traits is difficult to find embodied in individual candidates. However, starting with a good personal character as a base, many heads of organizations rapidly learn and adapt well in the high-stress job of a PM. As they grow in experience, the great ones will place difficult issues in context, describe the rationale for all their decisions, and continuously report progress to their senior executives as well as to their entire program team.

System Engineering

Visualize a three-dimensional puzzle with many small interlocking pieces that move fluidly, sing music, are of differing colors and temperatures, and are composed of different materials. All must somehow be harmonized into an operating whole to perform some exotic task. Some of the pieces will interact with others, changing size or shape to accommodate a piece that cannot change.

Solving a complex puzzle like this is similar to the challenge of harmonizing the many pieces of hardware and software in a command and control linkup for control of forward troops, a surveillance and tracking system aboard ship for managing a Naval task force, a sophisticated guided missile, or a nationwide communication satellite network. Numerous separate devices must rapidly perform complex functions that join together to carry out the total mission.

System engineering was the center for technical decision making within the program manager's team. Many tasks began after a thorough understanding of the overall requirements: devising the system's architecture; analytically setting performance and reliability goals for the overall system and each of its contributing segments; defining interfaces and interactions among subsystems and with other systems within the overall project; determining whether to develop a component in-house or subcontract it; specifying limits of size, weight, power, and cooling; negotiating with the system's carrier vehicle maker or user's site to accommodate the system's needs; constraining the hardware and software configuration to maximize repairability; prescribing manufacturing and field-maintenance standards; setting reliability and repair goals; and specifying the testing and evaluation of fully integrated prototypes. System engineers continually negotiated and compromised with the detail designers, making many adjustments in order that the sum of all the parts achieved the contract's overall performance level. This practice, called making tradeoffs, occurred when a better-performing device could offset a sister segment experiencing a shortfall or when an initial design approach proved unsatisfactory.

✸

Systems are typically made up of parts, or components, which are combined into units, which are in turn combined into subsystems, which then combine to make up the system. The physical segments are controlled by the system's central computer software, which is often more technically complex than any of the individual physical assemblies. The central computer software needs to be interactive with an operator to adapt to the particular situation. Either different organizations within the company or subcontractors can be responsible for separately developing each subsystem. System engineering's job is to ensure that the system comes together as a whole and performs as its customer intends it should, including melding smoothly with other customer systems.

Like Hughes's program management techniques, system engineering methodologies were continually improved over a span of years, were well documented, and were often emulated by other aerospace firms. Much to our dismay, by direct observation and customer suggestions, many of our competitors adopted these efficient and sophisticated practices.

Sustaining Engineering

Both customers and Hughes benefited from stable and continual funding for technical backup throughout the life of difficult projects. Programs begin with design and development, followed by rigorous testing and evaluation of prototypes, a manufacturing trial run and full production, then user training, field deployment, and long-term support for operations and repair. A large organization within the company was responsible to nurture customer satisfaction with the hundreds of products fielded. This Support Systems Group (later called Support and Training Systems Group), which grew to 14,000 people, set the stage for deployment and ensured the user's ability to quickly remedy operating problems, whether due to initial design error, periodic component failures, or operator misunderstanding. Early in the project's development, this set of professionals planned and prepared operator manuals, repair handbooks, training programs, logistical supply profiles, test equipment for field use, and training simulators. They were responsible for maintaining a compatible relationship with the operational customer.

In addition to all these important support efforts, a substantial contractor engineering pool was needed to solve problems that inevitably arose with new equipment, to modify interfaces to match changes in associated customer equipment, and to improve or expand the system's operating capabilities. At projects' inceptions, contract negotiators had to convince customers of the wisdom of this effort and persuade them to insert a well-funded program requirement, called sustaining engineering, for the full life of the program. Hughes successfully emphasized the importance of sustaining engineering, usually obtaining a higher proportion of total contract cost dedicated to it than did our competitors. The benefits were enormous: quick response to production or field operation difficulties, stability in our technology base, and a crew continually inventing relevant improvements. Results in the deployed military equipment assured the customer that growing combat demands were always met or exceeded with Hughes equipment.

We enjoyed a reputation of always caring about, and rapidly responding to customer concerns, thanks to sustaining engineering.

24

ENTRY INTO SPACE

ONE OF THE many branches that Hughes grew on its diversification tree began in the early 1960s and created worldwide interest and excitement. Because of it, Hughes became a major player in the international space race, considerably expanding its business base and greatly enhancing its reputation and prestige. As Pat Hyland put it at the time: "It is our extraordinary good fortune to be living in the space age, this infinitesimal speck of time when we are privileged to witness advancements earlier men of great wisdom thought impossible."

Everyone was stunned by the appearance in 1957 of the Soviet Sputnik racing along in a low elliptical orbit. That world's first artificial satellite could also perform limited communication with people on the Earth. As this was happening, an innovative forward thinker at Hughes, Dr. Harold Rosen, saw a way to satisfy the world's emerging appetite for real-time, worldwide transfer of voice, text, music, and video information.

Harold believed that active wideband microwave relays permanently positioned in space might accomplish this transfer. He felt that the optimum way to do so would be to use a satellite, placed in the Earth's equatorial plane, that orbited high in the sky at the same rotational rate as our planet. Antennas on the ground could then be set with fixed pointing angles and with precise narrow-beam shapes (Fig. 4.2).

Lower orbits with rotational rates different from the Earth's force the ground antennas to continually move to track the satellites. Relay-link interruptions occur as the satellites disappear below the horizon, and a search must be made to reestablish hookup as they reappear on the opposite horizon. Another advantage of a "fixed" position is that the better performance of the ground antenna's narrow, well-focused beam allows the satellite's relay equipment to use desirable radar-like frequencies and to function at low power. This makes it feasible for the satellite to carry only a modest array of solar cells to power continuous operation. The concept was called a geosynchronous, or geostationary, communication satellite.

A team of Rosen, Don Williams, and Tom Hudspeth eagerly pursued this idea, and they completed a paper design that promised a high probability of success. However, many requests for corporate funding to complete development were unsuccessful. Pat Hyland and Allen Puckett clearly visualized the potential long-term corporate benefit from this new endeavor. Because its advocates were unable to present a business plan showing risk-abatement and forecasting a high probability of success, they were reluctant to make the large and uncertain investment. Pat and Allen were most impressed when Don Williams wrote a personal check for $10,000 (big money in those days) to keep the work going forward. However, the executives urged an intensive search for funding either from the government or from private sources.

Figure 4.2. Geosynchronous Orbit ("Fixed" Satellite Position)

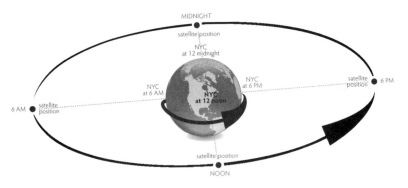

The team made numerous attempts to do this throughout the next year, without success. Finally, in late 1961, the deputy director of defense, Dr. John Rubel (who had formerly worked at Hughes), became excited about the project. Dr. Rubel revised a long-standing agreement between NASA and DoD that had precluded NASA from "competing" with the DoD-funded Advent, a geostationary satellite program whose development had so far been unsuccessful (and which was subsequently cancelled). The altered agreement permitted NASA to fund and oversee a geostationary communication project. Now, after a two-year struggle for adequate support, Hughes could begin full development of something called Syncom (synchronous communication satellite).

Syncom

The idea of a communication satellite had first been described in writing thirty years previously, before the technology was adequate to accomplish the difficult task. In 1928, a Slovenian rocket engineer, Herman Potocnic, discussed the challenging idea in *The Problem of Space Travel: The Rocket Motor.* Shortly thereafter, Britain's Sir Arthur C. Clarke further ignited public fantasy with his many science fiction stories. (In 1944, I was intrigued with similar dreams, and wrote a space fantasy story for a ninth grade school project.) Arthur Clarke also understood many technologies. In 1941, he was a radar expert for the RAF; in 1945, he defined how a workable satellite communication system could be created.

To attain geostationary orbit, a spacecraft must be boosted to 22,236 miles above the Earth's surface and retain a speed of 6,873 miles per hour. This velocity sets a centripetal outward acceleration force that exactly matches the Earth's gravitational pull, just like a child's whirling a rock attached to a string. The satellite's movement traces exactly over an equatorial spot directly beneath itself. That location allows the satellite to capture a ground signal to be relayed to a receiver placed anywhere within one-third of the world's surface. It was initially thought that a person talking through this relay would need a small mental adjustment to cope with a slight time delay: the signals traveling at the speed of light take a quarter of a second to reach the distant receiver. The concern was that people could be frustrated if the listener unintentionally interrupted the speaker—total confusion could result with neither able to complete sentences. The disadvantage of the time delay was actually so small that it was easily accommodated. (Previously, AT&T had warned of this alleged fault in its unsuccessful attempt to forestall competition by satellite communications with its profitable undersea cable business.)

Equatorial placement limits visibility from regions beyond the Arctic and Antarctic Circles since the spacecraft is below the Earth's horizon (Fig. 4.3).

When several satellites are placed in the same orbit circle, and relay data at the usual high frequencies, they must be spaced at least 3 degrees apart (a physical distance of about 930 miles) to avoid overlapping antenna patterns and to ensure proper linkup with the correct ground station. When using much longer wavelength transmissions like UHF (as was done with TACSAT, described in Section 45, "Global Communication; Increasing Payload Capacity"), only one satellite per ocean basin was permissible to prevent mutual interference.

Only the orbit altitude and velocity of the satellite determine its dynamic offset with gravity, not its weight or mass. The orbiter's mass does affect the size of the launch booster rockets: the heavier the delivery package is, the more lofting power or thrust is needed. It was found that the economical method for final position insertion uses three stages: first, placing the payload into a circular low altitude orbit, then thrusting it into an elliptical transfer orbit whose highest point (apogee) is the desired synchronous altitude, and lastly, applying a kick-boost at that peak altitude to achieve the needed orbital velocity. Launch sites far from the equator also need an additional satellite maneuver. If the launch is from Florida, for example, a 28-degree latitude shift must be made.

Figure 4.3. Beam Impingement Limits

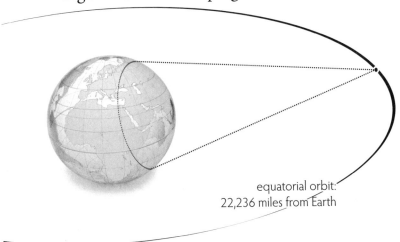

equatorial orbit:
22,236 miles from Earth

In the early 1960s, US launch rockets were just maturing in lifting power, imposing severe size and weight limits on their payloads. But achieving small size and light weight were only two of the many challenges for Syncom. Others were how to guide the booster stages to insert the satellite into the correct orbit; continuously control its alignment and attitude; provide enough electrical power; select the frequency bands for downlink telemetry data and uplink command instructions; choose the relay frequencies for voice, text, and video; create antennas with the proper beam shapes and placements to ensure adequate reception on the ground; and set power levels for the relay transponders for good linkup without overloading the power available. Photovoltaic solar cells were chosen to obtain the electrical power, coupled with batteries to span the times when the Earth's shadow obscured the Sun. Room had to be found for the canisters of hydrogen peroxide and nitrogen used for pulsing the thrusters to maintain spin stabilization and to adjust the spin axis for attitude control. The final design with its many performance complexities was a cylinder 28 inches in diameter and 15 inches high, weighing only 86 pounds.

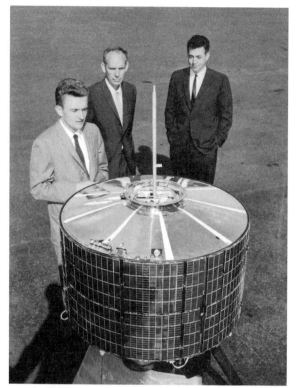

Williams, Hudspeth, Rosen with Syncom
(courtesy of Hal Rosen)

The ingenious team achieved many brilliant technology break-throughs that enabled Syncom to succeed, including attitude stabilization by spinning the entire cylindrical body to act like a flywheel, controlling the spin axis to remain parallel to the Earth's axis, and devising lightweight 2-watt traveling-wave tubes that gave enough output power for broadband data relay. The satellite's exterior cylinder provided enough area for the number of solar cells needed to satisfy the continuous power demand. The spin rate of about 160 revolutions per minute was rapid enough to stabilize the vehicle during its insertion into orbit as the final solid rocket thruster did the kick boost, and just right for long-term attitude stabilization.

The Sun sensors provided reference data to maintain axis control. Two small clamshell canisters on the spinning exterior cylinder each contained a solar cell. A small slit permitted the sensors to glimpse the Sun for a brief instant and to react by providing an electric pulse. The base-reference sensor had its slit parallel to the satellite axis and peered 90 degrees outward; the other had its slit at an angle to match the Earth's normal tilt relative to the Sun. Pulses from both were sent to the ground for computing corrections that would keep the satellite's axis parallel to that of the Earth. If the pulse from the tilted sensor came earlier or later than the one from the base-reference sensor, the satellite axis was not aligned correctly. Commands sent on the uplink then triggered Syncom's small alignment thrusters until the two pulses came at the same instant. Computer calculations always adjusted for the known wobble of the Earth's axis. The time information of the base-reference Sun sensor was also used to command another thruster to control the spin rate. The radiation pattern from the pole-shaped antennas determined the up and down orientation of the satellite's spin axis.

Syncom Satellite Reaching Orbit
(courtesy of UNLV)

William's and Rosen's astounding creation of both the spin-stabilization and the simple Sun sensor for spin-axis attitude control resulted in patent protection. These inventions became the basis of an infringement lawsuit several years later, with a settlement very favorable to Hughes (see Section 25, "A Different Kind of Business").

Syncom 1 did not reach the correct orbit due to an unknown failure. There was much speculation about the possible cause. Don Williams made one likely assumption, mathematically computed where the errant bird would be, flew to Australia, and, borrowing a large telescope there, discovered he was right!

Syncom 2, modified to avoid another disappointment from that failure and several other speculated ones in Syncom 1, was successfully placed in orbit in July 1963, followed by another the following year. Each was boosted by a three-stage Delta rocket from Cape Canaveral, Florida.

Syncom provided the first non-land-wire international telephone conversation: President John Kennedy interchanging greetings with Nigeria's prime minister, Sir Abubakar Balewa. It also transmitted real-time television broadcasting of the 1964 Olympic games from Tokyo, which was received throughout the United States—another world first.

Syncom 2 performed flawlessly for five years, although its forecasted life had been only one year. It finally perished after using all its stored thruster fuel.

Syncom was soon followed by the first worldwide business commercial communications using geosynchronous spacecraft relay links, which began with the Hughes Early Bird (also called Intelsat 1) launched in 1965; it relayed one TV channel and 240 separate telephone links. This satellite was the beginning of a long series of configurations for Intelsat (the International Telecommunications Satellite Organization, formed in 1964). By 1973, Intelsat had six hundred Earth stations located in 149 nations and territories. Satellite Business Systems (SBS) began in 1975. Intelsat and SBS provided US military and domestic services as well as services for overseas commerce. This business venture became a rewarding one for Hughes Aircraft Company, as further described in Part Seven. Spectacular proof of the value of satellite linkage occurred in 1972, when President Nixon's visit to Beijing was seen "live" by a worldwide audience of 600 million people. Hughes satellites were used, and the company prepared and operated a full-capability ground terminal in China, despite numerous difficulties with language and culture, and rigorous security restrictions.

With these new business thrusts, the company's long-term future was somewhat more secure. However, public attitudes about the company were still a mixture of little visibility, credit for technology achievements in only a few notable areas, and the continuing mysteries of organizations bearing the name of Howard Hughes. One media example can be found in a *Fortune* Magazine article of April 1968. It praised some achievements, but erroneously forecast a negative future.

Fortune Magazine Cover
(From *FORTUNE* Magazine, April 1 ©1968 Time Inc. Used under license.)

Hughes Aircraft: The High-Flying Might-Have-Been

It could have been the G.M. of electronics, say its distinguished alumni. It isn't, but in its unique way it keeps advancing the technological frontiers.

by Gene Bylinsky

Beginning of *Fortune* Article
(From *FORTUNE* Magazine, April 1 ©1968 Time Inc. Used under license.)

25

A DIFFERENT KIND
OF BUSINESS

MUCH OF THE reason for the company's remaining unknown to the public stemmed from the defense secrecy classification that draped a veil over the work done by Hughes for the CIA, DoD, NRO (National Reconnaissance Office), and other agencies, further described in Part Eight. These curtains had advantages. The "need to know" classification shut out many inquiries and potential interference with progress, as well as competitors keen to understand the intricacies of new creations that they could apply to their own projects. Patents also could protect company inventions, although the government had the right to pass on any discoveries engendered by a project for which it had paid the cost. This happened when such a new idea could solve a problem in a completely different government program. All contractors exclusively owned their employees' patents if the work was performed on site and was company funded.

Patents formed a significant revenue source. For many years, Hughes used more than 4,100 active and meaningful patents that it owned. It also could market to other companies the rights to use the unique designs or processes. In a number of instances, patent infringement lawsuits against "pirating" domestic and overseas firms could result in richly rewarding settlements. Some of our key officers jokingly considered setting up a separate product line organization called the Patent Infringement Division to search for liability opportunities.

One example of infringement lawsuits pursued by Hughes was the Williams patent mentioned above, which was issued in September 1973 (more than ten years after he devised the concept) and related to satellite attitude control using spin stabilization during insertion into orbit and in its lifetime positioning. Although the work was performed with company funds, the government allowed other contractors to use this design concept without recompense to Hughes. The 1973 lawsuit against the government (NASA was the defendant) and the manufacturers of the satellites contended that 108 designs had infringed. Hearings determined that ten did not infringe. Philco-Ford settled out of court in 1988 for thirteen Intelsat V infringements, leaving eighty-five in the suit. The Ford settlement was for $45 million. The government case had a series of court decisions followed by appeals and retrials. The case was finally settled in favor of Hughes, after an incredible twenty-six years, for $154 million. It took a mighty long time to harvest that crop!

Another infringement matter was the Bower's patent case, which had mixed results. In 1969, Dr. Robert W. Bower invented a new process for making semiconductor circuit devices while he was with the Hughes Research Laboratories. These clusters of hundreds of microelectronic elements were created by etching and altering the chemistry of silicon wafers. The new process was to perform oxide doping using a step called ion implantation, giving far better placement control and higher quality than any previous chemical diffusion technique. Bower's process is now used in virtually every electronics device throughout the world. Hughes filed an infringement suit against the Intel Corporation, claiming $200 million in damages. Unfortunately, Hughes lost, apparently because of a negative vote by a single juror, who later gave no publicly stated reason. Hughes decided not to try Intel again, but successfully negotiated out-of-court settlements with several Japanese semiconductor firms for almost $20 million. The Japanese apparently believed Hughes had a very strong position, so avoided risking a trial they thought they would be sure to lose.

26

PERSONAL PROGRESS

DURING THE 1960S I was fortunate to be directly associated with vital Hughes programs that were continuing technical successes. I progressed from section head through department manager to laboratory manager for the *Tomcat's* complex weapon control and missile system.

After personally witnessing three aircraft cancellations (the F-108, YF-12, and F-111B), helping ensure that Hughes won the Navy's competition for the extraordinary *Tomcat* weaponry was invigorating, challenging, educational, satisfying, and rewarding. (A senior Naval officer later complimented me, saying that a positive factor for Hughes in the competition came from a presentation I made demonstrating the large cost savings and greatly reduced risk to the proposed program that would result from Hughes's achievements on its F-111B contract.)

An amusing (only in retrospect) event happened during my time as the *Tomcat* system engineering laboratory manager. It was my first meeting with Dr. Albert (Bud) Wheelon, who had left his position as technical director of the CIA to join Hughes as senior vice president for technology. After a quick good-morning greeting, his first question was, "Tell me how a pulse-Doppler radar works." I felt reasonably comfortable at that point, since my boss, Walt Maguire, a world expert on that subject, was present and surely would answer this tough question in great detail. Oh-oh! Walt immediately turned to me saying with a smile, "Go ahead and tell him, Ken." That was going to be a real strain for a "big-picture overview" person like myself, but luckily I got through with apparently enough credibility. (Walt sometimes did such a trick in order to better develop his subordinates, yet he always saved the scene if things did not go well.) It was most likely that Dr. Wheelon already knew the answer to his question. My fear was risking reassignment from my spot as the *Tomcat* system engineering laboratory manager if I appeared to lack knowledge in the primary technical area for that project!

Operating Black

For many years, many critically vital defense and intelligence programs fell into a category known as "black," described in more detail in Part Eight. They were governed by the strictest security measures to avoid any leaks to foreigners (and even between rival US services!). Their purpose, existence, location, schedule, funding, and workforce were unknown or disguised from anyone without a "need to know" status. Documentation was usually limited, extremely protected, and often shredded as soon as possible.

Learning how to function properly for many months or years on a black program was difficult. The aforementioned Hughes program to adapt the *Rapier* ASG-18 weapon control system and Super Falcon missile to the YF-12 aircraft was highly secret, thereby black. One afternoon in 1961, I became the fourth Hughes person cleared to work the project; the others were Allen Puckett, Claire Carlson, and Walt Maguire. Black was new for all of us, since this was the first program of that type assigned to Hughes. With systems engineering authority, my job was to recruit a small but excellent staff to define all the physical configuration and design requirements for the entire system's redesign. That same evening I was secretly transported to the Lockheed Skunk Works in Burbank, California, to see drawings of the compartments assigned to our equipment.

Returning to Culver City, I spent until 2:00 a.m. on a drafting board. Using a new secure telephone, I asked Lockheed to extend the aircraft's fuselage by 12 inches (it already was 100 feet long) to make enough room. By 10:00 a.m. the same day, the famous Kelley Johnson called back and concurred. This was typical of the fast-track activity that contributed to so many Skunk Works triumphs in remarkably short time. All governmental and corporate bureaucracy was set aside. The operating credo was: "Find the best way to meet the objective, then proceed." There was no delay to request approval from many uninvolved people and agencies, and there were no papers to be filled in triplicate. When top-notch professionals were assigned, this technique got the job done in half the time and one-third the cost of other DoD programs. I never could understand why most other military development programs were so cluttered by unnecessary government oversight and paperwork! As in every tough project, things certainly do sometimes go wrong in fast-track developments, but tripling the cost and doubling the time in order to catch errors that happen in less than one in twenty tries seems awfully wasteful.

In these highly classified programs, employees could not tell their families about what they were doing or where they were going. About sixty Hughes staff members were security-cleared and worked "behind the green door," a secured area on the second floor of an aging Hughes building. Since more than 1,000 Hughes people were needed to perform the project, we renamed the ASG-18 the "Standard System" searching for an unknown aircraft home. Design requirements and equipment shapes were mandated to non-security-cleared engineers without discussion or debate. Often this non-negotiable demand could become awkward. Detail designers thought, "If the airplane space is not yet known, why push us so hard?"

When we completed the wooden mockup of all the equipment to be installed in the aircraft, it needed to be moved to the Skunk Works for a trial-fit in the YF-12 prototype. To do this clandestinely, I rented a large truck, marked it with the name of a bogus transportation firm, donned a trucker's outfit, and drove the empty truck to a Hughes delivery gate. Security guards (not informed about this black program) had been instructed to let this truck pass without question. A crane was used to grasp the large canvas-covered mockup (it was the size of a small automobile) and place it in the truck's cargo bed. In spite of my "disguise"a sharp security guard recognized my face, causing a real ruckus—intensified because I could not prove that I was a union member. This was very important since the Hughes labor contracts stipulated that only union folks could physically move equipment. A big bunch of lying ensued, the guard was sent away by his boss's boss, and finally an associate and I started for Burbank. Because of my inexperience with the multiple downshifting and double clutching needed to scale the ridge en route north, I almost destroyed the truck's transmission. All ended well, however, and the mockup fit perfectly. Since someone else returned the rented truck, I never heard (and didn't ask) what happened to that big vehicle with its ground-up gears!

Civilian in Military Disguise

Cultivating customer relations and earning their confidence is essential for success in any business. When the product is destined for military aviation, direct involvement by flying in combat aircraft leads to first-hand understanding of battle operations, adds reality to design decisions, and enhances open and friendly communications (one learns to speak their language). Many of these experiences also bolstered the ability to inspire and lead thousands of employees to commit themselves to invent, develop, and produce excellence—and perhaps to visualize themselves in a combat flying suit.

One educational flight opportunity was in 1971 aboard a Navy twin-engine Douglas TA-3B *Skywarrior*. (Navy personnel called it the "Whale" because of its appearance and for being the largest carrier-based aircraft in history.) The Whale assigned to Hughes was for early flight testing of the AWG-9 weapon control system destined for the F-14. Initial AIM-54 Phoenix missile launches were also done from this platform. Three test engineers rode in the compartments behind and below the pilot and copilot in what originally was the bomber weapon bay, operating banks of instrumentation. I was an observer, free to roam the aircraft while in flight. However, I was warned to beware of treading on an escape-hatch door just behind the piloting crew. Its latch occasionally failed, with disastrous results for someone foolish enough to be there at that moment. You can bet I complied with that preflight suggestion!

To qualify for real experience in fighters required rigorous medical testing and physical training. Experts at Pt. Mugu Naval Air Station in California performed comprehensive medical exams and taught me many survival lessons. The next step was exposure with seven other candidates in a vacuum chamber taking us to the extremely low air pressures existing at high altitudes. As we ascended (pressure decrease), reaching the equivalent of 10,000 feet, a young Navy enlisted man started to panic! We all returned to sea-level pressure so he could exit, and the rest of us were resealed and started upward again.

One exciting segment of this trial was to remove one's oxygen mask at 25,000 feet to see how long one could perform hand motions before blackout. I carried on for about two minutes, feeling early symptoms of tunnel vision, then I became unable to place playing cards properly on a table. Others only made it for thirty seconds. Another thrill was enduring a sudden pressure decrease of several thousand feet (simulating a sudden puncture of a pressurized aircraft), for checking one's eardrum reaction. It took a lot of trust that the chamber operator would avoid making fatal mistakes!

Real fun was an ejection-seat test from a fighter cockpit attached to a platform with a near-vertical travel rail and a stopping block at its top. After student strap-in, a small cartridge boosted the seat upward, at an acceleration of 3g (three times the force of gravity). After hitting the stop, the chair slowly returned to the surface with a delighted student. It was as good as the most exciting Disneyland fantasy ride.

Lessons to survive a parachute descent into the sea were done in a large outdoor swimming pool. My scheduled time was on Saturday, January 2. The pool had not been heated for the holiday week, and the water temperature was in the low fifties! The candidate, dressed in full flying suit with heavy boots, helmet, and parachute harness, stood poolside with his back to the water. A sturdy rope was tied to the harness where a full parachute would attach. On "go," the rope was rapidly jerked from the other end of the pool. The victim hit the water upside-down and dragged backwards while he tried releasing the parachute harness. To pass the survival test, he then had to stay afloat for ten minutes, hopefully enough time for a helicopter rescue in a real crash. It was an uncomfortable ordeal for me in that freezing water. The urge to remove my heavy gear to avoid sinking was offset by the strong desire to stay warm! It was a good thing that I was an experienced swimmer.

Author with Navy Lt. Conrad in F-4B *Phantom*
(personal files)

Now properly qualified, a ride in a Navy McDonnell F-4B *Phantom* became possible. I sat in the RIO (radar intercept officer) seat while Lt. Harry Conrad piloted the fighter.

We departed Point Mugu Naval Air Station early one morning, headed for the sea test range. As we left the runway, ground control requested us to pass close to a Chance Vought F-8 *Crusader*. Its pilot thought a towline had not properly re-reeled after the towed target had been released. Lt. Conrad approached close from the rear and executed a complete roll around the F-8 to see if the snagged line could prohibit a safe landing. We discovered nothing, so after reporting the *Crusader* was OK to land, we zoomed over the Pacific, performing many intense high-g maneuvers, reaching 55,000 feet altitude and a speed of Mach 2 (twice that of sound). What excitement for a civilian, especially one who somehow was impervious to nausea or altitude sickness! The very next week, Lt. Conrad and his RIO had to eject from that same *Phantom*; both survived, but the RIO sustained a broken leg. A good thing for me that my flight schedule had not put me on that unfortunate flight!

The Navy's Douglas TA-4 was the training version of the A-4 *Skyhawk* and was fully equipped in the rear seat for a student to operate flight controls; the combat A-4 attack aircraft has only the pilot's cockpit. Capt. Scotty Lamoreaux took me aboard for a flight from Miramar Naval Air Station near San Diego for an hour of maneuvers over the Pacific. This backseat tourist did OK during this flying opportunity, but his performance was pretty dismal in executing a controlled horizontal roll: we skidded all over the place! Doing it correctly requires much training in continuously changing the throttle, ailerons, and rudder. Operating agile and powerful military aircraft requires a lot of skill and practice. Success by a civilian rookie in his first attempt ain't easy.

Scotty had a most colorful Navy background. In 1959, flying an F-4 *Phantom* he set the altitude record for powered flight; both air-breathing engines flamed out at 65,000 feet, the F-4 zoomed ballistic to over 94,000 feet and was uncontrollable (without thrust or hydraulic pressure) until falling to 60,000 feet, when the engines found enough air to restart. In 1961, he was on a team that set a new transcontinental speed record (soon bettered by the SR-71 *Blackbird*). Scotty also performed more than 250 aircraft carrier missions in Vietnam, was a lead in directing the F-14 *Tomcat* program, and commanded the Miramar Naval Air Station, home of the famous Top Gun fighter pilot school.

The Navy assigned two *Tomcat* aircraft to Hughes to operate from Point Mugu for testing our developing weapon system. As the weapon control officer (formerly the RIO), I had two flight adventures that were professionally and emotionally rewarding; I got to do the "right stuff!" Both flights were far more than just routine observation jaunts for a lucky tourist. Because important engineering tests were involved, the weapon control officer had to do precise and difficult work, pretty challenging for this senior manager of the Hughes program. I would have to physically operate the equipment correctly while in simulated combat.

AWG-9 Controls and Displays in F-14 Rear Seat
(courtesy of Raytheon)

My first mission was a surprise. The previous day's flight test had uncovered minor design flaws in two Phoenix missiles that were scheduled to be launched the next day; overnight changes had to be checked before the real test shots. George Marrett piloted, and I was the inexperienced weapon control officer responsible for gathering the needed flight test data to verify the fixes. George was a retired Air Force pilot with many search and rescue missions in Vietnam as well as experimental work at Edwards Flight Test Center. Hughes hired him as a lead test pilot. In this capacity he set several world records using the Hughes AWG-9/Phoenix equipment, one of which was the shot against a simulated Soviet *Foxbat*—the target was at the highest altitude and fastest speed ever tried—with a resultant direct hit. George wrote four exciting books about his aviation career, including *Testing Death* about his experiences at Hughes.

On this flight, I manipulated the AWG-9 to detect and track air targets at 240 miles range. The test mission then began with tracking an F-8 *Crusader* at thirty miles, closing to eight miles, and performing a simulated Phoenix shot (the weapon electronics were active, but the missile was held captive to the fighter). I triggered the launch command while the *Tomcat* was turning at a preplanned 3 g's, making my arms and head feel as if they were three times their normal weight as I engaged the system controls. After target crossover, we turned sharply at 6 g's toward the F-8's tail. I then relocked the radar on using a clutter-fouled mode. For this pass, low PRF, not pulse-Doppler, was used since our closing speed was slow. (Low PRF from the old days had been included in this system to cope with encounters like this one). Missile "launch" of the second Phoenix in this tail shot was done at a range of one mile. George steered the *Tomcat* to the target within one wingspan each time so the missile seeker could track almost to impact, gathering data to see if the fixes had worked properly. They were judged to be OK, and the very next day two live missile shots scored direct hits!

Former Marine fighter pilot Bob Solliday was at the helm for my next *Tomcat* foray. This mission was to evaluate a new helmet-mounted sight, a device allowing the user to aim crosshairs at an object, then command several systems to align to that designated spot: radar, infrared tracker, laser pointer, or missile seeker. Combat engagements could proceed immediately without either the pilot or the weapon control officer looking at the instrument panels. The purpose of the test was to measure the distortions resulting from the canopy's swelling or shrinking from differing altitude pressures. The weapon control officer's job was to continually point the helmet-mounted display crosshairs at an F-8 *Crusader* (flying a mile off to our side), as both aircraft gradually ascended from 20,000 to 45,000 feet, then to repeat the procedure as we slowly descended. Angle data between the tracking radar and the helmet sight were to be recorded to provide real numbers to define software for computer compensation of those distortions made by the canopy. The helmet was heavy, and holding my neck in one position for so long (about ten minutes up, then ten minutes down) was a ghastly ordeal! Any head movements would invalidate the test. Most unfortunately, no data were recorded: I had not switched on the recorder! That switch was not visible, being far behind my right shoulder. I thought all aircraft switches move forward or upward to command on, and the opposite way for off. I don't remember being told that this temporary switch had been rigged backwards. Rats! In rechecking my activating push, done only by feel over my shoulder, I moved it from neutral to the off position. What a costly and embarrassingly wasted mission!

Unfortunately, I never got to fly in the Navy's McDonnell-Douglas F/A-18 *Hornet*, but I did try a training simulator against an expert Navy combat fighter pilot and was again embarrassed. To lose a dogfight to an opponent in only a few seconds makes one quite humble. Another eye-opener occurred in skippering a Boeing 747 simulator made by Hughes's London subsidiary Rediffusion. In the right seat was the leading commercial airline pilot from Brazil. A trip from Miami to Sao Paulo was chosen. All went well with the taxi and takeoff, but as I was increasing altitude while over Brazil, my eyes were glued to the instruments to correctly and smoothly execute the change. Without warning, we suddenly smashed into another huge passenger plane! The Brazilian pilot laughed, saying that I should have known that ground-based surveillance radars were still primitive in his homeland. Alerts from ground control systems were not always available, so visual observation by the pilot was essential. What a meaningful lesson for a novice! We were lucky to be in a simulator rather than in the real thing.

All these memorable experiences were helpful in my future customer contacts. I now could speak their language and at the same time feel extremely humble in light of what they do so well.

PART FIVE

MANY NEW BRANCHES

THE COMPANY'S STRATEGY for its long-range future continued to stimulate thrusts into many new business areas in the 1960s and 1970s. The aim was to invent and develop unique devices to overcome knotty performance weaknesses in all types of military hardware. These devices enabled new multifunctional systems with spectacular capabilities whose development gave Hughes a significant competitive advantage because the resulting equipment performance far exceeded that which other firms could deliver.

By this time, the company had become a most prominent part of California business enterprises and the western region's fascinating history. The firm was soon to be the state's largest private employer, as well as in the adjoining state of Arizona. As viewed by citizens of the eastern portion of the United States, Californians had long displayed a particular set of characteristics. These included nonstandard behavior, sporty dress codes, casual work habits, adoration of youth, and liberal politics. Not all these are fully deserved, although a brief label could be applied: "nonconformist." This can be an apt way to portray creative talent desired by Hughes: people who can think outside the box of traditionally perceived limits. Much of the Californian behavioral image that was over publicized arose from an extremely colorful influx of diverse peoples and dramatic events over five centuries. Unbeknownst to easterners, a substantial part of the state's post-European settlers' heritage is far older than those touted on the Atlantic shore. Many who migrated to California soon adapted their attitudes and behavior to a blend of cultures: Native American, Spanish, Mexican, Chinese. Spaniards and Mexicans had brought diverse agriculture and cattle ranching tended by vaqueros and had built the twenty-one historic missions. The 1849 gold rush attracted optimistic fortune seekers from all corners of the world, which greatly expanded the seaports of San Francisco, Long Beach, and San Diego. Soon to follow was the railroad building frenzy performed by thousands of Chinese. The early 1900s brought further riches from an oil-production boom, the movie-making bonanza, fruitful citrus and walnut orchards, and successful development of a large variety of recreational services. World War II caused an intensive growth in manufacturing industries, and Southern California became the nation's primary region for aircraft design and production. Douglas, Convair, Lockheed, North American, and Northrop thrived and became magnets for creative professional talent. A real estate development thrust changed the face of the whole Pacific Southwest. By 1980, the state was ranked as the world's sixth largest economic power. Hughes Aircraft beginning in 1946 brought electronic technology to aerospace as an essential way to solve complex problems and made economically practical the commercial use of satellites. Its success inspired many other corporations to also pursue advanced electronics in both military and commercial markets. Hughes Aircraft Company thus greatly contributed to California's dynamic and rich history.

27

UNLIMITED
CREATIVE CAPABILITY

THE COMPANY'S LARGE staff of development engineers had the breadth and depth in all areas of electronics design to make the breakthroughs possible. Airborne weapon control systems and guided missile design, development, and production encompassed virtually all physics, chemistry, aerodynamics, thermodynamics, electrical, electronic circuitry, mechanical structures, optics, propulsion, power management, materials usage, and hardware manufacturing realities. There were no limits in electronic designs to generate and amplify signals, interpret responses from targets, control mechanisms, compute complex operations, store data, and devise new ways to maneuver electrons to achieve almost any purpose. By the mid-1960s, Hughes had developed sensors that could operate in the entire spectral region: sonar, audio, radio and TV, radar bands, infrared, visual, laser, ultraviolet, and X-ray.

Former CEO Mal Currie expressed in 2008 his feelings of why Hughes became so successful:

> "The technology genius of the Hughes Aircraft Company was unique in its time, compared to all major technology companies in our nation's history. It derived from a culture of extraordinary professional comradeship and technology enthusiasm across a large and very complex company made up of a number of operating groups, each with its own distinct business and product lines grounded in advanced electronics and science. The constant symbiotic flow of knowledge and ideas across these diverse activities gave rise, in turn, to the stream of creative new kinds of systems that were the foundation and

hallmark of Hughes. The vision and leadership of Pat Hyland were responsible for this unique culture."

The diversification thrust was extraordinarily beneficial. The 1952 staff of 15,000, which ranked Hughes Aircraft Company as the twenty-second largest US defense contractor, had grown to 20,000 by 1959, putting Hughes in eleventh place. Effects on the company of the F-108 cancellation were short term, and employment had more than doubled by 1970.

Because of the unpopularity of the Vietnam conflict, however, national enthusiasm for defense spending declined sharply in the early 1970s. Furthermore, the long-standing US priority of landing on the Moon was satisfied in 1969, leading to political pressure to curtail NASA expenditures. The aerospace industry, consequently, suffered greatly. Sales at Hughes temporarily declined 27 percent, causing some reduction in employment, but the company soon found and captured top priority DoD programs and gained many new customers. Within three years, the downturn was overcome, even though other defense companies were still in deep depression.

Hughes engineers were not tightly controlled in their daily activities. Free spirited inventors, well supported by company funding, explored new device concepts. Other staff members discovered ways to apply these to pressing military needs. As mentioned previously, one of the hardest management jobs in this frothy work environment was to turn something off! Some believed that this task was beyond their own managerial capability or that a stop would be counter to their own innate never-give-up attitude. Throughout the company, everyone nurtured the "laboratory freedom" philosophy, fully expecting long-term business results from almost any new discoveries and always seeming to find and capture the top priority programs of our military and space customers.

28

FURTHER
DIVERSIFICATION

I$_T$ IS VERY difficult to describe all the branches taken by Hughes in its quest for product line expansion in every possible direction. This Part and Parts Six through Eight illustrate the wide variety of projects that were undertaken in many technical areas; they are grouped by the mission fulfilled or the technology advances made. This Part covers infrared, lasers, electronic beam scanning radars, reconnaissance, and inventive efforts of the Hughes Research Laboratories, as well as the continuation of the long series of airborne radars. In every project, success came from the dedicated efforts of several or many experts and supporters teamed together. One individual may have conceived a fresh approach, but completing a complex design always involved a team of engineers with various skills getting the job done together, even though their home bases may have been in different formal organizations. If it was impractical to separate that portion of the total system to a specialty organization, arrangements were made to loan staff members to the responsible team.

Searching for the Undone

Fundamental corporate assets were inventive genius and effective integration of new devices into large-scale complex electronic systems. It was very energizing for senior executives to witness each new concept in science and engineering, often on a daily basis. An enthusiastic staff of knowledgeable personnel usually assured success in any new branch of electronics. Unusual ideas could come from any source; detailed scientific expertise was not always necessary for someone to look outside traditional boundaries. Management always had to be ready to listen to and support its staff members, regardless of their experience or educational background.

A good illustration of invention from an unpredictable source is the creation of the now-popular glass elevator on the exterior of public buildings. The emergence of electrically powered elevators motivated hotels to install them to attract tenants; rooms above the third floor were usually not too popular. The multistory El Cortez hotel in San Diego, California, hired a large group of architects to find a reasonable way to add an elevator into that old building. Its interior was filled with structural supports with no vertical spaces large enough to accommodate the new feature. After more than a week of intensive discussion, no affordable solution had been found; too much reconstruction apparently would be needed, as the architects judged. A bellhop who had been hearing some of the group's frustrated debate politely offered a suggestion: why not put the elevator on the building's outside wall and make it possible for the passengers to see the sights as they moved up several floors? Bingo! The minds of the highly trained professionals finally "peered out of the box" of traditional practice. They then designed, in 1956, the world-famous "glass elevator." Credit the low-paid bellhop! I hope he was well rewarded for his breathtaking insight.

Another example of a fresh technology idea springing from an unexpected source was the concept of radio frequency-hopping. Famed movie actress Heady Lamar conceived the idea of confusing enemy wartime listeners by rapidly changing broadcast frequencies to transmit secret messages. The number of shift positions was the same as a set of 88 piano keys. The frequency switching was timed by using a player-piano activation scroll; the sender and desired receiver controlled these tapes. Her concept was patented in 1942, but not formally adopted by the US military until 1962. Apparently, a bunch of closed minds during WW II were unresponsive to sparkling fresh inspirations. ("Exotic Information Links" on page 203 reveals earlier usage in some clandestine projects).

Stretching Out

The growing inadequacy of the 1 million square feet of space at Culver City to house the increasing numbers of employees, let alone the specialized support equipment needed to match the new technologies, demanded new facilities at more remote sites. Company square footage exploded in the next two decades to almost 15 million in 1981 and then to 23 million by 1986. Each of the campuses developed a personality of its own, even though the different organizations were sisters in the huge Hughes family. Unique methodologies, customers, and priorities lent a characteristic signature to each product line enterprise. Entering an area, one somehow knew what type of product would be born there: a spacecraft, a missile, a surface-based radar—the staff somehow projected its products' characteristics.

We built an expansive campus on 480 acres in Fullerton, California, thirty miles east of Los Angeles, for large ground-based products. Opened in 1958, the facility eventually became headquarters for the Ground Systems Group and housed a workforce of over 17,000 with full design and manufacturing capability for products such as air defense radars, displays for combat ships, and sonar surveillance systems.

Ground Systems Group, Fullerton, California
(courtesy of UNLV)

The Space Systems Division, which would soon grow into the Space and Communications Group, was located in a twelve-story building just south of Los Angeles Airport adjacent to the airborne radar manufacturing plant. Unique laboratories, engineering offices, and final satellite assembly work areas were housed in this structure and several other nearby leased buildings. The main building was easily identifiable because of the two large spherical antenna domes visible on its rooftop—an unusual sight at the time.

In 1965, the headquarters staff of what would become the Missile Systems Group (with an eventual engineering staff of 2,300) moved to another campus thirty miles north in Canoga Park, a Los Angeles suburb in the west San Fernando Valley. Manufacturing continued in the large Tucson plant. The Canoga Park site truly looked like a college campus, with low-rise buildings and a large decorative pond in its central quadrangle, plus wildlife all around and beautiful views of a boulder-strewn mountain ridge (which had been a backdrop in many popular Old West movies!).

Missile Systems Group, Canoga Park, California
(courtesy of UNLV)

Most exotic of all was the new facility Hughes built for the Research Laboratories in Malibu on a hillside surrounded by chaparral and live oaks, with an extraordinary view of the blue Pacific Ocean and several offshore islands. What a perfect ambience for innovation. And only a short commute if one relished the storied Malibu beach. But look out for the Hollywood movie stars!

Research Laboratories, Malibu, California
(courtesy of Raytheon)

In 1956, we acquired the Santa Barbara Research Center (SBRC), a world leader in infrared detectors and sensor systems. Established by Dave Evans, the original manager of the Hughes Radio Department, after he left the company in 1952, it was located in open fields adjacent to the city airport and the University of California at Santa Barbara. The SBRC facilities had low-rise buildings set in lush landscaping. The staff enjoyed great beauty in their workplace, as well as nearby residential and recreational areas and close access to high-technology academics at the university.

Each working area soon found itself with a whimsical identifier, conveying some ridicule, but at the same time further strengthening the family bond. "Clever City" was Culver City, which was also known as "The Bean Fields" because of its former use as farm land; "Congo Park" was a natural for Canoga Park; Fullerton became "Disneyland East"; El Segundo South was named "El Stinkgundo" because of the nearby oil refinery; Santa Barbara Research Center suffered with "Santa Booboo"; "The Beach Boys" inhabited Malibu Research Labs; Tucson was besmirched as the "Cactus Curtain," probably because of its operating style; "Behind the Green Doors" was where our first highly secret design was done; and "Trouble With Torrance" afflicted the plant where TWT component designs sometimes had difficulties and deliveries were often late. Perhaps most endearing was the overall description of the company's culture: "A bunch of anarchists bonded by a common parking lot." All of these monikers provided relief from the stress of work as we tried diligently to meet our mission assignments.

29

TECHNOLOGY STILL
THE DRIVER

THE LIFEBLOOD OF Hughes was always technology advancement in almost any form. CEO Allen Puckett described this well in a 1972 *HughesNews* article entitled "Use With Great Wisdom":

> "There is a particular concept that underlies our interests and ambitions in our major national endeavors. It is a concept that must be of vital concern to everyone in our kind of industry: the role of technology in the evolution and growth of American society.
>
> "It is not uncommon today to hear criticism of the technologists, especially by some young people, of making the world unnecessarily complicated, of polluting the environment, and of making life uncomfortable or even dangerous. In the eyes of many laymen, the technologists have become the bad guys.
>
> "The fact is that life in this world has become complicated and sometimes uncomfortable simply because there is an enormously large number of people trying to survive and live together on the same small planet.
>
> "Technology provides the most powerful tool available for solving problems in the real world around us. Whenever technology has been presumed to make life more complicated, its primary function should be to make things more comfortable and economical. Technology occasionally has been abused, and has created problems, but I suggest that this abuse is generally the fault of others outside the profession.
>
> "At the same time, the engineer, the manager, or any mem-

ber of our industry has an increasingly urgent responsibility to study and understand not only the skills and tools peculiar to our trade, but the problems to which they should be applied, and the real objectives in the solutions.

"These thoughts relate very directly and very personally to each one of us as we view the projects in our current business. We are in the forefront of the technological world."

Practices, procedures, and even basic understanding of any technology discipline can change rapidly. University education can be almost obsolete within a very few years of graduation. Since the Hughes fundamental foundation and philosophy depended on the intellectual currency of the staff, an internal "university" was begun in 1965, called the Advanced Technology Education Program (ATEP). Its objective was to refresh and expand the technological and scientific capabilities of staff members. The school was fully funded by company money, and used internal experts and guest lecturers from the outside. Held at the Culver City plant during the first ten years, ATEP had 23,261 enrollments for 852 classes in 155 different courses, with 205 instructors and 115 lectures by guest experts. A notable frequent visitor was Dr. Richard Feynman from Caltech, who in 1965 was awarded the Nobel Prize in physics. As the company expanded geographically, the training facilities moved to El Segundo, and many classes were conducted at remote sites or were sent by videotape. In the next ten years, there were 39,775 enrollments for 928 classes in 240 courses, all done by 220 instructors. This program was a key factor in keeping Hughes at the leading edge.

Systems Expertise

As the company grew, Hughes successfully produced and marketed many singular hardware assemblies, electronic components of numerous varieties, computer software packages, and extensive support services. However, much of the company's competitive strength lay in its unique ability to form the architecture of complex systems. This latter term is used throughout this book, so what is a "system"? One definition by Webster is "a functionally related group of elements, especially: a group of interacting mechanical or electrical components." To this should be added "computer software packets," which perform the brainpower to properly operate the system.

An extremely complex example is the Hughes-developed NADGE (NATO air defense ground environment) air defense system used throughout the NATO nations, which is described in Part Six. Needed for this vital mission were at least two types of radars, aircraft identification transponders, central and dispersed computers, massive amounts of robust software, displays, operator controls, several types of missile batteries, communication links immune to interference, and power and cooling supplies, as well as all the protective shelter arrangements. Each of these pieces, such as one of the radar types, could be considered a "system" by its developer, having many internal complexities to integrate; that supplier's system, however, is considered by the next higher level integrating contractor as a "subsystem." Coordinating all the physically and electronically separate elements into a harmonious functioning whole, especially when each element may come from a different supplier, is exceedingly difficult. Hughes was able to do this tough system integration job to the satisfaction of the buyers and users. A most lucrative worldwide business resulted.

This and the next three Parts describe fourteen diverse product line endeavors by Hughes. Most of these were ranked among the best performing in the world, and all persisted as successful businesses for thirty years. Each description attempts to inform the reader about that particular technology's evolution and how the devices actually function.

30

EXPLOITING INFRARED

Successful military action often depends on surveillance, that is, knowing where the enemy is and what he is doing. If everyone has the same skills and equipment, then it's unfortunately true that "if you can see the enemy, then he can see you," and "if the enemy is within range of your weapon, you're within range of his weapon."

Advances in military strategy, technology, and training are intended to overturn this symmetrical situation. The development of radar during and after World War II allowed us to locate enemy targets through fog, smoke and dust, during both day and night. Radar, however, is not a perfect surveillance and targeting tool. It does a great job of pinpointing an airborne vehicle such as an aircraft, but when aimed at a target on the ground, the signal from the intended target is confused by the ground clutter (as mentioned earlier, ground clutter is unwanted reflections of the radar signal from other objects.) By 1980, this radar dilemma had been solved, as described in Section 34 under "Airborne Mapping."

Radar poses another problem: it is an active system; that is, it "sees" by sending out a strong signal and then detecting its reflections from a target. This strong signal may be detected by the enemy, however, who may use it to locate the radar and attack or counter it electronically. (This radar concern was eliminated by the late 1980s, because Hughes had perfected stealth designs that could scarcely be seen by the enemy, see Part Eight).

Enter IR, short for infrared. Infrared radiation is very similar to visible light, but is invisible to the unaided human eye. By building sensors that extend our vision into the infrared, we can often observe through haze, light fog, smoke, and dust. Because object emanations at IR frequencies differ from those at visible frequencies, with IR we may be able to perceive objects hiding in shadows or concealed with camouflage. Better yet, all warm objects—including people and vehicle engines—emit infrared radiation, so they can be easily seen at night using infrared vision equipment. Best of all, infrared imaging systems are passive—they receive meaningful signals, but don't emit energy that reveals their location to an enemy.

All electromagnetic radiation, from radio through visible to X-rays, travels in vibrating waves at the speed of light. Different forms are described by their wave spacing (length) or characteristic frequency; the higher the frequency the shorter the distance between their wave crests. The AM radio waves have 1,000 feet between crests when tuned to 900 kHz. The FM radio waves are about 3 feet long; radar microwaves are about 1 inch; and very shortwave infrared is only one five-thousandth of an inch between crests. Specific parts within the IR frequencies are described by their wavelengths in microns (also called micrometers); IR wavelengths are commonly considered to be from 1 to 15 microns. One inch is the same as 25,000 microns.

Radar and IR systems are often complementary. For example, radar can provide range and velocity information; IR systems do not broadcast their presence, and are useful in situations where radars suffer from ground clutter.

The earliest infrared systems (see Section 8, "Technology Advances") did not provide complete images: a single infrared detector, or just a few detectors, would be pointed in the general direction of a hot target such as an aircraft or a tank, and then moved at different angles until the target was detected. That signal could then be used to guide a missile to the hostile object.

By the early 1960s, Hughes had several years of IR experience with the Falcon missiles and the shoulder-launched FIM-43 Redeye missiles. The latter was a big disappointment for the company: a superb design, done under subcontract to General Dynamics, did not result in any production work because all 85,000 missiles fielded for the United States and many overseas nations were manufactured in-house by General Dynamics. However, we used this IR expertise to capture awards for other missile programs: the air-to-ground strike Maverick, the air-to-air SRM (short-range missile), and the ballistic missile defense kinetic kill vehicle (KKV) described in Parts Seven and Eight.

Hughes also eagerly sought new applications in other combat arenas.

Table 5.1. Infrared Technologies

Technology	Year of Introduction	Key Features
Search and track	Late 1950s	Four or eight detectors; gimbaled telescope with linear and circular mechanical scan
Cooling	Late 1950s	Cryogenic gases; Joule-Thompson cooling; Leyden frost-transfer; thermoelectric cooling
FLIR	Early 1960s	Mechanical scan with image display
HgCdTe and serial scan	1960s	Greatly improved detector materials; TV-compatible raster scan
Thermal imaging	Mid-1960s	IR imaging systems small enough for man portability, ground vehicles, and helicopters
Tank fire control	Early 1970s	Integrated gun control using thermal imager, laser and motion-compensated telescope
Staring arrays	Early 1970s	Large detector array mounted to silicon readout chip with indium bumps; electronic rather than mechanical scan

Our biggest successes were in search and track of airborne targets, forward-looking infrared (FLIR, pronounced "fleer") imaging, and surveillance from satellites. FLIR products at Hughes evolved from early scanning systems, to a unique method of serial scanning that greatly improved TV display compatibility, then to more advanced FLIR systems integrated with lasers, and finally to large arrays with thousands of detector elements that could obtain a complete detailed image by staring at, rather than scanning, the scene. These devices were produced and fielded in aircraft, tanks, and combat vehicles, for individual troopers, and in several commercial products.

Throughout its history, Hughes developed and manufactured a wide variety of infrared systems, a full discussion of which is beyond the scope of this book. However, Table 5.1 lists the principal technologies that were critical to this part of the company's business growth, and these are discussed in the sections to follow.

Search and Track

Hughes's prominence in airborne search and track radars prompted us to try doing a similar combat job using infrared. The initial infrared search and track (IRST) systems did not form images, but could precisely track a target's hot spot, such as the exhaust nozzle of a turbojet. Several designs begun in the late 1950s were installed in fighter aircraft: the F-101, F-102, and F-106, the F-8U, and the Swedish *Viggen*. The company produced more than 2,000 of these systems. The F-108, YF-12, and F-14 had more advanced versions. The IRST system was usually mounted immediately in front of the canopy or on the fighter's chin just below the radome. To lessen aircraft aerodynamic drag, two sets were used in the supersonic F-108 and the YF-12, each placed at a wing root; they shared the forward view since half their lateral sight was obscured by the fighter's nose.

An IRST system consists of a cylindrical container with a hemispheric protective dome transparent to IR radiation. Housed within is a telescope mounted on a set of gimbals, an IR sensing device, a cryogenic cooling set to obtain detector sensitivity, a signal processor, and a system-management computer. Since conventional glass does not transmit most IR frequencies, the dome and telescope lenses were made of a variety of exotic materials depending on the application: quartz, silicon, germanium, arsenic trisulfide, or magnesium fluoride.

The IRST telescope was initially pointed by the pilot or by the aircraft's radar. Incoming energy was focused onto a ceramic wafer with an array of IR detector elements or cells. Our first designs used four detector cells arranged in a plus formation; the target object was a hot spot. Later, high performance systems used eight cells also set in a plus array: four horizontal and four vertical to the planned scanning view.

As the gimbaled telescope swept across a target, the captured thermal energy focused on the detector array passed across the vertical line of cells and the hot-spot target was detected. Gimbal scanning then stopped at that angle and the telescope spun in a small circle (technically referred to as nutated), so the horizontal cells could sense the IR spot. When the time interval between signals from the center two vertical and the center two horizontal detector elements was equal, the seeker pointed directly at the target. This timing balance was maintained to give angular information for the tracking process and for display in the cockpit. In the later F-14 IRST systems, all eight cells were in a vertical line and always scanned horizontally. Detector cell pulses from several separate targets were sent to a computer, which generated individual tracks while the scanning continued. Eight cells were enough to measure elevation angles without nutating the telescope; a higher speed small field scan was used for accurate single-target track.

Unfortunately, unlike a radar, these systems did not directly measure the distance to the target. In later years, significant refinements in pulse-Doppler radar performance minimized the need for a supplemental IRST system since background clutter was no longer a problem. Although the systems were still useful for counting the number of targets in a mass raid, the market that had been quite lucrative for Hughes disappeared.

Detector Materials

Many research laboratories, with Hughes in the lead after its 1956 purchase of Santa Barbara Research Center, pursued the search for photon detector materials that would respond to IR energy better than the lead-sulfide detectors used since the 1940s. What emerged was greatly improved sensitivity and responses at longer wavelengths, which made it possible to separate target signals from background noise and to see very weak radiation sources at longer ranges. Detectors were fabricated by placing a very thin layer of an exotic material on a supporting crystalline or ceramic substrate. Different chemical compounds were responsive to different parts of the infrared spectrum. They were chosen to match the most likely targets and surrounding conditions. The longer wavelengths were most effective in separating cold objects from a background of outer space (needed, for example, in searching for an ICBM warhead before it heats up as it reenters the atmosphere in its terminal phase; see Section 53, "Strategic Warfare"). More than ten different exotic compounds were commonly used as the art improved; examples are lead-sulfide responding in the 1 to 3.2 micron wavelength band, indium-antimonide (1 to 5.5), lead-selenide (1.5

to 6), mercury-doped-germanium (2 to 14 or longer), and, most recently, mercury-cadmium-telluride, which can be chemically tailored to operate in any span of an incredible 0.8 to 14 microns depending on the cooling level provided.

Detector Cooling

The original lead-sulfide detectors in Sidewinder and early Falcon missiles operated at ambient air temperatures, but the more advanced compounds demanded extremely low temperatures to perform with maximum sensitivity. In many designs, the low temperatures were achieved by placing the detectors inside a vacuum insulated container (dewar) and exposing them or their mounts to cryogenic gases, specifically argon, nitrogen, air, or helium. These fluids were stored in a separate dewar flask. In other cases, liquid or compressed gas sent through a small opening generated the cooling when it expanded at the back of the detector, a process called the Joule-Thompson effect. These are called JT-cooling devices or cryostats (frost-producing without motion), a concept originated in England in 1852. More effective, however, was storing the coolant in liquid form and transferring it in droplets using the Leyden frost-transfer method. This is similar to small drops of water bouncing for a long time on a hot skillet; boiled-off gas forms an insulating wall around the droplet. This phenomenon enables the liquid to be transferred across the gimbal mount in flexible lines to finally evaporate in a metal mesh much like "steel-wool" at the back of the detector. Liquid argon cooled to -309°F; nitrogen to -320°F. Cool-down time was only a few seconds; the duration of cooling was limited by the size of the storage bottle. To attain optimum performance in surveillance from space for strategic defense, most detectors responding in the long-wavelength IR region were cooled to as low as -453°F with liquid helium!

Long-term operations that would not permit replenishment of coolant materials could be done with cryogenic engines or mechanical refrigerators of many types. Thermoelectric or solid-state coolers were also used.

To avoid the detecting of unwanted stray radiation by the sensitive super-cooled detectors, internal structures were specially shaped or the detectors were masked with cold barrier structures. In cold background space applications, cooling of the telescopic optics themselves was sometimes required to obtain maximum sensitivity.

FLIR Imaging

There has always been a strong desire to see things in real time at night as though there were no darkness at all. Vital combat jobs not done well with poor lighting are surveillance, navigation, terrain or obstacle avoidance, target detection and identification, stationkeeping, and weapon fire control. Without clear weather, moonlight, or strong starlight, the attempted solution had been artificial light using fires, lamps, flares, and focused searchlights. Such synthetic aids were difficult to place quickly and usually revealed tactical positions to the enemy. With the maturity of television and image intensifiers, it became possible to amplify very low light levels and present more clearly a visible likeness on a display screen.

Aided by optical magnification and more sensitive visual-wavelength detectors, a viable system called low-light television (LLTV) was developed by Hughes and many of our competitors. The LLTV system yielded reasonable displays of scenes illuminated by starlight, but the devices were large and cumbersome. Hughes realized that a far better way to solve the night vision problem was using passive infrared devices to form scene images under many conditions impossible for visible systems.

In the visual wavelength, object shapes appear by differences in color, three-dimensional characteristics, reflected brightness, shading effects, and distinction from their backgrounds, as well as changes due to their motions. These same features are present in the infrared wavelengths. Consider a person's nominal average internal temperature of 98.6°F: body highlights are notable, with higher temperatures in the chest and head, and much lower at the ends of limbs. Observing them with an array of detectors capable of seeing differences of one-tenth of a degree temperature can yield an easily recognized image. In addition, compared to nearby surroundings, a human can vividly stand out as very hot. Virtually every physical object has similar characteristics, due to either internally generated or reflected heat.

An inherent design problem for IR imaging was that of emphasizing the contrast in different parts of an IR image. Large differences can be made by processing, but remain very small compared to TV wherein black-to-white is a 100 percent contrast. An IR scene will have temperature differences of only 1 percent with variable backgrounds, so before processing it's like looking for an off-white dot on a white sheet. Fortunately, with refined processing details on the white sheet, the off-white dot can be made to stand out. Key subsystems in military TV or IR imagers properly analyze what objects are being detected.

An individual image sample is called a picture element, or pixel. Newspaper photos appear grainy or dotty if there are not many pixels per square inch; many smaller dots in the right places appear to blend into better picture quality, but this costs more to produce. TV cameras have traditionally used a vidicon tube that required no optical mechanical scanning. A telescope focuses the complete field of view onto the tube's faceplate. The

P-2 *Neptune* Patrol Aircraft
(courtesy of the National Naval Air Museum)

TRAM in Acceptance Test
(courtesy of UNLV)

A-6 *Intruder* with TRAM
(courtesy of Raytheon)

P-3 *Orion* Antisubmarine Patrol Aircraft
(courtesy of the National Naval Aviation Museum)

vacuum-sealed interior of the faceplate has a sensitive inner coating that emits electrons when stimulated by the light on the faceplate. The emissions are read by a single electron beam swept in a regular pattern (called a raster) across the sensitive surface.

To display what the camera has seen, a signal stream of these samples from the swept beam is sent by cable or is transmitted to a TV set with its display tube. That cathode-ray tube (CRT) has a beam that traces the same pattern; its faceplate film forms visible light spots as it is hit by the sweeping beam. The standard TV raster has 480 effective horizontal lines making a screen with a 3 by 4 size ratio format for the image 30 times per second. Although not actually processed as discrete picture element samples in early designs, the better quality sets had the equivalent of 345,600 pixels in the picture viewed. The line sweeps are done so rapidly that a human viewer is not aware of the raster scanning process; the display picture is formed quicker than the eye's response time.

In the case of IR imaging, it was not practical to place a detector film on a transparent screen to do a similar beam sweep as in a visible vidicon. Early attempts at IR vidicons failed because the response of the individual detectors varied more than the small temperature differences in the scene.

Texas Instruments (TI) built the first real-time IR imager with a TV-like image in the early 1960s. An adaptation of an existing line scanning reconnaissance system, the line scanner looked downward from an airplane, the detector scanned across the line of flight, and successive lines were made as the aircraft moved forward, eventually adding up to a two-dimensional image stored on film. The modification to make a real-time TV-like image was to use a high-speed mirror to replace the aircraft motion and provide a frame scan at the needed 30 picture frames per second. Since this design was converted from looking downward to looking forward, TI named it a forward-looking IR, an apt designation for all future systems performing this function. This nascent design was marginal in performance since it had only a single detector element. TI then tried three elements and a three-beam display gun, as used in color TV, so three cells could be scanned at once. It soon became clear that more elements were needed to obtain adequate performance.

During the same period Hughes, using internal funding, modified an IRST system with a lead-selenide detector linear array and specialized electronics for its first real-time imaging system. Although using more detector elements, our design operated in the less favorable atmospheric window of 3 to 5 microns instead of 8 to 14 microns, and in the early

1960s we lost the chance to build the first deployed FLIR to TI. This FLIR was destined for the devastatingly effective AC-47 gunship deployed in Vietnam. The aircraft was initially named *Spooky*, but soon adopted the charming title of "Puff the Magic Dragon," from the song currently popular in the United States.

Then in 1964, Hughes set out to leapfrog TI with an advanced FLIR using an array of 176 mercury-doped-germanium elements that operated in the longer IR wavelengths. (We also continued the 3 to 5 micron technology, which required less cryogenics, for Army ground-based operations, successfully applying it to an experimental integrated night sight for the antitank TOW missile described in Section 43, "Guidance Gains.")

This advanced FLIR was supported by company funds, but also benefited from a 36-element array technology developed at Hughes Santa Barbara Research Center under a contract from the Navy Ordnance Test Station at China Lake, California. Hughes won an Air Force contract (in competition with Aerojet-General) to develop the first such system with two fields of view and very high performance using an array of 176 elements. It had two fixed telescopes, with each field scanned by a set of counter-rotating germanium prisms placed in front of each telescope. Hearing of this, the Navy asked Hughes to adapt their 36-element system to a day-night bombing system for the P-2 *Neptune* antisubmarine patrol craft for use in Vietnam. Several were delivered and performed successfully, further building our practical experience base.

Variations of the advanced FLIR were attempted with very limited success for the Navy's A-6 *Intruder* in an early program called TRIM, and for the Army's UH-1 *Huey* helicopter, but the next important step came in 1966 when Hughes won a program to improve night vision in the UH-56 *Cheyenne* helicopter. This design, known as PINE (passive infrared night equipment), used a simpler version of the advanced FLIR array by rearranging the array in a simple line but still using interlaced scan lines. It had better optics and a much simpler internal mirror mechanism for scanning.

The helicopter project was cancelled but this design became the basis for the B-52 *Stratofortress* FLIR begun in 1968, whose purpose was to supplement a TV and ground-clearance radar during low-level flight. All three sensors would help the aircrew avoid terrain while the cockpit's visual openings were masked to preclude eye damage from a nuclear flash. It is interesting to note that before those devices were part of the B-52 fleet, aircrews were instructed to use a single eye patch, so they would be blinded in only one eye if they witnessed a nuclear weapon detonation.

That's frighteningly bizarre! This system became Hughes's first high quantity FLIR manufacturing run, with 350 units produced. An improved version was slated for the B-1 *Lancer* bomber in 1975, but that aircraft was scrubbed by government budget cuts.

The next step was to find other applications for this production configuration. The first was a system mounted in a turret for the Navy's P-3 *Orion* for antisubmarine patrols. The first set was delivered in 1972, with twelve more in 1973. This FLIR was very effective for eight years, flying over the Mediterranean Sea and finding Soviet surfaced submarines as well as wake detections of many that were cruising well below the surface.

Another production system based on the PINE was the Navy A-6 TRAM (target recognition and attack multisensor), a turret-mounted system combining a FLIR with telescopic zoom, a laser spot illuminator with range finding, and a laser receiver to confirm it was pointing to the selected target. This system provided the Navy A-6 *Intruder* attack aircraft comprehensive night viewing, a pilot-selectable high resolution zoom for acquisition and identification, tracking a selected target while continuing the area-wide night picture, and laser beam placement for range finding and spot-illumination for weapon guidance. We produced 300 of these high capability systems.

HgCdTe and Serial Scan

Throughout the 1960s and 1970s, DoD sponsored development of the material mercury cadmium telluride, or HgCdTe, as the detector material of the future. Progress was frustratingly slow, however prompting one DoD director to remark in the early 1980s that "HgCdTe is the detector material of the future and it always will be!" Finally, a great success: these new detectors could be tailor-made to respond anywhere within the IR band from 0.8 to 14 microns by varying the amounts of cadmium and telluride. In contrast to earlier materials, the detectors responded far more rapidly to incoming energy, so imaging could also be far more rapid. Cooling demands were only to -320°F instead of the -409°F required in previous sensitive long-wavelength sensors. This now could be done easily with a single-cycle liquid nitrogen cooler.

The HgCdTe made possible a significant advance in FLIR technology. PINE derivatives and other FLIRs of that generation scanned a vertical line array of detectors horizontally to simultaneously gather data in many parallel lines of samples. Much processing was required to convert these many samples into a single signal stream to operate the single beam within the display tube. Even then, while it appeared similar to a conventional TV image, the display raster was fast in vertical and slow in horizontal, ultimately requiring either a unique display or a scan converter (a special purpose computer), which reduced performance. Taking advantage of faster responding HgCdTe detector elements, a quicker scanning mechanization, and miniature digital technologies, Hughes developed a scanning method called serial scan, which generated a completely TV-compatible raster scan. This resulted in a lower cost FLIR system using two parallel rows of thirty-two HgCdTe detector cells cooled to -320°F in a dewar cooled with liquid nitrogen. Hughes perfected a new processing method called time delay and integration (TDI) in this design.

The two parallel horizontal linear arrays of elements were horizontally scanned by a rapidly rotating mirror. Each cell in a row would sequentially sample the same spot in the image being viewed. All these signals were then delayed and summed, for an output thirty-two times that of a single cell. The next viewing spot was then scanned and sampled. This procedure was done continuously for each parallel row of thirty-two detectors; the two rows were displaced horizontally as well as by one line vertically, and they were scanned in sequence to provide two lines of a TV raster. While one line was being sent to the display as it actively scanned, the adjacent line was being retraced. After completion of those two raster lines, the mirrors shifted downward to start the next two lines. This fast scanning of pairs of horizontal lines continued for a complete vertical field. The electronic signal was amplified and adjusted for brightness and contrast, and passed directly to a cathode-ray tube TV display. The optical scanning was synchronized for compatibility with a commercial 525-line TV raster and at the same rate of 30 frames and 60 fields per second.

Thermal Imaging

The phrase "thermal imaging," first used by the Army to define night vision equipment, became a generic term for all devices that create picture displays of objects radiating infrared energy. The Army tended to use the term for smaller imaging systems while other services still used the FLIR designator for all real-time IR imaging devices.

Supported by internal funding in 1964, Hughes started developing a night-vision concept both for the ground launchers for the TOW missile and to satisfy other Army thermal imaging requirements, including forming images with a visual display reading directly from the IR elements. These designs originally used a vertical line of cells, scanning the telescope image horizontally across that array with a mirror to form a complete image.

The new infrared imager used a simple and elegant design that eliminated the complex signal processing of previous FLIRs. The back of the mirror scanning the detector array was equipped with another mirror, which reflected a matching vertical array of visible light photoelectric emitters. The resulting scanned light sources provided a visible display perfectly synchronized with the IR image being scanned. Originally these IR detector cells were lead-selenide, but they were later changed to the more sensitive indium-antimonide; both responded in the 3.5 to 5 micron region.

The late 1960s saw the beginning of two new thermal imaging approaches, one by Hughes, the other by an Army laboratory assisted by TI. The Hughes objective was to find a less expensive way to generate a "TV-like" IR video raster signal to directly mate with a common TV display device. The Army's goal was to design a set of common modules to mechanize the previous Hughes 3.5 to 5 micron thermal night sight for TOW using the new 8 to 14 micron HgCdTe detectors. The Army was interested in two harmonious sets of modules to be used for either high performance or modest operating level systems, with emphasis on man-portable, ground vehicle, and helicopter applications.

In another thrust with the more sensitive detectors, Hughes developed a lightweight imaging system called TWS (thermal weapon sight), using HgCdTe detectors operating in the 3 to 5 micron band; cooling was done thermoelectrically to the temperature of dry ice: -78°F. This device was small enough to mount atop a rifle, and could be produced in reasonably high quantities. However, some critics thought it was so expensive that a soldier would feel reluctant to have it assigned to him for fear of being penalized if it were lost or damaged!

The Army approach became the "common module" FLIR, which could be integrated in selective ways to match differing mission needs. Hughes and TI continued to compete, with most of the business fortunately won by Hughes. The DoD made the common module a government standard for battlefield surveillance, target designation, and range finding. Systems were assembled from a mixture of separate subassemblies rather than being uniquely configured as a fully integrated system. The Army's desire had been to compete each module among several sources instead of purchasing a full-up system from one supplier. The DoD standardization goals forced this modular design on the Navy and the Air Force but few airborne uses resulted because of size, weight, and display difficulties.

Both high- and low-performance common module systems were fielded in large numbers for the Army, and, when coupled with a laser rangefinder, a soldier could provide accurate data for artillery fire. Coupled with a laser designator, they could provide target location information for laser weapon guidance. Several varieties could be both man-portable and carried in jeeps. They had the enchanting monikers of GLLD, MULE, and LTD.

Hughes produced more than 20,000 of these combat night sight systems; the public saw their many advantages on CNN during Operation Desert Storm. The Iraqi invaders had no chance when US systems attacked at night, since they themselves could see nothing. (An old saying attributable to the Dutch scholar Desiderius Erasmus in 1610 is: "In the land of the blind the one-eyed man is king.") We again achieved total dominance using the next generation of night vision equipment when we entered Iraq in the second Gulf War in 2003.

Tank Fire Control

Our largest production of thermal imaging devices came from our competing in systems for tank warfare in 1973. Texas Instruments had been more responsive to the Army laboratories' goal of modularity and had captured the initial development contract. However, Hughes prevailed in later competitions and won most of the Army production procurements.

Using the unique features of imaging infrared and laser pencil beams, these systems solved the ever-existent problem of tanks using a cannon against a maneuvering small target while racing at 30 miles per hour over rough terrain. In the North African desert campaigns in World War II, a critical element in tank combat and survival was the speed of finding the opponent, measuring target range and determining the required cannon elevation, forecasting its angle change with maneuvers, and firing the cannon at the correct moment. Seconds made the difference, but the optical distance measurement device with its mechanical computers took a skilled gunner up to half a minute to decide on the range and then shoot.

Hughes's new stabilized gimbal-mounted system teamed a thermal imager with a telescopic optical tracker, a laser coupled with a computer, and an operator's display. The tank gunner only needed to view the terrain ahead through the telescope, choose a target, select a weapon, and pull a trigger; the system's fire control automatically compensated for all motions, kept the laser pointed at the target, measured and predicted both the range and angle to the target, computed the cannon shell trajectory and expected impact time, and fired the weapon. Most astonishing in our design was the stabilization system that kept all sen-

Tank Fire Control System
(courtesy of Raytheon)

sor devices aligned as if the tank were motionless, regardless of speed or terrain roughness. Functions were done with such precision that first-shot destruction of the opponent was almost a certainty. Those deadly time delays in World War II tank battles were no more.

These systems gave tank crews day and night visibility through haze, smoke, and dust never before possible in the battlefield. Armor protection was maintained for the friendly crew since viewing was through a periscope. Another step forward was use of a laser beam to spot-illuminate the target for the newly developed Rockwell Hellfire guided missile. Hughes produced more than 15,000 of these tank fire control sets.

The hoped-for product line series came to pass when we won an Army contract in 1979 for a night sight to equip the M1-A1 Abrams 60-ton heavy tank and the M2/M3 Bradley Fighting Vehicles. These mobile land combat products became a business pillar for Hughes as these fire control products, added to other laser devices from Hughes, made us the world's largest supplier of military systems using lasers. We really capitalized on our perfecting that miraculous technology and the expertise we acquired in stabilization and pointing.

Because of these dramatic advances in fire control and guided missile technology, the long-held tactical advantage of battle tanks and armored

M1A1 *Abrams* Tank
(©iStockphoto/Rockfinder)

vehicles was reversed. Such equipment now could quickly become flaming armored coffins. Many times in Desert Storm, Iraqi tankers would immediately abandon their vehicles if they saw their commander's tank destroyed. They would leap from their tanks and surrender to helicopters flying overhead in the hope of being safe, even though it meant being captured. Gen. H. Norman Schwarzkopf remarked, "Our tank sights have worked fantastically well in their ability to acquire targets through all the dust and haze."

Staring Arrays

As solid-state technology improved, it became possible to make large two-dimensional arrays of very small IR detector elements. At the same time, silicon integrated circuits could be built to read out the signals from each element of the arrays. These would be called focal plane arrays (FPA), a small flat panel much like a thick playing card 1 inch square. In a DoD research project, Hughes attempted to make both the detector and the readout circuitry from a single material using silicon. It was successful for use in space, but impractical for tactical weapons because of its cooling demand.

The company then developed a hybrid format in which matching arrays were fabricated using two different materials and mated together; one array used detector material and the other was of silicon for the matching readout circuitry. Implementing these detectors and silicon technologies was most challenging since they needed to operate together at very low temperatures and with both analog and digital signals. Each detector and readout transistor was plated with a bump of indium solder before the wafers were pressed together to simultaneously form thousands of interconnects. This significant development took many years but is now an industry standard and is used for arrays with millions of elements. The center-to-center spacing of the bumps now approaches 25 microns!

With such FPAs, most of the IR imaging mechanisms can be greatly simplified; a very large scene can be simultaneously examined by a staring array without the need for mirrors or prisms repetitively scanning lines of detectors. There are enough individual detector elements to make a pixel-rich visual display.

Parts Seven and Eight describe other Hughes developments in infrared technologies, all relating to the emerging search for solutions to the difficult problem of defense against ballistic missiles.

31

LASERS EVERYWHERE

THE LASER, SHORT for light amplification by stimulated emission of radiation, is now a familiar and essential device throughout the world. The laser was first commercially introduced in 1974 as a barcode reader to quickly record grocery item prices at the supermarket checkout counter. Laser text readers appeared in 1978; the compact audio disc replaced the phonograph record in 1982; laser printers became available the next year, quickly followed by directional pointing flashlights, three-dimensional holographic pictures, and dramatic city-wide laser light shows displayed on buildings or hillsides—the latter first demonstrated by Hughes in 1973. (Don't miss the shows in London, Las Vegas, and Crazy Horse Monument in South Dakota!) Small DVD discs replaced fragile and bulky motion picture film and magnetic videotape. DVDs store digital visual and audio data on a tiny glass fiber, spiral-wound tightly in a flat circle. In the recording process, digital data bits are etched as tiny pits on the fiber by a laser tracking along the spiral; readout is by a miniature laser reading and interpreting those pits. A new reliable and secure high-speed communication link became practical and economical using glass fiber optics transmitting laser light data over long distances. Manufacturing processes use lasers for precise cutting, bending, marking, burnishing, and welding. Medicine greatly benefits from laser applications in microsurgery, diagnostic procedures, and many forms of physical therapy. Scientists use lasers for comparative wavelength measurements, for precise positioning, and for cutting and burnishing chemical films.

Achieving Practicality

Dr. Albert Einstein first publicly proposed the concept of stimulated emission as a physics phenomenon in a paper published in 1917. During the next thirty years, several laboratory experiments showed the concept's feasibility, and in the 1950s Dr. Alfred Kastler experimentally demonstrated a method called optical pumping to increase the output of radiation. Charles Townes at Columbia University demonstrated stimulated emission in the millimeter-wave band in 1954, a device later called a maser (microwave amplification by the stimulated emission of radiation). Townes was awarded the Nobel Prize in physics for his work in 1966, although many felt that Dr. Theodore Maiman deserved similar recognition for his technical contributions. Dr. Maiman achieved an important practical breakthrough at the Hughes Research Laboratories by demonstrating, on May 15, 1960, the first operating laser.

The idea was to use a pure solid crystalline material whose atoms were known to emit visible light when stimulated, shape it as a light-containing cylinder with reflecting ends, and provide a light flash to get it started. This first laser used a tiny 0.8 inch long, 0.4 inch diameter rod of ruby crystal as the light-emitting material. At each end of the ruby crystal was a mirror to reflect the light back through the material again and again. One mirror had a tiny hole at its center to allow a portion of the light to emerge from the device (later lasers used partially reflecting coatings to achieve the same result). Next to the rod was a powerful flash lamp whose bright pulse of light would excite the active atoms in the ruby rod, as well as a mirror to concentrate the light onto the ruby rod.

The light waves emitted by the ruby bounced repeatedly between the end mirrors, each time increasing in energy. Amplified light waves passed through the transmitting mirror for outward projection and use. The light's wavelength was very narrow or pure in color (monochromatic red, when using ruby). This feature resulted in a high intensity beam, spatially narrow and with very little angular divergence. A ¼-inch beam would expand to only 1 inch in a mile, or to only a 1-mile circle if the beam traveled 240,000 miles, as measured by the Hughes Surveyor 7 in 1967, as the vehicle rested on the Moon's surface (see Section 44, "Scientific Space Exploration"). In contrast, most light sources are noncoherent, or essentially disorganized in frequency and timing, causing great spatial divergence and loss of brightness.

The first lasers operated in the visible spectrum, but designers quickly found other lasing materials that could emit beams down to lower frequencies of infrared and microwave, as well as upward to ultraviolet and X-ray. Most of these materials emit radiation in a narrow frequency band (that is, a single pure color or frequency or wavelength, depending on one's choice of measurement); some others operate with

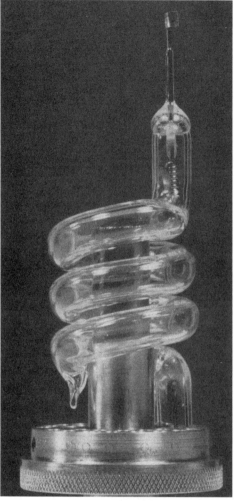

First Laser, 1960
(courtesy of Raytheon)

a broader band but are still uniformly coherent; still others emit several different distinctive wavelengths at the same time. Laser colors familiar to the public are red, yellow, green, and blue. The stimulated media can be solid such as ruby, sapphire, and crystals to which are added the rare-earth metals yttrium, erbium, and ytterbium; some gasses that work well are carbon dioxide, helium-neon, helium-mercury, argon, and nitrogen. Bill Bridges at Hughes perfected the use of ionized argon, now commonly used for eye surgery and laser light shows. The most commonly used solid material is called Nd:YAG (neodymium-doped yttrium aluminum garnet), operating in a near-infrared wavelength.

Several other chemical and physical methods of creating lasers have been developed for special applications. Other laser devices use a dye or free electrons, or operate as in a semiconductor.

Particularly interesting are fiber-hosted optical lasers, which consist of a central core surrounded by another glass layer; the inner strand forms the stimulated medium and the outer acts as the power pump. The active atoms are usually ytterbium or erbium. The long extending inner core also is an effective transmission line for the laser output.

Early designs, and many current lasers, when activated project a continuous uninterrupted beam. However, for some applications short pulses of high peak power are required. For example, for a radar to measure distance, the beam must be rapidly switched on and off. The same can be done with a laser. A most successful method called Q-switching (the Q is short for quadratic electrooptic effect, or QEO) was first perfected at the Hughes Research Laboratories by R. W. Hellwarth and F. J. McClung using a 1.7-inch-long ruby crystal medium that had a 0.3 inch diameter. This technique periodically alters the stable conditions for the bouncing light waves in the stimulated material, done by inserting a thin-film cell in front of the mirror at one end of the laser cylinder. The cell's material (in this case nitrobenzene) changes the polarity of any light passing through when it is electrically energized. This is called the Kerr effect, discovered in 1875 by Scotsman John Kerr. When the cell is not activated, there is normal laser operation; when electrically charged, the cell rotates the polarity of the reflected beam and thereby quenches further amplification. Switching times can be extremely fast and easily controlled for power management and exact timing intervals to ensure precise range measurements. The first prototype with Q-switching achieved pulses as short as an eighth of a microsecond and a peak power of 600,000 watts, which at the time was startling performance from such a small device.

The mature implementation of laser technology has resulted in many levels of power output: DVD players operate at only one-hundredth of a watt; monitoring and communicating devices range between 1 and 20 watts; surgical instruments emit 30 to 200 watts; industrial cutting machines spit out 100 to 300 watts; the behemoth of them all, first operating in 1998, is at the Lawrence Livermore Laboratories, emitting a peak power well over 1 trillion watts!

Entirely new combat methods came to the military with lasers: high resolution surveillance imaging; target designation, precision range-finding, target illumination for guided missile homing, and projection of destructive high-energy beams. Also, pilots could now be provided with

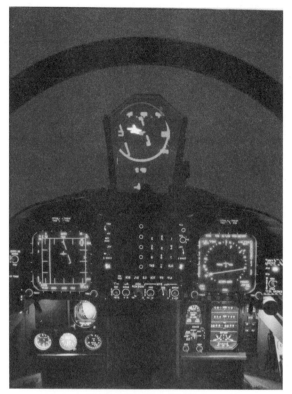

Cockpit Head-up Display
(courtesy of UNLV)

flight instrument data and active combat system information on edge-lit see-through displays so they can see the information with their eyes while still viewing the combat scene ahead. Hughes produced many of these head-up displays for many domestic and overseas fighter cockpits.

Measuring Range

As mentioned earlier, the precise measurement of the distance to target objects is vitally important in battle. The first laser rangefinder was prototyped at Hughes in early 1961 by Dr. George Smith (later corporate vice president and head of the Research Laboratories), using an Nd:YAG laser with Q-switching aided by a rotating mirror. It sent a single pulse to instantly find a target's range with an accuracy of 1/4 inch in ten miles. Laser rangefinders built by Hughes allowed US tank forces first-shot hits using many diverse weapons in the Gulf wars of 1991 and 2003.

A fascinating idea by astrophysicist Lowell Wood in the 1980s languished until 2008, when astrophysicist Jondin Kane at Lawrence Laboratories, motivated by Microsoft's interest, demonstrated a working device. The concept was to use a laser for eradicating mosquitoes and harmful farm pests, with the laudable goal of eliminating the use of insecticides. The device can rapidly search, identify, and zap the undesired creatures. If used extensively, this machine may solve the persistent threat of malaria, locust swarms, and crop damage without the use of chemicals. Household versions are now on the market.

First Laser Range Finder, 1961
(courtesy of Raytheon)

32

RESEARCH LABORATORIES
INNOVATIONS

THE PERFECTION OF fully functioning lasers of many types was only one of the many creations of the Hughes Research Laboratories (HRL), which for many years was one of the highest rated research organizations in the United States—indeed, in the world. During the 1980 decade, HRL employed 400 engineers and scientists, with 60 percent of its support coming from company financing (formally known as IR&D, independent research and development) and the rest from government contracts.

Many HRL innovations were critically supportive of company product lines, greatly increasing our competitive edge, and became the foundation of many of the world's high-technology and consumer products. Some examples: in 1965, ion-implantation and self-aligned gate designs, which permitted unprecedented numbers of electronic devices on a single semiconductor chip, enabling today's personal computers and mobile electronics; in 1969, creation of liquid crystal light valve displays, which form the basis for today's ubiquitous flat-screen displays; in 1977, development of gallium arsenide (GaAs) material to form complex ultra-high-speed microcircuits with very low internal noise, which greatly extended the performance of radar and satellite systems; high data rate fiber optics communication devices; advanced high performance detector arrays in visual, IR, and ultraviolet spectra, using the ion implantation technique; ion engines as propulsion and stabilization thrusters for spacecraft operating outside the Earth's atmosphere; and many artificial intelligence software assemblies for rapid and accurate analysis of IR and radar images used for military surveillance.

Despite our Research Laboratories' small size, its creativity was virtually unbounded and unmatched worldwide. It also served as a recruiting and training ground for technologists who later moved into management positions across Hughes, changes very harmonious with our family management philosophy. The American Physics Society named HRL a Physics Historical Site in 2010, principally because of the creation and applications of the nation's first laser.

33

THE WONDERS OF
ELECTRONIC SCAN

THERE ARE MANY types of radar antennas in use today depending on the mission to be fulfilled. Hughes was at the forefront of the evolution of antenna technology, perfecting conical scan reflectors, spaceborne pattern-shaping horns, gimbal-mounted planar arrays, beam scanning in all dimensions without mechanical motion, and large arrays of separate elements both actively transmitting and receiving. Many of these differing designs enabled new US dominance in artillery counter-fire, accurate air target intercept, precision mapping for reconnaissance, and stealthy radars, which are hard to detect by an enemy. Hughes products were world-class in all these missions. We also were well-known for supplying satellites whose high performance antennas had precise and unusual pattern shapes readable only by selected ground stations and continuously transmitting enormous volumes of data.

As described in Part One, early radars often used a parabolic reflector with a feedhorn spun to make a conical scanning pencil beam with a known pointing center. In the 1960s, we changed to what was called a planar array—a circular flat plate supported in a motion-stabilized gimbal mount. Like the parabolic reflectors, antenna beam sweeps were mechanical, using electric or hydraulic motors. The planar array faceplate had a large number of openings, or slots, each about 1/4 inch by 1 inch long, matching the wavelength of the radar's X-band frequency. Behind them was a complex network of waveguides that divided and distributed the transmitter power output pulses to each slot. The beam shape was formed by altering the phase and amplitude output of each slot to simulate the wavefront from a parabolic reflector. When the wavefront from each slot combined at a large distance from the antenna, it formed a beam much like that from a well-focused flashlight.

The operating performance of radars and communication networks is affected by the frequency used. Lower frequencies with longer wavelengths are used when high power is desired, but the equipment can be quite large and heavy. Shorter wavelengths provide higher angular resolution, but may be affected by water vapor, oxygen, and other atmospheric conditions. Beginning in World War II, easy-to-remember letters were used to designate different frequency band segments. Following are their meanings, wavelengths, and frequencies:

P: Previous or first designs; 40 inches, 300 mHz
L: Long wavelength; 12 to 6 inches, 1–2 gHz
S: Short wavelength; 6 to 3 inches, 2–4 gHz
C: Compromise between S and X; 3 to 1.5 inches, 4–8 gHz
X: "X-marks-the-spot"; 1.5 to 1 inch, 8–12 gHz
Ku: under Kurtz; 1 to 0.65 inch, 12–18 gHz
K: Kurtz, German for short; 0.65 to 0.5 inch, 18–24 gHz
Ka: above Kurtz; 0.5 to 0.3 inch, 24–40 gHz
mmw: millimeter wave; 0.3 to 0.1 inch, 40–100+gHz

Hughes used all of these in its many diverse products. Ground and ship equipment was usually L-, S-, or C-band; airborne and space radars were X-, or Ka- and Ku-band. Choice of a radar's primary frequency is done to match the desired operating mission and the size of the equipment, but it is also influenced by the susceptibility to enemy countermeasures or signal jammers. Hostiles attempt to hide themselves behind large amounts of electronic noise. Approaching target echoes may be masked beneath powerful jamming signals transmitted by the enemy at the same frequency as the radar. The effectiveness of this masking depends on the jammer's ability to match the radar's frequency and to radiate enough power to provide a continuous mask. It is very difficult for a jammer to transmit high enough power noise to cover the entire bandwidth, such as 4 gHz for X-band, and such a transmission provides a ripe target for a homing missile. Another effective remedy for jamming is to rapidly vary the radar's transmitting frequency in a random manner throughout the band (called frequency hopping). The hostile will have a very difficult time anticipating and tracking those changes.

The planar array was divided into four quadrants; the pointing center of an observed target reflection was found by comparing the target returns seen by the upper and lower quadrants and also the two side-by-side quadrants. When all were equal, the target was centered. Compared to the conically spun horn reflectors, these antennas performed with twice the power output (gain) and twice the sensitivity to incoming reflections from targets. Planar arrays were used in our radars equipping the F-14 *Tomcat*, F-15 *Eagle*, and F/A-18 *Hornet*, as well as many other US and overseas aircraft types. Some of these aircraft were later upgraded to special purpose active arrays, as described below.

Hughes used a planar array with a simple fan beam design for an air defense surveillance system applicable to all classes of naval combat ships from aircraft carriers to utility vessels. Called TAS (target acquisition system) it was a search radar with command and control computation and display for close-in defense. Its antenna, placed high on a ship to increase over-the-horizon visibility, was stable with respect to the ship's motion and was lightweight, placing less than 2,000 pounds on the ship's topside. A vertical fan beam 3-degrees wide reaching from sea level to 70 degrees in elevation was mechanically swept 360 degrees around the ship in about four seconds.

The system's pulse-Doppler radar operated at L-band with peak power pulses of 250 kilowatts. Tracks could be established for more than fifty targets at distances to thirty miles, including surface ships in the task force. Data passed to the system command and control computer, which characterized and designated targets, then cued the ship's fire control system to launch and control intercept missiles. System response was only a few seconds from initial detection to designation, providing enough visibility time for multiple defense missile engagements.

This capability was demonstrated in many fleet exercises with incoming subsonic and supersonic threats. Signal processing was done so well that virtually all clutter was rejected regardless of land proximity or sea conditions; countermeasures and noise blips were also quickly eliminated. The system integrated the radar information with target height data fed back from the missile's fire control radar when it made its lockon and with target elevation angle data from an IR tracker (if one was aboard that ship). A most important correlation task was to properly match each target with its IFF (identification friend or foe) transponder. This linkup was done with coded signals on a different radar frequency using separate antennas. Also critical was the ability to avoid or adapt to electronic emissions. The TAS display consoles gave a comprehensive view of the entire battle scene. In some task force groups, tracking data from all air defense radars, including TAS, were transferred and shared by several ships for coordinated battle actions.

The Mk-23 TAS program began in the late 1960s as a joint effort called IPD (improved point defense) for navies of the United States, eleven NATO nations, Australia, and New Zealand. The project's goal was to create a set of compatible systems for surveillance to more than 120 miles and self-defense to 10 miles using the Sea Sparrow missile, and later the RAM (rolling airframe missile) aboard combat ships of all classes. The IPD/TAS mission was to counter incoming hostiles that had leaked through the outer fleet air defense networks, with high priority on sea-skimming supersonic anti-ship cruise missiles. After a few systems were installed in lead ships, production contracts continued from 1977 through 1997; TAS was a most successful company product, with seventy-five deliveries placed on seventeen aircraft carriers, thirty-one destroyers, and many other ship types; twenty were deployed in the 1991 Iraq conflict. They were well prepared to cope with Exocet cruise missiles, but none were encountered. The CIWS (close-in weapon system) rapid-fire cannon for terminal defense, controlled by TAS, has been added to most ships. (Hughes assumed manufacturing of these after acquiring a portion of General Dynamics Corporation in 1992.)

Frequency Scan

Our big leapfrog in antenna technology was finding a way to scan a beam in at least one dimension without physical movement. Such a capability simplifies the antenna gimbal mechanism, reduces weight, and provides instantaneous repositioning of the beam look angle. The first method tried was similar to what happens in a wedge-shaped glass prism: a white light plane-wave beam splits into a rainbow through the prism, and each color's wavefront emerges from the wedge at a slightly different angle. This is because the speed of light in glass is slower than in air; the delay that light experiences at the wide bottom of the prism is greater than at the narrow top. Each of the colors in white light has an individual specific wavelength. At any level top-to-bottom in the prism, the delay through the wedge of glass is fixed. But that delay represents a different number of wavelengths depending on the color. The direction of the light wavefront exiting the prism is the angle at which all the wave crests line up. Since that alignment is a function of delayed wavelengths, each color exits at a slightly different angle. Because red has a longer wavelength compared to blue, it is less affected by the variable delay and is bent less. Blue has a shorter wavelength and the fixed delay represents more wavelengths, so the alignment angle is larger and bent more. Such a color separation effect is called dispersive.

Another effect associated with light or microwaves passing from one substance to another, such as from air to glass, is called refraction. The wavefront is bent so that energy is conserved. For example, a well-made plate glass window in your home bends light at the outside surface and then bends it again at the inside surface, so that the angle of arrival is the same as if you were outside. There is no color dispersion. These angle changes are exactly predictable and measurable, since they relate directly to each frequency and corresponding wavelength.

This dispersion phenomenon can be exploited in a radar antenna. The antenna feed is designed to be dispersive. The frequency (color) fed to a line of separate elements is stepped up slightly in sequence. The radiated beam angle shifts just as happens to light colors exiting a prism, without mechanical motion. The inverse process can be used for returning radar echoes. The radar's signal processor interprets the incoming data, correlates with the matching transmitted pulse, and determines the angle, Doppler shift, and range.

To implement this concept at Hughes, Drs. Nicholas Begovich and Nick Yaru perfected what became known as frequency scan, patented as "FreScan." Supported by company funds for three years beginning in 1948, then supplemented with government study contracts, the concept's first full demonstration was in 1953.

The first application was to perform elevation scan in surface-based surveillance radars. Previous fan-beam search radars such as TAS had to coordinate with a separate height-finding radar to enable a target track. By adding elevation scan, tracking could be done in three dimensions by a pencil beam of a single radar. Instead of handling only one target at a time, several could be tracked with operator participation; in later years, digital computers did multiple target tracking automatically. Electronic scan also was used to compensate for ship roll and pitch motions, stabilizing the radar view area.

FreScan Antenna, 1953
(courtesy of Raytheon)

The Navy deployed the SPS-26 shipboard surveillance radar using FreScan in 1957, and a similar MPS-23 (mission planning station) was delivered to the Army. Horizontal sweeps were done mechanically. An upright cylinder-like reflector focused on a vertical stack of waveguide slots for electronically scanning in the vertical direction. The beam squint angle frequency manipulation for "color" shifted up to 10 percent from the basic S-band frequency.

These radars were for long-range search and location of airborne targets. The information was used for aircraft vectoring or handed over to an illumination radar matched to air defense missiles. There was a long series of improved versions for all classes of US naval vessels and many naval vessels of friendly countries with SPS (designation for water surface radar search) identifiers -39, -39A, and -42, culminating in the fully digital SPS-52C in 1977.

These systems performed full azimuth target detections well beyond one hundred miles, with elevation scans up to 45 degrees. This search area was more than sufficient to stabilize the ship's motion and acquire all threat targets. High angles were not needed for this combat function (tracking a hostile overhead would be a little late for the defense game, unless it could be caught on its escape route), so, to simplify the antenna design, lower angle limits were implemented. Multiple target tracking by the digital SPS-52C radar enabled the first demonstration of handover to several intercept missile systems for launch against sets of hostile targets. Completely digitally controlled, it was used on guided missile frigates, destroyers, and cruisers of many nations. Cued defense weapon batteries were for the Tartar and Standard missiles. The SPS-52C was also used for friendly air traffic control by small aircraft carriers like the *Tarawa* (LHA-1) and for large amphibious vessels. The US Navy and friendly navies successfully used our systems until they were replaced in 2000.

SPS-52C Antenna
(courtesy of Raytheon)

The next concept for electronic beam manipulation, called phase scanning, used new solid-state components. The SPS-33 with its frequency scan had achieved a 70-degree elevation scan, but beams at larger angles were poorly shaped; the phase scan method can achieve much larger angles off broadside to the array face with better accuracy. Also, the frequency shifting needed for scanning sometimes creates slight angle uncertainties during target tracking due to frequency sensitivity in the target echoes and the limited bandwidth of the radar pulse. There also was concern about susceptibility to enemy countermeasures since there would be limited agility in changing the primary frequency to avoid jamming. But systems delivered to the fleet never experienced this anticipated problem.

Phase Scan

The newer way to steer the beam look angle without making frequency changes is to take advantage of the wave's phase. As mentioned earlier, a radar sends out a pulse of radio waves in a specific direction. A radar looks for reflections from objects as is done with a telescope: it looks in a desired direction and can only see objects within a narrow field of view.

When using an electronic signal, it is most helpful to know not only its frequency and its strength but also the arrival time of each part of the wave. This latter is called phase. If you watch a series of ocean waves approaching the coast, you will see that the crests and troughs are at approximately equally spaced distances from the shore. The crest's peak represents the wave's strength (amplitude). If the sand below is flat, halfway between the top and bottom of the wave the water is at the same level as a placid sea. Specific points (phases) of the wave can be numbered in degrees just like positions on a circle. As the wave approaches, the first point at sea level is defined as 0 degrees; the crest is 90 degrees. As the wave surface moves down toward the dip, it passes sea level again (180 degrees), and the trough is 270 degrees. Then the next wave set repeats this sequence. So every degree of phase defines an exact position in time and amplitude in the wave's surface (Fig. 5.1).

Similar to scanning a telescope in different directions to see all of the sky, early radars used rotating or tilting antennas to "look" with a narrow beam in search patterns.

Antennas pay a price of extra weight and design complications to achieve mechanical scanning, particularly if they must be large or mounted on a vehicle. Such configurations also may not be agile in scan timing or re-pointing of the beam. After using the frequency scan method, Hughes and other firms invented a way to change the beam look angle without moving the antenna with a concept called phase scan.

Visualize dropping a pebble into a quiet pond, starting a circular ripple that spreads in all directions (Fig. 5.2*a*). If several friends also do the same, each pebble makes its own circular wave, creating a jumble of confusing wavelets.

If everyone makes sure to drop the pebbles in a straight line and drop them at the same moment, instead of a confusing pattern of ripples, you will see a smooth blended wave moving across the pond, with the front of the wave parallel to the line of splashes. All the circular ripples have apparently joined in one direction to make a wavefront line (Fig. 5.2*b*).

Figure 5.1. Wave Phase Determination

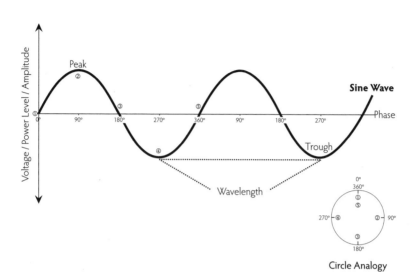

Circle Analogy

To point the wavefront in a different direction, drop the pebbles one at a time, in sequence from left to right. Instead of being parallel to the pebble drop line, the combined wavefront will move at a different angle: the ripple from the first pebble arrives at the second ripple just as that pebble hits the water. This dynamic event continues at each following pebble splash (Fig. 5.2c). By adjusting the timing, we can produce a plane wave traveling in whichever direction we choose.

In a radar, instead of using one large antenna, let's use a number of small controllable apertures and send out simultaneous signals, so that all the waves add up in the desired pointing direction. Similar to the pebble game, a group of antenna apertures can do the same kind of "beam steering" by adjusting the time delay from one small antenna outlet to the next one. Since a time delay moves to a later point of the signal wave's up and down cycle, we call it a "phase delay," and the whole beam control process a "phase scan." This phenomenon can be done whether transmitting or receiving energy.

The phenomenon can be exploited using antennas that are sensitive to phase as well as amplitude. For example, X-band crests are spaced about 1 inch apart. A line of elements (slots, dipoles, horns, etc.) evenly spaced in a flat array antenna can measure crest arrival time differences, and thus the tilt angle of the arriving signal relative to broadside to the array. A longer time interval means a larger tilt angle. In other words, the phase of the wave appearing at a series of slots defines the approach

Figure 5.2. Visualizing Phase Scan

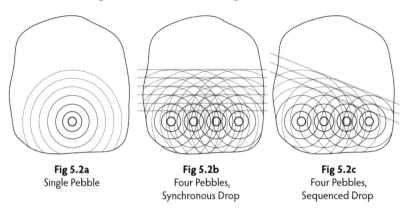

Fig 5.2a	**Fig 5.2b**	**Fig 5.2c**
Single Pebble	Four Pebbles, Synchronous Drop	Four Pebbles, Sequenced Drop

angle. Electronically manipulating the phase at each slot determines the beam shape and controls the squint (or scan) angle. This works both for transmit and receive. Phase shifting is done by inserting a controllable device (ferrite, diode, or dipole phase-shifter) between each slot or row of slots. Many later designs used far more effective microelectronic MIMs (miniature inline modules) designed by the company in the 1980s; these shifters can be commanded to change the phase of each wave slightly, so it differs from the previous beam formation. Programming a moving phase sequence causes the beam squint angle to shift as commanded.

Hughes combined frequency scan in one direction with phase scan in the other to attain a complete two-dimensional electronic scanning.

US Navy Cruiser
(courtesy of Wikipedia)

We also selected combinations of mechanical scan and electronic scan to best match the mission. This yielded a full horizontal quadrant, stabilized for ship pitch and roll, with electronic beam steering 45 degrees in elevation without physically moving the antenna.

Aboard the aircraft carrier USS *Enterprise* and the heavy cruiser USS *Long Beach* were two Hughes radars, each with four planar antennas to cover all horizontal quadrants. The first radar, SPS-32, with each antenna 20 feet high and 40 feet wide, was for air search; it operated at the since-abandoned low frequency P-band, with vertical fan beams similar to our TAS radars swept in azimuth by the frequency scan technique. Upon a target sighting, an operator cued SPS-33 (antennas 23 feet high by 19 feet wide) to precisely track the hostile for handover to a missile attack system. Operating in S-band, its antennas' pencil beams scanned in elevation using frequency manipulation and in azimuth by the newly developed phase-scan method.

Artillery Combat

An urgent problem that had plagued ground forces for centuries was ripe for a solution. For survival and forward progress, Marine and Army units have to find and destroy enemy artillery or rocket launchers assaulting friendly forces. Response in only seconds is essential.

The Army began a counter-fire radar program with Sperry in 1944, followed by work with General Electric, Sylvania, Emerson Electric, and ITT Gilfillan. However, performance was limited by poor analog processing, circuitry containing vacuum tubes, mechanical scan complexity, false alarms, and obscuration by background clutter. To eliminate these defects, the Army specified new requirements for a series of systems that eventually acquired the name of *FireFinder*. In 1972, Hughes won an Army contract to develop the TPQ-36, initially for locating hostile mortars. (TPQ is a designation for transportable radar, special purpose.) TPQ-36 had an antenna 3 feet wide by 7 feet tall, and weighed only 3,000 pounds, including its own 10 kilowatt power generator; mounted on a two-wheel trailer. The radar could be towed or quickly transported by helicopter. Later, a fierce competition for the larger TPQ-37 was resolved in our favor by an Army field "shootout" between prototypes from Hughes and Sperry.

The TPQ-37's mission was to find enemy artillery positions at ranges as far as eighteen miles away and rocket launcher sites to thirty miles; these distances were usually beyond the maximum reach of the hostile weapons. The smaller TPQ-36 performed at about half those ranges. TPQ-37 weighed in at 10,000 pounds; its antenna was about 8 feet wide and 12 feet high, and the equipment was carried in a four-wheel trailer

TPQ-37 FireFinder
(courtesy of UNLV)

behind a six-wheel field transportation vehicle. Both versions included a protective shelter for the operator and were qualified to operate at extreme conditions from -50°F to 125°F. Field setup times after transportation were fifteen minutes for TPQ-36 and thirty minutes for TPQ-37.

The Hughes mobile FireFinders solved the long-standing counter-fire problem. They could detect incoming projectiles as small as 4 inches in diameter and 18 inches long, verify them as hostile, and track them. The systems performed automatic acquisition, and their computers reverse-plotted the hostile shell trajectories and pinpointed the location of their source. Return fire could begin before the incoming enemy rounds hit their targets. Tracks were set up on all other enemy projectiles appearing within the scanned area. The systems also determined the impact points of the incoming round, and could assess friendly counter-fire accuracy.

The astonishing design of the data processing distinguished the real projectiles from the myriad of radar-detectable objects at low altitudes in the battlefield. Individual birds, insect clusters, and weapon shrapnel appeared similar in size; much larger targets such as helicopters and aircraft at many distances could overwhelm receiver sensitivity. The only way to sort all these targets out was to track them all and select rounds on the basis of their trajectory. That took an enormous amount of processing and virtually instantaneous decision making by the computer.

TPQ-36 FireFinder
(courtesy of UNLV)

The antennas of both systems formed pencil beams for searching and tracking projectiles. Operating at X-band, the TPQ-36's flat antenna array of slotted waveguide columns was frequency scanned in elevation, and phase scanned horizontally in 90-degree azimuth sectors. The S-band TPQ-37 used phase scanning in both azimuth and elevation. Each antenna's radiating element was fed by a vertical sub-array of six diode phase shifters to effect the elevation scan. These were mounted on removable circuit cards. For this construction simplicity, the elevation scan angle could be less than 10 degrees above the horizon; the hostile shell was immediately acquired as it ascended from the terrain, and the counter track was quickly computed, so the job was completed for that projectile. An operator in the control shelter could select the azimuth search sector. The TPQ-36 operator could command a 270-degrees search with an automatic rotation of the antenna in three successive timed scans of 90-degree sectors.

Initial deployments began in 1980, and in the next fifteen years more than 250 TPQ-36 and 100 TPQ-37 systems were deployed. They were used in live fire combat with excellent results in Bosnia, Grenada, Iraq, Lebanon, Panama, Somalia, and Thailand. Adaptations of the TPQ-36 for air defense search and missile launch control expanded the total production to 500 systems by the year 2000, equipping the United States and seventeen other friendly nations.

FireFinder used by our Army and Marines was not only most effective in directing accurate counter-fire against sources of incoming artillery or mortar rounds, but also terrified the enemy and virtually destroyed its ground troops' morale. (Another example of effective deterrence came from one captured Iraqi artillery officer, who said that it was very difficult to command his men to shoot a cannon, since they knew that immediate return fire would kill them even if their round hit its target. And from a trooper: "We couldn't fire our artillery; if we did, the steel rain would come . . . . All we could do was surrender.") One Marine FireFinder destroyed fifty-two gun-emplacements in a single day, as it advanced from Kuwait City!

HADR Electronic Scan Antenna
(courtesy of UNLV)

Improvements in the TPQ-36A created a portable air defense search radar called LASR (low altitude surveillance radar). It was most effective in short-range searches for "pop-up" of helicopters and low flying strike aircraft, and served as a gap-filler in large national air defense networks for cueing missile defense systems, particularly in Norway. The US version was identified as the MPQ-64 Sentinel radar.

As a further extension into ground-based air defense radars, the company created a more complete system called HADR (Hughes air defense radar), or HR-300. With its long-range performance, multiple target tracking, virtual immunity to countermeasures, and complete clutter rejection, it became a worthy competitor for international sales as the primary air defense sensor. It was the choice for the networks in Malaysia, several NATO countries, Norway, Switzerland, and Taiwan. The HADR's antenna was mechanically scanned for 360 degrees horizontally and phase scanned in elevation to provide the desired surveillance coverage. The Swiss system was similar, but its operating frequency was C-band rather than S-band and used frequency scan in elevation.

Lt. Gen. Donald M. Lionetti, Former Director of the US Army Ballistic Missile Defense Agency, complimented Hughes in 2008:

> "In 1984, I had occasion to work with Hughes Aircraft to modify a TPQ-36 mortar-finding radar for air defense use. Hughes delivered as promised in record time a prototype that was evaluated and later deployed throughout the US Army as the Sentinel air defense radar, which is still fielded. Hughes delivered more than just technical excellence, Hughes provided top quality support to the Army with highly qualified, dedicated professionals."

Active Arrays

The pinnacle in the evolution of radar antennas was a most sophisticated array of many independent transmit and receive elements. These modules became possible because advances in digital formatting, exotic software, and microelectronic miniaturization that enabled assembly of hundreds of small active elements into planar arrays shaped to fit fighters, bombers, and combat ships.

The beauty of these arrays was their unbounded versatility for any mode of radar operation. Beams of any desired shape could be formed; several pencil beams could be simultaneously sent at different angles; beam positioning could be instantly changed; commands could alter operating frequencies, pulse shapes, and transmitted power levels. Total power radiated could be much larger than in those fed by a single transmitter, since power output is the sum of many channels very close to the radiating elements, each performing at a comfortable output level without overheating or overtaxing waveguide feeds. Outputs of each were commanded at differing signal phases, forming a beam at the desired angle. These designs were particularly vital for the latest versions of F-15, F/A-18, F-22, and F-35 aircraft, as well as many other military systems.

34

SEEK AND
YE SHALL FIND

Throughout history, one of the elements most needed in combat planning has been knowledge of the opponent: his strength, position, movement, armor and weaponry, and ability to actively counter one's own combat systems, as well as his most likely strategic and tactical behavior. These data must be intertwined with detailed current information on terrain, weather, and visibility limitations caused by natural trends, camouflage, or stealth.

This complex job is called either surveillance or reconnaissance. The *New Oxford American Dictionary* describes surveillance as "close observation, especially of a suspected spy or criminal," and reconnaissance as "military observation of a region to locate an enemy or ascertain strategic features." Regardless of which term is used, the same steps are needed for success. First is gathering data, screening out unnecessary details and background clutter, then relaying the useful information to a control center. There, the data are stored for use and historic comparison, and the content is analyzed (perhaps automatically). The results are displayed to an operator who interprets the panoramic situation, manipulates the system's next actions, and reports results to upper-level commanders.

In many cases, superior forces have been defeated by their lack of knowledge of hostile movements or even their lack of knowledge of the hostile forces' locations. There were also times when the information was available, but pig-headed poor judgment by commanders made for failure: Napoleon's first "negative victory" in 1812 at Borodino, just west of Moscow, for example. Although reducing half of General Kutuzov's 104,000 Russian troops in a single day, the 124,000-soldier French force suffered 28,000 irreplaceable casualties, which crippled their campaign and caused a full retreat. Napoleon had insisted on personally studying the battleground before the engagement, ignoring his experienced staff; his resulting plan was deeply flawed. French cannons were placed beyond their effective range, and no protective trenches were dug at key spots. Napoleon also assumed that the hostile artillery would not use grapeshot, and that the Russians would quickly retreat as they had done in all previous encounters for the previous seven years. In this case, gathering of data was poorly done, and Napoleon's self-confidence overwhelmed his usual good reasoning. The lesson: as a leader, one should always at least listen to intelligent staff personnel.

Another example is General Lee's defeat of the Union forces at the 1864 battle of the Wilderness in Virginia. Confederate forces numbered 61,000 and opposed 101,000 Northern troops. Lee executed an end sweep with a quick thirty-mile nighttime march for a dawn surprise attack from the Union rear. Generals Grant and Meade had no reconnaissance in effect to discover this move. The result was devastating—and embarrassing for Grant: it was his first engagement after assuming high command of the Army.

A more recent experience is the quick capture of Singapore in early 1942 by the Japanese force of 36,000, led by General Yamashita. This victory astonished the British and Allied force of 85,000 led by General Percival. Instead of appearing by sea, where all the defenses were set in accordance with the forecast of traditional Allied thinkers, the Japanese used bicycles and fast moving foot soldiers to suddenly appear from the jungle across an undefended causeway (still visible today), completely to the rear of a formidable fortified defense line. Once again, both traditional stubbornness by commanders and lack of adequate active reconnaissance allowed a smaller force to cause 7,000 casualties and capture 50,000 prisoners.

Surveillance and reconnaissance in the old days were done by use of intelligence-gathering individuals or networks within the enemy's region—sending scouts forward, peering from mountain crests, in balloons (as one of my great-uncles did in the US Civil War!), and later on in scout aircraft providing visual reports or still photography.

In more modern times, information gathering has been done far more effectively from swift aircraft, satellites, or ground combat vehicles. In addition, a number of options are available to augment visual observations (which are limited in many ways and suffer from lack of accurate recounting): precise-tracking optics, TV and movie film cameras, as well as infrared imagers, laser scanners, high resolution radars, electronic listening devices, and undersea sonar arrays.

Presenting reconnaissance data quickly and in a usable format, so that rapid tactical decisions could be made based on hostile status and activities, led to the desire for an instantaneous transmission link from the observer to a command location. Early satellite and U-2 aircraft attempts to gather and store data used large masses of photographic film; returning these home and developing the results took uncomfortably long times. Although useful in a strategic sense, this method was impractical in tactical situations such as in Vietnam. Reconnaissance systems needed better processing and direct interlink transfer to their control stations.

In current systems, much of the information may be processed aboard the observing vehicle. In other cases, a data link transmits masses of raw data to a sophisticated computer to format, sort, and automatically analyze historical and current data of terrain, target identification, likely countermeasures, movements and forecasted positions, weather, and obscurations. The resulting information can be transferred by satellite relays over long distances. This practice was tried in Vietnam, with poor results because of decision-making time delays. But during Desert Storm, target images were seen in Washington, D.C., while the air strikes were under way, and there were instances when commands were sent back to a pilot not to attack a particular target seen on Pentagon viewing screens.

Many of the military systems made by Hughes involved surveillance, ranging from satellite overviews of the USSR for the National Reconnaissance Office (NRO); monitoring ballistic missile launch sites from orbiting spacecraft; radar and infrared searching for hostile aircraft from fighters, ships, and ground-based air defense networks; and mapping battlefield situations from airborne and ground vehicles using lasers, IR, and radar sensors. Some of these systems are described in other Parts of this book; the following paragraphs tell of our laser imagers, sonar surveillance, and precision radar reconnaissance experience. The company's work in the vital tasks of storing, analyzing, and displaying information is described in Section 40, "Command and Control."

Using its extensive knowledge of laser mechanisms, Hughes developed two types of airborne and satellite laser surveillance systems for the military and the CIA. Difficulties in mechanizing laser scanners included coping with internal reflections in the optical telescope—requiring special shaping and the addition of masking devices. To function without damage the optics also had to be cooled. Hughes later abandoned this approach as a product line, believing that thermal imaging and radars would be of greater operational utility and lower cost to produce and maintain.

The company's laser system used in Vietnam on an Air Force fighter helped in target planning at the home base, but, similar to the U-2s over

Russia, the information had to be processed after the aircraft returned from its mission. The pulsed laser pencil beam swept over the terrain on lines perpendicular to the flight path. Each single reflection was focused directly on a filmstrip moving at the right speed to form a row of pixels. Then the beam was scanned in successive lines to record a series of raster rows to construct a clear image of the full scene below. The high-resolution pictures, obtained from altitudes above 10,000 feet, showed details as small as 4 inches square!

The later version used a spinning mirror to capture return samples and impinge them onto a fiber-optic array, which had half a million fibers; the primary laser line scan was converted to a circular image that could either be viewed on the pilot's display or activated tiny laser beams in each fiber to be recorded on a passing film strip. Although viewable to the pilot, the reconnaissance information had to be returned to base for comprehensive analysis by the commanders. The unfortunate time delay was still not overcome.

Testing these systems at our Culver City facilities before their deployment engendered a great deal of public attention, but we were unable to reveal what was happening because of military security. On the side of the airstrip opposite our equipment test sites, we set up a mile-long plywood fence with a thin horizontal line painted in reflective white on its surface. The line had to be precisely straight for its entire length; it would be used to measure the tracking accuracy of the laser line scanner. Uninformed observers speculated that this unusual setup was the control strip for a new aircraft automatic landing system. However, the real thrills came during several nights when the test system somehow got out of kilter. The bright green beam, randomly reflected off the clouds above, was seen throughout Los Angeles, as it darted aimlessly around the sky. It stirred up scary flying saucer rumors, and some neighbors were terrified that an attack by aliens was about to begin! The press went wild, as usual, but because of the military security of the project, Hughes could not alleviate the people's fears.

Undersea Reach

Sound waves have always been of great value to animals for navigation, communication, warning alerts, and identification. For example, while in flight, bats can rapidly maneuver, avoid obstacles, and find flying insect food by sending and receiving high-pitched beeps. Humpback whale communication is astonishing: their very low pitch communication sounds made in Alaskan waters can be heard by other whales as far away as Hawaii! Many fish depend on sound in ways similar to those of humans. Humans are primary users of audio for the purposes cited above and for entertainment in many forms. Human audio perception ranges between 20 Hz and 20,000 Hz; other creatures and man-made sensors can extend the upper frequency to 100,000 Hz.

✳

Sonar, a term created in the 1940s, is an acronym for sound navigation and ranging. Similar in concept to radar, it uses audio sound waves in water to detect, locate, and track objects of interest. It can be done with active transmission or by passive sensing. In contrast to radar echoes that return at the speed of light, audio waves travel in seawater at over 3,300 miles per hour (about four times faster than in air), and with far less loss of power with distance. Power lost in transit does increase as the sound pitch rises; Jean-Daniel Colladon first measured this speed difference in 1826 using a bell in the waters of Lake Geneva.

Military uses of undersea sound now include navigation; communication; search, track, and identification; imaging; and terminal homing of weapons. Systems employed are both passive, listening for sounds created from vessels, and active, functioning like a radar using a controlled sound source and searching for echoes to interpret. Sonar operation was first invented in 1906 by Lewis Nixon as a means of finding icebergs; the first military device was created by Paul Langevin in 1915 using a quartz sensor to passively listen for submarines; and the first active sonars were made by Britain and the United States in 1918, just as World War I was ending.

Many of the problems that had to be solved by radars also applied to sonar systems: enough receiver sensitivity in the passive mode to detect sounds emanating from the target; enough transmitting power in the active mode to ensure that target echoes could be detected; correctly measuring range, angle, and speed; avoiding false targets and clutter confusion from undersea terrain, numerous natural fixed objects, and moving sea creatures; immunity to hostile countermeasures; coping with stealth configurations and deceptive maneuvers; and avoiding unnecessarily revealing one's own position. Solutions to these difficulties involved attempts at transmitting vertical and horizontal beam patterns, making frequency changes, using variations in transmit-pulse timing, and changing the sequences of different passive operations. Again, similar to radars, return signal confusion was eliminated by comparison with stored databases (such as the known undersea terrain) in the sonar system's high performance computers.

In addition to these radar similarities, sonar system designers must consider the various propagation paths that will be encountered. Sound speed in the ocean is affected somewhat by salinity levels, but measurably increases as temperatures rise and as pressure increases at lower depths. Sound rays will "bend" toward the slower medium: downward to lower temperature regions or upward at about 1,000 feet depth as pressure becomes the dominating factor. This bending must be considered in determining the path sound takes from a radiating source to a passive receiver or in the round-trip from an emitter to an object and back to the receiver in an active mode. Some temperature profiles can provide a direct path or long-range focusing of sound rays; such areas are called convergence zones. Similar to how whale sounds travel from Alaska to Hawaii, a deep sound channel could be available for exceedingly long-range detection of submerged objects.

Beginning in the 1960s, Hughes invested company funds to explore audio sensors, signal and data processors, and displays to meet the growing needs for high-performance sonar systems. As part of this effort, a 100-foot diameter redwood tank was built at Fullerton to evaluate towed-array acoustic and mechanical concepts before trials at sea. Experimental systems towed hydrophones responding in the frequency band of 50 to 1200 Hz. The array was oil-filled for neutral buoyancy. Individual hydrophone outputs were wired through an armored tow cable to reach the ship-based equipment. Tow depth was adjusted for variations in the ocean's acoustic condition by changing the ship's speed and cable payout. To prevent vibrational "strumming" of the cable from interfering with the hydrophones' sensitivity, automobile-like shock absorbers isolated the sensors from the cable. These experiments resulted in several varieties of sonar receivers and signal processing systems for the Navy. Derivatives of these devices eventually found their way into submarines, surface ships, and helicopters.

The company received a contract for a submarine intelligence towed array referred to as Tuba II, later designated BQH-4. The system had an array with hydrophones, a winch and handling equipment, and shipboard signal processing and display, all installed on an operational submarine. This led to subcontracts from IBM on two sonar systems designated BQQ-5 and BQQ-6 to be installed on *Los Angeles* and *Trident* class submarines.

In 1975, Hughes won a tough competition and became the prime contractor for SURTASS (surveillance towed-array sensor system). Hughes was awarded the contract to develop and produce twenty-three systems starting in 1980, and to assist in a 1984 deployment. The SUR-TASS's mission was to detect, track, identify, and report at long distances the population of diesel and nuclear powered submarines in a widespread area. Encrypted satellite links transferred the processed data from this very mobile equipment to sea and shore bases for real-time display to rapidly cue tactical defense weapon systems.

Finding and tracking slowly moving submarines in shallow water is quite difficult because of the low Doppler shift of the submarine reflection signal compared to unwanted clutter coming from many ships in the area being examined, as well as other sources. The company developed special signal processing to sort out real targets from all the false ones that might be seen. The software programming had to be particularly creative: much of the system's peripheral equipment was COTS (commercial off-the-shelf) from many different suppliers. Getting them all to respond compatibly as an integrated system was indeed challenging.

The SURTASS, designated as UQQ-2, consisted of a very long towline with many stems, each carrying highly sensitive hydrophones. Line length was chosen to maximize separation from the mother ship for improved quietness, but was constrained to minimize adverse towing drag. The hydrophones were carefully shaped so that the water motion would place them in a predetermined pattern when being towed. Data received by each hydrophone was sent by wire along the towline to a central signal processor aboard the ship. The processors aboard ship, or at a shore station, with their previous databases of terrain and sea conditions, sorted the targets from extraneous information and accurately located and tracked them. Precision was greatly enhanced by analyzing information from all the separately placed hydrophones. With the target sounds thus perceived from different angles, triangulation yielded an accurate measure of range and position. In later years, signal processing was so intricate that specific submarines could be identified by their distinctive primary engine, power-drive reduction gear, and propeller noises.

A 1992 Navy configuration used smaller hydrophones attached in two parallel towlines about ten feet apart. This configuration allowed vertical angle measurements (and thus the ability to determine the target's depth) and resolved the single-line uncertainty of whether the target emanations were arriving from the right or left side of the sensor string.

The arrays could be passive, listening for noises emanating from distant objects. They could also listen for target echoes coming from pulses by an LFA (low frequency active) acoustic transmitter mounted aboard the SURTASS vessel or operated from a remote site. Hughes won the competition to develop the LFA in 1987, followed by another award in 1992 to integrate the LFA and SURTASS into a unified system. This integrated system could detect extremely stealthy threats at long ranges (the lower the frequency, the less power loss as the sound progresses through the water). During initial sea testing, there were numerous reports of disoriented whales and distressed swimmers and scuba divers when LFA was operating, so such transmissions became a long-standing political controversy. The Navy has faced several federal lawsuits from environmentalists because the transmission frequency—between 200 and 1000 Hz—is close to the communication band of several species of whales, and the high sound power levels used by the system may be damaging to them. Prolonged investigation resulted in the Navy's being barred by the federal government in 1992 from using this new equipment. Although the dispute was partially resolved in 2002, discussions still continue. Some operation is now permitted in the western Pacific.

Initially the towed array systems were deployed in several types of single-hull ships. In other applications, the processors were aboard surface vessels and submarines, with the hydrophones hard-mounted to the exterior hull. The ultimate tow vessels were those in the SWATH class (small waterplane area twin hull); four of these ships were launched in the 1990s.

SURTASS Search Vessel
(courtesy of UNLV)

The fifth vessel displaced 5,370 tons, was 281 feet long with a 97-foot beam, and cruised at 12 knots. This design provided a stable platform for slow speed in adverse weather. The ship carried a full LPA/ SURTASS system, including the newly developed Hughes software to perform automatic track and identification of hostile threats with no false alarms. In 2000, the Navy SURTASS force had eight ships in the Atlantic and four ships in the Pacific. Over the years, shore stations operated in Norfolk, Whidbey Island, Pearl Harbor, Yokohama, and several other temporary locations.

Surprisingly, SURTASS tow ships are classed as noncombat vessels, and the crew consists of 20 civilians with Navy badges and 20 technical contractor personnel. Hughes had several long-term contracts to supply a total of 140 operators aboard ships and in shore stations.

The Navy also employed MH-60R *Seahawk/Seaknight* helicopters to seek and destroy hostile submarines, using a towed sonar network called ALFS (airborne low frequency sonar). Hughes and Thomson Industries, Inc., of France teamed to create this unique system. After a successful development program, eighty systems were planned for production. An array of staves is lowered from a hovering helicopter by a fast-reacting reel and expands below the surface to spread the sensors. Each stave contains several acoustic sensors; all data are sent to the helicopter for analysis and display. When targeting is completed and attack is authorized, the helicopter launches a Mk-46 or Mk-50 lightweight homing torpedo. As mentioned in the ADCAP description in Section 43, "Guidance Gains," these weapons also became a Hughes product when the company purchased a portion of AliantTech systems.

Since the submarine threat considerably lessened after 1990, other SURTASS useful applications were found for the Coast Guard and Drug Enforcement Agency in countering clandestine drug smugglers. Systems also aid in sea-environment research by the National Oceanic and Atmospheric Administration (NOAA).

The sonar systems product line, including the torpedo projects mentioned above and the ADCAP torpedo, was a significant Hughes business for thirty-five years, accruing more than $3 billion in revenue from contracts to develop, manufacture, operate, support, and continually improve system designs. Not only was this product line beneficial to Hughes, but also it helped increase the security of the United States by giving the Navy the means to cope with submarine threats in the twenty-first century.

Airborne Mapping

Hughes made a significant contribution to improving tactical airborne reconnaissance with its precision mapping radar for the TR-1 (tactical reconnaissance) aircraft, a version of the famous Lockheed U-2 "spy plane." The radar, called ASARS (advanced synthetic aperture radar system), was deployed in the 1980s. In addition to test prototypes, Hughes produced thirty-five radars.

As indicated by its name, this X-band radar had a "synthetic" antenna, which was shaped to create images of virtually unlimited areas of terrain. The hardware was a series of 2,250 active transmit and receive elements arranged in a line perpendicular to the aircraft's flight path and peering toward the Earth. This array was activated in a linear sweep, with received returns processed to form a single line for a video raster. As the aircraft flew forward, another sweep formed the next raster line. The term "synthetic array" thus meant that this antenna had a discrete series of separate elements in one direction and an infinite number of elements in the other: as long as the aircraft flew, another antenna scan line would follow the previous one. The only limits to the mapping size were the 120-degree swath width, the flight altitude (usually 55,000 to 65,000 feet), and the amount of fuel in the TR-1. The downward look angle could range from 20 degrees up to 70 degrees below the aircraft's horizontal plane.

TR-1 (U-2) Surveillance Aircraft
(courtesy of the National Museum of the US Air Force)

The high-speed data processing was quite sophisticated for that era. Information for the image was gathered accurately and with high resolution, since the radar knew its own position and could measure the locations of numerous terrain-feature echoes within a small fraction of the transmitted wavelength, which for X-band is 1 to 1-1/2 inches.

Any measuring uncertainties of position or the range of a motionless ground object were resolved by determining the Doppler shift at that specific observation point. As the aircraft moved, the apparent passing speed of each observed spot altered slightly from other spots when viewed from an angle different from the line of flight. This predictable change could be used to correct any uncertainties, resulting in mapping resolutions of 1-foot square for this system. (This process is called DBS, Doppler beam sharpening.) Think of seeing everything the size of a basketball in a map of a small city ten miles away!

Aboard the TR-1, the radar data were digitally formatted and coded for transmission by high-speed data link to the ground control station. An early version of a programmable signal processor (Hughes's evolution of this device is described in Section 51, "Processing Signals Digitally") received the data and performed the necessary computations to yield a real-time map for display to the control officer or to be stored or relayed to other stations. This processor, originally designed in 1973, achieved 225 million operations per second, an incredible speed for that time. The result: precise maps detailed to 1-foot squares and obtainable in any weather or under any battlefield conditions.

Airborne Radar Mapping Image
(courtesy of Raytheon)

Earlier Hughes synthetic aperture mapping test programs described in the signal processing portion of Part Eight (Section 51, "Processing Signals Digitally") demonstrated 11-foot-square resolution, and improved in 1973 down to a 7-foot square. Advances in on-board processing have now added ground-mapping modes to tactical fighters, with resolution cells as small as 3 inches square. These advances had finally overcome the old dilemma of tactical reconnaissance data being almost useless because of the many time delays between observing and using. The problem now was to rapidly derive useful information from the enormous amount of received data. This was solved with very high-speed computers with comparative reference data and diagnostic software to recognize and highlight on the display all meaningful targets in the overall panorama.

35

AIRBORNE RADARS FLY

MEANWHILE, CONTINUING EFFORTS on winning airborne radar programs yielded substantial successes. Performance improvements in each generation were passed forward and further embellished with new creations. These programs collectively represented major development opportunities for our innovators and were remarkably large revenue sources.

In 1969, Hughes and its perennial rival Westinghouse each won contracts for creating an engineering model of the APG-63 radar destined for the McDonnell-Douglas F-15 *Eagle* slated for the Air Force. The performance of two development models was to be demonstrated in a B-66 *Destroyer* flight test aircraft. The objective of the demonstration was to ensure acquisition and track of any airborne target regardless of its aspect, even if at low altitude with a lot of ground clutter returns. The radar modes selected were high (250,000 pulses per second) and medium (16,000 pulses per second) PRF to obtain clear Doppler separation with low fighter-to-target speed differences. The two waveforms were interleaved, so both modes were run simultaneously. When the resulting processed signal streams were combined in a clear and certain basis, the targets were displayed to the pilot without risking false alarms caused by weak target returns or unwanted ground targets. With its newly developed digital signal processor design (see Section 51), Hughes won the fly-off competition to begin a most successful product line with its next generation APG-70, which is still active forty years later.

In 1975, competition—again with Westinghouse as the opponent—began for the radar to equip the McDonnell-Douglas F/A-18 *Hornet* slated for the Navy; I was fortunate to lead the company's proposal effort. There was a lot of pressure on this contest, since we had just lost to Westinghouse the General Dynamics F-16 *Fighting Falcon* radar award, in spite of an all-out effort to offer a persuasive proposal. This time we held a better hand of cards. Our forte always was to bid high performance, and our internally funded research project had already demonstrated an innovative software-programmable signal processor (see Section 51, "Processing Signals Digitally"); it was the ideal match for this radar.

With this signal processor and an all-digital circuitry configuration, Hughes had a slight technology edge over our arch rival. But we were deeply concerned that Hughes would not be favored: we were already responsible for the F-14 and the F-15 radar systems. Our competitor was completing the final production lots of its electronics for the F-4, and although they were now active in the F-16 radar design, it would be their only fighter project. Perhaps both the government and McDonnell-Douglas would feel there should be an even division of development responsibility between the two radar suppliers; relying on Hughes for three of the four active US fighter designs might be too risky. That fear may have been unwarranted; we did win a real squeaker. This versatile APG-65 radar, later upgraded as the APG-71, eventually became the largest revenue source in Hughes history.

APG-65 Radar in F/A-18 *Hornet*
(personal files)

Table 5.2 summarizes airborne radars developed and produced by Hughes in over fifty years of dedicated effort.

Table 5.2. Airborne Radars

Aircraft	Year Begun	No. Produced	Principal Features*	See Part
F-86, F-89, F-94	1948	5,718	Pulse	One
F-102 F-106	1952	2,305	Pulse Doppler Digital Computer	Three
F-108	1957	4	Mostly digital	Three
YF-12	1961	6	Long range	Four
F-111B	1963	6	Track while scan; multishot	Four
F-14	1968	725	Track while scan; multishot; new dogfight mode	Five
F-15	1970	1,200	Multimode; all digital	Five
F/A-18	1978	1,490+	Programmable signal processor	Five
TR-1	1981	27	Synthetic aperture; high resolution mapping	Five
B-2	1982	21	Multimode; stealth	Eight
F-22 F-35	1986	187 In Produc.	Central integrated processing**	Eight
Global Hawk	1992	In Production	Synthetic aperture	Not inc.

* All positive performance features in fighters were carried forward to all succeeding generations.
** Hughes provided only this central processor, not the entire radar.

GSG Command & Control Brochure
(courtesy of UNLV)

PART SIX

THE BOOM YEARS BEGIN

T HE 1970S BEGAN with a significant decrease in the US defense budget, as the government tried to respond to the population's dismay and unrest at the difficulties of the Vietnam conflict. In turn, this caused business and employment reductions throughout the aerospace community. At Hughes, sales and staff size remained flat for three years, and then rapidly expanded. To further exploit the Sino-Soviet split, in 1972 President Nixon began positive overtures toward a new relationship with China, even though that country retained its firm commitment to communism.

In 1974, the United States withdrew from Vietnam, followed by the national political embarrassment of the Watergate scandal and President Nixon's resignation. In spite of these events, our new relationship with China put pressure on the USSR, motivating it to promote an East-West policy called *détente* in 1973, which achieved a modicum of peaceful stability. However, this mutual goodwill collapsed when the Soviets invaded Afghanistan in 1979. (It is ironic that twenty-two years later the United States entered that nation to combat the same political factions that we had supported against the USSR.) Nonetheless, with great hope, President Carter signed the Strategic Arms Limitation Talks (SALT) Agreement that same year. However, that invasion of Afghanistan and the subsequent test of a potent Soviet SS-20 IRBM (intermediate range ballistic missile) equipped with three powerful nuclear warheads were viewed by the United States and other western nations as preparations for a military conquest of Western Europe. These growing concerns motivated the United States to boycott the 1980 Olympic Games being held in Moscow and to dramatically increase its defense budget.

The eternal Middle East conflict heightened with the 1973 Yom Kippur War (known in the Muslim world as the "Ramadan War") between Israel and an alliance of Egypt and Syria, with secondary support from Iraq, Jordan, and Libya. This contest was somewhat alleviated by the Camp David Accords, sponsored by President Carter and signed by Egypt's Anwar Sadat and Israel's Menachem Begin. Further instability arose from worldwide fuel shortages in 1974 and the Muslim extremist overthrow in 1979 of US-supported Shah Pahlavi of Iran, followed by the Ayatollah Khomeini's retention of fifty-two US hostages. Goaded by this act, and by an increased truculence by the USSR in the United Nations, President Reagan pushed for substantial increases in US military capability as mandatory for national survival.

To decrease communist penetration in Latin America, in 1983 the United States invaded the Caribbean island of Grenada (oddly, I was on a sailboat cruise in the area, and I snapped pictures of the resort beach, not knowing that it would be used two weeks later by the US Marines; even the CIA had no reconnaissance data—but no one asked me for those valuable photos!) That year the United States helped the dictatorial Nicaraguan government defeat the Sandinista rebels, with a subsequent embarrassment about allegedly secret money transfers, called the Iran-Contra affair.

The public supported the Reagan military buildup, and the growth in available government funding provided numerous opportunities for defense contractors, starting what became known as the "arms race" with the Soviets. Also, an entirely new set of scientific and engineering objectives in space ignited a burst of development opportunities. Harvesting these fertile business fields was quite advantageous for Hughes.

National budgeting to support aerospace advances was made easier by the high regard of the public, who greatly admired those in that profession who already had achieved giant leaps forward in human endeavors. Politicians, eager to please their constituents, funded many daring technical ventures. Successes were heralded, and growing budgets for the DoD and NASA were considered worthwhile and necessary for the nation. This willingness resulted in part from the successful fulfillment of President Kennedy's commitment to land a man on the Moon within a decade, and the subsequent enhancement of our national technical prestige vis-a-vis the Soviets.

To paraphrase Ralph Waldo Emerson: Build a better mousetrap and the world will beat a path to your door. The growth of Hughes in the face of competition often stemmed from customer satisfaction with what the company did; buyers were amazed to see the large collection of technical professionals at Hughes who seemed to be extremely capable in their scientific and engineering fields. First the Air Force, then NASA, often went directly to Hughes for help, since it appeared that the only comprehensive set of skills resided there. Contractor selection in development competitions was usually made on the same basis: the buyer chose the only bidder he believed would meet all the requirements in a timely manner. Hughes could focus on winning against only a very few other firms: in missiles, Raytheon; radars, Westinghouse; spacecraft, TRW and Lockheed; command and control, IBM and Raytheon. Production contracts often were granted as sole-source to the developer, but sometimes were competed on a price basis.

Sunday, December 20, 1981   Los Angeles Times

'Cadillac' of Defense Contractors Purrs Along

Hughes Aircraft Posts Rising Backlog, Sales

By RALPH VARTABEDIAN, *Times Staff Writer*

When Defense Secretary Caspar Weinberger recently terminated the Roland anti-aircraft missile program at Hughes Aircraft Co., he wiped out an estimated $238 million in business at the Culver City-based defense firm.

Yet the phase-out of the Army program did little to mar the company's bright business outlook as a leading supplier of military radar, communications and missile systems.

Hughes Aircraft has become so large and diverse—no single program accounts for more than 5% of sales—that it is virtually immune to a disaster from any single contract cancellation, Hughes Chairman Allen Puckett said in a recent interview.

State's Top Employer

As one of the nation's largest private corporations, Hughes Aircraft has grown in recent years into the Pentagon's leading defense electronics supplier and the seventh-largest overall military contractor. In the process, it has become California's largest manufacturing employer with 54,000 employees in the state.

The company, which recorded sales of $2.61 billion in 1980, is a far cry from the relatively small electronics division that Howard Hughes separated from his empire in 1953 under pressure from the Pentagon and transferred to the Howard Hughes Medical Institute. The secretive, nonprofit institute still wholly owns Hughes Aircraft, although the institute may soon be forced to divest itself of a portion of the defense firm. Headquartered in Coconut Grove, Fla., it operates medical research programs in about a dozen university hospitals

some congressional observers say it is gaining a reputation for doing expensive work.

"Buying a product from Hughes is more like buying a Cadillac than a Volkswagen," says a House Armed Services Committee aide. "But you get what you pay for."

"Hughes has a corner on the radar market," he adds. "They are the top in military systems. They are expensive, but they are a first-rate operation. Their radars on the F-18, the F-15 and the F-14 are as good as any radar in the world today. There aren't too many engineering houses capable of doing that kind of work."

The company's reputation and relations with the Defense Department have improved dramatically since the World War II era when, under Howard Hughes' ownership and control, the company embarked on the disastrous XF-11 and flying boat (popularly known as the Spruce Goose) programs.

The two projects are widely judged as technical failures. Of the two XF-IIs completed by the company, one crashed in Beverly Hills during a test flight with Howard Hughes at the controls. Hughes sustained a crushed lung, extensive bruises and seven broken ribs, among other cuts and broken bones. The other XF-II was turned over to the Air Force, and later scrapped. The flying boat was mothballed after only one brief flight by Hughes and remains a curiosity of aviation. It is now being prepared as a tourist attraction in Long Beach.

The Hughes performance on the two projects, coupled with longstanding Pentagon objections to the use of laminated plywood in constructing the aircraft, ultimately led to a Senate investigation of alleged influence buying in the Pentagon by the Hughes organization. No action against Hughes ever resulted from the investigation, however.

After those bitter setbacks to Hughes' goal of becoming an aircraft manufacturer, his attention turned to different interests and the company began to prosper in the new area of military electronics.

Hughes Aircraft at a Glance

The company has provided advanced antenna technology on Intelsat satellites as well as beginning operations with two new types of satellites.

Work is under way to develop 'smarter' weapons and Hughes has won a $421-million contract for an advanced air-to-air missile.

Appraisal of Hughes Aircraft Company, 1981
(courtesy of *Los Angeles Times*)

Following a discussion of the company's response to the emergence of large-scale production, this Part describes the successful product lines in computers and command and control systems. It concludes with details of five significant operating problems that Hughes experienced.

36

THE COMPANY'S
BUSINESS BOOMS

THE BOOM YEARS from the early 1970s to the late 1980s were good ones for Hughes. The company blossomed from 30,000 employees in 1971 with $770 million annual sales to 84,000 employees and over $10 billion annual sales in 1986. Business diversity provided stability: Hughes products could be found in virtually all branches of electronics, and annual revenue dependence on any single product did not exceed 5 percent of the total; the top ten amounted to only 40 percent. The company became the preeminent US military electronics supplier, had the highest employee count of any firm in California and in Arizona, and in terms of sales and staff, ranked as the seventh largest US defense contractor.

In 1976, Howard Hughes passed away while in flight from Mexico to Texas. As previously mentioned, Mr. Hughes had had little effect on company operations since 1953, and few personal ties remained with any of the senior executives.

By the 1980s, with 22,000 scientists and engineers, most holding graduate degrees, including 4,000 of these with PhDs, there was a wealth of talent to meet any need. Emerging concepts from any source could usually be nurtured into a new product or an improvement of an existing system. This golden inventory of creativity was approximately evenly distributed among the seven major product line organizations.

Reciprocal sharing of expertise was an innate characteristic of every manager. If a program staff lacked a particular technical skill or temporarily needed extra staff, loans or transfers of the appropriate talents quickly solved the shortfall. When an organization lacked experience in a new sub-element of its product line, experts resident elsewhere would

When the company fully matured, it consisted of seven major product line organizations reporting to corporate. Each group, staffed with about 14,000 employees (Ground Systems Group reached 17,500 employees), had full capability to develop and manufacture its particular type of equipment. It carried the title of "Systems Group," and was also identified by its products. The groups were usually referred to by their initials: EDSG (Electrooptical and Data Systems Group), GSG (Ground Systems Group), IEG (Industrial Electronics Group), MSG (Missile Systems Group), RSG (Radar Systems Group), S&CG (Space and Communications Group), and SSG (Support Systems Group).

act as consultants or as temporary performers until enough expertise was established.

For example, when a Group with sonar experience once won an advanced torpedo program, the guidance design talent was loaned by the missile product line organization. Similarly, infrared talent from that electrooptical sector assisted the missile group in introducing new IR sensors into their weapon product line.

Adding More Workplaces

In these boom years, Hughes employment, especially in manufacturing, increased dramatically, requiring a large expansion of facilities (see the time-line chart, Fig. 9.1, at the end of the book for growth in personnel and sales). Selecting the right locations for new sites was not easy. Detailed analysis of many conflicting factors was necessary as was balancing those factors: cost of real estate, building construction and maintenance expenses, availability of skilled labor, prevalent wage rates, ease of communications between the engineering and manufacturing sites, and political support of a new enterprise in a specific region, as well as the need for direct foreign personnel participation in overseas contracts. Also, rental or lease of a site might be preferable depending on the expected duration of the manufacturing phase. By 1976, as part of its expansion, the company had established thirty-two subsidiary firms and twelve operating affiliates.

Radar Engineering Building Construction Next to Space
and Communications Group, El Segundo, California, 1978
(courtesy of UNLV)

Growth in the engineering staff by the late 1970s was accommodated by installing more than fifty large office trailers between the older buildings at the Culver City home base, coupled with some expansion into rental buildings in nearby Westchester. The trailer solution arose from the "no new buildings" restrictions in the Hughes Tool Company property lease. Finally, in late 1978, Radar Systems Group engineering moved into a new company-invested twelve-story building next to its production facility in nearby El Segundo, which had begun operations in 1955.

Also in the late 1970s, a mile south of Los Angeles International Airport, the company built a gigantic and costly campus, called El Segundo South, for its electrooptical product line's 12,000 development and production employees. A complex of four-story buildings, with panoramic views of the South Bay cities that are part of the greater Los Angeles basin, it featured underground trucking deliveries as well as decorative ponds and gardens—very first class. Full-capability facilities were also established in nearby California cities: Carlsbad, Rancho Cucamonga, Irvine, Newport Beach, Ontario, San Diego, San Dimas, Santa Margarita, Santa Maria, Sylmar, and Torrance, as well as in twelve other states. We constructed new Hughes-owned buildings in Tucson, Arizona(the others there had always been leased from Hughes Tool or the government), and continued trying to lure the Canoga Park engineering contingent there for an eventual completely integrated Missile Systems Group in Tucson. By 1980, the company occupied 22 million square feet of space, which increased another 10 million square feet in the next five years. To fund all this construction, management budgeted $1 billion for capital investment for the following five years and another $1 billion by 1986.

As noted above, much of the expansion was in Southern California. The cities' names came from the historic past, but it was astonishing to read in 2004 of a move by the ACLU (American Civil Liberties Union) to force California to change the names of many cities, based on the possibility that there was an improper religious connotation. Those communities were established in the eighteenth and nineteenth centuries by the Spanish or the Mexicans, and in those days there was indeed a deeply religious intent. It seems completely silly to think that the town name applied any religious pressure upon the current residents. How grievous it would have been to forever lose the mellifluous sounds of places like San Juan Capistrano, La Purissima, San Fernando, San Luis Obispo, Sacramento, San Buenaventura, and Santa Ynez. Fortunately, the ACLU did not prevail in the court hearing.

The largest of the thirteen out-of-state plant sites were in Eufaula, Alabama, La Grange, Georgia, Forrest, Mississippi, and Orangeburg, South Carolina; these were all fully equipped for sophisticated electronics manufacturing. Principal offshore centers capable of design and production were established in Canada, Scotland, and England. There also were three subassembly plants in Mexico defined as *maquiladoras*. These facilities were especially advantageous because of their very low labor costs, high product quality, and excellent workers, not to mention our amicable relationship with a nation that became a viable market for satellite sales. Additionally, Hughes placed about 250 engineering support personnel in Iran for two years in the 1970s to help its military personnel operate and maintain the weapon system and missiles for eighty Iranian F-14 *Tomcats*. Similar duties were performed by nearly 1,000 employees assigned in the 1990s to Saudi Arabia to support Peace Shield (described below).

In the early 1980s, corporate headquarters relocated to a leased high-rise office building in El Segundo, south of Los Angeles Airport, while construction began on a new headquarters on a hillside overlooking the old Culver City complex. This lavish four-story building featured complete underground parking and a central atrium open to all floors; half the offices were able to enjoy views of the Marina del Rey yacht basin with its 6,000 leisure craft. Senior officers and staff organizations moved there in 1984, but after Raytheon purchased a large part of Hughes in 1997, the building was sold and became part of the adjacent Loyola Marymount University.

Executive Offices, Culver City, California, 1990
(courtesy of UNLV)

37

LARGE-SCALE PRODUCTION

F ROM ITS BEGINNINGS as a large-scale producer of airborne radars and guided missiles in the late 1940s, Hughes sought to employ the most modern and effective manufacturing methods. Ray Parkhurst, an experienced production manager, led the setup of needed staff, facilities, and operating procedures at Culver City, initially for radars, then for missile production. By 1949, compared to previous manufacturers, Hughes had greatly improved the efficiency of planning the high-speed, high rate production of military electronics. The procedure was to divide the total process into stages and analyze the equipment and workforce size required, so that the elapsed times for each stage would be identical with all the others, ensuring an even and consistent flow down the line.

In 1951, John Black did the same excellent job of establishing a smooth-flowing production facility at the new missile plant in Tucson, as did Harper Brubaker in Fullerton in the mid-1960s, when Hughes began making large, heavy ship- and ground-based electronic systems. These manufacturing organizations had considerable management authority, with corporate executives pressuring the engineering design managers to place high priority on solving design-related difficulties discovered on the factory floor. Nonetheless, the inherent laboratory-like practices remained: creative engineers doing their initial design with little interest in, or knowledge of, the most productive ways to ensure easy, reliable, repeatable, and low cost manufacturing. This regrettable condition persisted into the mid-1950s until Pat Hyland, as he revealed in his autobiography, *Call Me Pat*, modified those erroneous engineering attitudes within a year, and far more producible designs emerged.

At Hughes, as in most firms producing tangible products, manufacturing is the key to business and financial success: it's the best source of earnings, customer satisfaction, and enhancement of one's reputation for future sales. In designing its production facilities, the company thought through many important considerations to ensure an organization that would yield low cost and high reliability devices on a predetermined schedule. Achieving this was particularly difficult when those devices were very complex, required extreme precision in their production, and might never have previously been manufactured anywhere. Such high-technology manufacturing particularly needs willing cooperation between design engineers and production personnel. Open ears and a willingness to adopt ideas from persons with differing skills can overcome many obstacles to achieving a producible product.

By 1973, Pat was well satisfied with the company's progress, as he commented in the *HughesNews*:

> "Hughes has long been recognized and respected for engineering expertise, and now manufacturing has moved into the same area. Simply stated, what we build works.
>
> "Regardless of what aspect you look at, you will find outstanding performance. This reflects the synergistic attitude we have where the total effect of our cooperative efforts is greater that the sum of our organizations working independently."

A fine example of design and manufacturing teamwork was finding a way to efficiently and correctly make the intricate center panel for a planar array antenna used in the F-14, F-15, and F/A-18 radars. A perfectly flat, 36-inch diameter aluminum sheet, less than 1/2 inch thick, had to be pierced with hundreds of cavities interconnected by channels cut into the surface. In turn, the cavities, 1/2- by 1/4-inch rectangles, had to be precisely shaped with absolutely square corners and placed with accuracies of one-thousandth of an inch. The outer veneer for the array also needed hundreds of precise rectangular openings matched in position to the inner panel cavities. The shape and sizes had to match exactly the electromagnetic wavelength of the radar's operating frequency. After a year of struggle (and quite a few animated disputes) the manufacturing staff, working with the design team, created a unique milling machine controlled by a computer to do this tough job in a low-cost, repetitive manner with accuracy better than the levels specified for product acceptance.

The best way to effectively transition from something defined on paper to the reality in production was to incorporate a preproduction "practice" stage in the program master schedule. One example of such a transition was that of a new infrared sensor system, a very complex mechanical, optical, electronic creation using exotic materials and requiring tricky fabrication and assembly techniques. For a year, overlapping the final prototype proof testing, a large team, half design folks and half with manufacturing skills, pored over the configuration details. They were empowered to alter designs slightly, invent new production processes, carefully outline operator instructional documents, define the timing sequence for information transfer, and conceive short-cut corrections if things went wrong on the floor. Test runs of fabrication and assembly processes refined their reliability and repeatability. As a result, full production experienced little difficulty, met schedules, and even achieved lower cost than anticipated.

That team effort proved a worthwhile investment. It avoided what often happens in similar situations: confrontation between advocates of either design or production camps. Even with a referee, such behavior breeds festering long-term ill-will, time delays, and higher costs, and even foments pervasive internal political warfare to establish a winner. The better teaming method, with its mutual understanding and communication methods, also helps the manufacturing staff respond rapidly and flexibly to the inevitable flood of future design changes that always occur in the development of leading-edge devices. Changes arise from incorporating remedies to problems discovered in further testing, reliability or producibilty improvements, field-use experience, and customer-desired performance improvements.

Once the product design is understood, a crucial manufacturing staff decision is whether individual parts or subassemblies should be made internally or bought from a qualified supplier. This decision hinges on the internal capability, the suppliers' reputations (they may already be the experts in making a particular component), the critical importance of each part in meeting the final product requirements, the quantities and delivery rates, the expected duration of need for the particular component (it might soon be eliminated by a probable redesign), the cost, the reliability, and the customer's preference for how much of the total work should be subcontracted.

It is important to establish and nourish effective, cooperative relations with many firms in the supplier base. When involved early in the design, subcontractors and suppliers can recommend alterations to match their capabilities or to lower cost. In the subsequent purchasing phase, many cost and quality upgrades can arise from such a relationship, as well as positively motivating the supplier to meet schedule and quality commitments.

What always made for lowest unit price was a contract for a multi-year purchase, but this was usually precluded by highly political government financial rules. The DoD, CIA, and NASA purchases were normally only year to year, being constrained by the uncertainties of annual budget squabbles with Congress. (I always thought this was crazy, since the government would clearly gain a cost benefit if multi-year commitments were permitted.)

A strategic decision was which manufacturing labor source should be used for each product. The choice depended on the necessary skills, worker availability, and labor wages. Sometimes government security rules limited the workforce locations; otherwise, several options were possible: use the home factory, set up in another state, establish an out-of-country source, or subcontract to a worthy supplier. Hughes selected among all these options to produce its many diverse product lines.

Smooth, reliable, and low cost manufacturing requires controllable processes, repetitive task sequencing, and adherence to safety and government-imposed standards. All process steps must be clearly defined and stated in terms understandable to the trained operators. Results of each procedure must be measured, recorded, and analyzed to ensure adequate yields. In the 1950s, the highest production rates at Hughes were to be found in missile manufacturing in Tucson. Yield charts were updated and displayed throughout the working floor to provide employee awareness; with this public visibility, individuals and teammates were highly motivated to improve their performance and to recommend changes to the task procedures being used. Follow-up actions to remedy flaws were well documented, studied, and used to alter the low-yield step. Most costly was rejection and discard of large quantities of "one-shot" devices, such as the tracking xenon lamp to be installed in the TOW missile's tail (see Part Seven). Fifty of each group of 5,000 were tested; if more than one did not operate, the entire lot was discarded.

Compliance with voluminous customer-imposed standards, specifications, and contract terms needed continuous attention and care. In spite of careful monitoring of all production processes, Hughes Tucson got in big trouble on the little things in the 1984 "Missile Quality" fiasco, described below. In all other Hughes manufacturing facilities, and certainly in Tucson after the 1984 difficulties, long-term high-quantity and excellent product performance earned high marks from all customers.

The high motivation of employees to doing our job for the nation was made dramatically evident during the first Gulf War in 1991. The manufacturing workforce in Eufaula, Alabama, became aware of a shortage of rail launchers that attach the Maverick missile (see Part Seven) to various strike aircraft. Most of them volunteered to work twelve hours a day without overtime pay for many weeks to double production output quantities. Management had to lock the doors on Saturday nights to prevent excessive wear and tear on the participants. Here was a location remote from the company's center that set working standards far above normal. Of course, they did this not wholly because they worked for Hughes, but also from a strong desire to contribute to a high priority objective of the United States. Whatever the cause, the deed illustrates the type of dedicated employees who were attracted to the firm.

38

TECHNOLOGIES
SWEEP ON

Not only did the manufacturing business blossom and prosper, but also the management and creative staff eagerly pushed forward on many technology fronts. Hughes captured more than 80 percent of the competitive bids it made in the 1980s. Parts Five through Eight describe many enormously important product lines, each of which could have been the proud output of a single high-technology corporation: global communications, command and control equipment, precision sensors, and top secret projects. Each product line was extremely complex in terms of what needed to be created to satisfy difficult missions, as well as in the business strategies and tactics needed to secure a place in the market.

The company's leap forward was well summarized in 2008 by former CEO Bud Wheelon:

> "The success of Hughes Aircraft Company arose primarily from individual initiative, and the interactions among many creative people. This accomplished far more progress than could have been done by central planning and iron control. Pat Hyland loosened the reins and let the staff make mistakes. It was a lot like a university laboratory: challenge and encourage each other to do exciting things. There was a large market for those achievements in satisfying US and foreign military needs. Few other companies were willing to try this complex type of business. The difficult tasks could only be done by Hughes. Our team was almost unique in working the leading edge of technology."

39

COMPUTERS
AT THE HEART

MOST OF MILITARY and civilian life now depends on the computer and its software. Readers may care to know what they are, how they operate, and how they function as the heart of modern military systems, including those developed by Hughes.

When we see the word "computer" today, what usually comes to mind is the personal computer residing on many desks, or the laptop carried by a business traveler. However, almost all of the computers that serve us are not so visible. There are electronic computers within cell phones, toys, iPhones and Blackberries, wristwatches, and home appliances. An automobile may incorporate dozens of computers, an aircraft hundreds, and a military or space system thousands.

A computer is a machine that manipulates data according to a set of instructions. Mechanical devices that do this date back to the Antikythera mechanism, an astronomical calculating device made by a Greek philosopher about 100 BC. More recent mechanical computers include the nineteenth-century Jacquard loom and the early World War II Norden bombsight.

The rapid modern development of computers began in the 1940s. Early devices whose behavior could be altered by inserting instruction changes include the 1941 German electromechanical Zuse Z3 and the 1944 British all-electronic Colossus Mark 1. However, the first fully programmable electronic computer, and the best publicized, was the US ENIAC (electronic numerical integrator and computer) designed at the University of Pennsylvania under a 1943 secret contract with the US Army. After its public revelation in 1946, news media colorfully proclaimed it the "Giant

Brain." Fashioned from 17,468 vacuum tubes and many thousands of individual resistors, capacitors, inductors, and transformers, it occupied two large rooms full of tall equipment racks. It could perform 5,000 additions or 385 multiplications per second. It had no separate memory, and could store only twenty 10-digit decimal numbers within its circuitry.

Later generations of computers rapidly improved speed, memory capacity, and number of functions performed simultaneously. Advances included great reductions in computational errors, less power consumed and heat generated, and improved reliability and life. Sizes shrank an astonishing degree. Large vacuum tubes were replaced by miniatures, then by solid-state transistors, and eventually by tiny wafers containing thousands of interconnected components, known as integrated circuits. Memories progressed from many vacuum-tube storage rings through spinning magnetic drums to magnetic cells infused on tiny paper-thin wafers as well as laser discs. What had taken two huge laboratory rooms in 1946 became the size of a half-slice of bread by 1995 with several million times more memory, and operating speeds jumped from hundreds to billions of computations per second.

Today, a computer generally includes a storage memory, an active temporary working memory, an information processor, and a set of preplanned operating instructions called a program. In addition, there are input-output connections that bring instructions and data into the computer and that make the results of its calculations available for display or use elsewhere.

Computers can accept and process a great variety of information, including words, images, tables of data, streams of signals from sensors, and countless equations. All of these are translated into sets of numbers, which can then be mathematically processed according to the instructions in the computer program. For example, an image may be encoded as a set of numbers that represent its shape, its brightness, and the color of each of the millions of picture elements that make up the image. A military application could then insert instructions for the computer to analyze the image details looking for objects that resemble specific shapes, such as buildings, vehicles, or aircraft. Similarly, a list of military targets might be stored in the memory as the latitude and longitude of each object, plus numbers that identify its important characteristics. These detailed data could be used to direct a missile toward a high-priority target.

Computering at Hughes

Hughes was very active in this rapidly advancing technology, creating the world's first airborne digital computer in the late 1950s. Regrettably, senior management decided not to enter the consumer market—who knows what would have happened had we tried.

In 1953, the company received a study contract from the Army to design a method for managing and controlling regional air defense networks containing Nike and Hawk surface-to-air missiles. This C&C (command and control) project, described below, led the company to become the foremost supplier of ground- and ship-based military computing and display devices. Initially, large capacity central control computers were packaged into drawers mounted in vertical racks; peripheral modular machines were configured into mobile containers about the size of an office desk. In the first configurations, electronic components were mounted on etched circuit boards that plugged into wired interconnections to form the complete device. Most of those for Navy ships were fully incorporated within the operator display consoles.

By 1970, as microelectronic miniaturization progressed, digital computers of various sizes and performance levels were included in virtually every product designed by Hughes. While at the forefront of designing and fabricating the hardware of high-performance military computers, the company also excelled at preparing the complex instructional software to manage massive amounts of rapidly changing combat data streams. These data were assembled and correlated with battlefield situations and presented to highly stressed combat operators in a fully understandable manner.

Signal Processing or Data Processing

Military and space systems frequently employ the terms "signal processing" and "data processing." Signal processing deals with interpreting incoming sensor data streams to determine their detailed physical meaning, such as an analysis to understand the structural behavior of an airborne target by examining the fine structure of its radar echoes. These sensor data streams were originally in analog format, gradually varying in content, and complicated in their technical structure; signal processors would contain functions tailored to a specific characteristic of signals coming from a particular sensor. In today's designs, sensor data are immediately converted to digital numbers, and a very specialized digital computer performs the signal analysis. A sample can even be stored for repeated examination.

General-purpose computers used in C&C systems perform what is called data processing. They make sense of a very broad range of information, including outputs from many signal processors and data files containing maps, missile capabilities, and expected target characteristics. This information is typically in sets of digital numbers. The gradually varying sensor signals have already been processed into numbers describing the size, shape, location, and motion of each identified target. The C&C computer then assembles these data streams into an overall battle scene, coupled with missile battery positions and intercept zones, all of this overlaid on terrain maps for comprehensive display on an operator's console.

In summary, a signal processor takes direct inputs from sensors and uses a special purpose computer to analyze the electronic material in real time, converting the sensor signals into digital outputs that describe target characteristics. Data processing combines the digital outputs from many sensors and from other sources, not always in real time, to provide a broad-based view of an entire battle scene.

Computers Think Binary

The ENIAC used our familiar "base-ten" (decimal) number system, with the ten digits from 0 to 9. Each digit was stored in a "ring counter" built from thirty-six vacuum tubes that could switch between two stable states. Each tube represented one of the digits from 0 through 9.

This method eventually made ENIAC an exception. Other early computers and almost all computers today use a "base-two" (binary) number system, in which numbers can be represented using only the digits 0 and 1. These symbols are often called bits, which is shorthand for binary digits.

To illustrate the differences, consider a number such as 185. In the decimal system, 185 means one group of 100, plus eight groups of 10, plus five groups of 1. Thus, each digit stands for ten times as many objects as the digit located to its right.

A binary system represents the same group of objects by 10111001, which means one group of 128, plus no groups of 64, plus one group of 32, plus one group of 16, plus one group of 8, plus no groups of 4, plus no groups of 2, plus one group of 1.

Thus, in a binary number, each digit stands for only two times as many objects as the digit to its right. Check that 185 (decimal) equals 10111001 (binary) by adding up the numbers: 100 + 80 + 5 = 128 + 32 + 16 + 8 + 1.

Why would we want to write down a string of eight digits when only three will do? Because when you use an electronic circuit to store a number, the circuit that uses the fewest components is the "flip-flop" circuit, which has two stable states. These two states may be used to represent the digits 0 and 1. The ENIAC used ten vacuum tubes to store the numbers from 0 to 9, but the same ten vacuum tubes could have stored binary numbers from 0000000000 to 1111111111, which in decimal notation cover from 0 to 1,023, more than one hundred times as much memory storage! Thus, almost every computer today finds it more efficient to store and manipulate numbers in binary notation.

Although binary notation is great for computers, it takes a lot of room on the page if it's printed, and it is difficult for a person to work with long strings of ones and zeros. As a remedy, two shorthand methods have been perfected: octal (base-eight) and hexadecimal (base-sixteen). Interested readers are encouraged to look elsewhere for a detailed description of these techniques.

Software Runs the Machine

Early computers had their operating instructions installed by physically wired connections between circuit assemblies, called hard-wired programming. By the mid-1960s, operating instructions were inserted by "software," in which numbered behavior codes are entered into the storage memory only as electrical pulses. This new approach was a design bonanza, almost unlimited in the amount of complexity that could be handled, and permitting much more flexibility, since instructions could easily be altered. Quick changes can be implemented to attain better end results or adapt to new external conditions or changes in the mission.

For example, imagine that you are writing computer instructions that will navigate an automobile through a small village. You might study a map of the village and find that there are five streets that transit the community, and one of these is obviously the shortest. Before 1959, a designer would place a hard-wire connection in the electronic circuit that would instruct the automobile to follow this chosen short route. All works fine until a surprising permanent roadblock occurs; a car can no longer cross the village on this path! The computer's wire connections must be physically reconnected to match an alternate roadway. This is very expensive, especially if many models of this computer have been distributed to widely spread users.

After software programming became feasible, alterations of this type became easy: one solution was to program all possible roadways into the computer memory and ask it to automatically re-choose a route if the driver tells it about the roadblock limitation. Another method was to revise the master program to use the new route and release a mobile memory device or electronically relay the revised software to all that family of computers to be installed into their storage memories. Instantly, all those machines would now guide the auto along the corrected route through town.

Today, most computer programs are stored in the memory as software. Hard-wired programming continues only at the most fundamental level within the machine. Examples are circuits designed to repeatedly perform a single storing or retrieving of a number, adding or multiplying two numbers, or efficiently digitizing the output from a particular sensor. Hard-wiring programs in specialized circuits for simple standard functions, and placing all other operations under software control, enable computer designers to achieve a combination of broad flexibility and rapid computation.

Creating Software

Designing the computer's brainwork involves several procedural steps, and is usually put together by engineers well trained in mathematics. Following the customer's specifications for required performance, the first step is to create the overall architecture defining a layout of sequences and manipulations to produce the desired results. Somewhat like a company organization chart, minor computations are combined with several similar calculations, this aggregation is married with another summary, and then on upward to a final conclusion. With an agile computer, many clusters can be independently computed at the same time. For example, different parts of the computer hardware might simultaneously track each of three targets, matching them to identification codes, and finding under these conditions the proper launch range of a variety of available missile batteries.

The second software design task is to select a programming language, that is, the format or writing style for the content; this is similar to deciding to write a book in English, Farsi, Sanskrit, or Japanese. This selection will ensure that all parts of the software program will be understood by this computer and its sisters, as they proceed through their architecturally determined operations. The earliest electronic computers were programmed in "machine language"; a single binary number is used to instruct the computer to execute a simple step such as storing a number in a particular location. This was quickly replaced by "assembly languages," in which easy-to-remember abbreviations signify each instruction.

After the entire list of instructions has been completed, a special process called an assembler translates the abbreviations into the machine language of zeros and ones. Modern computer programming uses many types of "higher level" languages, in which a single command may represent a long sequence of machine instructions; a program called a compiler converts each high-level instruction into machine-readable binary numbers.

The next jobs are to analyze what needs to be computed using mathematical equations and to decide what will be performed automatically or be assisted by an operator's interaction. Computations that are to be done repeatedly are placed into software packets labeled with a specific access address. For example, a target data stream sent from a radar processor will always be sent to a "track" packet, where the sequential progression of location changes and speeds is calculated and converted into a vector line for passing to an operator's display to show that target's course, speed, and altitude.

Finally, the mathematical equations are translated into a set of step-by-step instructions that will be stored in the computer's memory. Each instruction, after compiling and assembly, becomes a list of binary numbers. The computer will read each instruction, execute the appropriate operations, and then proceed to the next instruction. Most programs also include self-verification procedures to double-check the results.

Before the software is installed into the computer hardware, extensive validation testing must be successfully completed in a surrogate computer. Responsible programming efforts never end: during the computer's lifetime; software engineers provide the customer with continuous field support to train new operators, solve problems as they occur, and supply performance upgrades in response to changing requirements.

Softwaring at Hughes

Because of the nature of the software-intensive systems produced at Hughes, design emphasis was on computational methods, operating speed, and number of instructions. Program designers teamed with system engineers to fully define the functional requirements assigned to software, including operator-to-machine interactions, sequencing protocols, and overall system architecture. This interactive work balanced requirements with design alternatives. The limitations of available computer resources had to be determined because they affected the choice of software architecture and the selection of a programming language.

In the 1960s, with limited processing and memory in computers, most programming was done in a language peculiar to that project or in a specialized machine code. If a complete radar control function or automated tracking system was being programmed in a 16,000-word computer, this level of coding was the only feasible method. As computers became more robust with larger memory capacity and faster operating speeds, more sophisticated programming languages could be used, increasing the productivity of all software designers.

Complex functional requirements could be met with high-level software architecture. Discrete packages of the software structure were allocated for design to separate teams in the responsible organizations. Frequent reviews by experts discovered design problems as early as possible. The software development plan also defined the testing methods to be used at each stage of design.

The software effort was synchronized with the overall system test plan and special project needs such as providing early customer operator training. In-plant and field acceptance testing verified the software design. Lessons learned from late deliveries or excessive code reworks helped refine the entire process, and many years of practice fostered early problem resolution and project success, all of which ultimately gave Hughes a strongly positive global reputation for creating effective military software.

A fine example was the software development for Peace Shield (a complex air-defense project for Saudi Arabia, described below), which contained more than 1.2 million lines of code and was delivered six months early, exceeding all expectations. Design discipline had required weekly progress reviews, providing continual view of critical path status and immediate corrective action. The software processes we used were formally rated as a top-of-the-scale five by the US Software Engineering Institute.

NADGE/AEGIS Command Center Antenna in Turkey
(courtesy of UNLV)

40

COMMAND AND CONTROL

DURING WORLD WAR II, command and control (C&C) designated an integrated network of systems providing information to a commander for situational awareness and tactical responses. In the 1960s, command, control, and communications, or C3, added messaging links to assimilate information from a variety of sources, display current data with historical information, and relay a commander's combat responses. As computers became robust, much of the work was done automatically, and the moniker became C4, or command, control, communications, and computers. This C4 further expanded to include intelligence, then surveillance and reconnaissance, becoming C4ISR. An amazing current C4ISR enables a Predator drone controlled by an operator located in the United States to carry out an attack on a real-time threat on the other side of the globe!

A capable system must provide planning, effect target detection, make comparisons with historic data, recommend actions, assist in prompt engagement, and assess and correct results. The job is to exploit all available resources and bring order out of chaos to ensure mission success.

A well-informed commander can alter the future by rapidly communicating orders to activate widely distributed combat assets, delegate authority to lower command levels, and relay all information to regional sector commanders.

Top commanders must deal with crises, combat losses, fragile logistics, dynamic intelligence, and political constraints; then allocate and conserve resources, interact with other services, and forward intended actions. An effective C&C system is a vital tool to help manage this mass of interlocking demands.

The C&C system depends on adequate data gathering. Sensor devices that capture dynamic target and background information are usually not counted as part of C&C project equipment. Hughes was very active in providing sensors (described elsewhere in this book), supplying devices that functioned throughout the electromagnetic spectrum—visual optics, laser and infrared sensors, radars operating in several different frequency bands, crypto-secure radio links, and electromagnetic listening equipment, as well as sonar and atmospheric audio detectors.

Sensors for large-scale C&C programs present the system with an almost unlimited maze of thousands of objects. Important data must be identified and sorted from that hodgepodge, then be assembled and displayed to an operator in an understandable form; a field commander can then make the best decisions on deployment of friendly forces. The C&C systems can also show the status of all assets, including ammunition, fuel, troop reserves, and support units; even food inventories and available shelter can be displayed. In some situations, a computer can automatically make critical activity decisions, with a human controller having override authority.

The growing threat of the Soviet empire in the 1950s created a corresponding urgency in the United States to develop effective air defense systems. This situation prompted Hughes to invest significant internal funds in new technologies to prepare for future C&C competitions. One focus was to adapt a logic rationale that had been used to manage the dynamic positioning of Air Force fighter intercepts. These software equations, called modified close-control, had very successfully steered fighters to the optimum position for weapon engagement and thus had enabled accurate control of aircraft and missiles from ground-based systems. Several key people, expert in airborne radars, temporarily transferred to the C&C program offices in the Ground Systems Group to help adapt the modified close-control equations to C&C applications—a good example of the company's willingness to share unique skills across organizational boundaries.

The first C&C contract at Hughes, won in 1955, was a study and feasibility demonstration project from the Army. The effort incorporated that new software technique and resulted in our winning the MSG-4 Missile Monitor program, which became the foundation for a long series of substantial programs with the general designator ADGE (air defense ground environment).

Another company investment was in the major hardware building blocks comprising C&C networks: robust computers with complex software, effective operator displays, and secure communication devices. Nurtured by the company's continual technology advances in these four areas, supplemented by dedicated investments in three-dimensional radar systems, Hughes became dominant in C&C systems, particularly for the air defense of many nations. The company's skills in complex system engineering and software design became the key elements in competitive wins. The company also established a user-oriented training and logistic support organization that assured long-term customer satisfaction. Over a thirty-five-year period, Hughes delivered over forty systems ranging in complexity from a single sensor integration center to large systems that continuously inter-netted several countries. These installations were a major deterrent in countering the worldwide aerial attack threat from 1960 to 1995.

Failing to Tie
Tri-Service Together

By 1960, the DoD urgently needed a comprehensive communication and information exchange network to provide situation awareness for multi-Service battle groups in joint battle actions. The resulting project was appropriately named JTIDS (joint tactical information distribution system). The mission was to provide senior commanders in a combat region a comprehensive overview of the real-time locations and actions of all submarines, surface ships, aircraft, tanks, missile batteries, artillery pieces, and personnel groups. Other senior commanders would also be provided with displays showing activities in the sum of several combat regions. Mandatory performance requirements included accurately locating all participants, positively identifying them, and transferring battle commands; in addition, the data streams had to be invulnerable to enemy interception or jamming. Hughes won a very ambitious Navy-directed fixed-price contract to develop an airborne system for this mission. Long-range L-band, 1.2 to 2.0 gHz, was chosen for communication link operating frequencies; individual messages would be encrypted and spread over the entire frequency band. All messages were combined to use a common link data stream. Message sorting was done by time-shared multiplexing, described in Part Seven.

This task was especially complicated by the attempt to accommodate the very diverse technology types used in Army, Navy (including Marines), and Air Force communication links. The volume of data to be captured, analyzed, and displayed was massive and fast moving. After more than two years of intensive effort and considerable expenditure of Hughes funds, the Navy cancelled the project. The technologies that would have enabled mechanizing the tough JTIDS demands were too immature during the project's short life; the digital devices, random access memories, and component microminiaturization had not yet emerged as realities.

The same "JTIDS" designator was used a decade later for a program that was awarded to Singer-Kearfott in 1981. The needed component technologies appeared to have matured, but agonizing development difficulties delayed successful deployment for another eleven years.

Command and Control Project Details

Other than the JTIDS misfortune, a series of company C&C projects were developed, produced, and deployed, including the Army's afore-mentioned MSG-4 Missile Monitor, a mobile fire distribution project for managing the Nike and Hawk surface-to-air intercept missiles planned for overseas deployments. The equipment—the first three-dimensional surveillance radar bought by the Army (see Part Five); a radar data processing hub; a weapons monitoring center; and a maintenance shed with test equipment and spare parts—was mounted in four trailer enclosures.

Norwegian Air Defense Missile Launch
(courtesy of UNLV)

The MSG-4 digital computer had a hard-wired program (software was then in its infancy), transistor components, and a magnetic drum memory. Incoming radar target information was analyzed, stored, and processed to allow automatic tracking of up to one hundred targets. An IFF (identification friend or foe) antenna mounted on the main radar captured interrogator responses, which were then computer-matched to target tracks to sort out friendly aircraft. The operators viewed target position, velocity and IFF correlation on six plan view displays and two consoles that showed range and height. A hard-wired link sent track data to the weapons-monitoring center, which housed four operator positions and supporting status boards. Here, operators viewed an overall situation display; the nearest Nike or Hawk battery was automatically or manually matched with each incoming threat track. Handover to the selected battery's launch control system was by an electronic communication link; engagement status was sent back to the weapons-monitoring center.

Missile Monitor was first deployed to US Army units in West Germany in 1958; the second deployment was to South Korea. Each fielded system had two master control stations, both having four distribution centers, each of which controlled eight missile batteries of thirty-two Nikes or sixty-four Hawks. These two systems were in use until the Cold War threat ended in 1989. Table 6.1 outlines C&C programs with an air defense mission that were performed by the company over four decades. These projects served twenty-nine nations and greatly enhanced the free world's military posture. Four of them are described in more detail because of their significance in this important company product line.

FLORIDA Air Defense Network, Switzerland
(courtesy of Wikipedia)

Hughes won Switzerland's FLORIDA procurement in 1965, a very tough technical and political competition against Ferranti, Univac, and Westinghouse. The winning design had a three-dimensional radar, computers, processing to form video images, communication links, display consoles, and extensive operating and supporting software. The Swiss were very demanding in performance details, verification testing, and attention to schedules—all entailing special efforts on Hughes's part to finish the job to their satisfaction. Many different requirements were met, including establishing the first nationwide computer network in Switzerland; creating the real-time overall air situation from multiple reporting sources; integrating multiple voice and data links; managing all the country's air defense resources, including *Mirage* fighters and Bloodhound surface-to-air missiles; providing military air traffic control; and

Figure 6.1. NATO Air Defense by IPG Network

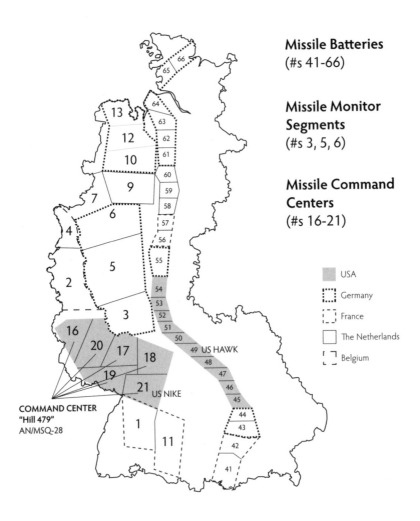

Figure 6.1 shows the air defense coverage provided by the IPG network in the mid-1960s of a segment of NATO with batteries of Nike and Hawk surface-to-air missiles.

Table 6.1. Air Defense C&C Programs

Program	Country	Start	Value	Notable Features
MSG-4	US Army	1953	$20M	First ADGE, mobile trailers; Hughes radars; controlled Nike and Hawk missiles
JBADGE	Japan	1960	$36M	First GP computer-based system linking 22 remote sites
TSQ-51	US Army	1962	$15M	Mobile trailer and radars; controlled Hawk batteries
IPG	Belgium Netherlands W. Germany	1964	$34M	First contract from Europe; integrated 14 sites located in 3 nations
FLORIDA	Switzerland	1965	$30M	Air defense and ATC; total country computer link; Hughes 3D radars
NADGE	14 European countries	1966	$79M	All-NATO coverage; 84 sites, 200 buildings; 14 nations
407L	US Air Force	1967	$59M	First portable system; difficult requirements
Project 657	Israel	1971	$80M	Nationwide air battle management
Combat Grande	Spain	1971	$161M	Advanced Hughes computers and upgraded existing radars
Project 10-1	Taiwan	1976	$161M	Hughes HADR 3D radars in surveillance gaps
JSS	US Canada	1977	$152M	8 centers covered northern approach to North American continent
GEADGE	W. Germany	1979	$162M	AWACS tie-in; Hughes HADR filled gaps
AEGIS	NATO	1979	$361M	NADGE upgrade; AWACs /JTIDS tie-in
Project Crystal	Pakistan	1980	$60M	National air defense
Project 222	Korea	1981	$135M	Data-bus architecture; led to ATC program

Table 6.1 (continued)

Program	Country	Start	Value	Notable Features
MADGE	Malaysia	1981	$116M	Multi-sector system
UKADGE	Great Britain and France	1981	$110M	Tie UK and France into NATO net
NECCCIS	Denmark Norway NATO	1981	$83M	Link Scandinavia into Europe C&C; very complex data streams
BADGE-X	Japan	1982	$95M	Used Japanese commercial computers
Project 776	Egypt	1983	$485M	Integrated radars and missiles made in US, Russia, China, and France
ACDS	US Navy	1984	$41M	First Hughes C&C for Navy; high data rate with new message format
IADS	Iceland	1990	$77M	Replaced JSS with Hughes AWACS Sentry
Other Projects	NATO	20 years	$50M	Updates using Hughes AWACS Sentry system
Peace Shield	Saudi Arabia	1991	$2,500 M	6 comand centers; 17 radar sites; robust communication net; earned large incentive award
PEWS	Kuwait	1991	$92M	Air defense with long-range radar

transmitting air-attack warning alerts to the civilian population. To ensure coverage of the entire country required two command centers with data processing computers, communication links, and thirty-two display consoles. The antennas of the three radars were mounted on elevators within mountain lairs, to be raised for operation or lowered into a secure chamber for environmental protection.

FLORIDA was operated and maintained for more than thirty years by the Swiss military and was replaced in 2000 by the FLORAKO system, developed by a Thales/Raytheon joint venture. (Raytheon's work was done by former Hughes employees after the company acquired Hughes in 1997.)

A quotation in 2009 by Lt. Gen. Walter Dürig, former Commander,

Swiss Air Force, gives an insight into the Swiss view of many years of working with our company:

> "During the long Cold War the Hughes Aircraft Company was an important supplier to the Swiss Air Force and its other military services. Following an intensive competition with European companies in 1961, Hughes supplied the electronics and Falcon armament for our thirty-six *Mirage III* fighters. In the next two decades, the performance of this weapon system was one of the most impressive in Europe, and was in active use until 2003.
>
> "In 1965 Hughes won the FLORIDA program, which included surveillance radars and a command and control system for nationwide air defense. This was the first computer network in Switzerland, and stayed in continuous operation until 2000. It was Europe's most effective air defense and military air traffic control network. The effective and high quality Hughes air-to-ground Maverick armed our *Hawker-Hunter* squadrons from 1982 until the aircraft was decommissioned in 1994. Following these successes many other Hughes products have played vital roles in equipping the Swiss Air Force and Army: F/A-18 *Hornet* radars, air-to-air AMRAAM missiles, combat training devices, TOW-2 antitank weapons, and the night-vision fire control system for our Leopard-2 main battle tanks. These excellent Hughes equipments have more than satisfied the military needs of Switzerland. All programs were completed, occasionally after some project difficulties, to a successful conclusion. The close collaboration between Hughes and the Swiss authorities led to many lasting friendships."

Hughes led a consortium of nine companies to win, in 1966, another European venture called NADGE (NATO air defense ground environment). Fourteen countries were directly involved and funded the coordinated program to expand and link the air defense system resources of nine NATO members: Norway, Denmark, West Germany, the Netherlands, Belgium, France, Italy, Greece, and Turkey. France and Great Britain partially participated in the final system network. Specific design and production segments had to be allocated to each country in proportion to their contribution to total project funding; this added political and business complexity to an already difficult technical challenge. Contract performance requirements were set quite high, since the survival of multiple nations was at stake. Hughes coordinated with Thomson-CSF in France, Marconi in Great Britain, Hollandse Signaalapparaten in the Netherlands, Selenia SPA in Italy, and AEG Telefunken in West Germany, with smaller roles by companies from Greece, Turkey, and Canada. This consortium won the competition over a strong team led by IBM, with Martin and a long list of European firms as members. Although the development program exceeded the original budget, reasonable funding increases were obtained from the participating nations, usually to maintain political honor.

The original NADGE system consisted of eighty-four sites occupying two hundred new buildings in the nine user nations. Hardware included thirty-seven data processing stations, forty command centers, and eighty-four remote sites with search radars. To maximize the use of existing resources, the radars were a mixture of old and new systems built by Marconi, Plessey, Thompson-CSF, and Hughes. By 1973, all sites were successfully activated.

The NADGE system gave the ability to coordinate air and surface weapon responses to any hostile threat. Extensive cross-referencing was done between observation stations in several countries to integrate track data into a composite European air surveillance picture. Radar tracks were sent by data link to the command center for automatic analysis and identification; the central computer managed time history and clutter mapping to minimize signal interference and jamming. IFF responses, pre-filed friendly flight plans, and voice communication assured that the targets identified as hostile were actually so, and the commander could order engagement by fighters or surface-to-air missile batteries.

To capture the mobile 407L air control system in 1967, Hughes had to overcome a tough competition with Litton Industries. The Air Force's role in a joint task force (JTF) mission was to plan, coordinate, direct, and control the resources assigned to tactical air operations. The fixed-price 407L contract contained significant cost and schedule incentives and embodied both development and production elements. The paperwork submitted for the competition was astonishing: 7,293,601 pages weighing 22 tons! This win was based on Hughes's system engineering expertise, unique hardware and software solutions, and laboratory demonstrations that responded to five major technical issues. Of prime importance was proof of our advanced technology computer with very sophisticated mission-related software; additionally helpful was the valid demonstration of our newly developed lightweight digital sweep display console.

The 407L enabled the Air Force to fulfill its role in a JTF mission with a mobile system. Its central command center received airspace

407L Operations Center
(courtesy of UNLV)

target data from the E-3 AWACS (airborne warning and control system) aircraft, other friendly aircraft, and many ground-based radars. A real-time view of a large tactical area was displayed on fourteen operator consoles. An audio and electronic communication network linked this center with other stations and transmitted operating commands to airborne pilots.

Two shelters 40 feet apart and joined by an inflatable overhead cover housed the equipment. This design enabled the system to meet two difficult mobility requirements: (1) setup or teardown in less than three hours; and (2) equipment module size and weight compatible with transport by C-130 *Hercules* aircraft or transport helicopter. Full performance was required in 65 mile per hour winds and temperatures from -65°F to +160°F.

To complete the development phase, Hughes spent $23 million of company funds to cover the overrun of the fixed price contract. Production was authorized in 1972, but our staff members forecast that producing the fourteen systems and two trainers would result in a further loss of more than $20 million. Fortunately, a special manufacturing and engineering team devised new factory processes and procedures, and timely deliveries were made without further financial reversals. Follow-on efforts made this a profitable business; the gains more than offset the development overrun.

One 407L system, sited in Phnom Phanom, Thailand, was used in the Vietnam War as a command center for the seismic and audio detectors placed on the ground looking for movement on the Ho Chi Minh Trail. C-130 *Spectre* gunships were successfully routed to those sites where guerilla movements triggered responses from those sensors (the notable AC-47 *Spooky*, or "Puff the Magic Dragon," was too vulnerable above that trail).

Peace Shield was the comprehensive C&C network for Saudi Arabia, a program, managed by the US Air Force, to provide the capability to plan, coordinate, and control air operations across the entire kingdom. Following a competitive loss to Boeing in 1985, Hughes was awarded the prime contract in 1991 for an impressive $837 million. Boeing's partially completed work had been cancelled in 1990, and the Air Force had granted $10 million feasibility demonstration projects to Univac, Westinghouse, and Hughes. Based on excellent performance in all sectors of the demonstration, Hughes was selected for this enormous project: a fifty-four-month development with a $50 million incentive to deliver three months early. The system was to contain seventeen remote radar sites, five sector command hubs, a centralized command center, and a complex voice and data communication network.

This was a tremendous undertaking: to deliver an integrated system to that remote country, the company, in addition to developing the hardware, software, support, and training elements, had to complete construction of the radar, communication, and command center sites partially completed by Boeing. As mentioned earlier, the final software required more than 1.2 million lines of code and the total project required 2,700 discrete pieces of equipment: high-performance computers, advanced operator consoles, and the new Hughes liquid crystal light-valve projectors (described below in "Consoles for Sea Vessels" and "Large Screen Viewing"). The data processing architecture was totally made up of COTS (commercial off-the-shelf) equipment. A fiber optic communication backbone allowed robust linkage between sites, and all equipment was housed in underground bunkers.

An extensive training program was established for operators and maintenance personnel both in California and Saudi Arabia. (At one time more than 1,000 Hughes and US subcontractor employees were supporting Peace Shield in Saudi Arabia.)

A dedicated project organization focused company resources on all program aspects. The entire system was operationally accepted six months ahead of the official milestone, earning Hughes the entire $50 million incentive. Company executives allocated $25 million of the incentive money to the team of employees who had achieved this extraordinary success.

Peace Shield was an almost perfect business venture for Hughes: the original $837 million award grew to more than $2.5 billion with many follow-on contracts. The company's management approach was selected by the Air Force as a model for the defense industry.

Safe Air Traffic Control

Hughes enjoyed success in US and overseas marketplaces because it supplied customers with systems that met their requirements in a timely manner; in doing so, the company also enhanced its reputation for proven advanced technology products and robust system architectures. This reputation, plus its well-demonstrated capability in development, operation, and support of extremely complex hardware and software systems, encouraged Hughes to enter commercial competitions for air traffic control systems—a business plagued with political and technical challenges.

The ATC mission objectives are to safely manage flight space used by thousands of aircraft moving at many different speeds from 80 miles per hour to more than 2,000 miles per hour. To ensure adequate separation, aircraft are required to be at least 500 feet apart in altitude, with eastbound birds using odd-numbered thousands of feet and west-bounders at even numbers. Horizontal spacing must be at least two miles. This enroute control is applied until handover to a local terminal area to manage the descent for landing; different rules then apply.

This mission continues to present major challenges for all nations faced with rapidly growing commercial aviation. During the 1990s, annual global flights doubled to 2 billion; at any given instant, as many as 100,000 aircraft were airborne going somewhere every day. In the United States, 800 million passengers were served during 2000, and there were 23,000 daily commercial airliner flights along with numerous private and military aircraft. More than 550,000 aircraft cross the US and Canadian airspace each year. Those staggering numbers demand sophisticated management by somebody with adequate authority, and much must be automatically computed and executed. Additionally, international flight rule agreements and variations within national boundaries require vigilance and flexibility in formulating the computer software.

Similar to the military C&C networks, ATC systems consist of three segments: large-scale computers, panoramic operator displays, and a reliable communication network. The computers process incoming data, monitor rapidly changing conditions, compare flights with their stipulated flight plans, and determine optimum solutions to surprise problems that arise. Aircraft location observations usually come from radar surveillance sensors, which are generally purchased separately from national ATC systems. Much of the ATC project effort is in designing copious and complex software to maximize results and minimize operator stress.

The system accepts information on each aircraft's location, based on radar, aircraft data link transmission, satellite relays, or radio voice links. Predetermined flight paths, terrain maps, airports, and national borders are in the computer's storage memory. The dynamics of weather, airliner-requested flight routes, fuel consumption, and flight-schedule timing are continuously computed and monitored. After overview by a control station operator, command instructions go to the aircraft by voice and electronic link to execute any alterations. Confirmation of receipt of all instructions is mandatory.

It is expected that the ATC system database should always contain all adequate landing sites, even for unexpected emergencies. In a spectacular occurrence in 1983, however, Air Canada Flight 143 (a Boeing 767) was at 41,000 feet altitude on the way from Montreal to Ottawa when it suddenly ran out of fuel; an error in fuel loading had not been detected before takeoff. The result was the famous "Gimli glider." Pilot Bob Pearson was able to control the plane's rapid descent of 2,000 feet per minute, but the closest large airport, at Winnipeg, was too distant to be reached with this precipitous glide. The ATC screens showed no nearer runway long enough to stop the giant craft after touchdown; ground controllers could offer no routing advice. Luckily, copilot Maurice Quintal remembered his military training years earlier at a subsequently-abandoned airstrip at Gimli, only twelve miles away, and Flight 143 made a safe landing with no casualties among the sixty-one passengers and eight crew members. Even after this scary landing with nose gear up, the aircraft returned to service a short time later with only minor repairs. A vivid example of intelligence, skill, and courage, coupled with wild luck! Hopefully, even abandoned airstrips are now in every ATC database throughout the world.

The first Hughes ATC program was KATS (Korean air traffic control system), which started in the mid-1980s, with a mission to coordinate and control national and international civilian aviation. KATS is currently operating successfully in the city of Taegu.

In 1984, the Federal Aviation Administration (FAA) issued contracts of $200 million each to teams led by IBM and Hughes. The objective was to design and demonstrate the technologies for a completely new ATC system for the US airspace. The Advanced Automation

Korean Air Traffic Contol Console
(courtesy of UNLV)

System (AAS) proof-of-design project tasks were completed in 1988, leading to a brutal competition with very high stakes: the winning team would be awarded a multi-billion dollar design contract, to be followed by long-term support and performance upgrade projects. There was also a possible extension to add international control networks. The Hughes team included Sanders Associates, a unit of Lockheed, for controllers' equipment and displays; Unisys for dispersed computers and data communication devices; and a division of IBM for central computers.

The Hughes team lost to the IBM team and subsequently filed a formal protest on the grounds that the IBM bid had not complied with stated requirements in six major performance areas; also, IBM's price was higher than the Hughes offer. After prolonged dispute hearings, the contract award remained at IBM. It was speculated that much political pressure had been brought to bear, and that the conservatives in the FAA feared more risk with "startup" Hughes, compared to using the iconic IBM. The United States suffered because of that decision, since the desired performance was not attained, schedules were delayed for years, and costs greatly increased. Would Hughes have done any better? The question is moot; however, the company's track record on many other complex systems was excellent, and we surely would have achieved those six major performance requirements that our opponents left out.

Canadian air traffic control system (CAATS) was awarded to Hughes in 1990, in spite of IBM as the domestic incumbent and Raytheon and Thompson as strong international competitors. We proposed that a new subsidiary located in Vancouver, British Columbia, would develop the system, with most of the 300 personnel being Canadian citizens. This operating plan was a positive factor in winning the competition (it reduced the bid price as well, due to lower Canadian salaries).

The Canadian air traffic control system used commercial computers and advanced Hughes color displays. The system experienced multiple delivery delays because of changing requirements, regional political disputes, and some design difficulties, finally becoming operational in 2002. As it was being deployed in the civilian sector, an adjunct network for the military was added to the contract, and it became operational in parallel with the civilian CAATS.

Hughes also won an extremely difficult Swiss ATC program, aided by the continuing success of the FLORIDA project. However, the company's direct participation was short-lived when Thomson-CSF of France regained its traditionally dominant position in that European market. Regrettably, the company had already completed the major development phase.

The *Guardian* was created by Hughes to respond to smaller scale ATC needs. With a lower cost modular architecture that could be tailored to regional areas, it was attractive to nations with small airspace or traffic volume. Versions of this modular concept were deployed in Germany, Saudi Arabia, Taiwan, and Indonesia.

Hughes systems operating in Europe had computer software that continuously suggested in-flight rerouting to optimize fuel consumption. When the new routing was acceptable within national and safety practices, it resulted in an estimated saving of at least $1 billion per year in fuel costs compared to the standard routing in previous ATC systems.

C&C Hardware and Software

Complex C&C networks require very competent computers, displays, and communication devices. Hughes vigorously pursued each of these hardware elements, using its own funding, to capture a sizable segment of the marketplace along with continual development and advancement in efficient software designs.

Computers for C&C

In 1953, as mentioned above, Hughes began an Army study for what became the MSG-4 Missile Monitor, forming a cornerstone in C&C. The MSG-4 computer instruction set and input-output structure focused on radar control, tracking, and weapon management. It used a spinning magnetic drum as a memory storage device and individual electronic components mounted on printed circuit cards. The device, now seemingly primitive, began a three-decade series of general-purpose computers for C&C (see Table 6.2). Some of the effort was internally funded, resulting in smaller size, increased capability, and substantially lower cost by exploiting the latest in microelectronic design.

Computer for Command
and Control Network
(courtesy of Raytheon)

Large Scale Integrated Packages
(courtesy of UNLV)

The final entry in the table shows the effect of substantial leaps in the design of commercial computers, making them completely adequate in performance and more cost-effective for use in Hughes systems beginning in 1985. The appearance of commercially available smart workstations changed system architecture from central control to a central monitor watching many distributed operating sites. For three decades, Hughes had enjoyed a successful and lucrative specialized computer product line that supported its worldwide C&C programs. Innovative designs provided high-level processor and input-output performance with the flexibility to satisfy a myriad of difficult customer requirements. The company would not have attained its global business success without this internal

Table 6.2. C&C General Purpose Computers

Designator	Date	Use	Features
MSG-4	1953	Army air defense	Magnetic memory drum
SPS-33	1958	Ship radars	13-bit; 1 MHz clock rate; core memory; hard wired instructions & logic
H3118	1961	Radar control; SPS-52; TSQ-51; ICBM reentry	18-bit; 2.2 MHz; diode transistor logic (DTL)
H3324	1961	Large scale C&C; JADGE; FLORIDA	24-bit; 131k core; 2.2 MHz; DTL
H3118M	1963	Combat Grande; Project10-1	18-bit; 131k core; 2.2 MHz; dual processors
HM4118	1967	Combat Grande; Project10-1	18-bit; 131k core; 4 MHz flat-packs; Freon cooled
H4118R	1970	IPD/TAS upgrade	4 NTDS channels; conductive cooling
H5118M	1974	AEGIS; JSS; Project 657	18-bit; 512k solid-state core; 5 MHz
H5118MX	1978	Project 776	18-bit; 512k; 5.5 MHz
Use of commercial computers	1985	UKADGE, 10-1E, IADS, Peace Shield	Lower cost; higher performance

capability. The commercial computer designs finally caught up; nonetheless, Hughes still retained its competitive edge in system engineering and software development.

Copious Software Demands

While designing and fabricating the hardware for high-performance military computers, the company also excelled at preparing the complex instructional software in C&C networks to manage massive amounts of rapidly changing combat data, assembling and correlating incoming information with battlefield situations and presenting it in real-time to combat operators in a fully understandable way.

Software programs for military C&C networks must incorporate many functions to achieve the desired mission objectives, as shown in Table 6.3.

Table 6.3. Typical C&C Software Requirements

- Mission planning
- Operator interface
- Real time detection, tracking, correlation, identification
- Correlation of data with stored reference data
- Comprehensible display outputs
- Communication procedures
- Threat priority assessment
- Response to hostile countermeasures
- Interceptor aircraft routing
- Weapons management
- Interaction with other friendly resources
- Evaluation of results
- Recording of important events
- Performance monitoring
- System training
- Fault detection and isolation

In many networks, it was a complex undertaking just to accommodate the dynamic information inputs from multiple sources including separate horizon and elevation scanning radars, identification transponders, electronic surveillance systems, infrared trackers, missile and gun directing batteries, and link data from other friendly command centers.

Program sizes are usually measured by counting how many instructions are needed to perform the entire set of tasks. These instructions are also called lines of code. One line of code to define an instruction may include as many as ten machine instructions. To achieve all the functions listed in the table above, Hughes C&C software packages would include between twenty-five thousand and one million instructions to be programmed, tested, incorporated, and supported in each system.

Connecting Operators to Machines

An adequate display is essential to any tasks involving interaction between human operators and computers. By the 1940s, television had made electronically distributed moving images of live events commonplace. Television soon performed in full color and with greatly increased picture clarity. This well-funded commercial technology was directly applicable to the demands of the military. Defense companies further advanced the electronics for higher operating speeds, miniaturized size, and handling and environmental ruggedness. These firms also vigorously pursued new technologies to substantially enlarge the viewing screens. In addition to its extensive work in the latest aircraft displays, Hughes was very active in these efforts, particularly for its diverse C&C product lines. The displays were either stand-alone militarized ones for the US Navy and other countries' navies or high-performance equipment as an integral element of major C&C systems.

Displays are the portal to visualizing the overall situation and controlling responses to dynamically changing conditions. Computers sort and diagnose the large masses of incoming data. Operating stations allow a human to plan, develop alternatives, monitor activities, and command optimum system behavior. Information can be accurately placed on terrain or naval task force maps with target positions, altitudes, velocities, and friendly weapon positions and their intercept ranges. Suggestions for possible tactical movements are often included. Operators use keyboards, touch screens, trackball or cursor pointing devices, as well as clearly marked command pushbuttons to interact with the system.

In the late 1950s, displays were radar output repeaters with little ability to show computer-generated symbols or highlighted data. Faceplates were limited to 12 inches in diameter, with sensor data shown in flat x/y coordinates much like a terrain map, using what was called PPI (plan position indicator) to indicate distance and angle to targets. Since all electronic signals were analog rather than digital, continual signal adjustments were needed. The consoles simply acted as repeaters and were refreshed 20 times per second.

In the 1970s and 1980s, displays used internal microprocessors and solid-state memories and no longer required high rate refreshes. The operator could select different display presentations with central computer participation. Brighter and larger CRTs (cathode ray tubes) with high resolution color made displays more robust and maintainable.

In the 1990s, commercial workstations began to displace the customized Hughes products, prompting the company to virtually abandon its display product line and concentrate on competitions requiring innate system engineering and software skills, just as had happened with computers.

Seeing Is Believing

Hughes developed and produced a series of displays supporting its extensive C&C product line, beginning with the traditional analog radar data in PPI format, a few with an overlay of computer-generated graphics.

The JBADGE, FLORIDA, and IPG had computer-driven and refreshed 16-inch CRTs; the operators also had a separate auxiliary readout that could show larger and more tracking information and other system data. Manual switches selected the desired display content. To permit continuous operation, the consoles were cooled by air circulation from an under-floor chamber.

The 407L tactical standard display consoles featured a magnetic beam-deflection technique that greatly improved display legibility on 16-inch CRTs. Now, both radar data and computer-generated graphics could be presented.

The next generation HMD-22 display was chosen for C&C projects begun in the 1970s. These used a 22-inch commercial CRT and an auxiliary monitor; both were internally refreshed rather than by the main computer. The screens showed live radar video overlaid on a tactical situation scene prepared by the computer. The consoles were built to commercial standards, enabling licensing to foreign manufacturers as an aid in overseas C&C competitions.

The HMD-33 was the last custom-built C&C display. It had a very high-performance embedded computer processor and an additional memory to dynamically refresh and to instantly respond to operator requests. The machine was especially rugged and ideal for the Egyptian Project 776 for installation in both fixed land sites and in transportable shelters.

In the late 1980s, Hughes teamed with Sony Electronics to apply its commercial 20- by 20-inch square-faced CRT with touch-screen control surfaces for future C&C and ATC projects. Hughes provided the electronic circuits for computer interaction, display generation, and refresh, as well as the overall console enclosure. Designated AMD-44, it was applied to Peace Shield, IADS, Taiwan Project 10-1, and CAATS.

Many later Hughes C&C projects contained large-screen displays, altering conventional projection systems with the company's patented liquid crystal light valves (see "Consoles for Sea Vessels," this section). Peace Shield used these in the command center and in five regional sectors.

Consoles for Sea Vessels

In the mid-1950s, the Navy began intensive efforts to modernize C&C aboard its combat ships. The acquisition plan was to separately compete computers, displays, and communication equipment, and select suppliers by promised or demonstrated technology to match very tough performance goals for the integrated system. Hughes aggressively competed for the display equipment. We soon became noted for our design techniques, meeting Navy needs and its delivery of reliable equipment on time and within cost, all of which kept customer satisfaction at a high level.

The SSA-23, awarded in 1956, was the company's first Naval Tactical Data Systems (NTDS) contract, and became the cornerstone of a long series of successful Navy display programs. The follow-on SYA-1 was installed on five ships for operational evaluation, resulting in the multi-segment SYA-4 display system. Univac provided the computers and Collins the Link 11 communication devices to form a complete NTDS network. The SYA-4 had a 12-inch CRT, an auxiliary status display unit, a range-height indicator, symbol generators, radar azimuth converters, video simulators, and switchboard controls. Two hundred fifty consoles were built and placed on seventeen Navy ships and several shore-based training sites.

After losing a UYA-1 build-to-print competition to Hazeltine, Hughes recaptured the business when Hazeltine was unable to perform adequately. Similarly, a Navy competition awarded Sylvania a build-to-print order for the Univac-designed computer. In both of these cases, the Navy reverted to the original contractors to satisfactorily complete the work. After this adverse experience, the Navy continued the Hughes/Univac/Collins industrial team for NTDS programs throughout the 1980s, serving NTDS needs for all US combat ships and those of many overseas navies.

In 1965, UYA-4 became the first military display system to fully utilize microelectronic integrated circuits. The 12-inch CRTs were computer-refreshed, very reliable, and operator friendly. The system matched with many military radars and computers. A 20-inch horizontal display enabled situational viewing by groups of observers. The UYA-4s were installed in 175 US ships, as well as 42 ships from Australia, France, West Germany, Italy, and Spain. The company continued to upgrade and support these systems for two decades.

Hughes competitively won UYQ-21 in 1972, a modular console accommodating a second CRT for an auxiliary readout. The 13- by 11-inch CRTs showed either radar or sonar data with superimposed symbols and instructional data. The 5- by 5-inch circuit cards were cooled by circulating water tubes, eliminating the irritating fan noise in the operator's control room and significantly increasing reliability. For NTDS and Aegis, and for several sonar surveillance programs, UYQ-21 added acoustic memory and presented a wide variety of active and passive sonar display formats on either of the two CRTs. Some versions were equipped with large screens, using liquid crystal light valve projectors for Aegis cruisers and guided missile destroyers.

In 1969, the Navy selected Hughes to develop and produce a digital display for the newest 688-class submarine, an upgrade to the Mk-113 fire control system. The effort included Mk-81 weapon control consoles, signal data converters, status panels, and operational software that enabled manual or automatic tracking of sonar-detected contacts, determined threat levels, and engaged the hostile with weapons. The system gave overall situation assessment, including the sea environment's effect on sensor performance and own-ship detectability by the enemy. This program was the start of many Hughes products for attack and ballistic missile classes of submarines, yielding more than $500 million in sales.

Large Screen Viewing

The public has often seen movies of the 1950s depicting the aircraft carrier control room with a petty officer marking target positions on the rear side of a transparent panel embossed with a clock-face-grid. The petty officer's job was done in reverse, so the observing officer viewing from the panel's other side would see the scene as geometrically correct. Marks were made by chalk or removable crayon to enable rapid changes—not very easy to attain completeness and accuracy when plotting a large combat melee! Perhaps many tactical and fatal errors occurred, especially in the frenetic naval air battle engagements of World War II in the Pacific.

Hughes's large screen projectors provided full graphics and many types of target symbols. First deployments, showing only black and white, went aboard several aircraft carriers and in several Air Force strategic air command and NORAD (North American Aerospace Defense Command) bases. Later designs were in full color, using three projectors, each with a CRT imaging in a primary color (red, blue, or yellow), with their outputs combined on the viewing screen to form the full visible spectrum. Screen sizes were tailored for the application and sometimes were up to 45 feet square! Hughes produced more than 500 projectors installed in most aircraft carriers, cruisers, destroyers, submarines, and in many land bases.

Large-Screen Displays Aboard USS *Enterprise* Aircraft Carrier
(courtesy of UNLV)

The projectors used an LCLV (liquid crystal light valve) perfected and patented by the company's Research Laboratories. Materials were organic compounds in differing mixtures to match the intended application, from a simple wristwatch display to the control device for a large-screen projector. The compounds become liquid crystals based on the temperature and electronic inputs, and behave as valves to alter light waves being imposed. The device is constructed with nineteen thin-film layers sandwiched between two transparent plates that respond to electrical signals; these films are liquid crystal, dielectric mirror, light blocker, and a photosensitive film. A desired image of low intensity light from a CRT is imposed on the photosensitive layer, changing the electrical field, which activates the liquid crystal to match the impinging light intensity in each image pixel. Light from a high intensity xenon arc lamp passes through the liquid crystal layer, which modifies the brightness of each pixel, and is reflected from the dielectric mirror and optically expanded to the viewing screen several feet away.

Exotic Information Links

Most essential in establishing a robust C&C network and for any system requiring high flow of complex data is the presence of versatile devices to transfer massive amounts of information from remote sites to each other or to central control stations. Features must include accuracy, reliability, immunity to interference, security from intercept and interpretation by hostiles, and adequacy in capacity and speed to handle the data streams. Where possible, such links can be done with electrical wires or fiber optic lines; much more flexibility and mobility are derived from free-space transmission with radio, IR, or visual light-beam links. The evolution of such long-range devices is described in Part Seven.

Secure links using varying radio frequencies or encoders in connecting wire lines for C&C networks began at Hughes in the mid-1950s under the inspiration of Dr. Sam Lutz; the company won a number of small DoD contracts for clandestine portable radios and wire-line link encoders that enabled the birth of what became a significant product line as well as a major contributor to the many successful C&C programs described above.

In the 1960s, as the digital age matured, providing transmitted data links secure from enemy interference or intercept became easier to accomplish, beginning with the "spread spectrum" technique of rapid changes in transmitted frequencies. Hughes pioneered the introduction into military use of spread spectrum methodologies using the high frequency (HF) radio band. Messages requiring signals only a few kilohertz wide were sent briefly at one frequency, then rapidly hopped about within the HF band of 3 to 30 mHz, a space many thousand times wider than the message signal. Friendly receivers were matched in timing with these position sweeps using a pre-coded sequence, which appeared random rather than orderly and thus not possible to be analyzed and tracked by the hostile. Visualize that the signal's information is all contained within the color dark blue. The transmitter quickly converts the data stream to green, then yellow, then purple, green again, followed by many other colors. The enemy cannot decipher these changes, but the intended receiver matches the sequence and restores the signal to dark blue. When operating in HF, attempts to jam are foiled, since the only means for complete success would be to project enormous power levels over the entire band, an impractical possibility.

ManPack in Antarctic
(courtesy of Raytheon)

In the late 1970s, the next-generation design used a more secure full spread spectrum technique. The relatively narrow frequency needed to convey the desired signal content was stretched hundreds or thousands of times wider in frequency. This was accomplished by dividing the message into segments; each part was multiplied in frequency by amounts that varied with time in a manner that appears random but is known to the friendly machines. The resultant multiplied frequencies to be transmitted spanned the entire HF band. The intended receiver used the coded sequence to interpret what it detected and reconstruct the segments into the proper message signal. The energy level at any point on the HF band was so small as to be undetectable unless decoded by a knowledgeable receiver. Without the cryptographic key, the entire signal energy could not be distinguished from naturally occurring electromagnetic noise. Now visualize the previous "dark blue" message signal at low power intensity being transmitted as white (all colors), with the resulting power level of any discrete single color one thousand times less than the original single color message. Then the friendly receiver reconstructs it back to dark blue. This spread spectrum architecture permitted several signal messages to be transmitted at the same time, being separately interpreted at the receiver by matching decoding sequences. The designs also included an error corrector: if a jammer interrupted a message by focusing at one frequency position, that spot would be avoided and the lost part of the message could be reconstructed. Designing these complexities was made easier by the emergence of very capable tiny microcircuit chips. Spread spectrum was a real boon for clandestine operations.

These special designs made the company the leading supplier of tactical communications for the military, with more than 10,000 units fielded throughout the world. In addition to providing the vital links in many C&C systems, projects included man-portable combat and clandestine radios, satellite ground terminals, and a most capable network to inter-tie active ground troops and mobile equipment.

The culmination of the radio products was ManPack (PRC-104), a rugged and very reliable device that, using integrated circuits, weighed 14 pounds and was the size of a single encyclopedia book. Although not using spread spectrum (other than a special secure variant for the Army), it tuned from 2 to 30 mHz in 1-kHz steps, transmitted at a 20-watt power level, and could operate for sixteen hours with its silver-zinc battery. Portable by individual troopers or carried in any vehicle, it provided unlimited combat communication coverage and versatility. It was deployed with the Marines beginning in 1978, and with the Army in 1982.

AWACS/JTIDS Monitoring Station
(courtesy of Raytheon)

The PRC-104 was designated as the US military standard, and replaced many varieties of unreliable and difficult-to-operate equipment dating back to the 1950s and 1960s. Air Force forward-area air controllers, Navy Seals, and Army Rangers also adopted the Hughes HF radio product family. Other nations using them are Indonesia, Jordan, New Zealand, Oman, Spain, Sweden, Thailand, and even Bangladesh.

As part of early national efforts to create long-range communication using satellites, the Air Force began associated projects in the late 1950s. In 1960, Hughes was tasked to develop a ground terminal to automatically link with both active and passive orbiters using all of their operating frequencies. Successful usage began in 1963. This program contributed many technology advances including solid-state L- and S- band amplifiers, a new X-band power-conversion device, microwave step-tuning in 10 mHz increments from 1 to 10 gHz, and high performance tracking antennas. In 1966, the Army awarded Hughes the MSC-46 development contract to provide ten ground terminals for its global defense communications system. Each terminal had a 40-foot diameter antenna that was controlled to automatically acquire and track low-orbit satellites. Any sister terminal, even thousands of miles distant, would also track that satellite to give a continuous voice and teletype inter-tie between the stations. The ground terminals were portable, and an eight-man team could assemble one and begin operations within forty-eight hours.

In 1974, Hughes won a Boeing-managed competition for the rejuvenated JTIDS program. This time we were to provide terminals to link with the AWACS aircraft, providing a sophisticated data link to integrate the early warning network. In 1975, the Air Force awarded the company, assisted by Mitre Corporation, an engineering design project to create the "B-waveform," which incorporated the foremost of every covert or deceptive trick in communications coding. The frequency hopping was extremely fast, and messages were formed into 32-bit symbols, each of which was frequency hopped to fill the full 150 mHz of spread-spectrum at L-band. Jammers were completely ineffective. By 1978, these B-waveform designs were being provided as upgrade kits to the Boeing terminals. Production of two hundred JTIDS terminals began in 1982; in 1983 co-production agreements with Siemens of West Germany and ITALTEL of Italy provided JTIDS terminals for the NATO E-3 AWACS program. The JTIDS waveform created by Hughes remains today the world's most sought-after tactical data link.

Spread spectrum, frequency hopping, and multiple message coding were combined to achieve a winning bid in 1976 to the Marine Corps for the position locating and reporting system (PLRS), which later became the backbone of the Army's tactical internet. The system is a unique form of C&C for land force maneuver control, but is described here as principally a communications product.

Position Locating and Reporting System

Produced in the mid-1980s, PLRS contained all the needed ingredients for managing actively engaged Marine or Army field units. It included

EPLRS Field Unit
(courtesy of Raytheon)

EPLRS Command Center
(courtesy of Raytheon)

position sensors, two-way communication links, computer information processing, and operator displays. The PLRS enabled a field commander to witness real-time placement and movement of all the small troop squads and weapons superimposed on terrain features and available resources throughout the battlefield.

Individual troop squads or vehicles in the field automatically reported their positions and status using jam-proof portable ManPack radio units. The links used the span from 420 to 450 mHz (UHF). Each unit provided a "user readout" so the operator could receive his location and other navigation information, as well as exchange text data messages with other ManPacks in the area. Such exchanges were most likely the first version of "texting," now a standard service feature in commercial cellular networks.

All the many PLRS data transmissions were received and separately monitored at a master station housed in a truck-mobile trailer enclosure, usually assigned to the division command level. If necessary, several easily portable relay transceivers were positioned atop ridgelines to ensure contact over the horizon. Effective ground-to-ground ranges of many miles were attained.

Integrated PLRS, TOW, and Tank Fire Control
(courtesy of UNLV)

The master computer sorted and processed incoming data streams, analyzed them, correlated them with stored information, and formatted the entire battle scene. A large color video display showed troop positions overlaying terrain map details, with supply chains and combat plans clearly indicated for the field unit commander. The system also triggered audio and visual alarms whenever position deviations occurred. Corrective instructions were then immediately sent to the appropriate squad or vehicle. Systems were deployed by the Army in 1987 and by the Marines in 1988, and PLRS were distributed in later years to many friendly foreign nations, garnering more than $2 billion in sales for Hughes. PLRS and distributed ManPacks were crucial in controlling the rapid end-around movement of thousands of tanks and support vehicles during the 1991

Desert Storm invasion. Misplacement and directional confusion were avoided by accurate location information provided to the commanders.

In the 1990s, significant performance improvements were developed to create EPLRS (enhanced PLRS). With an emerging "digitization" emphasis on data communications on the tactical battlefield between combat elements, the EPLRS radios were usually placed only in vehicles rather than with individual infantry troops. Using the giant advances in digital technology and microelectronics, the central stations became much smaller, cell-phone size radios rather than ManPacks were introduced, and the data capacity of the system was significantly increased. In EPLRS, each message is sent in packet bursts at different frequencies, and the spread spectrum code is changed between each burst; the content of each packet is protected by digital encryption. Network data capacity is maximized by simultaneously using three different methods of time-sharing of the total link by many data streams. The network is capable of handling one thousand different operating radio nodes at the same time, and Earth reference is ensured by a GPS tie-in. Currently, all fielded systems have been replaced or upgraded to an EPLRS configuration.

41

SOME OPERATING
PROBLEMS

Not everything could be done perfectly in the reach for new technologies. Even with the best of intentions, Hughes sometimes fell short in performing contracts with overly ambitious goals. (CORDS and JTIDS were described earlier.) Stretching too far often hinged on an unpredictable weakness in a single but essential building block—development of that component or basic element just took too long to match the system's schedule. In other cases, the excellent reputation of the company's products caused a customer to try using the equipment in a way never intended, to the embarrassment of all.

Some programs were unpredictably cancelled even when evaluation tests had demonstrated an excellent design. These scrubs usually happened because the carrier vehicle program did not survive. Hughes's electronics often did not stand alone, they depended on that vehicle in order to proceed toward production. In many cases, cancellations caused significant financial losses that were difficult to recover—for example, equipping a factory to efficiently manufacture a new product required company investment and lead-time. These costs may have been part of the original government contract, but usually they could be recovered only by a reasonable future production volume. Fortunately, with a bit of company funding to fill a time gap, a new application for the product or the production machinery could often be found, resulting in an outstanding business outcome. I personally went through this agony for ten years, bouncing from the 1959 F-108 cancellation through the YF-12 scrub in 1964, and that of the F-111B in 1968, to, finally, award of the F-14 *Tomcat* program in 1969! Major program casualties also spurred intensive searches for product diversification, many of which bore profitable results.

Falcon Misapplication

Attempting to use the Falcon missile on the F-4 *Phantom*, though well intended, was an embarrassing misapplication. During the Vietnam conflict, the Air Force was compelled by the DoD to deploy the *Phantom* as its principal tactical fighter. Designed for the Navy, the fighter's armament was the semiactive-radar-guided Sparrow and the infrared-guided Sidewinder. Both of these missiles also had been developed under Navy direction. The Sparrow was matched to the *Phantom*'s Westinghouse radar, so the Air Force procured a large inventory of these radars for deployment. Rather than choosing Sidewinder for its IR missile, however, the Air Force "top brass" decided to use their large inventory of infrared-guided Falcons. Results in combat were most disappointing. Near misses did not damage targets, since the Falcon had only a contact fuse. Direct hits were few; most shots passed through the engine exhaust plume aft of the target. Most noticeable was the unhappy experience of the famous Col. Robin Olds. He had been an ace in World War II, missed the Korean conflict, and had already achieved four victories in Vietnam. If he could down one more hostile, he would be the first ace in both of those wars. He didn't make it; several Falcon shots were misses! As a highly regarded wing commander, he demanded that Air Force change to Sidewinders for use on the F-4s. That took place soon thereafter, but Colonel Olds did not get the chance to score that magic fifth.

Why such a calamity? As stated by Ed Cobleigh, who had performed the third highest number of Air Force F-4 *Phantom* sorties in Vietnam and later joined Hughes as an expert missile marketing manager, "Try using a perfect football in a soccer game!" This was a classic case of applying an almost flawless bomber intercept weapon to the very different dog-fighting arena. Falcon missiles, carried internally in their mother aircraft, had to be externally mounted on the *Phantom*'s wings, causing erosion and vibrating flutter damage to their wings. The Falcon was also a segment of a fully integrated weapon control system in the air defense F-102 *Delta Dagger* and F-106 *Delta Dart* aircraft; primary targets were slow-maneuvering bombers. These interceptors were vectored by ground radars; the systems in the aircraft cued the pilot into an optimum firing position, calculated the launch time, aligned the Falcon seeker, and started IR sensor cooling by releasing bottled nitrogen; the pilot could then select an automatic Falcon launch.

None of these integrated features was incorporated in the F-4. The missile's long range was nullified by the doctrine of visual identification of the target before shooting; since 95 percent of airborne vehicles over North Vietnam were US military, this standing order made good sense. The pilot had to manually steer to a firing window, command detector cooling to start (realizing the cooling would be limited to two minutes), slew the seeker to find the target, assure by audio tone the seeker's lockon, and trigger the launch. These many operations, performed with five separate switches, were most difficult in highly maneuvering combat with a hostile fighter.

The two-minute sensor cooling time limit was determined by the size of the missile's internal liquid nitrogen flask, and was often exceeded as the pilot tried to reach the optimum launch position, rendering Falcon blind. (Cooling was required for the Falcon's detector material, which had been chosen to increase the sensitivity of the missile in order to extend its range to seven miles. A remedy could have been to try a costly retrofit using a non-cooled detector element like the one in Sidewinder, and sacrificing the extended range.) Also, direct hits to trigger the Falcon's contact fuses were usually precluded by evasive maneuvers. These made the exhaust plume the dominant hot target. Sidewinders had proximity fuses that triggered while passing through the plume, and so achieved many more successes. The Air Force change to that weaponry was the right thing to do. However, the prestige of Hughes was tarnished for some time by the whole unhappy experience.

Espionage

Thousands of employees at Hughes had many opportunities to commit espionage, since more than 80 percent of the company's products had military security classifications. The Soviets desperately desired to know performance limits, design details, and countermeasure vulnerability secrets about US hardware. Since the biggest design capability gap between the two great powers was in electronics, Hughes was naturally a chief target. Nevertheless, I am aware of only one unfortunate espionage success in the company during my forty years there, and I was unknowingly personally affected.

The national media became excited in 1981 when the FBI announced the arrest of William Bell for selling significant classified documents to the USSR. For some time, Bill, an engineer in the Radar Systems Group, had managed to remove documents containing unique radar design and performance details from his office. After smuggling them past the security guards, he was able several times to arrange company-sponsored travel to Switzerland, where he transferred the documents to a KGB agent in exchange for rather minimal fees.

Bell's decisions apparently had been first triggered by his son's suffering fatal burns from a portable cooking stove while camping on a remote beach in Mexico. This tragedy was soon followed by an unpleasant divorce; his wife and daughter had departed without warning, with all the furniture and bank savings, while he was on a business trip. Perhaps to recover from this blow, he expanded his already established fancy life style of overspending, showing off in flashy cars, and chasing unattached women. This behavior demanded funds far in excess of his salary, leading to his personal vulnerability for exploitation. Bill's emotions were somewhat eased by a "brunette bombshell" he had met in Europe and brought home, but she placed even more pressure on his modest income. Bill met a neighbor, Marian Zacharski, on the tennis courts. Mr. Zacharski, supposedly a Polish trade negotiator for the Southern California region, was actually a clandestine Polish intelligence agent helping the Soviet KGB. He was planted to induce aerospace engineers in the Los Angeles area to sell technical information.

A likeable and well-organized engineer, the fifty-eight-year-old Bell was working in highly classified radar stealth projects. He had previously been active on the Hughes TARAN radar program for the Swiss *Mirage* fighter and was often used as a technical advisor in Switzerland. During a period of several months, Zacharski persuaded Bell to copy unclassified documents, beginning with the company telephone directory. This transitioned to low-level technical data with a "Confidential" classification, with payment promised for the future. More highly classified papers were then solicited, with the request that Bell personally carry them to an agent in Switzerland on his next trip there. Many genuine documents were transferred in this manner, although Bell also had the ingenuity to create and pass some bogus ones as well. Apparently, the Soviets paid Bell only half of what they had promised, and no more than $100,000 for all of his espionage efforts.

The FBI investigations began in 1980 when a double agent (allegedly a Polish representative to the UN, seeking asylum in the United States) reported that the KGB had somehow obtained significant radar information. Hughes was the most likely source because of its lead in air and surface military radars. With the cooperation of senior Radar Systems Group management, the FBI narrowed the suspect list to two candidates and began close twenty-four-hour monitoring of both. Only three people at Hughes were aware of this investigation.

An arrest required detailed evidence sufficient for a trial by jury. Since these suspects spent much of their time each day in a protected "tank," direct surveillance could only be done by a supervisor. The process took the FBI agents about twelve months to narrow down the investigation to Bell and make the arrest; Bill's flashy personal life style and profligate spending helped point the finger. During that year, to avoid compromise of more classified data for which Hughes could be held legally liable, supervisor Jim Easton had to gradually ease Bell away from highly classified projects without his discovering that he was under suspicion. A tricky business!

What caught my attention after the arrest was that Bell's most significant transfers were complete copies of our proposal to McDonnell Douglas for the APG-65 radar for the F/A-18 *Hornet*. The proposal's security classification levels ranged from "Confidential" through "Secret"; nothing was tabbed "Top Secret" or the dreaded "Eyes Only." Each of the eight volumes had an introductory page authored and signed by me as the program manager. The KGB must have become very familiar with my name! That became clear to me years later when I hosted a dinner for a KGB defector, during which I learned a lot more about how espionage is conducted. That ex-spy seemed to have an innate ability to read minds. I felt almost transparent each time our eyes met!

Media frenzy about the Bell affair was most evident when a well-known television anchorman demanded entry to the radar manufacturing facility in El Segundo. The network wanted to film where the espionage had occurred. (None had occurred at that facility—so much for accuracy in reporting!) In spite of aggressive network objections, with accusations of denying the rights of the "free press," Hughes denied access, based on stringent government security rules. A helicopter then appeared overhead to film the anchorman at the gates as he illustrated to the nation that the public was being deliberately denied information by one of those evil military-industrial-complex defense contractors.

When the FBI had gathered enough evidence, Hughes fired Bell on grounds of travel-expense fraud. The arrest was made, fortunately not in any Hughes facility. During the trial, Bell confessed and was sentenced to serve seven years in a federal prison. The fact that he had recorded all of what he had transferred to the KGB in his personal logbook enabled rapid and effective alleviation of the damage. The confession and record files also enabled the arrest and conviction of Mr. Zacharski. Bill retained a peculiar sense of personal balance in prison; as if fully exonerated by his confession and logbook, he often asked for Hughes's help in obtaining computer-program discs and in writing his autobiography. William Bell, the one-and-only Hughes spy, died of natural causes in 1993, after his release from prison.

The Missile Quality Dispute

The biggest business injury in the company's history was what became known as the Missile Quality Problem, which flared up in 1984. The Tucson facility was actively producing the antitank TOW, air-to-ground Maverick and Walleye, surface-to-air Roland, and air-to-air Phoenix missiles, plus ARBS (angle rate bombing system) bombing sights, and several other high performance products. William "Will" Willoughby, a dedicated civilian bureaucrat in Washington, D.C., was head of quality for all Navy equipment procurements. His push for quality improvement was most appropriate, but seemed to ignore terms of existing contracts being performed at a fixed price. He announced that until Hughes improved its manufacturing quality, the Navy would no longer accept deliveries of Phoenix missiles.

Supreme quality is always a meaningful and high priority objective. However, perfection can be costly: infinite quality usually can come only after infinite expense. Missiles are weapons, so product quality must not be treated casually or unduly compromised, and there must be a continuous effort to control and improve manufacturing processes, both in-house and by suppliers. The defining element is the contract, which dictates the level of performance demanded for the product's price. The Tucson plant had continuously met or exceeded all Phoenix contract terms and conditions. Flight test results were far better than stipulated in the contract, with a far higher success rate than had been experienced by any other missile manufacturer.

The Air Force, which was in charge of quality monitoring, and the Army were both very satisfied with the products Tucson delivered to them, but they had to join a government alliance with the Navy. The government confrontation with Hughes was difficult to accommodate, since the company was exceeding contract requirements and was most willing to implement changes to improve quality, but was unwilling to bear the additional cost of the latter or be denied delivery acceptance. It was always possible for an inspector to find minute and meaningless deficiencies. Analysis of the plethora of government specifications applicable to Phoenix for materials, processes, and tests revealed 675,000 pages of documented requirements! Total "compliance" was impossible, especially since many items specified in one page conflicted with requirements in other documents, and some statements in those documents were obsolete. It would seem very reasonable to judge total quality based on end-item reliability and performance accuracy rather than on the little itty-bitties.

As president of the Missile Systems Group, I made a very regrettable mistake by fostering in the company an overly defensive attitude. The worst blunder was accepting an interview with Ralph Vartabedian, an excellent aerospace reporter for the *Los Angeles Times*. During the interview, I described our manufacturing practice: if an error is found in the hardware it is fixed before the next manufacturing step, and if that happens again, either the process or the design is changed. The example I showed Ralph was a small scratch in an aluminum frame that had a preservative coating added, which should be acceptable if the total product meets its contract requirements. A government inspector, however, had concluded it was of "insufficient manufacturing quality." The interview was a lively one, and unfortunately, the next day the *Los Angeles Times* featured a passing remark I had made: "After all, it's just going to be blown up when it's used." That foolish statement infuriated authorities in Washington, D.C., and I think triggered the big firestorm that lasted for more than a month. Government officials apparently thought I was too blasé and had assigned a low priority to superb quality. That perception was certainly untrue, but I soon felt a bit paranoid and unloved!

With concurrence from corporate executives, I shut down production of everything and assigned the entire staff of 8,500 people to find and remedy any processing flaws that workers could find. No suggestions would be ignored. Blaine Shull, an expressive and persuasive executive with immense people skills, was selected as the new manager for Tucson operations and his personal relations talent became vital to quick progress as he reassured both the distressed employees and the unhappy customers. (Blaine later became president of Ground Systems Group.)

The shutdown caused great dismay in the Army and Air Force—and cost Hughes an unrecoverable $300 million—but many outstanding improvements resulted in every product. After three weeks we were able to restart deliveries. The events were actually therapeutic throughout all segments of the company. The manufacturing personnel on the factory floor did an excellent job of perfecting processes and fabrication procedures to greatly improve end-product quality. In Ground Systems Group, one team so excelled in producing high quality assemblies that the boss of the government inspection squad reassigned his people elsewhere in order to keep them busy—the inspectors continually had found not a single manufacturing discrepancy to report. (This astonishing decision so excited the Hughes staff that they made large logo buttons to clip on their shirts proclaiming: "We Don't Need You." This provocative display horrified the company's marketing personnel, who feared customer retribution. They finally had the buttons eliminated, but our quality stayed top-notch.)

My personal irritation came from our being forced to greatly exceed contract requirements at our own expense; the government zealots mandated changes without spending a nickel from DoD coffers. Nevertheless, if I had taken a more positive, cooperative, and enthusiastic approach, it is likely that much of our large unplanned expenditure would have been reimbursed. This was a good lesson for me to learn! Hughes ultimately benefited from having far better manufacturing capabilities within the next few years, including shorter cycle times and a 30 percent cost reduction in some products!

Second Sourcing

Most probably due to discontent with Hughes's production pricing, or perhaps stirred by the emotional missile quality disputes of 1984, the government pursued an intensive "second-source" approach to awarding complex article manufacturing contracts. The second-source approach was intended to lower prices by requiring competition for annual procurement quantities. Principally focused on guided missiles, this new approach might have had a sensible government objective, but a thorough review of all the expenses involved actually reveals a large increase in total DoD budgets expended. Establishing another source can reduce the unit-price offers because of competitive bidding. However, the additional cost to provide customized tooling, fixtures, test equipment, and written procedures; train staff; and qualify a new supplier for producing that article is quite high for complex devices. Those huge set-up costs were separately paid by DoD to the new factory, but adding a pro-rata portion of that investment to each missile produced to reveal the true unit cost was not done.

The concept works for high quantities of simple bullets and bombs, but not for electronically guided weapons; the annual and total quantities are far too small. Enormous production quantities would be needed to accrue enough savings to offset the investment. Such quantities were never ordered, so second sourcing never paid off. But it allowed many companies to set a goal to become the primary manufacturer of unique equipments designed by Hughes. This could become a galling result for us: competitors would avoid the financial risks during development and garner most of the profitable segment of the business with all implementation expenses borne by the government.

Unit prices could have been reduced more effectively by increasing the quantity ordered each year from a single source. Lack of competition may not generate low-price bidding, but the contractor's actual costs are so carefully audited that rapacious monopolistic pricing cannot be sustained. Manufacturing plant overhead and engineering support each year do not increase much at higher delivery rates. The portion of those "fixed" charges allocated to each missile declines rapidly as delivery quantities rise. Assume the fixed cost to keep the plant open for a year is $50 million. If the costs of labor and materials for a missile are $50,000 and the rate that year is 1,000, the unit cost will be $100,000. If 2,000 missiles are produced, the unit cost will be $75,000; the fixed cost is parceled into more pieces. When the separate factories of two firms each produce only 1,000 missiles that year, fixed costs are duplicated, so those parceling savings are not realized. The second sourcing master plan requires both firms to continue production operations; therefore, each annual lot is split. If equally split, and to make the concept worthwhile, both competitors would have to reduce the unit cost from $100,000 to $75,000 to deliver only 1,000 missiles, and even more if that second company's implementation cost had to be recovered by the government. Those are very unreasonable expectations!

Spurred by this competition, Hughes made many positive improvements in facility operations for Phoenix and AMRAAM (described in Section 52, "Perfect Intercept"). But the loss of a total business base and the required transfer of unique Hughes technology to our most formidable competitor really hurt. Perhaps the much larger cost to the government by using two sources was viewed as a good motivational investment, but this certainly cannot be substantiated as a total budget reduction concept.

Hubble Embarrassment

In 1990, first results of the orbiting Hubble Space Telescope were mind boggling to the entire world. Never before had such detailed images of remote objects in far space been seen so clearly. Scientific examination of the origin of the universe could proceed with vigor! Unfortunately, it was soon apparent that in some observations the images were a bit distorted or fuzzy; analysis showed that the extreme periphery of the telescope's 94-inch diameter primary mirror was slightly misshapen.

Before Hubble's launch, Hughes had proudly proclaimed that we had produced this precise device, although truthfully we had not actually done the work: Hughes had purchased the Connecticut segment of PerkinElmer Inc. just as that entity had completed the mirror. Records showed that the fine grinding and polishing of the periphery was off by a few microns, and the flaw had not been revealed during final inspection. Having erroneously claimed public credit for this remarkable device, we now were terribly embarrassed. The remedy—insertion of a compensation element in the optical train—was made in 1993 by space-walking astronauts tethered to a Space Shuttle. The outcome was perfect, with spectacular images from objects far deeper in the universe, but the Hughes embarrassment remained. This was a good example of inappropriate advertising.

Hubble Space Telescope
(©iStockphoto/jamesbenet)

PART SEVEN

BOOMING IN MISSILES, SPACE, AND COMMERCE

Hughes continued its business expansion in many diverse fields in the two-and-a-half decades beginning in the mid-1960s. Most national and international markets were usually well funded, with increasing demands for the technologies nurtured at Hughes. This Part tells of our successes in many varieties of guided missiles, the expansion from Syncom into space exploration and world dominance in geosynchronous satellites, and our efforts to penetrate the consumer marketplace. It concludes with personal impressions and experiences of operating within the aerospace industry.

Continuing growth was certainly a great benefit to Arizona. Our guided missile manufacturing had been performed since 1951 in Tucson. As the demand for these products grew, two other plants were set up in Alabama and Georgia. Nonetheless, Hughes became Arizona's largest private employer, and by 2008 (the plant was part of Raytheon by then; see Section 62, "Doomsday and Remembrance") was generating $5 billion in annual sales revenues. The opener to Part Five mentions the peculiar characteristics of Californians; those in Arizona also projected their own special aura. New arrivals usually proudly adopted these traits as their own. Most prominent of these are self-reliance and pride in personal accomplishments. An employer can greatly benefit from this, since constant supervision is seldom required, although it is a real challenge for a manager to keep everyone going in a desired direction.

The state's natural features of aridity and craggy mountains originally were inhabited only by nomadic people who could not sustain an agricultural life. As the Spanish prospectors arrived and discovered large deposits of silver, lead, and copper, they devised ways to obtain sustainable water sources to support small towns. Unstable economics and politics in the late 1800s stirred pulp-magazine portrayals of gunslingers, vigilantes, and tough rustlers, as cattle ranching joined mining as a means of population support. The image of self-reliance was bolstered by tales of John Wesley Powell exploring the Colorado River through Grand Canyon and of Wyatt Earp shooting the bad guys at Tombstone's OK Corral. In the 1900s, tourism thrived from the wonders of the Grand Canyon, Sedona, Flagstaff, saguaro cactus forests, and ghost towns such as Jerome, Fool's Gulch, and Bisbee.

During World War II, many individuals from coastal areas fled to this inland territory to be remote from possible attacks coming from the Pacific Ocean. In the following years, the state boomed from military bases near Phoenix and Tucson, expanded agriculture, and a blossoming of warm-weather retirement communities. As mentioned in Part Two, Hughes and the government chose Tucson to have a sophisticated production plant far from the sea, just as many individuals had done. Another goal was to exploit adjacent real estate properties as residence developments. It certainly became an excellent place for the manufacturing of electronics and special assembling of explosive weapons in remote safety zones. The company also benefited greatly from individual employees projecting that Arizonan self-reliance creed.

42

PURSUIT OF
OVERSEAS MARKETS

A GREAT DEAL OF business could be mined in distant lands; as the old saying goes: "Thar be gold aplenty in them thar hills." Success came from cultivating friendly relationships and maintaining a reputation for consistent customer satisfaction. Part of establishing good relations was to avoid the term "foreign," which other nations can consider offensive. Better terms are "ally," "overseas customer," or "international business." For Hughes, overseas military sales controlled by the US government were a significant part of the international market, but most satellite sales resulted from competitive commercial wins. By 1985, Hughes had dealt successfully with forty-two governments other than that of the United States, sometimes as a provider of a subset of a vehicle sale made by another company.

Success in international market contract execution, hardware acceptance, and long-term support demanded an understanding of the diverse cultural values and behaviors of other countries. This was often difficult, since the United States educational system usually ignores most other cultures and their languages. Hiring consultants who could advise proper contact with international customers was vital, but careful attention was needed to avoid the corruption that was often prevalent in some nations; such corruption could be carefully disguised and almost impossible to detect. What may be corrupt by US legal standards may be normal business practice elsewhere.

From the 1960s until the early 1980s, NATO nations bought much of their military hardware from the United States. During those years, Hughes was the only firm able to consistently satisfy the particular electronics needs of these European countries.

Naturally, the countries nurtured their own internal firms, and so placed "offset" requirements on contracts to purchase US equipment. Offset is a term meaning initially that for every dollar of purchase, the United States had to buy European goods valued at least half that amount. As time went by, this offset percentage grew. By the 1980s, offset demands had increased to a one-for-one amount of trade to cross the Atlantic, and the European products had to be sophisticated ones rather than just ironmongery or services.

The unique military system that fit this description perfectly was the mobile Roland surface-to-air defense weapon system. This short-range missile system had been created and manufactured by Euromissile, a French-German consortium.

Roland System (second from left, NM Governor Caruthers)
(personal files)

The US Army selected Roland instead of the Crotale (French for rattlesnake) developed by Thompson CSF and used in fourteen countries, to perform what our Army called all-weather, short-range air defense (AWSHORAD). In 1975, Hughes, with Boeing as a partner, won a competition to produce the system in the United States, paying license fees to Euromissile. The hardware consisted of search and track radars, an optical telescope, a central computer, electronic command links, and a missile with a ten-mile range. The weapon was guided by radio command link from a computer in a launch trailer, which tracked the target seen by the radar or optical sight. The hardware was packaged in a small set of modules so that the system could be fitted into several varieties of armored vehicles that could keep up with maneuvering troops and defend them from marauding aircraft.

Dr. Elliot Axelband, the Hughes manager on this project, remembers the job of transferring the manufacturing to the United States as a real adventure. Hughes should have been forewarned: as told in the early great French epic poem, *La Chanson de Roland*, Roland was Charlemagne's brave knight who fought heroically but perished in a narrow pass in the Pyrenees in 778, as he was commanding the rear guard defending the Franks from the pursuing Saracens. The poem also relates that his magic sword Durandel was flung into a deep lake; legend says that it could be retrieved only by a person as noble as Roland. (Some less colorful epic versions say he tried to break the sword, was unable to do so, and finally collapsed upon it.) We got only to the first page of a more modern European epic adventure, nonetheless one filled with numerous surprises.

Significant impediments to progress were metric versus English measurements; drawings with strange formats; technical details that were not revealed because they were judged proprietary by Euromissile; and language differences between French, German, and US personnel. Some of the formal documents defining specific procedures on the factory floor might contain the footnote "See Otto." Investigation revealed that Otto was an experienced technician who performed the final adjustments of a production subassembly, but who would not reveal how they were done, nor would he come to the United States to do them! We spent a lot of time experimenting before we figured out what had to be done to that device before its delivery.

The Hughes challenge was not just to build Roland, but also to alter it to meet unique US Army needs, some of which were security classified and so could not be discussed with Euromissile. The Europeans feared the United States would use any performance enhancements to win competitions with them in future short-range air defense markets. A new government memo of understanding that essentially precluded US external sales eliminated that valid concern. To make any modifications, Hughes also needed an in-depth technical understanding of the system's design rationale, test procedures, and verification methods. Difficulties in acquiring this understanding are described in the last section of this part, Section 48, "Observations on the Aerospace Business; Human Relations Abroad," where the vagaries of overseas relations are discussed.

A slight misunderstanding of Roland's system operating architecture caused a problem in validation testing at White Sands, New Mexico. The test director, shortly before the event, altered the plan for the first missile shot, specifying that the guidance computation would use the optical sight instead of radar track steering. He also decided to leave the radar turned off. Launch was triggered, but the missile did not respond. The surprise was that a hang fire would always occur if the radar was off.

This was such a serious design peculiarity that it was astonishing that the very smart US team had not detected it previously. A critical lesson was learned at significant cost!

All finally went well, and the Hughes cultural education spread to many other business enterprises. The US Roland was successful: performance exceeded expectations; the unique US modifications worked; manufacturing was high quality and on schedule; and Hughes even made a profit.

Although Roland equipped only one air defense battalion; the original planned quantity was cut drastically, partly because of the end of the Cold War, but also because of the total cost invested. Twenty-seven fire units and 714 missiles were produced. The project had been selected at the Secretary of the Army level, but the Army's technical staff in Huntsville, Alabama, considered it a threat to their future. That agency was assigned responsibility to monitor and approve Roland's progress. It imposed inordinate demands on testing, required the requalification of all components, and forced an excessive application of any known government specification, each interpreted in the minutest detail—in spite of a signed agreement with Euromissile for technical reciprocity, which entailed automatic acceptance of what had already been done by the French. Insistence on these excessive procedures greatly inflated the development and initial production costs. After a few years, the operating systems were reassigned to Army Reserve units. Several years later, Roland was retired. It is strange that the US Army did not enthusiastically embrace this affordable equipment that satisfied all requirements. As a result, for at least ten years the Army was not equipped to perform the important AWSHORAD mission. Roland, you deserved a better fate.

The US Roland work was performed by Hughes as part of a widespread guided missile business, much of which was done with substantially fewer stressful cultural interactions, since design and production were managed within the company. Diversification in this product line expanded from our traditional air-to-air weapons to those for air-to-ground strike, antitank warfare, undersea attack, and ICBM intercept, as well as submarine-launched ballistic missile guidance systems. These are described below and in Part Eight.

43

GUIDANCE GAINS

Building on its long experience with the air intercept Falcon and GAR-9 missiles, Hughes sought not only to maintain world preeminence in air intercept, but also to use that expertise to solve many other combat strike problems. Weapons incorporating precision guidance brainpower could, from a safe distance, destroy or inflict fearsome damage to well-protected hostile objects of any type both day and night.

Hughes explored many possibilities; customer needs, technical feasibility, cost, and combat effectiveness determined the final choices. With significant advances taking place in electronics design, numerous technical concepts were becoming practical: command guidance from the launch site by wire or radio transmission; target tracking by an internal TV or IR imager; weapon response to radar or laser spot illumination; accurate inertial navigation to fixed targets; and passive, semiactive, or active sonar for undersea warfare. Independent guidance by GPS (Global Positioning System) satellites and use of fiber optics came along in later years.

Air-to-Surface

Accurately attacking protected ground targets from fast flying fighter-bombers was always difficult. Identifying the desired objective, avoiding ground defenses, and actually destroying the target by cannon fire, rockets, or free-falling bombs was problematic. Hitting the wrong object, missing a maneuvering target, inflicting ineffective damage even with a hit, or causing undesirable collateral damage to friendly forces, civilians, or historic artifacts were common.

One Hughes program to improve delivery of unguided bombs was the ASB-19 ARBS (angle rate bombing system) developed for the Marine's A-4M *Skyhawk* and AV-8B *Harrier* aircraft. A laser scanner and TV tracker either were locked onto the target by the pilot or automatically found a laser spot on a hostile object that had been placed there by a remote operator of a laser designator. The tracker provided steering instructions for the pilot to reach the optimum release point, and automatically dropped the bombs when the aircraft reached that point. The computational equations were greatly improved versions of the World War II Norden bombsight, using measured angular changes between aircraft and target to determine future positions. In contrast to 1944, the ARBS system provided all functions automatically after lockon, no longer requiring a bombardier to manually keep the crosshairs precisely on target and personally decide the correct release time. Many systems were produced in Tucson, successfully deployed, and are still in use today by the United States, Spain, and the United Kingdom.

To obtain even more accurate bomb delivery, the Navy funded development of the AGM-62 (air-to-ground missile) Walleye, a 250-pound warhead glide bomb produced by Martin Marietta with a Hughes TV guidance system attached at its nose. The weapon was extensively deployed in the 1960s, and Hughes produced thousands of these guidance systems in Tucson. The Air Force also began development of a 2,000-pound guided glide bomb, the GBU-15 (guided bomb unit), in 1974. It, too, used a Hughes TV seeker and later an interchangeable Hughes IR seeker. The company produced both of these GBU-15 seekers, which had many features in common with our Maverick missile seekers.

The Air Force awarded Hughes a contract in the late 1960s to create the AGM-65 Maverick, a new rocket-propelled air strike missile. The primary mission for this fire-and-forget weapon (also called launch-and-leave or launch-and-maneuver—different ways of saying the weapon was completely self-guided once fired) was as a tank-buster. As its outstanding performance became known, other strike missions were added, including a special heavyweight antiship version. Maverick replaced the Walleye glide bomb; its precision accuracy made a smaller warhead more than adequate. The deployed Mavericks weighed 462 to 670 pounds, depending on the warhead size, and were 12 inches in diameter and 8 feet long.

They were hung on launcher rails on the aircraft's exterior, usually beneath the wings.

The first-version Maverick had a telescopic television camera in its nose protected by a hemispherical glass dome; the sensor was mounted in a gyro-stabilized gimbal that could scan in a 60-degree-wide cone.

As the fighter approached the enemy area ahead, the pilot scanned the seeker across the ground while viewing the scene on a cockpit display. He placed a cross-hair pipper (predicted impact point marker) on his chosen target; that designation point was transferred to the Maverick

Maverick Missile
(courtesy of UNLV)

sensor as a lock-on command, which set a tracker gate around the chosen target spot on the weapon's internal video image. When the missile was launched, its rocket motor propelled the weapon as far as seventeen miles, providing comfortable separation for fighter breakaway to avoid defensive ground fire. The TV video tracker remained locked on the image point all the way to impact, even if the target was a rapidly moving tank. The video tracker kept the small gate on the target and the gimbals moved to maintain that gate centered in the sensor's field of view. An internal computer followed the gimbals' motions and steered the weapon to a target hit.

With rapid advancement in IR sensors and detector coolant mechanisms in the 1970s (see Section 34, "Exploiting Infrared; Detector Cooling"), day and night use of Maverick became possible, as did better penetration of the battlefield smoke and haze that obscured TV visibility. This IR version came well before full-scene thermal image scanning or staring arrays were available. The challenge was to create a low cost sensor that could form recognizable scene and target images for the pilot's display and for the missile to use for steering, just as in the TV version. Instead of directly creating a TV-like image raster by mechanical sweeping, this compact seeker used a rotating series of mirror facets, each slightly offset from its predecessor, mounted on a gyroscopic ring that also stabilized the seeker's pointing axis. Thermal energy focused by the telescope impinged on a mirror facet and was reflected onto a four-by-four array of sixteen HgCdTe (mercury-cadmium-telluride) detectors cooled to -320°F. The changing offset of each mirror piece generated successive samples for a swath of four lines of video pixels, which were stored for later conversion into a total scan pattern. The mirror spin axis then tilted up slightly to form the next set of four lines. The stored lines were then interlaced to finalize a complete scene and converted to a TV format. These pictures were similar to those made by the TV seeker, and the lock-on and flight guidance were also done in the same manner. This unique IR design was typical of the innovations that were essential to creating the extremely compact components needed to fit within a small missile, while keeping the missile affordable with low cost production.

We also perfected a laser Maverick for close air support for the Marines. They considered it a ground-soldier support weapon: when the Marine called for a strike, a forward observer pointed a laser designator spot on the specified target, which the Maverick in a strike aircraft acquired, tracked, and hit.

Other adaptations of the IR seeker and tracking system upgraded the Walleye and the GBU-15 missiles mentioned above, giving these weapons night and day capability with attack ranges beyond fifteen miles. Hughes produced many hundreds of these systems in Tucson, Arizona, and La Grange, Georgia.

Initially used in the Air Force F-4, F-5, and A-10, as well as the Navy A-7 aircraft, Maverick entered service in 1972 and is now used on fourteen aircraft types in twenty-four countries. Hughes delivered more than 40,000 of seven different types of the missile.

The United States' use of this weapon was extraordinarily successful in both Iraq wars. An Air Force captain piloting an A-10 "Warthog" described one dramatic illustration: his mission was to nullify a large air defense missile array that was defending the Iraqi border with Kuwait. This objective was vital to ensure that this set of missile batteries would not cripple large strikes heading for Baghdad. He had never fired a Maverick, even in training. The target was the central control facility, well protected by antiaircraft weapons. He made a direct hit on a single pass. He later praised our company with words that could have been adopted as a Hughes motto: "You're the one that makes stuff that really works!"

Antitank Solution

Tank warfare began with the British invention of heavily armored vehicles in an attempt to overcome the deadly trench warfare of World War
I; greatly improved versions of such mobile weapons were most difficult

TOW Launched from *Bradley Fighting Vehicle*
(courtesy of UNLV)

to counter in World War II. Lethal hits by artillery and unguided rockets
(the celebrated World War II shoulder-fired bazookas) were infrequent
because of the tanks' evasive movements, the poor visual conditions in
smoke and darkness, and the limited warhead effectiveness against increasingly tough armor. Survival of the soldiers using these antitank devices was risky because of the very short ranges of available weapons.
The Army urgently needed an extended range, lightweight, man-portable
guided missile with a focused, deeply penetrating warhead to "always"
decommission an agile and heavily armored tank.

Beginning in 1961, Hughes met these requirements by perfecting a
weapon called the BGM-71 TOW (tube-launched optical-tracked wire-
command-link-guided) missile, which was man-portable and later applied to the Bradley Fighting Vehicle and several varieties of helicopters.

The missile, 3-1/2 feet long and 6 inches in diameter, weighed 44 pounds and could reach targets up to two-and-a half-miles distant. Carried in a short launch tube canister (shaped so the rocket plume did not strike the gunner when shoulder-fired), its four flight wings and four control fins were recessed into its cylindrical body; immediately after it emerged from the launch tube, these panels flipped out for flight control. The TOW used a unique two-stage rocket motor; the high-thrust launch kick lasted only one-thousandth of a second, the sustainer burned until target impact. The foot soldier searched the battle scene with a tripod-mounted TV-enhanced telescopic tracker. The gunner scanned the telescope sight until fixed crosshairs, inscribed at the optics center, pointed to the chosen target's most vulnerable spot for warhead penetration.

After a trigger pull, TOW flew a few feet above the ground, trailing a steel wire pair that maintained contact with the launcher. A two-and-a-half-mile-long wire spooled within the missile was rapidly dispensed by its own tension as the TOW flew toward its target. An optical sensor in the launcher tracked a pulsed xenon arc lamp beacon mounted at the missile's aft end (xenon was chosen because its brilliance could penetrate battlefield smoke and the TOW's rocket motor plume); electrical commands sent to the missile from the launcher's computer through the trailing wire directed TOW to steer so as to match the beacon's position with the fixed crosshairs in the viewer. The gunner kept those crosshairs on the moving target for the missile's entire flight. On impact, a shaped charge triggered by a contact fuse deeply penetrated tough armor.

In previous years, the French had attempted to perfect a wire-trailing guided missile but had been unable to solve three major challenges: finding an adequately high tensile strength wire material; extruding several miles of wire pairs without flaw; and configuring a reliable spooling mechanism to avoid tangles as the wire rapidly unwound. Our attempts also failed many times, until a team effort with US Steel Corporation finally succeeded. By 1986, TOW had demonstrated an extraordinary performance record of 93 percent hits in twelve thousand launches!

The TOW 2, begun in 1980, had a longer launch range and improved warhead shape, plus an extending probe to trigger the fuse before impact. In 1984, at the Army test range in Huntsville, Alabama, I had the privilege of firing a production-test TOW 2; my bird hit the moving tank shape more than a mile away! First used in Vietnam in 1972, by 1991, more than 500,000 TOW missiles, of five different types, had been produced, purchased, and deployed by forty-two nations. They routed hundreds of Iraqi armored vehicles in both Gulf Wars.

Helicopter Strike

To increase the combat opportunities for TOW, a helicopter-launched capability was highly desirable, but some experts thought that the trailing wire would be sucked into the spinning rotor blades. Many tests with highly maneuvering helicopters demonstrated there was no hazard since the rotor downwash was strong enough to ensure clearance.

In 1964, we handily won the Army contract for the optical launch-track set for the AH-1 *Cobra* helicopter in competition with Philco-Ford. The objective of the program, called M-65 TSU (telescopic sight unit), was to combine the visual viewfinder with an IR imager and a laser rangefinder. The missile guidance concept was similar to that of the TOW ground version, with the pipper target designator, the tracker of the missile xenon beacon, and steering commands sent through the despooling

Cobra Helicopter
(©iStockphoto/chapin31)

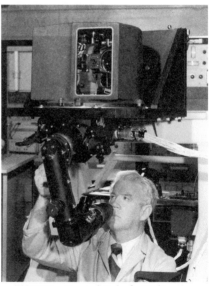

TOW Fire Control Sight for Helicopters
(courtesy of Raytheon)

wire. Later improvements added a laser rangefinder and a night vision IR imager with target tracker called C-NITE. The optical sight, thermal imager, and laser rangefinder were cradled on a gimbaled mount stabilized and isolated from the violent helicopter movements. Our design demonstrated extraordinary motion stability, with the IR and visual tracking angles coordinated with less than 2-1/2 degrees deviation, a remarkable achievement of precision. Concept evaluation TOW shots from the UH-1 *Iroquois* (the famous *Huey*) helicopters in Vietnam successfully destroyed many hostile tanks. That experimental program had the amusing moniker INFANT (*Iroquois* night fighting and night tracker). Since IR imaging was just evolving, the sensor was an LLTV (low light TV). The final M-65 TOW *Cobra* design performed exceedingly well, and Hughes produced almost 2,000 *Cobra* helicopter sets for the US Army and thirty other countries, including an adaptation for the British Lynx helicopter.

Submarine Attack

In the late 1970s, the Navy urgently needed an effective weapon to counter the very sophisticated Soviet Alfa-class submarine, with substantial performance improvements compared to the Mk-48 torpedo already deployed: higher speed, operation at greater depths, homing in at longer range, and far greater lethality. It was also desirable that the sonar detect targets at twice the Mk-48 range in a very complex acoustic countermeasure environment. Hughes's well-proven capability in doing intricate system engineering, creating many types of smart missiles, and developing sonar surveillance systems for the Navy (see Section 34, "Seek and Ye Shall Find") led to its capturing the exotic guidance system for the new weapon, the Mk-48 ADCAP (advanced capability) torpedo.

In entering into this new product field, the company made a wise decision to team with the incumbent Mk-48 prime torpedo contractor, Gould Industries; Hughes also promised to build a new plant in Forrest, Mississippi, to manufacture the resulting Hughes hardware—politically very beneficial in the competitive win.

The program's goal was to ensure high hit rates against deeply submerged nuclear-powered submarines and high-performance surface ships using evasive tactics. The company's responsibility was to develop a unique new internal guidance system for the torpedo and its companion fire control electronics and displays to be installed in the submarine. The 21-inch diameter ADCAP was 19 feet long and weighed 3,695 pounds. Launch range was in excess of five miles (specifics are still security-classified).

Midcourse guidance was by commands sent from the launching submarine through a despooling wire (similar to the TOW concept) from both the torpedo and its mother ship. Terminal guidance used an active sonar mounted within the torpedo. Similar to Hughes's air intercept weapons, the sonar array seeker tracked the target regardless of hostile evasive maneuvers or ADCAP's own course changes, and the internal computer determined the proper guidance navigation after midcourse commands from its own submarine ended. A set of electromagnetic sensors on the ADCAP skin triggered the 650-pound warhead. For maximum effectiveness, the torpedo steered to a point just beneath the target's hull; an explosion here would likely break the hostile ship's spine-like keel.

After a successful first phase of development, Hughes's business position was enhanced when the Navy requested that our company become overall technical integrator of the Mk-48/ADCAP weapon. Management by Hughes of the entire system was proven most effective in extensive testing. With production beginning in 1985 and first deployment in 1988, more than 1,000 had been made for the Navy inventory by 2007. Hughes further expanded its torpedo product line in the late 1990s to include the Mk-46 and Mk-50 lightweight torpedoes after the company acquired the Marine Systems Group of Alliant Techsystems located near Seattle, Washington.

ADCAP Torpedo
(courtesy of UNLV)

Table 7.1. Principal Weapon Programs

Designator	Name	Year	Est.# Built	Key Features
JB-3	Tiamat	1945	3	s/a radar
AIM-4A/C	Radar Falcon	1946	25,000	s/a radar
AIM-4B/D	IR Falcon	1952	27,000	IR
AIM-47	Super Falcon	1959	20	s/a PD radar
BGM-71	TOW	1961	660,000	Wire command
AIM-54	Phoenix	1963	4,600	Multi-shot, active
AGM-65	Maverick	1968	70,000	TV, IR, or laser
MMM-115	Roland	1975	714	Optical & radar
Mk-48	ADCAP	1979	1,000	Wire & act. sonar
AIM-120	AMRAAM	1981	16,000	Many modes
(none)	KKV	1988	10	IR
(none)	Agile	1989	6	>180 deg. IR
AIM-9X	Adv. Sidewinder	1995	10,000	Hi- res. IR
RIM-162	ESSM	2000	1,100	Cmd. & s/a radar
Guidance system by Hughes				
SM-62	Snark	1946	25	Star tracker
UGM-27	Polaris	1956	250	cmd/inertial
FIM-43	Redeye	1959	30	IR
AGM-62	Walleye	1960	950	TV or IR
M-67	Davy Crockett	1961	20	IR
UGM-73	Poseidon	1963	250	cmd/inertial
GBU-15	Glide bomb	1972	10,000	TV or IR
UGM-96	Trident	1975	250	cmd/inertial
Added by Purchases from General Dynamics 1992 & Alliant Techsystems 1996 **Advanced Cruise, Mk46, Mk 50, Phalanx, Rolling Airframe,** **Sparrow, Standard, Stinger, Tomahawk**				

44

SCIENTIFIC SPACE
EXPLORATION

MANY DEMONSTRATIONS OF complex technical excellence led to a large number of Hughes ventures into space for scientific exploration. The company was a strong advocate of achieving such information using unmanned space vehicles. Such spacecraft could be developed in far less time and at only one-third the cost of manned vehicles to obtain the same amount of data—the difference being the extra size, weight, and provisions needed for safely sustaining any humans aboard. However, the public emotions stirred by films such as *2001: A Space Odyssey*, *Star Trek*, and *The Right Stuff* persuaded politicians to provide enormous financial support for the more colorful and costly approach. The same situation prevails today, almost fifty years after "place a man on the Moon" was stated as a national objective. Ironically, the first Hughes program in space exploration was directly related to the astronaut program.

Surveyor Lunar Landing

In 1966, a spectacular Hughes product made the first American soft landing on the Moon. The primary results from the Surveyor spacecraft (of which there were seven) were twofold: as a precursor to Apollo, to demonstrate the feasibility of a lunar soft landing and to investigate possible landing sites for the manned flights. Surveyor actually accomplished much more.

The spacecraft had a storybook appearance, with tripod landing legs and a body that looked like a crouching spider.

It was designed so that, as it neared the Moon, its radar determined the distance to the surface and the approach speed; the vehicle rotated to an upright landing position and retrorockets ignited to slow the touchdown to a gentle soft landing on its cushioned feet. To determine more about the Moon's structure (and its origin), Surveyor's probes measured soil chemistry, density, grittiness, and load-bearing properties. A television camera scanned the surroundings.

Surveyor I responded to 158,000 instructions from the Earth station and transmitted 11,500 photographs of the Moon's surface. People all over the world were amazed to finally see what they had only dreamed of: what is "up there?"

Surveyor Soft Lander
(courtesy of UNLV)

In undertaking to validate technologies that would enable the first human landings on the Moon, Surveyor achieved many firsts—precise guidance to a predetermined landing spot far from Earth; autonomous control of a remote object; radar reflectivity data about a hitherto unknown surface; and a radar-controlled soft landing. Also notable were long-distance microwave performance in space conditions; flawless data transmission both to and from the Moon; and remote chemical analysis of materials collected by the soil probes. And finally, the functioning of electronics, optics, mechanical devices, scientific measurement instruments, and materials performed in the harsh vacuum of space and their survival of exposure to unfiltered sunlight.

In the succeeding two years, four more Surveyors soft-landed and did their assigned tasks without a hitch. One of them returned images of the Earth showing beams from two Hughes lasers, their spacing, and the angular spread of their beams at this great distance.

Like many other company programs, credit for success was due to the technical skills of the program's team members. For example, the configuration of the radar that measured Surveyor's approach angle, speed, and distance to the rapidly approaching surface of the Moon during the last flight phase was unique. Also, the autonomous performance of the spacecraft's control system in assuring an upright and soft landing was especially noteworthy because interaction with an Earth station during this short but crucial phase was precluded by the two-way signal delay of two-and-a-half seconds at that 236,000-mile distance.

Carrying out the development of Surveyor on its optimistic schedule, however, caused considerable embarrassment for Hughes senior executives, as viewed by government agencies. The ambitious program was fraught with uncertainties; new scientific and engineering discoveries were necessary to attain the difficult performance goals under conditions never before attempted. The project was directed by NASA's JPL, which in turn was managed by the California Institute of Technology. Detailed design decisions, program sequences, testing methods, and budget details were closely monitored and often revised by these agencies, accompanied by endless discussions. This management complexity engendered a good deal of confusion about the lines of authority. (Who is in charge today, please?) The original Hughes cost and schedule forecasts were extremely optimistic, as were those of NASA about the launching rocket vehicle's capabilities and schedules. Progress shortfalls provided a continuing basis for criticism. The final spacecraft results were spectacular, but completion took $360 million rather than our original bid of $60 million! A bit embarrassing, but extraordinary technical success overcame government dismay.

Preparing for the unknown involved many unusual ground tests to see if various devices would work on the surface of the Moon. Scientific assumptions and speculation both had a part in the attempt to simulate the foreign lunar surface, hostile temperatures, Sun exposure, and vacuum conditions. One challenge was to design the drill that would extract soil samples for analysis by the onboard laboratory. One morning a security guard noticed a number of holes drilled in the parking lot asphalt and in adjoining sections of earth and sandstone. As he was considering the possible cause, along came an engineer carrying strange-looking bits of hardware and about to begin that day's experiment. The guard did his duty, however, and prevented further damage to the parking lot in this creative attempt at space exploration!

The young professionals managing the dynamic control system design became very concerned about a potential catastrophe during Surveyor's first flight as it sped in its sixty-hour transit to the Moon. In the midcourse, or coast, phase, the spacecraft was continually stabilized in attitude by sensors in each of three axes that triggered cold-gas thrusters to correct deviations. Surveyor relayed telemetry signals to the ground staff, so they could monitor the performance of these sensors. One periodically indicated an errant orientation, which, curiously, did not seem to trigger corrections. The home folk were exceedingly worried that Surveyor could soon tumble out of control and be a costly disaster. Yet there were no other indications of instability. After careful but anxious analysis, the team concluded that the telemetry monitor for that axis sensor had been wired backwards; the sensor and its thruster were working properly, but the signal sent to the ground was showing a reverse correction. Hallelujah!

Other Journeys

During the 1960s and 1970s, Hughes participated in many other scientific explorations of the solar system in projects that usually were unprofitable from a business perspective, but greatly enhanced the company's reputation for excellence in the space industry. The company's renown was due in part to 186 spacecraft launches in a quarter century. Following is a sample listing:

- *Orbiting Solar Observatory-8 (OSO)*, orbiting at 345 miles altitude, measured X-ray and ultraviolet emanations from the solar corona.
- *Multispectral Scanner* and its higher-performance follow on, *Thematic Mapper*, have been the payloads aboard NASA's Landsat Earth resources satellites since 1972. These Hughes instruments have provided images of the Earth in visible, infrared, and, in the case of Thematic Mapper, thermal spectral bands, showing visually the state of the land surfaces over the entire globe and making valuable contributions to scientific and Earth-management endeavors throughout the world.
- *Geostationary Operational Environmental Satellite (GOES)* has provided continuous vital global weather information and severe storm tracking, as well as meteorological research data, since 1975. Hughes supplied five GOES spacecraft for NASA; NOAA was the satellite systems' operator.

- The *Pioneer Venus*, a technically challenging mission managed by NASA's Ames Research Center, conducted the first in situ measurements of the atmosphere of that cloud-covered planet.

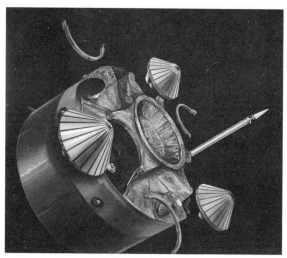

Venus Probes
(courtesy of UNLV)

Hughes designed and developed the mission's two separately launched vehicles: an orbiter and a multiprobe, the latter carrying one large and three small probes. In addition to its measurements of the upper atmosphere and ionosphere, the orbiter recorded measurements of the Venusian surface (including a surface plateau the size of Australia and a mountain 8,000 feet higher than Everest) and later performed celestial mechanics and other scientific measurements. The four probes recorded, in widely separated areas, the structure and composition of the atmosphere down to the planet's surface, the nature and composition of the clouds, and the radiation field and energy exchange in the lower atmosphere. Two probes operated for a short while on the surface instead of burning up on their descent as anticipated. All these new data altered scientific theories about the creation of the solar system.

- The *Galileo Probe*, the first probe to enter the atmosphere of one of the outer planets, was also built by Hughes for Ames Research Center. In 1995, the probe was ejected from the orbiting *Galileo* spacecraft into the extremely hostile atmosphere of Jupiter; during its 58-minute descent, it relayed back to Earth data on the nature and composition of the atmosphere, including wind speeds greater than 400 miles per hour, before succumbing as expected to the extreme environmental conditions.

- *Visible and thermal imaging devices* made by Hughes have mapped the surfaces of Mercury, Venus, Earth, our Moon, Mars, Saturn, Jupiter, Neptune, and Uranus; all data were successfully returned to scientists on Earth and shown to an astonished public. Our imagers are also on Pioneer 10, launched in 1983; it has now become the first man-made object to physically leave the solar system.

Virginia Norwood was senior scientist in the Electrooptical and Data Systems Group when she received the 1979 Pecora Award from NASA and the Department of the Interior for her leadership of the Hughes team that developed the Multispectral Scanner and Thematic Mapper. Here are her remembrances in 2010 of her years at Hughes, especially those associated with space programs:

"During my thirty-five years at Hughes, I worked in the Research Laboratories and in the advanced design areas of diverse product lines: guided missiles, space, communications, and electronic defense systems. I was well rewarded by close association with many creative people and participated in several unusual design breakthroughs. Following are some examples.

"Hughes jumped into the space age in several different areas with different teams of people. Syncom, designed by Harold Rosen, Don Williams, and Tom Hudspeth, was not only the forerunner of today's worldwide communications satellite industry, it was also very small and inexpensive. (If Don Williams had had his way, Hughes would have leased an island in the Pacific near the equator and provided the entire launch hardware and procedures; the government would not allow that much autonomy to one company, however, so the US facilities in Florida had to be used, increasing the cost of putting Syncom in orbit.)

"Shortly afterward, Hughes began to build Surveyor, the first soft-landing probe for Moon terrain research. It used three-axis stabilization. Dick Cheng's team perfected a novel landing system (conceived by Bob Roney) for Surveyor as well as the orbital dynamics needed for the spacecraft to traverse the path to the Moon, be injected into lunar orbit, and descend to the surface. The TV and data communications link to Earth, the responsibility of my microwave organization, used a novel planar array, designed by Roger Anderson, to allow compact storage during flight. The transmitter was driven by the world's first solid-state signal source to produce 2 watts at X-band frequencies.

Before contract award by NASA/JPL, during the last week of the proposal period we triumphantly demonstrated the signal-multiplier chain to JPL. (It had been widely rumored that our chief competitor had warned JPL that this electronic process could only be done with conventional vacuum tubes.) We thus proved the feasibility of a solid state approach with a bit of drama!

"Different groups within the company competed among themselves to make the best technology advances. For years, the synchronous orbit was considered to be the private domain of Hughes. I remember the gibe: 'If it don't spin, it won't win.' In the mid-1960s, I began the design for an orbiting Earth imager to provide good resolution, multispectral images on a repetitive basis to serve a wide range of users for a number of environmental assessments. A Sun-synchronous orbit was selected because it allowed uniform lighting and imaging anywhere on Earth; company advocates of the Earth-synchronous placement championed their preference. After we showed the massive optics that would be needed at that high orbit, and the impossible viewing angles, everyone was convinced our choice was right. With the persistence of Steve Dorfman, we got our company funding, and NASA initiated the project.

"Another example of the extraordinary diversity at Hughes was the scanner invented by Webb Howe for a spacecraft-borne multispectral imager. The company had always been known for advanced electronics; however, this very clever linear scan was done mechanically, and gave us precision that was far superior to the three RCA vidicons that were also flown with our system on an early Earth resources satellite. The mechanical scanner, at first heartily scoffed at by many, allowed precision registration of the multispectral pixels, without which the separate data streams would lose much of their comparative value. After the launch in 1972, a diverse group of users found that these data could be applied to areas that were undreamed of when we had set up the original requirements."

These Hughes ventures were most exciting, educational, and scientifically rewarding. As mentioned above, none was profitable financially, but all enhanced the Hughes reputation for reaching beyond. The real profits in the space business lay in providing large-scale national, industrial, and public services.

45

GLOBAL COMMUNICATION

Until the nineteenth century, true long distance communication at high speed had only been a dream for commerce, military operations, or personal conversations. Smoke signals, colored flags, and timed light flashes were helpful, but were greatly limited in transmission range and message content. One amusing example of ingenious long-distance messaging occurred in 1815 when financier Nathan Rothschild in London received news of Napoleon's defeat at Waterloo one day ahead of anyone else—by using carrier pigeons!

Communicating Electrically

Electric signals passed by wire at the speed of light became practical in 1833, perfected by William Weber in Göttingen, Germany. Words were formed by coded "on and off" signals that could be interpreted by the receiving individual. This was called the telegraph, and landlines were strung through and between many nations' government and business centers. The US military made early use of the telegraph during the Civil War, when both Union and Confederate sides passed enormous amounts of information in this way. Transoceanic communication became possible by the laying of insulated, environmentally protected wire cables between shores, the first being across the English Channel in 1850. A trans-Atlantic line began operations in 1866.

Voice communication required the conversion of spoken sound into electrical signals that could be converted back to sound at the receiving end. Air pressure caused by incoming sound vibrated a thin membrane whose motion stimulated a stack of carbon granules to emit an electrical response that traveled along wire to a receiver. The first words telephoned were from Alexander Graham Bell to his associate, "Mr. Watson, come here, I want to see you." At least five innovators claimed credit for the set of related inventions; most likely demonstrations by Antonio Meucci or Johann Reis in the early 1860s should have been designated as "firsts" making the telephone practical, but the Scotsman Bell, working in the United States, was granted the first US patent in 1876. (Bell just beat the American Elisha Gray in the rush for that patent.) Long-range voice and music communication soon became possible everywhere. The undersea cables were also able to interconnect overseas telephones, but with limited capacity for the huge volume of desired traffic.

The next leap in communication came with the invention of radio, discovered by Germany's Heinrich Hertz in 1887. The Italian Guglielmo Marconi made the system practical in 1894. Signals at frequencies in hundreds of cycles per second could be radiated from an antenna and received at great distances. These signals could be coded, similar to telegraph messages, or be spoken words. The latter was done initially by changing the power levels emitted in a way that matched the sound waves of each word (amplitude modulation). At the higher frequencies (short wave), the radio signals bounced off an electromagnetic layer that encases the Earth, thus permitting international linkups between sender and receiver. Marconi demonstrated the first commercially practical transatlantic radio transmission in his 1907 startup of wireless telegraphy between Glace Bay, Nova Scotia, and Clifden, Ireland. There were several generations of marine radio design technology, and my father used them all, beginning in 1919 with spark-gap transmitters and crystal-detector receivers, and finally with audio and telegraphy linkups by satellite during the Vietnam conflict in 1969.

Fully operational commercial television transmission in the United States came in 1938. Many inventors throughout the world in the 1920s had been intensively working the needed technologies to render fast-moving images into electrical signals, broadcast large amounts of data, and convert the images onto viewing screens to satisfy a massive demand for household reception of video news and entertainment.

Worldwide communication of national security data and the burgeoning demand for public transfer of voice, television, and digital information became prime inducements for technology focus and investment.

Communication Satellite
Design Advancements

The strategy and tactics for Hughes to capture a large part of the global communication business through the use of satellites were effectively directed by Bud Wheelon, at the time president of the Space and Communications Group. (He became Hughes CEO in 1986.) With a strong international reputation gained from the success of Syncom and Early Bird, Hughes had a firm foundation upon which to build.

To maximize the voice- and video-carrying capacity of each satellite—the more the "throughput," the greater the return on the investment needed to develop, build, and launch the satellites—satellite design advanced in three stages. The first stage was to increase the payload capacity to carry more relay transponders—and thus more telephone and video channels—while keeping the patent-protected, low cost spin-stabilized satellite configuration. The second was to increase the data flow through each transponder, in particular, by advancing an electronic architecture called multiplexing. The final stage was to substantially increase the amount of continuous power available from a replenishable source. More power meant more transponders operating.

Increasing Payload Capacity

In 1958, JPL created and launched Explorer I, the first US satellite to orbit the Earth. Its cylindrically shaped body was intended to spin stably about its longitudinal axis, much like a pencil spinning about its central lead strip. Classic mechanics textbooks at that time dealt with rigid bodies, and calculations showed that this spinning configuration would remain stable. But to everyone's surprise, Explorer I did not. After a short time in orbit it began to tumble end over end. JPL ultimately figured out why: unlike the classic-rule examples, Explorer I was not a perfectly rigid body due to the effects of its four whiplike telemetry antennas. JPL found that a non-rigid body will spin stably only about its axis of highest inertia; in the case of Explorer 1, this was a flat spin about the axis perpendicular to the long dimension. (The altered spin did not end the mission, although it did produce periodic fadeouts of data sent back to Earth.) Therefore, any spinning satellites, including Syncom and its later Hughes family of descendants, had to be squat cylinders with diameters greater than their lengths. This stability rule was also thought to apply to any cylinders containing nonspinning (called despun) segments—imposing a perceived limit on the future usefulness of spinners, since their launch vehicles were growing more in length than in diameter. This diameter limit meant that "squatty" satellites could not become much bigger.

Also, by 1964, the DoD and federal intelligence agencies were aggressively pursuing the use of synchronous and high orbit satellites for communication and data gathering. These ambitious missions, of necessity, would require large antennas and electrooptical sensors probing specific targets on the Earth's surface. In spite of their well-demonstrated robustness, reliability, and relatively low cost, the Hughes satellites appeared to be inadequate for these new missions because of their fundamentally limited size.

Accordingly, Hughes and its competitors studied stable, nonspinning configurations for the more demanding missions requiring more power from large solar arrays. Some of these designs used reaction wheels in each of the three spacecraft axes of roll, pitch, and yaw, and some incorporated a single large flywheel for stabilization. Hughes proposed such a design in 1964 for a significant highly classified mission in competition with TRW, a company then more experienced in fully stabilized satellites. We lost.

At that time our fully stabilized Surveyor Moon lander design was progressing well; it was very sophisticated in all its features, but it could not be easily adapted to long-duration orbiting satellite demands.

Equally troubling, in 1965, TRW pushed into our territory and won Intelsat III, a spinner featuring a small despun antenna. Although the TRW design worked, it was limited by the area its antenna beams could cover and by its short cylindrical solar-power array. Nonetheless, the loss was our wake-up call. The future was going to be tough and Hughes needed to find a winning edge.

To compete effectively for the large payload programs, the company had to find a way to continue using our spin stabilized concept. If we could solve the wobble problem that pestered elongated spinning cylinders, a much larger spacecraft could be produced—one whose outer spinning drum could support an array of many solar cells sharing their spinning exposure to sunlight, and whose nonrotating (despun) center body could support precisely pointed antennas and optical assemblies.

Tony Iorillo (who later became president of the Space and Communications Group), had begun his Hughes career with an assignment from Don Williams during the design of Syncom. His job was to check Don's extensive analyses of Syncom dynamics. Later, during the unsuccessful 1964 competition with TRW, Tony began to study the wobble characteristics of a non-rigid satellite with a rigid flywheel. Using company funding, he expanded to the more general case of a non-rigid satellite configuration that incorporates a Syncom-like non-rigid flywheel. In particular, he analyzed the mechanical stresses in each part of the satellite during a wobbling episode and how these parts would flex. In the process of flexing—similar to the sloshing of fuel in gas tanks—mechanical energy is lost.

Tony discovered the rule that relates the overall wobble stability of such a satellite to the energy dissipated in its various component parts. His study found that if the mechanical energy lost in the non-spinning part is greater than that lost in the spinning part, the wobble will subside and the satellite is stable. The conventional wisdom was not correct.

To illustrate the concept, a series of laboratory models were built that could be made stable or unstable at the tester's will by balancing the amount of component flexing and the subsequent energy dissipated in each part. Fortunately, this balancing of energy loss proved to be easy in practice, accomplished mechanically by countering fluid slosh and inserting tuned damper springs between the outer drum and the core. Happily, the virtues of spin stabilization demonstrated by Syncom could be carried over to the more ambitious missions using much larger satellites.

In 1965, armed with this work, Hughes convinced the Aerospace Corporation (the technical consultant to the Air Force) that, when designed correctly, cylindrical spin-stabilized satellites of any length were indeed capable of carrying large, accurately pointed antennas and precise electrooptical sensors. The only limit now was launch vehicle lifting capacity. Hughes named this generic design the Gyrostat system. First used for the Air Force's TACSAT 1, a synchronous orbit tactical communication satellite launched in 1969, this configuration was later used for many other Hughes satellites, including the popular HS-376 family. A typical satellite in the latter category weighed 1,000 pounds and could support twenty-four transponders, each of which could relay a TV channel or two thousand voice lines. A telescoping cylindrical solar array—which extended to its full length once the satellite was in orbit—nearly doubled the number of solar cells available to supply power.

The TACSAT was gigantic compared to our original 86-pound Syncom; weighing 1,600 pounds, it was more than 9 feet in diameter and almost 30 feet high, including a large array of antennas. The cylinder's spin rate was set at 60 revolutions per minute. The resultant flywheel momentum was easily able to resist the disturbing forces of sunlight and provided a firm base for the mission-required slewing of five UHF antennas.

In 1968, before the launch proof of TACSAT 1, Hughes won two other major competitions using the same Gyrostat concept: Intelsat IV and a still classified program. These awards were in the nick of time for our space business survival. Surveyor funding was ending and our other

NASA and Intelsat programs were quite small, meaning only a few short months of backlog for the workforce. The two projects sustained us, led the way to virtual dominance of this market, and allowed the company to move toward providing and operating complete communication satellite networks. Those were exciting times!

TACSAT Satellite in Orbit
(courtesy of UNLV)

Increasing Data Volume and Flow

The second design stage focused on increasing the volume of information that could be carried by each satellite transponder. A number of improvements were made. The data streams were handled through electronic links operating at the high frequencies of Ka or millimeter wave (see frequency band listing in Section 33, "The Wonders of Electronic Scan"); these widely spread frequency bands gave enough space for several separate data streams. Precise antenna pattern shapes and focuses minimized the power level needed to ensure uninterrupted reception by the ground receivers. Furthermore, the operating efficiency of each transponder's transmitter and receiver was greatly improved, reducing demands on the satellite's power source (which in turn allowed more transponders aboard, if there was enough mounting space). The technique of timesharing of many channels on the same transponder (described below in "Multiplexing") was exploited to greatly increase the amount of information relayed.

The large advances in the intricate design and construction of the transponders were made by a team superbly led by Howard Ozaki and Tom Hudspeth; the team's ability placed the company in a good competitive position whenever the communication payload was the user's primary consideration.

Multiplexing

Transfer of as much data as possible can be done by handling message streams sent by the carrier in such a way that they can be separated and properly interpreted at the receiving end. This is called multiplexing, and can be accomplished in several ways. To visualize one process, think about your hearing ability. Most people can detect and interpret sound waves as low as 20 Hz and up to 20,000 Hz; this is called the audio range. While listening to the blended performance of an orchestra you can still, if you choose, perceive the separate "message" being sent by a single instrument. Suppose the oboe is really a computer, as are the violin, cello, and flute, each sending a different data stream to a group of "listening" computers; each receiving computer is tuned to a transmitting mate and ignores the other three data streams. We now have four separate sets of messages flowing within a single audio frequency range.

Now instead of using sound waves let's change the link transmissions to much higher frequencies, such as radio or radar waves. If we use a Ka-band microwave carrier there will be a lot more room for separate data streams, each at widely-spaced frequencies: the Ka band is 4 gHz (gigahertz or billions of cycles per second) in width, from 27 to 31 gHz. A lot of room for hundreds of narrowband data streams operating at the same time.

Besides using different frequencies for different messages, it is also possible to time-share a single data stream among several ongoing messages. This is commonly called time-division multiplexing. Visualize ten computers simultaneously sending ten different movies over a single transmission link. Each movie is assigned one-tenth of the link's sending time. The signal for movie number one is converted to digital data in computer number one, which stores it and squashes each second of video by ten times into a one-tenth-of-a-second packet (this is called data compression). The link sends that packet in the first assigned time slot. Movie number two is assigned time slot number two, and in one second, all ten movie packets have been sent. That sharing process is repeated in each following second. At the receiving end, a computer matched to number one captures packet number one in that first time slot; it then expands that information back to a full second, and translates it from digital to video. Other movies are caused to do the same thing during their assigned time slots. The reconstruction job is done so smoothly that viewers enjoy a chosen movie without any hiccups or burps in the quality of the received images and sound. The same time-share technique can be used for TV and high-content computer data streams. Massive amounts of complex information can be transferred by a relay carrier with many channels separated by frequency, each using time-shared data streams. Communications engineers have developed sophisticated mathematical techniques that permit sending as much information as possible over a given link, while preventing "crosstalk" interference between the separate data streams.

Overcoming Power Limits

For stage three of Hughes's effort to increase satellite capability, the company decided in 1987 to invest $100 million of its own money to develop a three-axis fully stabilized spacecraft, using electrically powered gyroscopes to control each axis. Such a design would greatly increase the allowable number of solar cells compared to spinners and thus provide enough renewable power to support double the number of transponders in the payload, as well as increase their output power levels. This HS-601 spacecraft became very popular with satellite purchasers and provided the base for the company's entrance into the business of supplying TV services directly to consumers. Within a few years, it became the best selling fully stabilized communications satellite in history.

The new 3,630-pound HS-601 had two giant flat wings that unfolded after the satellite was in orbit; the total span was 56 feet, and each wing consisted of three 7- by 8.5-foot panels containing thousands of silicon cells fastened to Kevlar sheets. The wings were always maneuvered to be perpendicular to the Sun's rays. The panels had thirty-five times the solar cells of the HS-376 spinner and, because of a change in cell material from silicon to gallium arsenide, 24 percent higher output efficiency. Total power produced was 3.3 kW. Rechargeable nickel-hydrogen batteries ensured continuous operation during times when the Earth's shadow blocked the sunlight.

The HS-601 could carry between twenty-four and forty-eight transponders, each of which relayed one thousand telephone lines and five to seven TV channels, in contrast to Early Bird, in which each transpon-

Communications satellite power chiefly comes from simple and reliable solar cells—the more cells the Sun illuminates, the more power produced. Before HS-601, all Hughes satellites had these cells mounted on the exterior of their enclosing drums; because of the drums' rotation, fewer than half the cells faced the Sun with full exposure at any one time. With the despun core design, satellites grew greatly in size, complexity, and performance, and available power became the upper boundary for the addition of more transponders. This fact forced a different design approach.

The alternative was to mount cells on flat panels attached to a non-spinning bus, requiring a three-axis stabilized spacecraft. Competitors had already chosen this more expensive concept, being precluded from using spinners by a number of Hughes patents. Achieving vehicle stability was more complex, but larger and larger solar panels could be accommodated as power requirements increased.

der carried only one TV channel and 240 telephone connections. This astounding improvement came from the use of multiplexed digital data streams. In 1976, the Hughes Intelsat IV-A provided six thousand telephone lines or twelve color TV channels, twenty-five times the capacity of any other satellite to that date. Only a few years later, capacity had increased another twenty-five times with HS-601!

The antenna beam patterns could be shaped to provide line-of-sight signals to subscribers' tiny home antennas in a specific assigned service territory. All geosynchronous satellites, when viewed from the ground, appear fixed in space, so those personal antennas did not have to perform tracking maneuvers, as required for satellites in lower orbit arcs.

Long Life Up There

To warrant the large investment needed to create and operate a satellite, the longest possible life of its equipment was a critical factor. After solving the many problems of hardware survival in frigid space, providing stable electronic devices, and housing enough solar cells to create sufficient

HS-601 Communication Satellite
(courtesy of UNLV)

electrical power, it was mandatory to assure long-term spacecraft attitude control and stationkeeping. This was done with small thrusters using fuel stored in a bottle large enough to last fifteen years. That might seem to be an economically long time, but usually electronic obsolescence occurred well before the fifteen years were up, prompting a complete replacement by a better performing satellite. In later years, ion engines using electrical power were developed to do the stabilization "forever," but before the mid-1990s their cost was so high that they were favored only for deep space scientific probes. Ion engines developed by the company's Research Laboratories did replace chemical thrusters aboard the Hughes HS-601 communication satellites when the cost became affordable.

46

THE COMMERCIALIZATION
OF SPACE

Syncom proved the viability of worldwide communications via geostationary satellites. It also opened up new directions for Hughes in developing both commercial and scientific spacecraft, as described above. The company's most ambitious—and arguably most risky—space-related venture, however, was the expansion of its business from supplying the satellites for commercial voice and television services to providing those services directly to millions of consumers throughout the United States. This venture, which took more than twenty years to accomplish, can be divided into four phases.

Phase 1. Satellite Manufacturer

The Communications Satellite Act signed by President Kennedy in 1962 opened the skies to commercialization and established Comsat (Communications Satellite Corporation) as the administrator of satellite communications for the United States; part of Comsat's mission was the development of a worldwide communications network. In 1964, Comsat joined with seventeen other countries to form Intelsat, a consortium of communications companies. With Comsat as manager, Intelsat would own and operate the global satellite system.

Hughes supplied Intelsat with its first spacecraft, Intelsat-1. Nicknamed Early Bird, it was the first geostationary commercial communications satellite. When launched in 1965, Early Bird was expected to last eighteen months; it actually performed successfully for four years, and was later reactivated twice for special duties. Intelsat completed its global coverage in 1969 with a constellation of four satellites, three of which Hughes supplied. (TRW provided Intelsat III.)

Some countries, however, preferred independence or had special geographic problems. When technology advances included satellite antennas that could shape and focus beams on smaller areas such as a single country, desires for national systems quickly emerged. Canada was first, in 1972, followed in 1976 by Indonesia. Hughes built families of satellites for Canada (Anik) and Indonesia (Palapa). A dramatic example of what satellite communications could do, Palapa helped bond together Indonesia, a widespread country of over seventeen thousand islands with over seven hundred different languages.

In the United States, the traditional communications companies—AT&T, Western Union, and RCA—all put up separate national systems. Hughes supplied the spacecraft for AT&T and Western Union; RCA built its own. An eager demand for these types of systems quickly grew throughout the world. Hughes remained the leading supplier, but other companies became noticeable competitors.

Phase 2. Satellite Supplier and System Operator

The Navy's LEASAT procurement in 1978 gave Hughes an opportunity to expand its business into providing the hardware segments for an entire communication system, rather than just the satellites, and operating the equipment rather than delivering it to a using customer. For LEASAT, or-

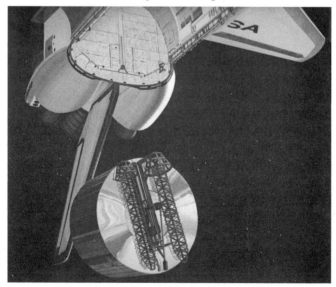

LEASAT Ejected from Space Shuttle
(courtesy of UNLV)

bit injection was to be from the Space Shuttle, necessitating a significant spacecraft redesign to fit the Shuttle's payload bay. (A model of that result can be seen today mounted in the Shuttle displayed at Cape Canaveral.)

The company's new business twist was to convince the Navy to lease, not buy, the total network: spacecraft, ground stations, and operation of the orbiting and Earth-based segments. In successfully performing this contract, at considerable technical and financial risk to itself, Hughes established its credentials as both a communications system supplier and operator.

Phase 3. System Owner and Operator

President Nixon's "open skies" policy in the late 1970s extended owner-ship of communications satellite systems to any qualified company that could obtain FCC approval. Hughes made another bold but risky busi

Satellite Network Ground Station
(courtesy of UNLV)

ness move. Forecasting that owning and operating satellite networks and providing commercial services would be far more lucrative than just sell-ing spacecraft, the company formed a subsidiary, HCI (Hughes Com-munications, Inc.), to provide the ground stations, sell usage rights for each transponder, and be a service provider. HCI would operate at arms-length from the Hughes satellite manufacturing unit. Initially created to start the LEASAT program, HCI became a direct competitor of some of

It is interesting to view this twenty-year venture as an evolution of a willingness to accept and conquer formidable risks. Initially, as a supplier of spacecraft, the risks to Hughes were chiefly technical and schedule: providing, on time and at a fixed price, satellites that satisfied or exceeded different customers' performance requirements. As the requirements grew, Hughes kept pace with increasingly more powerful vehicles. The customers took the risks of operating the system, marketing transponder usage, and making a profit. The customer base was relatively small, and Hughes's reputation for reliability and technical expertise went a long way. If there were enough contracts, their fixed-prices made the financial risk relatively small and controllable.

For LEASAT, Hughes accepted more risk. Although there was no marketing risk (the Navy leased all the satellites' capacity), there was some technical risk in developing a Shuttle-compatible vehicle. But now added were considerable risks in providing and managing the entire space and ground system while still eking out a profit.

Developing and operating the company's own Galaxy system through HCI added the risk of marketing the usage of a large number of satellite transponders in competition with several of Hughes's long-time customers. There also was a large financial risk in setting up, owning, operating, and maintaining the system itself.

Expanding one's marketing base to millions and millions of individual users throughout the United States, devising the equipment to do so, pricing the services, maintaining the services, and marketing them was a formidable undertaking. Several years of successful operation would be needed to regain the funds invested. A risky set of business decisions, indeed, but fortunately in this case culminating in extraordinarily lucrative gains.

the mother company's best customers such as AT&T, Western Union, and SBS (Satellite Business Systems), but the company correctly bet that the profits from commercial services would more than compensate for the lost opportunity for profits from spacecraft sales.

Transponders of Galaxy 1, HCI's first commercial satellite, were wholly subscribed to by the cable industry. Beginning with the success of HBO (Home Box Office) in using satellites to distribute its TV products to the cable industry, eagerness for product delivery by satellite spread rapidly to all the cable companies. Today, the US cable systems are completely dependent on communication satellites for program distribution.

Rather than leasing transponders as the competition did, HCI sold the property rights to use each transponder relay. HBO bought the first six, followed by Disney, Cinemax, The Movie Channel, Showtime, Turner Broadcasting, Viacom, and MCI, providing Hughes with cash to build Galaxies 2 and 3. HCI launched seven satellites in all, and set up ground stations around the world. Each satellite provided eighteen transponders, each with the capacity for five to seven TV channels and one thousand voice and data linkups.

Selling the services was quite beneficial to Hughes: the cost to get each transponder fully functioning was $3.5 million and revenues were $16 million. When paid up front, this cash provided a comfortable financial pool for ongoing and future expenses. The success of HCI confirmed the wisdom of entering the service business, its profits soon surpassing those of the satellite design and manufacturing efforts.

The company-funded development of the HS-601 satellite provided the foundation for further growth of HCI's services. Also, through a new subsidiary, Hughes Network Systems (HNS)—formed from a mid-1980s purchase of a segment of Microwave Associates in Greenbelt, Maryland—Hughes greatly improved the performance and manufacturing quality of the ground-based portions of the relays.

Phase 4. Direct Sales to Individual Customers

The company's culminating step in space commercialization was to provide services directly to individual businesses and homes, competing with cable distribution companies. The basic technology for DirecTV was well in hand—high power satellites broadcasting over a large area into small antenna dishes.

Selling to individual subscribers was rather easy; homeowners purchased small black-box adapters for their existing TV sets, added 18-inch antennas to the exteriors of their houses, and paid a modest monthly fee to continually capture up to 250 TV channels.

Household DirecTV Antenna
(courtesy of DirecTV)

To spur initial signups and thus proclaim a market surge, Hughes provided the adapters free to new subscribers. The first HS-601 satellite for DirecTV was launched in 1994; a ground station in Colorado provided the digital uplink at a rate of 1 billion bits per second.

This new public offering quickly captured the US market, gaining over 3 million subscribers within two years and soon reaching 14 million, more than were served by any other surface cable company. The company took enormous risks in attempting such a new and different venture in spite of very little consumer marketing and distribution experience. This leap in faith proved to be an extraordinary business triumph.

A key strategist who contributed immensely to making a success of this ambitious venture into a new marketplace was Eddy Hartenstein. He was named managing director of DirecTV, and in his later career became chairman of the board of Sirius XM Radio Inc. In 2008, he was appointed publisher of the *Los Angeles Times*. In 2010, he expressed these views about his experience at Hughes:

> "The hallmark of success for Hughes was its unique approach to problem solving at the system level. Whether a ground-based radar project for the military, an outer space mission for NASA, or a communications infrastructure program for the commercial sector, the approach was always systems oriented. And that's where the men and women of

Hughes had few equals. From these roots, combined with the willingness to abandon the NIH (not invented here) syndrome, came even greater breakthroughs in successful business development opportunities.

"Firmly guided by the principle that a successful undertaking cannot be a technology in search of a marketplace, and taking advantage of the confluence of outside developments and trends in both existing and forward-looking businesses and technology developments, opportunities such as direct broadcast satellite television materialized. DirecTV was such an example. Five favorable stars were aligned: asleep-at-the-switch cable company monopolistic franchises, breakthroughs in digital video compression, very high-powered communication satellite developments, consumer dissatisfaction, and finally, that special DNA of systems engineering.

"Fortunately, we made all the right moves to create an entirely new and very successful business enterprise, which today has almost 19 million customers generating more than $20 billion of annual revenue as a company whose market cap is almost $40 billion."

47

OTHER COMMERCIAL AND CONSUMER ADVENTURES

MOST OF HUGHES'S business through the 1960s was keyed to the company's mission of government support. The United States or overseas nations funded projects as part of their military, intelligence, communication, and scientific endeavors. Other markets existed, however, that could yield growth in revenue and earnings, such as manufactured products sold directly to consumers; competitive sales to governments, with research and development expenses paid by company investment; commercial offerings to other companies who would provide development funding; internally-funded products for consumer services sold to distributors of those services; and complete systems developed and operated with services sold directly to consumers.

During its early expansion years Hughes made many attempts to enter the highly competitive commercial world, targeting both consumer and industrial customers. The company made substantial inroads into the industrial sector, but was quite unsuccessful in the consumer sector. Selling directly to millions of individuals can be very lucrative if large quantities can be rapidly produced at very low cost. Hughes had no experience in this kind of manufacturing, nor in forming the marketing network needed to survive in a world of fickle customers with quickly changing desires. As soon as Hughes built a newly invented device and placed it on the consumer market, another company quickly copied it (outside the reach of our patent protection) at a much lower cost. To grab maximum market share, that competitor set its price well below its unit production cost; its well-established marketing network drove our product out. It then increased the price as it became the dominant or single source, and quickly repaid its own investment loss. Hughes could not compete because of the enormous investment that would be required. Even if we signed up with a major distributor with consumer marketing prowess, our top executives were unwilling to take on the unknown risk of establishing the needed production facilities. They decided the company was better served by focusing its venture funds on research and development for government systems. Nonetheless, the company did invent some pretty ingenious products across a wide variety of technical disciplines. Perhaps if there had been a string of successes, confidence and maturity would have resulted in quicker investments in, and entry into, commercial ventures. Speed is of the essence in this bubbling marketplace.

A good example was the computer-driven digital watch with its innovative liquid crystal display. Other attempts were initially successful, but few became long-term viable product lines. In many cases, Hughes led the way in introducing these innovative devices to the public, but the same manufacturing and marketing limits existed. Nevertheless, the company applied its strengths in some interesting and diverse ways. Here are some examples:

Digital Watch
(courtesy of Jeff Grant)

- *Digital watches* were not like anything that had existed before, and the public's enthusiasm blossomed into fruitful sales and earnings. But the company was slow to set up a low cost, higher output manufacturing plant. In the meantime, large-scale domestic and foreign competitors made close copies and willingly invested in automated production lines; their wide distribution nets soon captured the frenetic market. Patent holdings were insufficient to stem the tide, so we abandoned this marvelous small product in less than two years, making $50 million and then losing $50 million through pricing pressures. (Some of our competitors also retreated much later after losing their shirts.) It had become apparent that we could not sustain ourselves in this particular consumer market; we had the electronics competency to jump ahead with new designs, but we could not compete in what the buyers perceived as a jewelry business, where, not surprisingly, fancy appearance counts more than the product's operating features.

Typical Airliner Seat Entertainment
(courtesy of Wikipedia)

- *Airline passenger entertainment* used a single-wire network for distributing video and audio from a single source to display screens and headsets at each seat. The single-wire feature significantly reduced the system's demand for airplane space, weight, and power; that single wire simultaneously carried many independent music and TV channels by multiplexing digital-format data streams (see Section 45, "Global Communications; Multiplexing").
- *Flight simulators* were used for effective ground training of military and commercial aircraft pilots. A cockpit pod attached to a powered stand gave the pilot a physical sense of an aircraft's response to any motion command. The pod's interior was exactly like the real aircraft's cockpit, but had a large curved reflective screen beyond the windscreen upon which moving images of the flight regime were projected, giving a visual feel of reality. A computer managed the whole simulator, and the instructor could command it with any possible flight conditions. The 1988 Hughes acquisition of the British Rediffusion Corporation gave us a lead in providing flight simulators for the airline industry. However, although our simulators were ex-

cellent performers they were expensive and had a limited market. (A sister design by Hughes is very popular with the public: the exciting Disneyland *Star Wars* space flight).

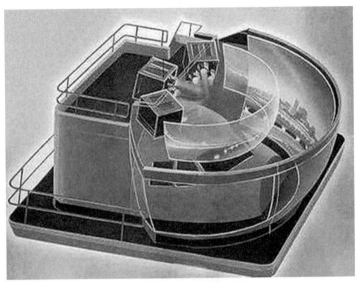

Typical Flight Training Simulator
(courtesy of Wikipedia)

- *Stereo retrieval systems (SRS)* enhanced the sense of direction that a listener experienced from only two stereo speakers. Sound appeared to emanate from beyond the width of speaker separation and under certain conditions would seem to be coming from behind the listener. This was done by digitally reprocessing the audio stream to recover directional information that is inherently lost in the recording process. (I was enthralled by a demonstration that used the dogfight scene from the film *Top Gun*; I had a most convincing illusion that I was actually flying that *Tomcat!*) One fairly obvious application was television sets where built-in speaker separation is limited; SRS gave the impression that the speakers were substantially farther apart. SRS today is incorporated into many products including Microsoft's Windows Media Player.

- *High-definition large screen projectors* developed by Hughes used liquid crystal light valve technology (see Section 40, "Command and Control") with picture clarity many times better than the video and graphics projectors existing in the 1980s. Again, commercial companies in the United States and Japan overwhelmed us; this performance jump was essential for their main line product and their giant research and development resources were difficult to match.

- A *laser fabric cutter* was intended to reduce the cost of high-volume shaping of garment sections prior to sewing. It used a moving laser beam to precisely cut many layers of material simultaneously. The laser device moved by computer instructions programmed to a predetermined pattern. The hardware design was excellent, but software flaws and lack of maturity were fatal; occasionally, a great quantity of material was lost, the victim of incorrect cuts. One garment firm complained, "Those pants only had one leg!" Software remedies came a bit late to restore universal market acceptance.

- *RealScene* converted two-dimensional photographs or filmstrips into digital format, analyzed the patterns seen, and created a video with all details in 3D. The scene could then be examined from any approach angle or from any distance. In a significant military application, RealScene images of aerial photos of the buildings in a town, projected in a theater, allowed tacticians to perfect the best and safest flight approach for the release of weapons against the tiniest of targets. The Israelis successfully used this procedure for a missile strike on a single room on the eighth floor of a Gaza Strip building, causing little collateral damage. Incidentally, the missile used was the Hughes TV Maverick, the only weapon accurate enough to hit a chosen single window in an air strike. Hughes failed to pursue the RealScene market with vigor, so only a few were sold.

  In addition, Hughes developed and produced many sophisticated display devices for both military and commercial applications: high performance cathode ray tubes, signal storage tubes, image processors, image memories, thermal image screens, and edge-lit see-through cockpit panels. In 1969, we were at the forefront in developing liquid crystal light valves to form large-screen panels that became the primary information displays in naval ship combat centers (see Section 40, "Command and Control; Consoles for Sea Vessels"); the perfected technology became part of the commercial marketplace. Hughes successfully teamed with Japan Victor Corporation to produce and market more than 3,500 displays with ten-foot square viewing screens.

- *Regenerative power devices* were produced by Spectrolab, located in Sylmar, California. This acquired subsidiary was preeminent in advanced design and manufacturing of solar cells, solar cell arrays, and panels. It also produced specialized searchlights and very high power light sources.

- *ProScan*, a product with enormous market possibilities, was a hand-carried IR thermal imager using indium-antimonide detectors and a throttled argon cryostat cooler with fiber optic connections to its display screen. It was perfect for, and very popular with, many city police units for night patrols and search and pursuit of criminals; for firefighters searching for hot spots and rescuing occupants; and for the US Bureau of Mines looking for potential hazards and other safety-related conditions. Architects and insulation repair companies used these imagers to scan heat flow from structures and properly plan improvements. ProScan sold well, but once again Hughes did not push ahead with an appropriate manufacturing base or reach beyond modest sales efforts in widespread domestic and overseas markets.

ProScan Thermal Image
(courtesy of UNLV)

- *NightVision*, a Hughes device to match into General Motor's primary automobile product line, was an IR thermal imager display to assist drivers after sunset. An IR-derived image of the scene ahead of the car appeared on an edge-lit transparent glass plate in the driver's view. This image was positioned on the windshield to appear the same as it would look visually in daytime. Even with the car's headlights off, it provided clear views for safe driving. (I had the exciting opportunity to test a prototype while driving in pitch-dark with the headlights off in forested terrain; fortunately, with no other traffic in the area. After some mental adjustment, I drove almost a mile without crashing into any of the trees looming around me! This ingenious product worked very well, but failed to attract the marketplace; perhaps it seemed too exotic for most drivers. 'Twas sure easy to sell to ex-fighter pilots!

- *AML (amplitude modulated link)*, one of the most successful industrial products, was a point-to-point microwave link for cable TV systems. A typical installation started at the head end or satellite receive station and distributed TV signals to outlying communities by microwave link; from there, cable distributed the signal to individual homes. Hughes basically had a monopoly and enjoyed exceptional financial returns.

At the electronic component level, the Hughes philosophy was to invent unique items and install them in large and sophisticated system products. Selling these components was often thought to be too helpful to other companies competing for those same large projects. In spite of this, outside sales of TWTs were very profitable—including some coming from government mandates to supply a competitor, and others for systems that did not encroach on our mainstay product lines. The same was true for many microelectronic devices, flat-screen displays, IR detectors, and laser elements.

Fortunately, the Hughes adventure in the seemingly unlikely attempt to capture the individual TV consumer market with DirecTV became most successful after a twenty-year strategic effort.

48

OBSERVATIONS ON THE
AEROSPACE BUSINESS

REACTIONS TO, AND conclusions drawn about, almost anything vary from one observer to another. The Japanese 1950 movie *Rashomon* gives a superb portrayal of this phenomenon. In the story, a woodcutter, a priest, and a commoner express completely different rationales after separately seeing the body of a dead samurai in the forest. No "true story" was presented for the many possibilities of what might have happened; each observer perceived events based upon his own personal life. Such interpretational differences stem from many causes, including cultural expectations, personal involvement, historic analogy, or individual personalities and likes or dislikes.

Advanced technology organizations rely on creativity, high motivation, experimental practices, and sometimes violation of traditional rules. Staffers must be willing to tackle something that appears to be almost impossible. As progress is made, unusual happenings may occur which appear entertaining to outsider observers, even if there's an unfortunate outcome. An effective team is a large cluster of unconventional innovators. Many anecdotes can be described; here are a few from my personal observation.

Combative Arguments

The Navy expected Grumman, as the manufacturer of the *Tomcat*, to verify that missiles could be safely launched from the aircraft while it was maneuvering in a reverse to normal—that is, while "pushing over negative g's," an unusual maneuver, rarely used except in emergencies. In this test, the plan was to be at minus 3 g (negative gravitational force).

Whether or not the ejection launchers would have enough force to physically separate the weapon before rocket motor ignition was uncertain; in this condition, a weapon carried beneath the airframe would have a force three times its weight trying to push it back against the F-14's fuselage.

Grumman and Raytheon agreed to try with the Sparrow missile, but our analysts calculated that the Phoenix missile would not safely separate in such a maneuver. I had to make the unwelcome telephone call to the Deputy Chief of Naval Operations for Air (Navy 05), hopefully to prevent a test with our missile. Two weeks later, Grumman proceeded with the Sparrow. The missile's rocket fired while the weapon was not yet separated and its wing fin sliced the *Tomcat's* underside, cutting fuel lines. A giant plume of flames 300 feet long gushed aft; the pilot tried to save the aircraft, but that was not possible. Fortunately, both crew members ejected safely and were rescued from the sea. For a while, I had been in the customer's doghouse, portrayed as a "real wimp," but after the Sparrow disaster our dissenting posture was regarded a heroic stance.

Another time, Raytheon attempted to persuade the Navy to cancel the Phoenix missile and select the Sparrow as the primary *Tomcat* weapon, instead of its then-current role as secondary backup. Raytheon almost convinced Navy officials that the Phoenix was too slow and clumsy; their bird could make faster turns in closing for target impact, and thus better counter aggressor evasions. Packed with information by our analysts, I had a one-on-one meeting with Naval Aviation's prime technical chief, Dr. John Rexroth. Our data showed that the Phoenix was far more maneuverable than Sparrow over a much larger operating range and altitude. Although its speed was only Mach 3 (going faster meant more frictional air resistance, which shortened the missile's flyout range), the added drag generated when its rear flippers turned caused little speed and energy loss. In dramatic contrast, the faster Sparrow's center-mounted steering fins generated a very large drag when turned, drastically decelerating the bird and reducing energy available for turning to impact. Abrupt turns resulted in shorter range and loss of continued maneuverability. The discussion results with John were positive for Hughes and our archrival failed to win the day.

Both of these emergency events showed the magnificence of competent technical analysts. Hughes had many people with these talents.

Another bizarre experience was when the company was summoned to appear at a hearing of the Senate Armed Services Committee. The topic related to progress in contracts for the F-14 weapon system and missile. Appearing in the Senate Committee Room were our CEO Allen Puckett, president John Richardson, program manager Walt Maguire, and myself, the program's system engineering manager. We had been informed that three Soviet technical experts would be in the large audience for this public hearing. The three thought they were clandestine, but the CIA had a clear track on them as being from the KGB.

Most of the Senate staffers' questions were about technical design details, which my bosses always passed to me to answer. Luckily, being well acquainted with most details, I could give satisfactory answers. Many queries, however, involved security classified information, so I had to say, "I am sorry, but I cannot answer this due to classification rules." This was very irritating to the Senate team, although written answers with security stampings would be accepted. However, I thought it incredible that senators and their staff would try in a public forum to ask questions potentially damaging to the country. Several of those astonishing probes concerned which electronic countermeasures or combat tactics would be most effective to nullify the system! On whose side were those federal politicians?

Gender Alerts

Adapting to the national desire for more fair and balanced employment rights for women took a lot of effort by many men who were inexcusably ignorant of the actual problem. The need for change was long overdue, but rather than trying to educate the uninformed males, many radicals loudly pushed demands for immediate improvement in everyday behavior. In that era, men who tried to open doors or step back for ladies to enter an elevator first, as taught by their mothers, were rebuffed and publicly scorned. Many men were criticized for glancing and smiling at any female and were accused of lecherous intentions. (That claim was sometimes valid, but surely not always.) Hughes tried hard to rapidly adjust the personnel rules for better hiring and professional opportunity for balance and fairness, but the task facing the company to achieve gender equality had to evolve, just as overall behavior in US society evolved. Most men and women in the 1960s were the product of television's *Ozzie and Harriet* stereotype: the man went to work and the woman dutifully stayed home to raise the kids. Hughes had to work to overcome this stereotype at the same time that it was surrounded by a society not fully adjusted to the new reality for women.

Some relevant events from that era:

- Executive Order 11375 expanded President Johnson's 1965 affirmative action policy to cover discrimination based on sex, resulting in federal agencies and contractors taking active measures to ensure that all women as well as minorities had access to educational and employment opportunities equal to white males.

- Robin Morgan led members of New York Radical Women to protest the Miss America Pageant, which they decried as sexist and racist.
- The first national women's liberation conference was held in Lake Villa, near Chicago.
- Coretta Scott King assumed directorship of the African-American civil rights movement and expanded its platform to include women's rights.
- Shirley Chisholm was elected to the US Congress, the first African-American congresswoman.
- For the first time, feminists used the slogan "Sisterhood," and NOW, the National Organization for Women, celebrated Mother's Day with the slogan: "Rights, Not Roses."

It was also true that engineering at that time was a male-dominated profession. Technically talented women were not encouraged by anyone to enter that profession; few, if any, universities welcomed females to such study programs. The Society for Women Engineers in the late 1960s reported that less than 1 percent of engineering degrees went to women. Fortunately, today that has increased to 20 percent, and is still increasing. This very short supply of technically educated women greatly hampered company efforts to achieve staff gender balance, remuneration equality, and promotional progress. Focus had to be in the administrative areas.

Fortunately, Hughes was able to attract and promote many high-performing female staff members; several achievers set great examples for resetting compensation and position rating standards. Many women career professionals could be cited; three whom I admired for many years were Georgia Oleson, who led the human resources staff in the Missile Systems Group and later became corporate vice president for human relations; Sue Baumgarten, an excellent electronics systems engineer who rose to the position of vice president of Raytheon Technical Services shortly after Raytheon acquired Hughes in 1997; and Louise Langlois Francesconi, a finance professional who became president of Raytheon Missile Systems Group at a time when that organization's annual sales exceeded $5 billion. Virginia Norwood, quoted in Section 44, "Scientific Space Exploration," was another of the company's great achievers. Throughout the entire organization, as time passed the problem of gender balance was reasonably corrected—not perfectly, but far better than it had been in the turbulent 1960s.

A very difficult "gender" task was to accommodate bisexual or transsexual employees. Once a male staff member was trying to become a woman through hormone treatments and behavioral training. "He" soon tried to use the restrooms designated for females. This caused the women to protest; the men were also a bit uncomfortable when "he" was forced to return to their comfort stations. I resolved the problem by having a unisex restroom installed. An expensive remedy, but at least it was an acceptable and permanent solution to a potentially disastrous morale problem. (And potentially hazardous from a legal standpoint.)

More significantly, one of the firm's passenger-transport pilots decided to switch gender through chemistry and surgery. His resume included a well-decorated military service and a family with two children. His flying skills were exemplary, with no accidents, and he had heroically saved an aircraft after an engine failure in flight. However, the other pilots strongly objected to his presence, and refused to be scheduled with him on the same flight, either because they feared his treatments might affect his concentration and flying abilities or simply because they did not sympathize with gender switching. After I made many unsuccessful attempts to pacify the dissenters, the pilot resigned, probably due to ostracism, took an extended medical leave, and then was hired elsewhere as a female pilot. His voluntary move erased the difficult management job of trying to preserve an excellent performer while facing a virtually irresolvable set of emotional conditions.

Ethnic Blindness

Assuring ideal human resource contentment in ethnic or minority employees was a more difficult goal than that of gender. Years of effort in the United States have made some progress, but the pace is slow. The strongly stated policies and intentions of the government were mirrored at Hughes. What is desired in this society, especially in a creative organization, is to judge people by what they can do and be completely blind to what they look like or where they originated—usually called a meritocracy. The stated national ideal was that the entire workforce reflect the same minority ratios as the entire population. Government regulations and monitoring procedures could apply sanctions on suppliers of products and services if there were significant discrepancies.

Hughes undertook intensive efforts to achieve these goals with strongly written policies, hiring practices, management training, encouragement and support of universities, engagement of consultants, and involvement of an active staff managing human resource policies. Nevertheless, achievement was extremely difficult. Corporate emphasis in staffing and rewards stressed technology. Even though only one-quarter of the total employees were engineers or scientists, most management emphasis on recognition, prestige, and promotional advancement was focused on education and performance in high technology. Rightly or wrongly, even a university name added status; you likely had a career head start if you possessed a degree from Caltech, MIT, or Stanford.

Attaining ethnic balance in the engineering workforce was handicapped by the limited supply of qualified candidates, a situation similar to the gender balance problem. Whatever the reason, in the United States, the percentage of minorities with college degrees in engineering and science was far less than the national minority percentages. And this issue continues today. The National Action Council for Minorities in Engineering reported that among the 68,000 US engineering bachelor's degrees awarded in 2006, only 8,500 were denoted as minorities. This ratio of one in eight is far less the total population ratio of one in three.

The company could not hire if there were few available candidates. Attempting to improve their monitored employment ratios, defense companies staged bidding wars to attract minority engineers. New college graduates were offered starting salaries far greater than for non-minority candidates. This created internal pay pressures when some new graduates received higher salaries than engineers with several years of experience. Fortunately, good sense finally ended this unwise practice. Nationwide demand for engineers in the booming 1980s again saw the law of supply and demand drive up starting salaries, but this time for any engineer bearing that magic new engineering degree, rather than just a few. Fairness to experienced staff members was obtained by adjusting overall salary levels; a bit inflationary, but there was little choice.

The minority supply imbalance was partially alleviated in one category by the boom in Asian-American technology graduates beginning in the 1970s. Hughes hired large numbers of highly skilled people with this ethnic background. It appeared that, by the late 1980s, there could be no doubt that any analysis of human resource statistics would be most favorable with respect to number of staff, promotional standings, compensation levels, and prestige. However, as a corporate executive, I was stunned and dismayed by a report authored by the notable UCLA professor Dr. William Ouchi. He had conducted extensive interviews with many Asian-American employees and summarized his findings as indicating that those interviewed personally felt great discontent and unfair treatment in the company. These findings were astonishing, since many of these folks were in senior management positions and others were recognized as being essential to the success of many product lines. Meaningful steps for remedial actions by management were not obvious, and little was done in the remaining two years before I retired.

The supply line for African-Americans was particularly small. This situation led the company to focus on stimulating interest in the engineering profession, and to directly support several schools with high African-American enrollment, such as Howard University, Grambling State University, Alabama A&M, Tuskegee University, and Morris Brown College. Support came in the form of funding grants, discussions with university faculty and administrators, and participation in hiring fairs with senior students. To appraise the company's internal status, consultants interviewed many of the company's professionals and found considerable discontent. My personal discussions with several key managers who were African-American revealed a universal feeling that unspoken attitudes by most other managers and staff members were a significant barrier to progress. A long interchange with William Grier, author of the 1978 book *Black Rage*, further detailed the depth of racial bias problems throughout the United States. He implied that things were the same at Hughes; although he was probably correct, I am not sure if he had conducted any interviews to confirm the magnitude of this issue at the company.

I also had a personal taste of how an attempted communication of sincere intentions can be foiled by a preceding emotional speaker. I was to make the key address at a convention of about 450 African-American college students in Los Angeles. My intent was to openly describe current difficulties at Hughes in ethnic human relations and relate our planned improvements. Before my turn at the podium, a flamboyant minister described in fiery words how evil all corporations (and especially their executives) were in ignoring the well-being of the employees in order for the company to gain financial profit! After that rampage, it was impossible for an executive of an "evil" organization to capture the attention of the agitated audience. There were a lot of hoots and whistles. What a way to engender progress on a tough national problem!

In an effort to better understand and remedy the issue, the company placed several excellent African-Americans in key human resource management positions to seek ways to change employees' behavior in ethnic matters. Results were not clear when I retired, but, hopefully, at least the increase in eligible professional staff candidates had a favorable payoff.

An exemplary role model who broke through both perceived barriers of gender and ethnic identification in our fast-moving high-technology driven organization was "Eddie" Murphy. Coming from Ohio and a graduate of the University of San Francisco, she performed with outstanding abilities. She showed a magnetic personal charisma in performing the difficult task of communicating plans and implementing policies for employee retirement. Senior executives wanted this emotional process to be fair and matched to the unique circumstances of each individual. Eddie also was involved in counseling, done with both charm and foresight. There was a continual and growing stream of people starting a new and uncertain phase of life. In her role as corporate manager of retiree relations, she shepherded the company's more than 25,000 retirees. Her excellence resulted in her being selected to direct this vital function for UCLA.

The Hispanic community, a large and rapidly growing percentage in the US southwestern region, did not seem to show the same degree of discontent. Hughes employment numbers in the manufacturing area, where many Hispanics worked, were quite healthy, and recognition and promotions did not appear restricted in any way. There was a reasonable population of this ethnic group among the engineering staff, and there was little evidence of bias causing limitations. However, the supply side in engineering was quite low, so Hughes lent support to a number of universities with high proportions of Hispanics, such as University of Texas in El Paso, Florida International University, University of New Mexico, and Texas A&M University in Kingsville. Once again, I did not observe results before retirement. Statistics after 2000 show that some progress has been made, but that there is still much to be done.

Interesting Personalities

An opportunity for Hughes aircraft Company to enter the entertainment business occurred in the late 1960s. The notable Irving Kahn approached our senior executives, offering a teaming arrangement with Time Warner to spread cable-TV networks everywhere. He had been a founder of the TelePrompTer Corporation, which created the display panels that cue television performers if they forget their lines. He was also beginning to install underground cables to relay television signals in several large US cities. Kahn wanted to obtain access to the sizable Hughes line of credit, and also to gain better prices in purchasing Hughes satellites. In return, he offered half ownership of the newly formed HBO enterprise. Our executives declined, feeling handicapped by the company's lack of experience in public entertainment and consumer marketing. A loss of a possible big future! However, teaming with Mr. Kahn would have been uncomfortable after he was convicted in 1972 of bribing three Trenton, New Jersey, politicians to grant the right to install cable TV in that city.

In our huge workforce of more than 80,000 people, there were bound to be individuals with physical and psychological differences from the expected "norms" of US culture. Some of these could be dealt with, others not, and many could be amusing to observe. The real management challenges were to ensure fairness and to maximize excellent personnel performance.

Alcoholism was an infrequent problem, partly because of the thorough screening done to obtain government security clearances. When an individual suffered from this disease, it was usually well hidden, and often the creativity and work output of that employee were above normal expectations. Other observable aspects were not tolerable; organized assistance was most important. First, the medical staff would arrange external clinical rehabilitation paid by the company. This step, however, required the employee to agree to such medical help. In one case involving an excellent engineer, his supervisor and several others had personally tried persuasion without success. The man's family had then revealed the problem to Hughes management, asking for help. His supervisors implored me to try, even though three layers of supervision separated us. My approach was straightforward, using what is now called tough love. After gentle talk and praise for his work, I stated that unless he accepted rehabilitation, I would have to discharge him, and his family would suffer deeply. That was enough; he agreed to start at a clinic, and two months later he returned, cured.

Another somewhat scary request to me involved an excellent system analyst who had long ago been diagnosed as manic-depressive. One day he locked his office door and refused to respond to pleas for access. A call to his wife revealed that he had failed that morning to take his prescribed dose of lithium; in such cases, some untreated persons can become violent. I guess he trusted me, so, with a knock on the door, I courteously asked for admittance. After some time I was admitted, closed the door, and chatted for a long time until he was quite calm. By then, someone had brought a lithium pill, so very quickly all was well. It had taken a bit of courage to enter the office and try to be gentle and persuasive while facing the potential of a violent outburst. It was of long-term benefit to the company that this employee continued performing well and there was no recurrence of his breakdown.

One of my own quirks was adoration of technology advances and inventive breakthroughs. It seemed that every day there was an amazing invention to hear about, and then decide whether to risk investment in developing a new product. I was usually a pushover for someone to obtain a project go-ahead because technology wonders overwhelmed my business judgment. After retirement, the senior vice president for research told me that whenever there was a presentation to me requesting funding support, the words "technology advance" were always used. That phrase guaranteed that I would agree to the financial request. What a presidential "patsy"! My weakness was the gain of others, but I don't think the business suffered much.

I did have a business side, however. In an important meeting on the progress of the vital F-15 *Eagle* radar, an outstanding engineer in charge of its development proudly announced a new, higher performance modification to the design, which he had already caused to be tested and incorporated. Since we were performing on a fixed price contract, I asked whether the customer had paid us for this improvement. Had we gotten a signed contract change order? He replied, "I don't know, but I got my paycheck last week." My retort was, "Are you sure you'll get one next week?" After much laughter, an immediate contractual remedy was sought. As a business, we just could not do magnificent things for free!

Dr. John Rubel, who managed the Aeronautical Systems Laboratory in the 1950s, was an excellent, technically bright and communicative manager. He was energetic and committed to inspiring greatness in his organization. One of his attempts to enforce staff discipline, however, was to personally monitor the arrivals of the engineers each morning. The official starting time was 8:15 a.m. (set to differ from that of other companies to reduce commuter traffic congestion). Many engineers believed in more flexibility, feeling that if they contributed at least the expected forty-five hours per week, specific times did not really matter. Many actually contributed sixty or more. But John perched in an obvious second floor spot overlooking the security gate through which, each morning, every employee had to pass to enter the fenced facility. Although thousands of staff members were involved, anyone who came late could see Dr. Rubel checking his or her tardiness on a no-no list. This effort quickly taught John the names of every staffer and did correct the habit of some to be late; however, it became a great source of amusement as "Rubel's 8:15." It is a good illustration of an inappropriate style of leadership: methods to reach worthy objectives should not look foolish or make the boss appear "quirky."

Although he clearly could have been a top candidate for CEO at Hughes, John left to become the assistant secretary of defense for technology. A catchphrase praising him was that if he had the same job in Moscow, the USSR would get "more rubble for the Rubel." Unfortunately, instead of returning to Hughes, he started a career in the movie industry. What a loss to the United States!

Customers also sometimes had quirks that could be amusing or unfortunate. Some senior military officers always wanted to be known for being in charge and smarter than their subordinates. At the conclusion of a three-day design review of the aircrew displays for the *Tomcat*, three hundred people from three contractors and several Navy commands gathered to hear the decisions of Navy officers who were in charge of the conference. Written "chits" with comments about the design had been submitted by expert reviewers and sent to an executive board of senior officers for review and resolution. When the admiral in charge announced the rejection of one chit, the author, a Navy lieutenant, made an immediate appeal. The admiral sneered, "Who are you, are you an expert, have you ever flown a fighter plane in combat?" The young officer quietly replied, "Yes, sir, I just returned from 260 sorties over North Vietnam." What a perfect put-down for an arrogant superior officer! As I recall, the rest of the review board then approved the chit, and the admiral was silent.

Senator Strom Thurmond from South Carolina (in his time, the oldest serving senator in history—since then, Senators Byrd and Inouye have set new records) once visited the Tucson plant to view missile manufacturing activities. Hughes was in the process of establishing a subassembly manufacturing facility in his home state. The facility would be a meaningful economic boon to his constituents, so he naturally wanted to take credit. As I briefed him about the helicopters equipped with TOW antitank weapons, he interrupted in his delightful Southern drawl, "How many launchers are there?" The design had four launch-tube assemblies on each side of the helicopter, each containing a single TOW, so I replied, "There are eight launchers, sir." He then said again "How many launchers?" Thinking he now referred to the aircrew, I said, "One, sir." He now demanded in irritation, "No, how many launchers?" The photograph projected on the screen showed the four tubes on one side clustered as a group, so I now guessed he thought of each cluster as a launcher, so I tried, "Two, sir." He was still dissatisfied, so asked the same question again. Now completely bewildered, I told him we would look into the matter and send the answer to his staff. I still don't know what I should have said to satisfy his question: what had he really wanted to know?

Human Relations Abroad

Overseas business was a large portion of Hughes growth, and the company supplied equipment and ongoing support to forty-two nations. Inevitably, amusing happenings occurred during our transactions abroad, as the following examples illustrate.

Japan purchased the F-15 *Eagle* fighter containing the Hughes APG-63 radar. Co-production was prescribed as a condition of sale, and Japanese industry was well able to produce electronics. Hughes considered the programmable signal processor proprietary and the Air Force stated that its details be secured for military reasons, however, so its specific drawings were not released for Japanese manufacture, an act that remained contentious for many years.

Japan also selected Hughes to develop and deliver-in-orbit the weather surveillance Geostationary Meteorological Satellite (GMS). As always, different languages and technology complexities foiled accurate communication. When our interpreter was temporarily absent during negotiations, Japanese participants would exchange their personal viewpoints in Japanese, assuming the Americans did not understand. It was a great help if one of our team was fluent in that language but had not revealed this skill. Harvey Palmer, a Space and Communications Group division manager, was adept in Japanese, which he had learned during the American occupation of Japan in 1946, and was thus able during the GMS negotiations to direct his team's position to blend comfortably with the thought-to-be private leanings of the GMS bargainers.

F-15 *Eagle* Containing APG-63 Radar
(©iStockphoto/CT75fan)

In the same way, my limited understanding of Japanese, learned in my Honolulu youth while listening to a favorite radio series *Cherry Blossom Melodies*, was helpful in *Eagle* radar negotiations. But it was especially humorous when I was the honored guest at a banquet sponsored by the CEO of the giant Mitsubishi Corporation. In accordance with protocol, I gave a thank-you speech, with a translator nearby. Beginning with flowery phrases in English, I switched to Japanese for several sentences. Amazingly, that translator, who did his job simultaneously as I spoke, instantly switched my words from Japanese to English! I had given him no warning that I would try both languages. I received much praise from the chairman, but an associate of his later whispered, "You did a fine job by using the female version of our language." Little did I know!

On another occasion, I was taken to the elegant Mitsubishi management "retreat" in Tokyo. As we toured the gardens, I remarked that the French Renaissance style building looked odd; it was shaped like a cube, rather than the traditional Parthenon 2.8 by 5 proportions. My host had been the company's quality chief in the 1940s, as they produced famous *Zero* and *Zeke* aircraft that I had watched attacking Pearl Harbor. He quickly said with a chuckle, "So sorry, B-29 bombing not very accurate; only hit half of building." When Mitsubishi repaired the building, they built one new wall and reused the remainder of the mansion's structure.

Most difficult was a "business" dinner meeting with that company's officials at their private geisha house in the Tokyo Ginza. I was the principal guest, and had been warned by friends that my duty was to enthusiastically proclaim enjoyment of the first dish served, as the hosts politely observed. Very fortunately, the elegant geisha assigned to me refilled my sake cup several times before that unknown dish arrived. It was a beautifully arranged art piece, with flowers and green leaves in a red lacquer bowl, upon which was a complete pickled trout. My task was to lift it with chopsticks and bite off the delicious head, showing great delight while crunching that lovely morsel! Luckily, the sake had made me a bit mellow so that my "uncivilized Western" tummy did not react improperly. Since my hosts knew this show would be a real trial for me, they promptly gave a hearty round of applause for my stellar bravery.

Another experience occurred in Spain when the Navy, McDonnell-Douglas, Northrop, and Hughes were making final marketing presentations to persuade the Spanish to select the F/A-18 *Hornet* for their Air Force. My task was to describe the segments of our radar that could be co-manufactured by Spanish electronics companies.

On the last evening, the Spaniards gave an elegant dinner for the US team at Madrid's outstanding Zaragosa Restaurant, a place with Renaissance era décor and costumed waiters. The Spanish hosts and their American guests were interspersed; I sat next to the Spanish assistant secretary of defense. After complimenting him as a look-alike with King Juan Carlos (he really was!), I spoke several sentences in my "Spanish" jargon. In the four days of discussions, I had shown no response to Spanish words, but perceived much about what others had assumed were private discussions. He smiled, quickly raised his hand for attention, and announced, "I caution my countrymen: Mr. Richardson speaks 'Mexican' Spanish!" He thought this a perfect put-down, since the upper crust in Spain use only the refined Castilian version of the language. Even Catalan, used by one-third of the country's population, is scorned by the privileged folk and a Mexican dialect is considered a step below that.

F/A-18 *Hornet* Preproduction Model
(personal files)

By contrast, my Mexico style of Spanish came in handy when I met with President Carlos Salinas de Gortari in Mexico City; my mission was to persuade him to overturn the actions of his federal procurement director. At issue was the selection of synchronous communication satellites to service the nation. The competition was a French company subsidized by its government, in contrast to our company, which had no US funding assistance. Although the resulting lower price made the French system attractive, it had very limited capability compared to our satellite. Three times, a Mexican government review team had selected Hughes but had been overruled by the procurement chief; rumors abounded that perhaps someone was offering him rewards if the French system was selected.

I was most impressed by the president, who was Harvard educated, able to comprehend much of the technical jargon, and spoke flawless English. (In an attempt at rapport, I tried my jumbled Spanish and was praised for trying.) I cited several major advantages that favored our offer. The most significant, which had not previously been suggested in our proposal, did the trick: with a simple ground receiver at each elementary school nationwide, a single, and ideally the most excellent, teacher in the country could reach every child. As an enhancement, I offered three of these receivers at no cost. President Salinas ruled the next morning that the Hughes offering would be selected. The educational idea was successfully implemented in the next few years. I rejoice at thinking of something to aid Mexico's educational system, and sincerely regret that Salinas de Gotari was subsequently accused of malfeasance during his presidency; he exiled himself to Ireland.

HS-376 Communications Satellite
(courtesy of UNLV)

The French are magnificent hosts, even in business situations, as was evidenced in the Roland program. These enjoyable occasions, however, are often used as a negotiation strategy not obvious to their guests. Luncheons at an elegant restaurant in Aerospatiale's headquarters near Paris were extravagant three-hour repasts enhanced with glasses of at least five varieties of wine.

The French practice was to raise important issues for discussion and agreement by the participants just before dessert was served. Naive Americans were frequently disarmed and readily agreed to contract or schedule changes, instead of more wisely choosing to take the French suggestions under advisement and providing a response the next morning. The encounters were always very amicable, but the French always reaped any resulting benefits.

German team members were also present; they had already experienced this ritual for three years and had learned restraint to protect their own business interests. When the Americans began to attend, the Germans were quite amused, remembering their own trials; fortunately, they soon taught the newcomers how to behave properly—shortening our learning time in how to cope with a unique segment of European culture.

Another illustration was our difficulty in communications involving a complex product like Roland that came from an overseas source. Euromissile sent a senior engineer whose native tongue was French. Cultural and language differences caused a six-month delay in completely transferring the necessary knowledge. When asked to prepare an information package within two weeks, the senior engineer would respond, "*d'accord de principe*." We assumed that when he said that, he meant, "Yes" (its literal translation is "of agreement in principle"), but the phrase actually is a polite French way of saying, "No"—so he did nothing in the time before he next appeared. Surprisingly, some vital technical information was given only after a license fee increase was agreed to. Nevertheless, the program turned out extremely well, in spite of the three-way cultural differences and our initial weakness at the lunch table.

Imperial Iranian Air Force F-14 Squadron
(personal files)

Iran was a most unusual encounter. Although Farsi is closely akin to English, Hughes had few experts in that language or in the ancient country's very different culture. Attitudinal differences are dramatic. What formerly was Persia is deep in historic treasures, folklore, Muslim heritage, and classic art; especially notable are the cities of Isfahan, Persepolis, and Shiraz.

The seventy *Tomcats* the Iranians bought were based at two new airfields, and Hughes sent 200 support experts to train Iranian Air Force personnel to operate and repair the weapon control system and its companion Phoenix missile.

Unfortunately, many of the trainees had a working philosophy very different from that of our staff. Those differences were almost impossible to overcome: if there was an electronic component failure, for example, attempts to repair it were thwarted by the local belief that the failure was "an act of Allah's will, so must not be tampered with."

A challenging mission on one of my visits was to provide analytical data to the Iranian Air Force Commanding General Khatami on how many Phoenix missiles should be procured to properly equip the Iranian squadrons. The Hughes staff had prepared a graphical method of calculation whereby the needed quantity could be obtained by finding the intersection of several values chosen by the IAF: for example, number of potential hostiles, replenishment time, probability of successful intercept, and total cost. We knew that two primary reasons for the purchase of this weapon system were to defend against the Iraqi threat and deter further USSR surveillance overflights. While I watched, General Khatami applied the graphical method to choose the number of missiles to purchase: the answer was 600 missiles. (Interestingly, that particular value was identical to the one I had used to illustrate how to use the graphical method.)

General Khatami was a most impressive man—talented and well rounded in most subjects; regrettably, he perished shortly after our meeting in a recreational hang-glider crash. Rumors circulated that a wing-support wire had been partially severed by a dissident subordinate. I also got to know General Rabi, commander of the Iranian Army, who taught me many things about the fascinating Persian culture. I liked him, and I grieved when he was shown on worldwide television being executed by a firing squad during the Islamic revolution.

Business with Israel was also a revelation of differing cultural and operating styles. Many US weapons had been purchased or given to Israeli combat forces; American defense contractors, including Hughes, did a great deal of consulting and initial training. There also were opportunities to market improved designs or completely new products, if given the OK by the US government. When I tried to excite the Israelis about a possible purchase of the same systems chosen by Iran, it was astonishing to see their intense zeal for information: many well-informed technical questions and excessive probes into what I knew of effective countermeasure methods. I concluded that their main interest was not in a purchase, but rather in ways to counter Iran's *Tomcat* fighter squadrons. To their dismay, US security rules kept me pretty mum.

Bright technical minds were apparent in Israeli Air Force officers regardless of age or rank; I was amazed to see junior officers frequently interrupting, contradicting, and debating with their senior officers, including the commanding general! It is very interesting to speculate on when such behavior is permitted when a direct order is given; in most military organizations even foolish orders must not be questioned.

In 1988, Hughes was marketing the RealScene system to Israel. As described above, this equipment provided full-color three-dimensional moving images of target areas to help strike aircraft pilots prepare a correct approach for accurately delivering guided weapons. In this potential purchase, all contract terms between Hughes and Israel were agreed to, except the final price. A senior director of that country's military procurement approached me to arrange closure. We had priced the effort with some margin to cover design uncertainty, since the system was not fully developed. A very modest profit was also included. He wanted—virtually demanded—a substantially lower price, saying, "This is for the good of Israel, so you should be willing." He also hinted that US government pressure could be brought to bear on Hughes unless I conceded. My quick response was, "Although it may be for a great cause, the money you will be using for this purchase will come from the annual US-to-Israel aid package. Those funds are partly drawn from federal tax payments made by this company. This program will cost your country nothing. It's already a donation from the United States, and our company does not wish to add a further donation by assuming the entire contract risk." He was infuriated, but his unsuccessful ploy seemed a bit outrageous to me. The contract was awarded the next day at our price. As described earlier, RealScene was applied very effectively in Gaza against Fatah militant bosses housed in a high-rise building. No civilian losses occurred.

I was delighted in the 1990s to meet Maj. Gen. Yeshayahu Gavish, who had led the Israeli tank force through the Sinai Peninsula in the 1967 Six-Day War against Egypt (then UAR), Syria, and Jordan. That advance, against a much larger armored combat force, was quickly victorious and the Israelis soon crossed the Suez Canal, causing international pressure for a cease-fire. Remarkable to me was the rapid destruction of the many Egyptian Army Soviet-built tanks, which apparently resulted from the Israelis' tactical genius and superior equipment, including Hughes tank fire control systems and missiles. I congratulated that tank-force general on setting a world-record time for eliminating an opposing tank force, "It was amazing to hear that 370 tanks were destroyed in only one day!" With a large, proud smile, he modestly replied, "Oh no, it took two days."

Marketing communication satellites to individual nations usually required direct contact with each country's political head. On one such visit to Indonesia to help sell the Palapa satellite network, our team, upon arriving on schedule, was told that the meeting was delayed two days. Negotiations could not start until the Hughes people went to a distant

Palapa Communication Ground Station
(courtesy of UNLV)

town and returned via a test flight of a newly designed small airliner, the
first airplane ever constructed in Indonesia! The apprehension of the
team about surviving the flight lessened a little when they stepped aboard
and met a senior US FAA inspector, who had been asked to evaluate the
craft on this same flight—if this experienced expert was willing, why
be queasy? However, the flight itself seemed a strange precondition for
marketing a completely unrelated product. Perhaps the premier wanted
to advertise the successful introduction of airline service for traveling foreigners. Fortunately, the Palapa sale went through, with lucrative benefits
for everyone.

And then there was Italy, the marvelous land of enthusiasm and joy
of life. With the US Army promoting it, the Italians decided to purchase
the antitank TOW missile. One requirement was that portions of the
weapon had to be built by in-country companies, a common practice in
all such sales to gain the benefits of economic and technology transfer.
The final unresolved issue in 1983 was choice of the Italian firm to supply
the rocket motor.

Two very competent Italian contractors vied for the job. I was summoned to a meeting in Rome with the Italian Army general in charge of
all national military procurement. Discussions were held in an elegant

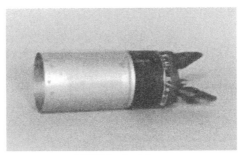

TOW Rocket Motor
(courtesy of UNLV)

Renaissance building with high ceilings, low lighting, and loud echoes. After a half-hour of routine chatting, in swept a most handsome, debonair, white-haired executive in a flowing sash and overcoat. He was the CEO of one of the two rocket motor contenders. He said to me, "You must select our company, or the TOW purchase will not be made by our government." This statement was then endorsed by the procurement general! Astonished, I replied, "We have quoted a fixed price for the total weapon system, but do not yet have a quote from your company for your portion of the manufacturing cost. I cannot select a supplier until we can compare your price with that of your competitor." The meeting was quickly adjourned and the elegant CEO angrily stormed out.

That night I received a telephone call to be ready at 7:00 a.m. for further discussions. I was met at the hotel entrance at that hour by a long limousine, escorted by several motorcycle police. Seated next to me was the Italian minister of defense. He apologized, saying that, because of his schedule to appear that morning before the Parliament, this was the only time he could meet with me. He asked for details of the previous day's meeting. The entourage raced down the crowded Via Veneto in Rome, with the motorcycle police clearing the path, sirens screaming. What a thrill to be doing business in this manner! As we reached the Parliament building, the minister exited with an elegant bow and a thank-you. The next day, the full purchase contract was signed, with the exclusion of that CEO's firm from supplying the rocket motors. We were comfortable with the other supplier's price, which we had received a month earlier.

❋

PART EIGHT

THE BOOM CONTINUES

Previous parts of this book have described numerous Hughes product lines and technologies. Over three decades, the company excelled in airborne and surface radars, guided missiles of many types, infrared and laser trackers, sonar networks, sophisticated digital computers and signal processors, a wide variety of reconnaissance systems, scientific spacecraft and communication satellites, and command and control systems for nations around the world. In the 1980s and early 1990s, these successful product lines prospered and led to increased technological and business complexities. Competition became more intense as the federal defense and space budgets declined, and as the electronics design capabilities of many other aerospace firms greatly improved. Following are descriptions of three exciting mission areas wherein the company expanded its leading-edge strength: performing projects with high security classifications, including stealth radars; creating an almost perfect air intercept missile; and successful experimental efforts in solving problems of defense against strategic ICBMs.

49

TOP SECRET
PATHWAYS

THE US EXPERIENCED many security breaches in World War II and in the nuclear weapon design race with the USSR; vital technology concepts prematurely "crossed over to the other side," with very unfortunate results. Accordingly, an intensive effort began to strengthen security controls over programs intended to advance military strength. Specific levels defined the degree of security to be used: confidential, secret, top secret, special compartmented information, special access required, eyes only, and others. As the procedural methods were perfected, some projects were unknown to the public; and even the federal budget to support them was unlabeled and deeply hidden. The concept was to cloak everything in an impenetrable "black" darkness. Black programs, such as the YF-12 project described in Part Four, are formally designated as special access required—SAR.

The YF-12's security code name was KEYLOCK, although that designator was never used within Hughes. Over the next thirty years, we received or initiated numerous government-contracted programs in the clandestine classified category, and Hughes was often a team member with several other defense contractors to get the total job done. Unfortunately, details of most of these projects still cannot be revealed. The company scored many significant technical breakthroughs for which there can be no public recognition. It isn't even permissible at this time to acknowledge company participation in any code-named programs unless the government has released that information to the public.

Revealed programs can be found on the Internet with a little searching. A few colorful names of airborne vehicle projects and the years of their first flights are: AQUATONE (U-2 surveillance aircraft, 1955);

OXCART (SR-71 surveillance aircraft, 1962); KEYLOCK (YF-12 interceptor, 1963); TAGBOARD (ramjet cruise missile, 1966); SENIOR BOWL (follow-on to TAGBOARD, 1967); HAVE BLUE (single seat aircraft for testing radar low observables, 1977); SENIOR PROM (a flying drone, 1978); SENIOR TREND (YF-117 fighter-bomber, 1981); TACIT BLUE (low observable aircraft, 1982); and SENIOR CEJAY (B-2, 1987). Programs whose purpose was primarily exploratory, exploitative, or experimental were often performed at the Nevada Area 51 test site, also known as Dreamland, described below. Many of these testing programs also had code names beginning with HAVE, as in HAVE DONUT, HAVE DRILL, and HAVE FERRY. These were evaluations of fighter tactics against many different types of captured Soviet aircraft during the 1960s and 1970s. Other examples were HAVE GLIB, the operational testing of many aircraft with stealth features against simulated Soviet ground-based air defense networks, done in the 1970s and 1980s, and HAVE GLASS, F-16 fighter low observables testing in 1982. Although of very serious and vital national importance, all these code names added a feeling of arcane humor to projects with a deadly purpose.

To simplify the identification process, Hughes often labeled highly classified projects with only three- or four-digit numbers. By doing so, a person could admit to being assigned to "2386" or "7583." Competitive intramural sandlot softball teams by company employees often identified themselves by a number on their baseball caps, without compromising security. How were such numbers selected? Perhaps randomly, or perhaps they stood for the date that the government contract had been awarded, or perhaps it was a composite of several lucky numbers. The latter would surely help guarantee the project's success!

Work on such programs had to be done in specially protected and isolated rooms, suites, or buildings. All work, documentation, and communication took place there; personnel without the appropriate security clearance were excluded. Metal wall construction barred acoustic or electromagnetic listening; thermal, TV, and motion detectors set off alarms if cleared staff were not there. Cryptographic telephones linked these "tanks" with authorized sites on the outside, and a completely isolated electrical power supply system was often used. As mentioned in Section 26, "Personal Progress: Civilian in Military Disguise," the Hughes version of such a tank used for the KEYLOCK project was humorously called "behind the green door"—probably an extension of employees' feelings about the bilious "Hughes green" building exterior paint, or from the popular 1956 song *Green Door*, composed by Bob Davie and Marvin Moore. Access was possible only by first passing a special security guard, then going through an outer locked door, followed by a second identity verification before passing through another barred door to finally enter the workspace.

In the beginning, metal keys were issued daily from the vault to cleared staff members. Once, an individual going to lunch elsewhere within the building lost his key; upon his return, everyone had to exit the tank and wait until all the locks were altered and a new set of keys was issued. The key system was soon replaced with coded number keypads with the access code changed frequently. Many programs required that at least two cleared people be present in an area for any occupancy to be permitted.

A difficulty in maintaining proper security clearances arose when an engineer unintentionally performed above his approved security clearance level. Projects usually were compartmented into layered segments, each higher layer having increasing clearance requirements. An engineer working on segment A, for example, might report about his work and include his creative idea about a device that could connect to his segment and make it perform better than its stated objective. This discovery actually placed the designer into a higher security level than he had been authorized for. Now there was a real administrative dilemma: had this engineer personally made a new technical discovery, or had he violated the need-to-know rules? A tough procedural difficulty, but fortunately no one ever went to jail. There were even many special procedures for classified invention patent applications.

The extreme security rigors often triggered a certain amount of cynicism among the engineers, who sometimes believed that security people, who did not create or build anything, were simply there to place as many obstacles as possible in the path to getting the job done—an attitude that was a bit arrogant and most inappropriate, since the security force performed a vital role. Despite the presence of this attitude about their coworkers, thousands of professional engineers earnestly and effectively toed the line, except for one, the infamous Bill Bell (see Section 41, "Some Operating Problems; Espionage").

People working black programs had significant personal frustrations, since they could not disclose to their family or friends what they were doing or even where they were spending their time. This situation and its consequences were well understood by former base commander at Area 51 Dreamland, Col. Larry McClain:

> "Such work is not for every man. But those who accept the burdens implicit in this silent labor realize a camaraderie and sense of value known to few. These memories cannot be stolen. They will last always, untarnished, ever better."

50

THE EVOLUTION
OF STEALTH

Combat can be much more effective if the enemy is unaware of your presence either by deception or by becoming nearly invisible. One animal well adapted to stealthy behavior is the small domestic black cat. It can be very difficult to see this creature at night: its fur absorbs light, it crouches within masking shrubbery, it stalks prey quietly, and it can only be spotted momentarily if light is reflected directly from its eyes. Furthermore, the cat makes that reflection instantly disappear by shutting its eyelids or by rotating its eyes a bit, deflecting the light beam elsewhere.

In trying to emulate a cat's stealth maneuvers with equipment, several aspects must be considered. "Be not seen" can be done by approaching from an unpredictable direction, hiding behind terrain features, absorbing impinging light, suppressing heat outputs, or reflecting hostile radar beams in an unexpected direction. "Be not recognized" can fool the opponent by adopting a bland shape, blending into the background using camouflage, appearing among many other nearby non-stealth moving objects, or generating clutter or a masking "white noise" to confuse searching sensors. "Be not heard" comes from doing the attack job passively using sensors responsive to visual, infrared, sonar, physical vibration, audio, magnetic attraction, or even aromatic vapors. If forced to send communications or use active laser or radar emanations, these must function in ways virtually undetectable or unnoticed by the hostile.

Aircraft Stealth Designs

As the Vietnam War was winding down in the early 1970s, the US DoD began an urgent exploration of ways to build aircraft that could be made less visible to hostile radars, especially those on the ground in air defense systems. The U-2 *Dragon Lady*, piloted by Gary Powers, was shot down in 1960 by a Soviet radar-guided surface-to-air missile. That surprise spurred the effort to create surveillance aircraft undetectable by radars. The desired technologies came under the title of LO or VLO, meaning low or very low observables.

The US experimental prototyping efforts initially focused on "be not seen"—revising traditional airframe shapes to divert reflections and adding exterior coating materials to maximize absorption. The objective was to radically decrease aircraft radar cross section (RCS), which is measured by comparing the target radar return with the reflectivity of a polished aluminum sphere a little over 4 feet in diameter that has a cross section of 1 square meter (slightly less than 11 square feet). Fighters at the time usually had an RCS of 2 to 5 square meters (21 to 53 square feet), making them easily detected and tracked by radars to well beyond one hundred miles range. Something had to be done! The desire was to pose an unsolvable problem to the enemy, "How can we pick out a stealth vehicle that reflects our radar search beams no more than does one of those many pigeons in the sky?"

The first two manned aircraft programs were the 1975 Lockheed HAVE BLUE and the 1978 Northrop TACIT BLUE. These projects led the way to the extraordinary configurations of the F-117 *Nighthawk* fighter-bomber fielded in 1983 and the B-2 *Spirit* bomber successfully deployed in 1997. The same concepts are embodied in today's F-22 *Raptor* and F-35 *Lightning II* fighters (and in many surveillance drones and cruise missiles). Even Lockheed's *Sea Shadow* stealthy SWATH (small-waterplane-area twin hull) ship for the Navy benefited from those aircraft technologies.

Low RCS can be achieved by shaping the aircraft fuselage to reflect incoming radar beams at oblique angles, so that no reflections are detected by the enemy's receiving antenna. Successful tries included flat-plate facets at odd angles, strangely curved skins, and saw-toothed surface edge structures covered by nonreflecting and partially transparent materials. Early low RCS vehicles often resembled an arrow or had squared platypus bills.

Intensive research at many laboratories sought to find the most effective radar absorptive material (RAM) for exterior coatings. Most practical were asbestos-fiberglass, carbon loaded foam and honeycomb layers, and phenyl-silane composites. Finding the optimum material and its finished texture was most difficult: besides having the toughness necessary to survive the flight environments, the RAM could not generate excessive aerodynamic drag, sustain damage in ground handling, or add unacceptable weight. Coatings also had to be repairable in the field even when the aircraft were carefully protected to preserve RAM performance.

Concept Testing

Determining the value of new structural and material designs in reducing RCS required extensive and expensive exposure of full-size aircraft models to active radar illumination. This procedure was particularly difficult because of the need for top-level defense security; hopefully, no one outside the need-to-know projects would even be aware that such testing was under way. Large spaces had to be found in remote regions of the United States. Accordingly, in addition to a few small outdoor ranges and enclosed spaces in secure contractor facilities, the government established two evaluation sites having the capacity to test large targets.

The first, named RATSCAT (for radar target scattering), near Alamogordo, New Mexico, was used for testing stationary objects. Prototype aircraft, large-scale models, and experimental body shapes were mounted on tall pylons to separate direct target reflections from the effects of ground clutter. From significant distances, radars of all conceivable types took turns illuminating these objects, and responses were carefully measured. The work was usually performed only at night; test objects were removed and totally enclosed in storage sheds when not on the test pylon. This daily practice masked the work from prying observations, especially from Soviet satellites passing overhead. Design alterations could be done in the sheds during the day to improve the low observable results during the next night's testing.

A troublesome but most amusing annoyance came from interference by mother nature during RCS evaluation of the antenna for the B-2 radar. To obtain comparative measurement values, the antenna was attached to a mounting device that was uniform in reflectance from all angles. This assembly was then rotated atop a supporting pole during illumination by many different types of radars. The effect of the antenna's presence could be easily compared with the opposite side of the mounting device.

On several occasions the data was badly garbled and returns from parts of the mounting device varied significantly as the testing proceeded. On later inspection, it was found that families of local burrowing owls had discovered that by perching on the rotating device they could enjoy a complete 360-degree scan of the desert for rodents. Each bird would bring its prey back up to the device, dine, and leave copious droppings. The material splattered the exterior of the test mount, and was found to be both electrically conductive and very reflective of impinging radar energy. After a short time, the owl-work precluded any useful RCS measurements. The only acceptable solution was to clean up each morning, and then to hope the birds would not return the next night. The owls gave no heed to ardent pleas from the test team. Fortunately, their appearance was for a few evenings randomly spaced throughout each month, very likely matching the availability of prey. Sometimes unavoidable natural events increase the cost of defense-equipment development!

Pylon work of this type also began at a second secret test site, in Nevada, starting with mockups of the SR-71 *Blackbird* brought up in 1959 from Lockheed's Skunk Works. This site, with the improbable name of Dreamland, was also uniquely capable of evaluating low observable aircraft while airborne. It became the primary in-flight RCS test location for the United States.

Experimenting at Dreamland

Sponsored and controlled by the CIA and set up in 1955 by Lockheed for a project with the code name AQUATONE, Dreamland has been the

Dreamland, Groom Lake, Nevada
(courtesy of Wikipedia)

center for test and evaluation of many highly classified projects, evaluation of fighter tactical encounters with captured Soviet aircraft and other equipment, and radioactive fallout measurements. Most notable was its role in the evolution of stealth techniques to render combat aircraft and surface vehicles virtually invisible to hostile radars, electronic intercept receivers (known as "sniffers"), infrared seekers, and visual observations. The location at Groom Lake, northwest of Las Vegas, was selected because of its close proximity to the large and already highly secure Atomic

Energy Commission (AEC) test sites at Yucca and Frenchman Flats, thus expanding the enormous keep-out zone that was free from public or hostile intrusion.

This vital test station was known by various names: Paradise Ranch—a name chosen to attract workers to this remote desert location, perhaps because there were several well-known "entertainment ranches" in this general territory; Watertown (named after CIA Director Allen Dulles's birthplace in New York); Dreamland; Area 51; and Det 3. The latter two were Air Force designators begun in the late 1970s. The project AQUA-TONE, tasked to test the *Dragon Lady*, became known there as "the Angel from Paradise Ranch," and many cleared personnel simply referred to the test base as "The Ranch." The Dreamland moniker began in the late 1960s, taken from an Edgar Allen Poe poem of the same name: " . . . But the traveler, traveling through it/ May not, dare not openly view it!/ Never its mysteries are exposed/ To the weak human eye unclosed." Although in 1961 senior command was assigned to the Air Force with a CIA deputy, it remained a CIA facility until 1979, when it was designated an Air Force Base.

Over the thirty years, Area 51 Dreamland expanded enormously, confirmed by a 1987 Congressional mandate denying any future public access to the entire Groom Mountain region. One runway was 150 feet wide and 13,530 feet long, paved with concrete. Many hangars, storage sheds, and residential buildings were constructed or moved from other government sites.

Except in times of schedule urgency, workers usually resided there for five days a week and were ferried by passenger aircraft to Burbank or Palmdale, California, or Las Vegas, Nevada, for weekends. Of course, none of the families or friends of those who worked there knew where they were during the week. By 1965, when most of the housing facility was complete, the transient population reached more than 1,800. Although several companies had permanent spaces assigned for long-term employees, many workers were there for only short periods. Upon completing their planned and approved work, they were no longer allowed to be anywhere on the site.

An expanded Air Force team for evaluation of the YF-117 *Nighthawk* in 1980, formally known as the 410th Fighter Test Squadron, was humorously dubbed the "Baja Scorpions," since they were located on the south part of Groom Lake, a place richly populated with hundreds of native scorpions.

Significant systems evolved at Dreamland include Lockheed's *Dragon Lady*, the SR-71 *Blackbird* and its sister YF-12, the HAVE BLUE experimental stealth fighter prototype (two made, but lost in crashes), the F-117 *Nighthawk*, and the F-22 *Raptor*. Also, Northrop's TACIT BLUE stealth prototype (only one completely made, now on display at the Dayton National Museum of the US Air Force after 135 flights), and the B-2 *Spirit* stealth bomber.

TACIT BLUE Stealth Evaluator
(courtesy of the National Museum of the US Air Force)

Additionally, low observable improvements of the McDonnell-Douglas-Boeing F-15E *Strike Eagle*, Lockheed's F-16 *Fighting Falcon*, and Lockheed-Martin-Northrop's F-35 *Lightning II*, as well as a number of stealthy cruise missiles from several contractors were developed at Dreamland.

Other Dreamland Adventures

During the *Dragon Lady* flight-testing, Dreamland (then called Watertown) had to be evacuated when above-ground detonations of nuclear weapons took place at nearby Yucca Flat Proving Ground. The wind pattern caused radioactive debris to pass over Groom Lake—although by 1957 much of that project's flight-testing had ended, so a complete site evacuation of Dreamland for a long period did not interfere with vital CIA work.

The nuclear weapon's 74-kiloton hoop warhead was activated while suspended from a balloon 1,500 feet above ground. The CIA base at Dreamland, fourteen miles downwind, evaluated the effects on building materials, shielding effectiveness, and physical damage to structures similar to many found nationwide. The shock waves caused substantial damage to the Dreamland structures. Fortunately for us all, this type of nuclear testing was soon banned throughout the world. Dreamland reopened in 1961, in preparation for OXCART.

Beginning in 1968 with project HAVE DONUT, for two decades Air Force and Navy squadrons conducted tactical fighter combat experiments against captured Soviet MiG-17, MiG-21, MiG-23, Su-7B, Su-22, and Su-29 fighters. Crews flying the Soviet fighters were known as "Red Hats." From 1974 to 1978, this intensive work was called AIM-VAL/ACEVAL (air intercept missile evaluation/air combat evaluation), and involved dozens of aircraft in spectacular group combat trials. One clever French unit, operating F-5 *Freedom Fighters* to simulate a Russian squadron, realized that their aircraft were not equipped with radar detection equipment. They purchased some automobile speed-trap "fuzz busters" from an auto shop, mounted one on top of each fighter's control console, and successfully detected incoming radar illumination, which they used for effective evasive maneuvers.

Substantial benefits accrued from these trials in setting new design objectives and tactics for fighters, radars, and missiles. Understanding the results was also helpful to Hughes in maintaining its long-term dominance in the air intercept product lines of fighter radars and air-to-air guided missiles.

Beginning with KEYLOCK (the YF-12 weapon system testing), Hughes had a large role in many of the Dreamland projects, especially those involving radars and weaponry. No details can yet be revealed, but Hughes had transient staffs assigned to the evaluation of many hardware and software stealth programs, as well as extensive advisory efforts in operating hostile defense systems and mimicking enemy operating doctrines.

According to the Internet, another major task at Dreamland was HAVE GLIB, which evaluated simulated and actual Soviet ground-based air defense tracking and missile control radars. The objectives were similar to those of AIMVAL/ACEVAL, wherein all types of US aircraft were pitted against Soviet fighters to develop countering tactics and equipment improvements. The HAVE GLIB was particularly valuable in appraising the low observable characteristics of candidate stealth aircraft by testing them against genuine hostile air defense systems. Sophisticated US ground-based radars were also used to verify aircraft stealth behavior. Known on-site as Project 100, DYCOMS (dynamic measurement system) was an RCS measurement tool to evaluate all US stealth vehicles and weapons with very low observable features as they flew by the array of DYCOMS radars.

Invisible Radars and Antennas

Even if an aircraft has achieved a satisfactory low radar cross section, many of its missions require a radar; this is particularly true of multimission fighters. Radars by their very nature emit electromagnetic energy that may be detected by hostile listening receiver "sniffers." The radar hardware may also affect the aircraft's total RCS if it presents a bright reflection of enemy radar search beams.

While Lockheed and Northrop were busy competing for what would become the F-117 *Nighthawk*, Hughes received a modest technology demonstration project from the Air Force and DoD with a stealth objective. The desire was to demonstrate an airborne radar performing useful missions without being detected by the most sensitive threat sniffers in the Air Force inventory. As described below, results were spectacular, and Hughes soon was at the industry forefront in perfecting combat radars that were extremely difficult to detect while performing their targeting or surveillance jobs. The technology demands for these LPIR (low probability of intercept radars) were intense: both "be not heard" and "be not seen" objectives had to be met with no reduction in radar performance. Since "be not seen" partially depended on an unknown aircraft configuration, the "be not heard" work began first. Designers also took advantage of "be not recognized" features to confuse hostile sensors that could not sort this radar from similar things detectable in the airspace.

The early projects exploring airframe stealth prototypes were soon accompanied by intensive efforts to attain the vital "no hear" objective. Hughes was invited to create the stealth radar technologies for use in the *Nighthawk* and TACIT BLUE aircraft. The company's rapidly growing expertise was nurtured by these programs, six other major code-name projects, and many smaller secret efforts, some supported by internal research funding. Neither Hughes, rival Westinghouse, nor anyone else was able to develop a practical radar for the *Nighthawk*, for reasons that remain classified.

What was done? The demonstrated performance numbers and design details are still classified, for good reason. However, the following thoughts derive from my musing and reasoning twenty years later about the technical possibilities that might be tried to effect stealth. Anyone with a general understanding of radars could do the same.

In addition to shielding the radar RCS by its location in the aircraft and minimizing the antenna's RCS, several other steps could be taken to make it very difficult to detect radar transmissions: change frequency often, alter transmitted power levels, switch pulse repetition rate, modify the electronic waveform or pulse shapes, and place the beam on target only intermittently. If all these are done with random timing, it will be almost impossible to "see" a series of emanations. One instantaneous emission may be seen as a flicker, but there will be few subsequent samples to confirm it as part of a series or to establish a track record for analysis. With a robust central computer, what appears from the outside as random is understood and tracked, and return echoes can be matched to the pulses that mothered them.

A high priority task is to substantially reduce the antenna's RCS. The rest of the radar equipment is housed within the aircraft's stealth skin, but the radar antenna is exposed through an electromagnetically transparent radome. Hostile radar illumination must be either absorbed or deflected in a direction not detectable by the enemy's receiving antenna. Hughes successfully invented new shapes and construction techniques to create several types of "be not seen" antennas with very little reflectivity; again, details are classified.

While shaping the antenna to reduce RCS, engineers also stressed the "be not heard" objective by carefully molding the antenna output pattern to avoid sending energy in any direction other than the narrow-angle main beam. Non-stealth radars have patterns with the main beam surrounded by successive cones of energy, called sidelobes. If the main beam is about 3 degrees wide, the first sidelobe cone plus the main beam cone forms a fan of 9 degrees; the second, a 15-degree fan and so on. Power levels weaken considerably with each successive fan cone. Although the energy of the first sidelobe was at least a thousand times less than the primary beam, sensitive probing sniffers could still easily detect it at appreciable ranges.

Hughes began an LPIR technology demonstration project in the late 1970s to radically reduce those sidelobes. The demonstrator was fashioned with a unique new antenna coupled with a modified version of the company's radar prototype that was used in the design fly-off competition to equip the Air Force F-16 *Fighting Falcon*. (Westinghouse won that lucrative development.) Results of the airborne demonstration in an A-26 *Invader* test aircraft were spectacular, which motivated both the Air Force and the airframe companies to select Hughes for LPIR programs.

To control pattern shape and ensure random search patterns and instant changes in beam angles, electronic frequency scan had been chosen for wide look angles in the horizontal (azimuth) direction. In the A-26 experiments, mechanical scan was implemented in the vertical (elevation) direction for cost savings, and because large look angles in this direction were not vital for the primary ground-mapping objective.

In stealth bomber applications, however, space limitations and aperture openings necessitated electronic scanning in both sweep directions, providing unlimited agility and full viewing angles, both very important for fighter-bombers. Stealth antenna designs based on this technology were eventually deployed in US fighter aircraft and as an upgrade in the B-2 *Spirit* in the late 1990s.

The next LPIR step was to redesign transmitters to respond to rapid commands to change power levels and output waveforms, as well as pulse shapes and timing. If the waveform resembles electromagnetic noise in the atmosphere, how can it be recognized and separated? It cannot. The radar power output is controlled by the computer to emit only enough power to perform the job at hand. For example, upon observation of a single echo from a new target, pulse power is immediately reduced in subsequent randomly timed samples to the lowest possible output power that will obtain a detectable return echo. Lessening the power combined with the intermittent observations makes the stealth radar very difficult to trace.

The computer can also command the transmitter to rapidly alter the pulse timing, waveform and shape, contributing to the "do not recognize" objective by frustrating the listener, who is unable to track repetitions and confirm initial flickers. Consider comparing successive pulse sets with languages: the first word is in Swahili, the second in German, the next in Farsi, then Hindi, followed by Bantu and Mandarin; all these and many "waveforms" can be selected in random sequences and be extremely difficult for an observer to understand.

Changes of output signals in power and appearance attempt to place the perceived transmissions into the familiar phenomenon termed "white noise," in which background conditions mask the visibility of point sources. Perhaps it would be possible to further confuse the enemy by using transmitted radar waveforms identical to its own, in which case sniffers would be foiled by identity uncertainties. This is an effective "be not recognized" tactic.

The ability to make all these changes rapidly necessitates an extremely agile and high-capacity signal processor. As the transmitter alters each pulse set in many diverse ways, the signal processor must sense each output set and correlate any target returns with the specific illuminating pulse that caused it. This vital signal processing function, and the ultimate programmable signal processor (PSP) that enabled that agility, are described below, after the following stories about the large production stealth radar for the B-2 *Spirit*.

B-2 *Spirit* Stealth Bomber
(©iStockphoto/telegraham)

B-2 Radar Program Legends and Tales

The Hughes radar (with its own security classified designator) for the *Spirit* bomber became the first true stealth airborne radar to be fully developed, thoroughly tested, produced, and successfully deployed. The radar's multimission requirements called for providing the flight crew with super high quality target imagery, extremely accurate position locations, precise munitions delivery, low-altitude terrain-following performance, air-to-air targeting, and several other difficult functions. All these tasks were to be done while remaining almost invisible to any enemy search devices, with statistically insignificant probabilities of detection. Very high reliability, crew safety, nuclear radiation resistance, and easy maintenance were also challenging requirements. The resulting design significantly exceeded all these performance goals and truly demonstrated low probability of intercept in many laboratory and airborne tests.

The bomber radar development program was cloaked in high-level security, with all work performed in secure double-locked tanks, and with the enormous constraint of laboratory testing with absolutely no radiation into free space until the hardware was shipped to a remote flight test hangar. The company's normal experimental roof-house laboratory operation viewing distant targets could not be done.

The 1981 radar development contract to Hughes from the Air Force stipulated overall procedural control by the aircraft's designer, Northrop.

The initial contract value was $145 million cost-plus-fixed-fee, and was based on a mutual assumption by the Air Force, Northrop, and Hughes negotiators that existing security facilities and procedures would qualify, since the company had already satisfactorily performed many other black programs over the previous twenty years. However, the new crushingly severe security restrictions—probably necessary because of Soviet spying efforts—were significantly tighter than anyone expected. Hughes flunked the intensive compliance survey by the Air Force, and all operations were suspended until substantial facility reconstruction was completed and procedural doctrines were sufficiently upgraded. To do this properly cost an astounding $60 million above and beyond the basic contract value. Fortunately, the government absorbed the cost because all the required improvements came in the form of command direction from the Air Force security organization. Hughes completed the work within a few months and passed the government compliance inspection with flying colors and many compliments.

Northrop also failed its initial security compliance inspection even more poorly than we did. In attempting to solve those difficulties, plus manpower shortages, Northrop hired many experienced people from Rockwell International (which had successfully developed the B-1 *Lancer* bomber) and many retired Air Force officers. This new assembly of talent was jokingly known as "North-Rock-Force!" Northrop also borrowed the new Hughes-developed security procedure documentation that had been assessed by the Air Force as the ideal model for security-requirement compliance. Eventually, they passed too, so the complex stealth program could proceed.

In spite of these security setbacks, plus some fundamental design difficulties, to the astonishment of both Northrop and the Air Force, the first radar flight test in January 1984 aboard the KC-135 *Stratotanker* flight test bed made recognizable high resolution SAR (synthetic aperture radar) ground map images. Each additional complex radar operating mode added into the equipment also performed successfully in its first flight. Such an achievement was a first in the history of radar full-scale development flight testing.

There were few instances of security errors at the company during the rigid B-2 radar design and test. However, one incident did happen because of poor supervisory communication with a cleared staff member. The event is amusing in retrospect, since no project or financial damage occurred.

The first flight test antenna was undergoing verification evaluation in a tank at the El Segundo facility. Without prior notice, Northrop telephoned at 5:30 on a Friday afternoon with orders to immediately transport the antenna to the B-2 flight test hangar at Edwards Air Force Base. This move had been scheduled for two weeks later, and no shipping arrangements had yet been made. The estimated construction cost for this prototype antenna was about $20 million, and, of course, required the ultimate in security protection. The carefully disguised antenna was fastened down in the covered truck bed of an unmarked rental truck, and a chase car driven by a properly cleared security guard followed behind. Half an hour after the northbound truck departed, a distress call came from the chase car: "The truck has been parked on a residential street east of our planned route, and the driver has entered a house. What should I do?" After being told to just observe for five more minutes and to allow no one except other Hughes men to approach the truck, he called again, reporting that the driver had returned. When confronted, the driver apologized profusely for the delay, stating he had to stop at home to pack an overnight bag. When he had volunteered to drive the truck, he had just been scheduled to work at the remote test site the next week. He was not told of the truck's valuable contents, nor of the strict need to proceed directly to the destination. Fortunately, no harm resulted from this classic foul-up, and the unique antenna arrived safely before dawn.

In 2010, Dr. John Cashen, former vice president and chief scientist of Northrop-Grumman and co-designer of the B-2 *Spirit* bomber, reminisced about his dealings with Hughes. He was the customer's taskmaster of our company's contract efforts leading to the B-2 stealth radar. Prior to becoming a key figure at Northrop, John had been a staff member at Bell Labs as well as at Hughes (as a Hughes advanced-degree Fellow).

> "One of Northrop's first stealth projects, TACIT BLUE, was also America's first experimental stealth aircraft designed to do a mission: carry a very new technology—a synthetic aperture radar that produced imagery in 'real time.' The DoD asked Northrop to include the unique low probability of intercept radar experience of the Hughes Aircraft Company in its radar design, development, and flight test team. This was a 'special access' program, maintained secretly for twenty years. When it was finally revealed and placed in the Dayton National Museum of the US Air Force, the Air Force stated that the TACIT BLUE team had conducted one of the most successful flight test programs in history: 132 flights were made without any adverse incident. All of the multiple objectives were achieved successfully, including many aviation 'firsts.' None

was more noteworthy than the radar with the first low radar cross-section antenna and with very low probability of intercept to boot. The radar included the ability to collect real-time SAR images, with the digital processing done in a ground station and tied to the aircraft by data link, just as *Global Hawk* does the job today; surely a pioneering first.

"Shortly after TACIT BLUE was under way, a parallel lower-security classified program at Hughes called PAVE MOVER was initiated by DoD to extend the development and testing of airborne battlefield surveillance using an MTI (moving target indicator) radar. The combined outcomes of TACIT BLUE and PAVE MOVER were then used as the technical 'proof-of-concept' necessary for the development of the JSTARS (joint surveillance and target radar system).

"Hundreds of dedicated Hughes employees pioneered a new chapter in airborne surveillance. The team at Northrop Advanced Projects found both the outstanding cooperation and the challenge of managing such technical excellence to be exhilarating. The program created many lifelong friends within and bridging the two companies.

"In 1980, Hughes competed with Westinghouse for the contract to design, develop, and manufacture the B-2 stealth bomber radar. Both companies had outstanding radar divisions in those days, and it was a very close competition. Both proposed radars would have met all the specified requirements. I was part of the selection board at Northrop's B-2 Division and my recollection is that the deciding factor was the detailed design of the first 2-D airborne electronically scanned antenna to be integrated into a combat aircraft; it also had to be very stealthy. Hughes's unique design was not the most advanced, making use of decades-old antenna technology. The elevation scan plane featured a unique adaptation of the old mechanically-driven dielectric phase shifter concept. The azimuth scan plane employed a state-of-the-art digital ferrite phase shifter, first fabricated as part of the TACIT BLUE radar. Contrary to my doubts, the design proved highly reliable and it gave Hughes the winning edge with an antenna whose weight was significantly less than the competitor's design. The B-2 became operational with that design and for twenty years performed with distinction. It was subsequently replaced with a robust active element phased-array.

"In 1981, the B-2 was the most costly Air Force full-scale

development and manufacturing program in its history, and also its riskiest project. In contrast to normal practice, there was no prototype flown, nor any comprehensive technology risk-reduction efforts undertaken, nor alternative component tested. Northrop accepted and managed the significant technical risks by identifying the highest uncertainties prior to the preliminary design, and planning for each an alternative risk-reduction project. The unique Hughes radar antenna was one of those; another was the 56-foot-long all-graphite composite structure used for each outer wing. The one 'failure' in the eleven high-risk projects was the antenna. Surprisingly, I was asked by both Northrop and Hughes to temporarily take off my Northrop badge and again pin on a Hughes identification badge to take on the technology investigation at the design source. The technical excellence of that remedial team, drawn from throughout Hughes, was awe-inspiring. (Author's note: our company's family philosophy was thriving!) In short order, the team conducted interviews with the engineers involved with the design and fabrication of the full-scale risk-reduction antenna and reviewed its detailed documentation. We came quickly to the conclusion that the design was sound, but the fabrication process was flawed in its inability to maintain extremely precise tolerances during assembly. Hughes's manufacturing engineers creatively changed the tooling and assembly procedures, and after I reported this to Northrop's B-2 program manager, he ordered a second antenna to be built. It tested most successfully.

"That first antenna failure could have been a major disaster to the B-2 cost and schedule plan, and ultimately could have caused the bomber not to perform some of its vital missions. The collegial attitude and technical excellence of the senior Hughes antenna engineers, along with the confidence demonstrated by Northrop and the Air Force, led to an exceedingly successful program outcome, greatly enabling America's premier strike capability, the B-2 *Spirit* bomber."

51

PROCESSING
SIGNALS DIGITALLY

A VITAL SEGMENT OF stealth radars—as well as of any high performance systems—is the ability to fully analyze the data being seen. Briefly mentioned in Section 39, "Computers at Heart," signal processing is the function of analyzing the information details in the signals captured by a sensor such as a radar. Target echoes have distinctive features that can be used to understand the location, behavior, shape, and identity of the object being observed. Signal data to be diagnosed are energy level, primary frequency and changes in it, phase changes, time duration, and repeatability; all these are compared to the transmitted signal and previous responses from that object stored in the radar's computer memory. Each echo must be correlated with the specific transmitted pulse set that had caused it. (Determining target speed by examining the Doppler frequency shift of the echo from the transmitted pulse carrier frequency was described in Section 17, "Technology Advances.")

The high-performance signal processor can minutely examine the echo structure down to a fraction of the distance between wave crests (much less than 1/4 inch for X-band) and use this to develop an image of the target—perhaps even precisely locating its section most vulnerable to attack.

Early signal processors were analog devices for measuring and recording the data stream from the radar receiver. The previously-mentioned performance of CORDS suffered because of the relatively crude components available at the time; poor dynamic range allowed weak target signals to be overwhelmed by strong clutter that could not be eliminated by timing or frequency filtering.

Progress in digital computers in the 1960s stimulated the idea of performing signal processing in a similar mathematical way. The first challenge was to convert the analog signals into binary digits rapidly and accurately. This conversion was done by measuring the magnitude, phase, and frequency of continuous samples of the received electromagnetic wave as it passed a time-clocked position. The measured values were transformed into digital numbers, passed to the processor, and combined into a data stream for subsequent examination. A number of unknowns had to be addressed and resolved in those early days of digital signal processing. Among them were the difficulty in achieving the required sampling width, determining how many samples to accrue for each signal and how to avoid clipping the peak values, determining how many digits to use to ensure adequate detail, and achieving the needed conversion accuracy.

The first government-funded project to implement digital signal processing was in 1966, when study contracts were awarded to Hughes and Westinghouse. Milt Radant (later corporate vice president for research and development) led the creative Hughes team. They won subsequent competitive demonstration projects with airborne radars operating in X-band and the higher resolution Ku-bands. One project for the Air Force, called FLAMR (forward looking advanced multimode radar), flew in a B-47 *Stratojet* test bed, and another, labeled MMRDSP (multimode radar digital signal processor), for the Navy, flew in a T/A-3 *Skywarrior*. These experimental devices demonstrated digital signal processing for the three important radar mission modes: air-to-air search and track, SAR ground mapping with real time imagery, and Doppler beam sharpening (DBS) for precise ground mapping.

The early airborne SAR processor, for example, performed analog-to-digital conversion, and achieved mapping resolution of 10 feet at ten miles range. Signal processing requires only very simple repetitive computations, but it has to keep up with the high-speed real-time radar data input of 2-1/2 million operations per second, which was really speedy in the late 1960s. As noted in Section 34, "Seek and Ye Shall Find; Airborne Mapping"), the TR-1 aircraft system reached speeds of 225 million operations per second. Today's general-purpose computers usually operate at about 1 billion operations per second!

During the competitive 1969 fly-off of the fighter radar model slated for the F-15 (see Section 35, "Airborne Radars Fly"), the performance of the signal processor was astounding, with over 10 million operations per second. Construction was in one "black box" the size of three loaves of bread, using plug-in multilayer printed circuit boards supporting flat-pack integrated circuit packages.

Programmable Signal Processors

In the early 1970s, it became possible to satisfy the urgent need for far more signal processing agility, which would enable the radar to switch rapidly from one performance mode to another—providing much better performance in tactical situations. Highly capable multimode radars also contributed to the creation of a single aircraft that could execute several different mission assignments such as reconnaissance, air intercept, and ground attack. This was a revolutionary development in combat aircraft.

Advances in semiconductors and new generations of integrated circuit devices made construction of complex high-speed digital electronics possible. The desired flexibility could result from designing the processor to be managed by software programs similar to the way data processing is done in computers, which were rapidly growing in technical sophistication and breadth of performance in that era.

Up to this time, signal processors had limited performance and lacked agility to change operating functions because each operating mode was hard-wired. Hughes invested large amounts of company funds in a project to solve this performance shortfall, deriving what became known as the programmable signal processor, or PSP. This project's purpose was to confirm the concept by fabricating and demonstrating PSP hardware and software that could perform multiple air-to-air modes. Dave Lynch (later the father of Hughes stealth radars) and Lee Tower patented the design architecture in the early 1970s. By 1974 a PSP was integrated with an AWG-9 fire control system in a Culver City roof-house test laboratory. All operating modes were confirmed against flyover and flyby targets.

Competition for the F/A-18 *Hornet* radar began the next year. The company was still reeling from its loss of the F-16 radar program, which had been snared by Westinghouse. In that contest, prime contractor General Dynamics, desiring low cost, had mandated a hard wired processor with modest performance compared to what was already in the F-14 and F-15 systems. The *Hornet* radar requirements were considerably more challenging, in both performance levels and the number of operating modes. This made our new PSP a natural, and it could be advertised as "off-the-shelf," with the AWG-9 roof-house demonstrations as proof. We won that close competition, and the first PSP deployed was aboard the F/A-18 *Hornet* in 1983. PSPs are now in radars for the AV-8 *Harrier*, F-4G *Phantom*, F-14 *Tomcat*, F-15 *Eagle*, F-16 *Fighting Falcon*, F-22 *Raptor*, F-35 *Lightning II*, U-2 *Dragon Lady*, AC-130 *Hercules*, French *Rafael*, Swedish *Viggen*, British *Typhoon*, and several other combat aircraft.

APG-70 in the F-15E *Strike Eagle*
(courtesy of UNLV)

Offspring of these devices using the same breakthrough architecture are used by much of the world's population today: in CD audio and DVD video players, second- and later-generation cell phones, and digital cable decoder units, among many others.

By the mid-1980s, Hughes PSPs had a central core computer to govern the type of signal processing and separate the echo samples into processing segments. Its unique software contained long instruction words containing multiple procedural commands. One complex calculation could be done in the extremely short time of 140 billionths of a second at a clock rate of 7 million cycles per second; 98 million operations were usually performed each second, and in one particular application it achieved an incredible 225 million! In the intervening years, circuit chip speeds have increased dramatically; this architecture today is achieving 4 billion operations per second for less than $50 per chip.

Robust PSPs now made it possible to transform any type of radar into multipurpose sensors. For fighter aircraft varieties, such modern processors removed all intercept geometry limitations, adding missions formerly assigned to specialized vehicles such as tactical bombers and reconnaissance aircraft.

The first air-to-air and air-to-ground multimode radar to be deployed was the APG-70 onboard the F-15E *Strike Eagle*, an upgrade to the APG-63 begun in 1988. This system could perform everything: SAR reconnaissance maps, Doppler navigation, detection of mobile ground targets using MTI (moving target indication), missile guidance illumination and command communication, precision bombing delivery, and noncooperative target recognition. Many modes could be performed simultaneously, or rapidly activated by pilot commands.

These features were then added to the *Tomcat* and *Hornet* radars and were design requirements for the *Raptor* and *Lightning II*.

The PSP fifth generation, reached by 1993, was the CIP (common integrated processor) used in the *Raptor* fighter. This adept machine performs all the signal and data processing for the aircraft's numerous sensors and mission avionics. It has the same operating throughput of two of the world's fastest general-purpose supercomputers. The integrated circuits have hundreds of thousands of digital gates per chip with operating part sizes less than 40 millionths of an inch in width. The equipment has inherent hardware data security protection, employs compensation to provide in-flight fault and damage tolerance, is constructed in modular form for easy growth, and supports the Air Force two-level maintenance concept (if a component fails, the small circuit card containing the failure is replaced in the aircraft, rather than sending the entire processor box to the repair station).

This significant technology evolution, which remarkably went from a concept to a fifth generation of unmatched performance in only twenty years, has application to all combat aircraft, surface, and ship radars as well as to the numerous essential devices used by the public.

52

PERFECT INTERCEPT

FOR THIRTY-FIVE YEARS, Hughes was very active in America's five-generation evolution of air-to-air guided missiles; Raytheon and the Navy's China Lake laboratories also performed state-of-the-art technology advances. Generation zero in the late 1940s was the Hughes Tiamat missile, which began the proof of semiactive radar guidance by steering to target echoes from the launch aircraft's tracking radar. Three missiles were tested successfully, but Tiamat was never manufactured and deployed. The subsequent generations are grouped below by guidance method and complexity, not necessarily by their evolutionary sequence. Production samples of all five generations, with explanatory storyboards, are on public display at the Estrella Warbirds Museum in Paso Robles, California; this is the only place in the world where they can be viewed together. Ed Cobleigh and Ben McRee, both retired from the Hughes Missile Systems Group and great contributors to this book, were the heart of our three-man team that assembled this notable exhibit.

Generation 1: China Lake's AIM-9 Sidewinder and Hughes's AIM-4 IR Falcon were small infrared heat-seeking birds that provided short range, tail attack capability. About 23,000 IR Falcons were produced by Hughes, and by 2006, 110,000 Sidewinders had been built by three manufacturers, with Raytheon making the most.

Generation 2: The Hughes radar Falcon and Raytheon's AIM-7 Sparrow used semiactive, low-PRF radar guidance and provided all-weather, longer range, and all-target-aspect attack against single targets that were not obscured by ground clutter reflections. The fighter radar tracked and illuminated the target until missile impact. By 2006, more than 39,000 Sparrows and 25,000 radar Falcons had been produced.

Generation 3: The Hughes GAR-9 (later called AIM-47) missile had semiactive guidance, but now with a pulse-Doppler radar providing long-range attack with immunity from ground clutter. This first look-down-shoot-down missile was never operationally deployed, but the Raytheon Sparrow was upgraded to pulse-Doppler radar compatibility for production in the 1960s.

Generation 4: The Hughes AIM-54 Phoenix missile was a giant leap in capability. The fighter radar gave illumination samples every two seconds to allow sampled-data, semiactive midcourse guidance by as many as six missiles in flight attacking different targets at the same time. During the final ten miles to intercept, a radar transmitter within the missile for final guidance allowed the fighter to maneuver away when the last missile was homing on its own.

Generation 5: The Hughes AIM-120 AMRAAM (advanced medium range air-to-air missile), the Raytheon AIM-9X, and the British SRM form this latest generation.

AMRAAM

The AMRAAM is the ultimate intercept weapon. It is 12 feet long and 7 inches in diameter, has a 25-inch wing span, weighs 335 pounds when launched, and can be shot against multiple targets at all aspects and at ranges well beyond twenty miles. The fighter's fire control radar searches and tracks several hostile aircraft, then transfers the selected target's location to the missile's onboard computer. During flight, AMRAAM steers by its internal inertial reference system (adjusted by GPS references captured from that satellite network) and by receiving target position updates directly from the fighter's radar. Its own internal radar acquires the target in the final approach, providing accurate guidance. Nearing impact, a radar proximity fuse triggers a 48-pound lethal blast-fragmentation warhead. Multiple AMRAAMs can be launched by a fighter and guided simultaneously to separate targets.

This spectacular intercept weapon was sponsored by the Air Force, which in 1981 awarded a full-scale development contract to Hughes after a hotly contested validation phase fly-off with Raytheon. Government funding for the program had been minimal, so both companies had to make major investments in their attempt to win an extremely important contract. Furthermore, the Air Force plan required that both companies manufacture the final configuration, so the winner had to share its data with its future production competitor! Thus, Hughes, upon winning the fly-off, had to take all the development program's financial risks and still had to give away most of its brainwork. There was an annual price contest for the larger manufacturing share of that year's lot. Faced

AMRAAM Missile
(courtesy of UNLV)

with the decision to commit the large corporate investment anticipated (would we ever earn those self-funded expenses back?), Allen Puckett, in a memorable demonstration of his long-range vision, said, "This is the opportunity of the decade—no, it is that of a lifetime, so move ahead full speed." Thankfully, that risky commitment was made and we did recover the funds after several years of production.

Hughes won this closely matched development competition for a fixed price of $421 million, far less than was needed to complete what the difficult requirements demanded. For the benefit of its concerned stockholders, as well as its own pride, Raytheon publicly said, "Oh well, we always get to build whatever Hughes designs," fully anticipating being awarded much higher manufacturing quantities than Hughes would in the annual competitions. That's where the real profit opportunities lay.

So what happened in the first five years of production? The initial three of the quantity splits were determined by the Air Force to assure that each company could achieve a sustainable ability to produce, and to encourage cooperation between the rivals to fix technical problems as they emerged. Each firm strategized its annual offer to balance the conflicting objectives of being awarded a prestigiously higher share versus maximizing profit. Higher quantities result in lower unit manufacturing cost, permitting a possibly more favorable unit price in the competition. However, by losing at the unit price level, higher total profit may be attained (increased cost due to smaller quantity produced, but a higher profit tagged to each missile in that bid, resulting in a higher total earnings for that year). Hughes was awarded the following production portions in successive years: 58 percent of 180; 52 percent of 423; 59 percent of 906, 50 percent of 900, and 67 percent of 810. Annual competitions continued through lot 11, after which, in 1997, Raytheon acquired Hughes. That was certainly one way to get 100 percent of the annual production award!

The Hughes development win came in large part from offering a TWT transmitter for the missile's active radar, thanks to the insight of Mal Currie. This transmitter provided dramatic improvements in power output, frequency bandwidth, and efficiency; whereas, Raytheon proposed a solid-state device that suffered in power output. The missile needed a high level of output power so it could acquire the target early enough that its final steering time was sufficient to correct any midcourse errors. The Air Force had stipulated a solid-state transmitter, but accepted the Hughes nonresponsive proposal when presented with adequate substantiation. Many stalwarts together made this tough but "lifetime" award possible: Mal Currie, Walt Maguire, Ben McRee, and Jimmy Jonokuchi, to name just a few.

The physical packaging of all this capability was enabled by jumps in super-miniaturized electronics (for example, AMRAAM's digital computing unit started as four test bays 24 inches wide by 6 feet tall, but was shrunk into a 6-inch cylinder only 1 inch long!); the high power transmitter; great improvements in rocket motors; new fabrication materials; an ablative skin for temperature control; the GPS link; excellent reliability; and efficient data inter-tie between the fighter and the in-flight missile. (It is noteworthy that after great improvements in device technology, all recently produced AMRAAMs have solid-state transmitters with excellent power output, just as the Air Force originally desired.)

The AMRAAM can be matched to most modern radar-equipped fighters as well as to ground-launched air defense deployments; all US military services and fifteen overseas nations have the missiles in their arsenals. More than 15,000 were produced by 2006. First used in 1991 in Desert Storm, AMRAAM has compiled an extraordinary combat record of 38 enemy aircraft shot down using only thirty-eight missiles. There were no misses or failures, and no successful counter-fire by hostile aircraft. You can't do better than that!

The philosophy of deterrence by weapon superiority was obvious when many Iraqi pilots refused to take off if an AMRAAM-equipped fighter was within one hundred miles!

ASRAAM

While AMRAAM was moving ahead as the perfect mid-range radar air intercept weapon, things were seething in the short-range missile sector. To cope with increasing concerns about highly maneuvering dogfight engagements, the Air Force and Navy began a number of experimental programs and funded study projects with many contractors. The last three decades of the twentieth century were a fertile time for the development of IR technologies to satisfy numerous combat missions, including solving the difficult dogfight problem. Advances in optics, telescope stabilization and tracking systems, and detector designs in IRST and FLIR imaging, as well as the ability to achieve full IR imagery with staring arrays (see Section 30, "Exploiting Infrared; Staring Arrays"), produced attractive candidates for missile guidance improvements to overcome the performance limitations of the prior generations of IR-guided missiles.

Sophisticated electronics enabled amplification and processing of very small signals to gain effective weapon steering intelligence. The seekers for Sidewinder and Falcon in the 1950s used simple optics with a reticle to sample and focus target energy onto a single uncooled detector. These seekers were sensitive to IR wavelengths very near those of visible light. Since this was well before the digital age, analog vacuum tube electronics were used.

In the early 1960s, Hughes was strongly pushed for improved IR guidance for air-to-air weaponry by developing a cryogenic cooler, longer wavelength detectors, an improved reticle, and better optics. The Navy Sidewinder, however, became the dominant dogfight missile in all free-world fighters, and was closely copied by the Soviets. Even though Sidewinder was quite effective in most tail attacks, the machine gun was still the favorite of pilots in "furball" dogfights (large dogfights involving many friends and foes).

In the 1970s, the ability to cope with effective countermeasures that used flares to deceive simple seekers became increasingly urgent. Tactical experts also desired the ability to engage on the target's nose and with wider tail offset angles, as well as better interpretation of target features by the sensor. The Navy particularly wanted a seeker with a very wide look angle to cope with the missile's "weathervaning" that occurs when it is fired in a tight turn. Hughes built an experimental seeker called Agile with an unusual cylinder dome that allowed the seeker to see beyond the full frontal hemisphere and peer back over its shoulder! It used an array of IR elements similar to those in IRST systems to provide better resolution to discriminate a target from countermeasures. Adding short wavelength detectors was considered as a second backup sensing band to reject very hot flares.

Government motivation to fund these missile solutions was considerably lessened by the 1973 Yom Kippur War. Israeli pilots were so adept in dogfight encounters with Egyptian fighters flown by almost novice pilots that victories were virtually assured with cannon or machine-gun fire, or even by forcing the opponent to maneuver himself into the ground. "Who needs a missile? All you need is a good airplane and a well-trained fighter pilot." This, of course was nonsense in the bigger picture, and to learn more, extensive evaluations were undertaken of interactions between wide varieties of fighter aircraft with opponents using Russian tactics and well-trained pilots. The results of these projects from 1974 through 1978—HAVE DONUT at Dreamland and AIMVAL/ACEVAL (see above)—coupled with concern that the new Russian AA-11 short-range missile performance was exceeding that of similar US weapons, spurred a new urgency. The Dreamland encounter analysis helped establish detailed requirements for AMRAAM and ASRAAM (advanced short range air-to-air missile) in 1978. Cooperative agreements were made with the Europeans to participate in the development programs.

The short-range missile goals included nose-on attack capability for first-pass shots before the dogfight maneuvers began. The seeker thus needed wide-angle acquisition, improved sensitivity to detect the lower intensities of targets encountered in a nose attack, and adequate resolution to avoid distraction from flares.

In 1975, using internal funding, Hughes had begun developing a digital method for tracking chosen objects in video images that was suitable for missile guidance. The resulting method showed an outstanding ability to track a target through the interference of multiple flares and in conditions of very high ground or cloud thermal clutter backgrounds. The Navy quickly started to build a TV seeker for Sidewinder that could exploit this new tracker, while Hughes pursued IR focal plane staring arrays for target lockon after launch. The latter would enable shots without the undesirable delay needed for pilot lockon before launch.

Intense work began in the early 1980s in several high-security projects. (Another possible concept was to create an IR version of AMRAAM, but no serious program was started.) In the mid-1980s, electronic compensation for the rapid temperature changes in the IR dome as the missile accelerated to high Mach numbers was successfully demonstrated.

All these efforts led Hughes to capture a contract to develop the focal plane array sensor for the British IR SRM (short range missile), which would enter production in the late 1990s. Hughes then won the Navy's competitive program to develop a sophisticated IR focal plane array for the exotic AIM-9X Sidewinder, which began production at Tucson in the 2000s.

AIM-9X Missile
(courtesy of the National Museum of the US Air Force)

These seekers use unusual optics to place the field of view image onto an array of hundreds of thousands of detector elements, providing extremely fine-grained details of the entire scene. The element signals are amplified, multiplexed, and processed using embedded microelectronic chips. The seekers analyze and track to the most vulnerable spot on the target and are seldom distracted by countermeasures or thermal clutter.

Hughes IR imaging and intercept technologies became vital in SDI programs beginning in the mid-1980s, as described in the next section.

53

STRATEGIC WARFARE

Hughes's experience in the early phases of digital computing in the late 1950s had placed the first airborne digital computer into the MA-1 fire control system destined for the F-106 *Delta Dart*. The next step was achieving electronic data conversion from analog to digital, enabling the first all-digital radars of the 1960s (see Part Six). These skills enabled a meaningful entry into the attack portion of strategic warfare and gained the company primary responsibility for the solid-state digital computer guidance subsystem for submarine-launched ballistic missiles (SLBMs).

Attack Guidance

The Navy's weapon series has had four generations: UGM-27 Polaris, first deployed in 1961; UGM-73 Poseidon in 1972; UGM-96 Trident I in 1979, and then UGM-96A Trident II, first deployed in 1990 and still active in the fleet.

The computers stored strategic target locations, provided missile stability in all three flight phases (boost, midcourse, and terminal), and commanded the trajectory and dispensing of decoys and warheads from the reentry bus, as well as performing warhead control and management. They were the missiles' genius brains.

Hughes also gained experience in the control of two other nuclear warfare weapons. Fortunately (from my point of view), neither went into production. One, in the late 1950s, was the GAR-11, a version of the GAR-9 (later designated AIM-47) air-to-air intercept missile described in Part Three. The Air Force Air Defense Command anticipated that the big boom of a single missile could be sufficient to destroy many Soviet

Trident SLBM Missile
(courtesy of Wikipedia)

bombers attempting a mass raid on the United States. The idea was probably to expend such a weapon well offshore as the raiders approached, to minimize collateral civilian damage. A number of flights demonstrated that the guidance system worked very well (no warheads were used in these shots), but the project was abandoned as an inappropriate defense weapon.

Another device fell into the tactical combat category. In the 1960s, the Army began a program called the M-67 Davy Crockett, providing artillery commanders the opportunity to use a guided short-range nuclear weapon if desperate times arose. Our company was awarded a contract to develop an IR imaging seeker and guidance system. Once again, testing proved the design successful, but this weapon was never fielded: its range was so short that friendly forces firing the missile would be threatened with possible radioactive hazards.

The Strategic Defense Initiative

The US began a politically controversial set of projects in 1983 called SDI (Strategic Defense Initiative), managed by a directive office called SDIO. The efforts were compliant with international treaties, and shared the goals of finding technologies that could provide defense against the global ballistic missile threat. Included were extensive analytical studies and prototyping of many devices to test their effectiveness. All projects were restricted to experimentation and test and did not include any production planning, which would have required both a difficult internal US acceptance as well as almost impossible international negotiations. Deploying anything of this nature, even though only for defense, is still politically sensitive in 2011.

When SDI (publicly nicknamed Star Wars after that popular movie) began, Hughes was in an ideal position to capture demonstration contracts in all three segments of the mission: (1) detecting and locating an ICBM launch; (2) finding and tracking the ICBM and its subsequent dispersal of warheads and decoys; and (3) intercepting and destroying the reentry pods containing warheads.

The company had demonstrated technical capability in every aspect of the job. One key performance need was for long-wavelength infrared to see launch sites surrounded by widespread Earth radiation and—the opposite technical challenge—to find very weak IR emanations from ballistic missile objects appearing in the extreme cold of a space background. During the 1970s, under the direction of George Aroyan, Hughes had many times shown the feasibility of detecting such targets in tests sponsored by the Army Ballistic Missile Defense Agency (BMDA) and DARPA, the research unit of DoD. Experiments with Hughes devices had demonstrated sufficient practicality that President Reagan could make his famous "Star Wars" speech and announce the beginning of SDI as a high priority US policy.

Detecting and Locating

Detection of an ICBM launch would seem easy when observed and reported from a satellite. But think about the difficulties: possible hostile ICBM sites spread over an enormous land and sea area that must be watched continuously, and sensors that must see the booster's radiation and not be bewildered by copious background emissions and objects such as active power plants. Furthermore, the system must remember what it had seen on its previous look and recognize a change; small pointing errors will totally confuse any memory comparison.

Surveillance Satellite about to Launch,
Cape Canaveral, Florida
(courtesy of UNLV)

Details of what the company designed and delivered for the satellite portion of this SDI project are still classified, but some things can be surmised. Sensors used detectors matched to three portions of the IR spectrum to distinguish thermal radiation coming from possible booster emissions from those coming from Earth backgrounds and known heat sources. To do a minimum job would require each observation pixel (the sensor's discrete image resolution) to resolve at least a 1,000-foot-square area from all nearby areas. Observing land regions the size of Kansas would mean many millions of pixels per look. The data processing task to handle all this information was the opposite of the normal practice of recording images: in this case, perfect and complete large-scale images were made, compared to the previous images, and everything was discarded unless a small spot had changed. Each second look required analysis of these millions of pixels without error!

Finding and Selecting

After an ICBM booster burnout, it's a very tough job to find, track, and correctly report the bus vehicle that carries sets of powerful warheads and a bunch of decoys. As the bus nears the terminal area, the detecting and tracking tasks go from one object to dozens as the many warheads and decoys are widely dispersed. Hughes won the SDIO contract to develop a very sophisticated machine, the AOA (airborne optical adjunct), to be flown at high altitudes in a Boeing 747 to scientifically measure faint IR signatures of various targets contrasted against the cold background of space.

AOA Ready for Mounting in a Boeing 747
(courtesy of Raytheon)

Large telescopic optics focused incoming thermal energy onto a many-element IR detector array. The focal point was horizontally scanned across a long line of IR cells only 2-degrees wide, then moved slightly upward to sweep another line, thus generating a large field of view. Three cell types, responding in three different IR wavelengths, were intermixed in the detector array to provide video contrasting features of the bus and its terminal vehicles, and to distinguish them from any space background clutter. Range was not directly measured, but was computed from scene geometry and a target's track history.

Enormous amounts of signal processing were required to analyze all the incoming data. Stabilization of the device for angular accuracy was also a major design challenge. Accounting for the Earth's curvature, re-entry vehicles could appear at more than several hundred miles range, or even farther if there was an ideal geometry from the 747 to form an optimum look angle to separate the bus from interfering background.

Mounting the 6,000-pound AOA in the aircraft was most complex; the entire assembly was continuously moved on a support rail to allow wide scan through a small fuselage aperture. Three-axis spatial orientation was stabilized with a set of gyroscopic gimbals. The AOA performed exceedingly well in extensive airborne testing for twenty years, proving all the functions needed for finding and tracking warhead reentry vehicles and distinguishing them from decoys. Hughes owes much credit for this accomplishment to the managers of this difficult project, George Speake and Bernie Skehan.

Intercepting and Destroying

The ICBM defense is best done by destroying the missile during the boost phase or in the midcourse phase before it disperses the clusters of reentry vehicles with warheads and many deceptive objects. In midcourse, the hostile warhead carrier is traveling at 15,700 miles per hour above the atmosphere. If this opportunity to track is lost, it becomes mandatory to intercept and destroy all the reentry warheads before the nuclear blasts are triggered. To avoid wasteful intercepts, decoys must be identified and ignored.

Solving this challenge required solution of many difficult subordinate problems: the defensive missile's seeker finding and tracking the hostile; distinguishing targets from background interference; having agile steering at closing speeds of Mach 10; and striking the most vulnerable part of the target to maximize destruction.

In the late 1980s, Hughes won the KKV (kinetic kill vehicle) experimental prototype program to demonstrate such intercepts. Ted Wong (Missile Systems Group president at that time) related in 2009 his memories of the resulting design: KKV was cylindrically shaped, about 8 inches in diameter and 2 feet long, with no aerodynamic wings or steering control vanes. Closing velocities would be 2 miles per second. The bird, boosted to more than 90 miles altitude from a ground base or ship, had an internal rocket motor for its final stage. Since it would travel in extremely rarified atmosphere, flight direction was governed by eight hydrazine gas nozzle thrusters on its periphery: four at the weapon's center of gravity for direct lateral shifts, the other four at the tail to control pointing and roll attitude.

After separation from its booster, KKV used two "bug-eye" IR imaging sensors to lock on to the oncoming target. Those protruding domes were so placed that the sensors would not be obscured by the intensely hot stagnation temperatures at the KKV nose in case of use within some amount of atmosphere. Reentry vehicles were detected at sixty miles range; with both target and interceptor rapidly decreasing their separation, the KKV traveled thirty miles until impact. Fine-grained thermal imaging resolution provided enough data for the internal computer to assess the target's shape and command steering to the most vulnerable spot. Agility and accuracy in terminal steering assured a direct hit. No warhead was needed; mass and speed yielded enough kinetic energy to vaporize the target upon collision. That feature was a blessing, since a nuclear blast by the hostile warhead was no longer possible.

Many test launches against ballistic missile reentry vehicles confirmed this intercept concept. The design was especially well demonstrated in 2008 when a KKV derivative, boosted from a ship by a Navy Standard Missile, intercepted and destroyed a US satellite that was decaying from its orbit. The satellite contained a large tank of unexpended toxic hydrazine fuel. To ensure vaporizing that chemical before it polluted at ground level, the missile software was preprogrammed to place the impact point directly on that fuel tank. Intercept occurred at 153 miles above the Pacific Ocean and the shot worked perfectly, much to the relief of many of the world's inhabitants.

A big disappointment came to Hughes as it was working the KKV project: the Army set up a program called THAAD (terminal high altitude area defense) that also needed a terminal intercept device. Lockheed won this very difficult competition. We were told that the Army's technical evaluators favored our design, whose working concept had already been proven in many KKV test shots. It appeared to us that Lockheed won on a political basis by promising to establish a new manufacturing plant in a state represented by influential congressmen. In the ensuing test program, Lockheed's design failed miserably, and the Army directed that the configuration be altered to mimic the one Hughes had proposed! Such are the ways of government competitions in which the loser's design is hijacked by the winner, but at least we still had the Navy's SDI version of the Standard Missile programs. (As noted in Part Seven, Hughes itself had politically benefited by promising a new plant in Mississippi to win the ADCAP torpedo program, but at least, in contrast to the competitor's THAAD, our design in that project worked perfectly.)

High Energy Beam Experiment

In the 1980s, many defense experts hoped that a high-energy electromagnetic beam might be the optimum way to destroy both tactical and strategic hostile objects: results could be accomplished at the speed of light and a missed shot could be quickly repeated, doing the job faster and cheaper than traditional guided intercept missiles. Hughes captured an extensive Navy experimental program, the SEALITE beam director, whose objective was to gather technical data and determine performance limits as a precursor to creating a new close-in ship defense against anti-ship cruise missiles or aircraft.

High Energy Laser Weapon Evaluator
(courtesy of *UNLV*)

Could a big operating laser actually be directed to repeatedly shoot down small and rapidly moving targets? Military applications of laser technologies had progressed through target designation, range finding, and spot-illumination for guided weapons, and for forming surveillance images. Could sufficient laser power be generated, adequately focused, pointed, and beamed long enough to effect mortal damage? It was visualized that laser beam impingement could nullify or confuse optical seekers, cook their electronics, or severely damage structures, airframes, or control surfaces. Estimates of laser power needed for success ranged up to hundreds of kilowatts with a duration of at least one second of contact in a small area of the target.

The Hughes working model used a purchased laser element, and was

20 feet high and weighed 23,000 pounds! It had a 58-inch aperture for output from its 70-inch primary mirror. The mechanism adjusted for optical diffraction and protected its elements from overheating. One taxing design challenge was to mechanically stabilize and precisely point the huge telescope mass: 18,000 pounds had to be rapidly shifted to counter targets crossing with fast angular rate changes.

Highly accurate tracking of small targets at ranges well beyond thirty miles was done with a FLIR mounted atop the full assembly. It had 16,384 IR cells in a 128 by 128 array, sensitive in the long-wavelength 8 to 12 micron band. Laser beams could be swept 290 degrees laterally and 90 degrees vertically. Pointing of the high-energy beam by the FLIR tracker was adjusted for unwanted movement or heating effects by electronically steering eight agile compensating mirrors. In early tests, the tracker could hold the beam on the target for more than fourteen seconds; later, the time was extended to seventy seconds. These dwell-times ensured physical destruction of any military target. Laser power levels were as high as 1 million watts and could be sustained for the entire seventy-second dwell time.

This project took five years to design and three years to integrate with the MIRACL (mid-infrared advanced chemical laser). Although it was never mounted on a ship, successful tests in the late 1980s and 1990s at New Mexico's White Sands Proving Ground "killed" many kinds of missiles, including a tiny darting TOW, and several helicopters. In 1997, a beam from this high-energy laser weapon disabled an obsolete US military satellite orbiting at 268 miles altitude, as a dramatic demonstration of a laser weapon's ability against distant small targets.

Preventive Defense

The international community continued its strenuous efforts to find ways to limit the chances or outcome of a disastrous nuclear weapon conflict. In the late 1980s, a new segment of the SALT agreement set to curtail production of IRBMs (intermediate range ballistic missiles) allowed in-country inspection by foreign teams of the manufacturing outputs of those weapons. Doing this job properly was difficult because, to avoid design and construction secrets being revealed or sabotaged, an inspector was not permitted to directly observe the production line. Only the material inputs and final product outputs of the entire production facility could be seen and recorded.

Hughes was selected to design and operate an adequate monitoring system for the principal USSR IRBM manufacturing site located in the Ural mountain range. The giant building had protective security fences and windowless solid walls. The workforce was confined to a nearby isolated living compound when they were not in the plant. Incoming materials moved through a single large entry passageway; final products were brought out through another portal with a rail car loading ramp. Back in the United States, Hughes was given detailed drawings defining the building and all its exterior construction.

We sent several experts to the Urals to view the actual building and surroundings. (I never heard how anyone verified that underground delivery tunnels did not exist, but this must have been done.) Our team then designed a reliable inspection technique using weight, shape, dimensions, aromas, and radioactivity emanations to accurately quantify the production rate. Several of our inspectors were to be present at all times, recording all data, analyzing input and output relationships, and reporting gathered information to both Soviet and US officials.

To practice and perfect these routines, a full-scale mockup of the entry and exit portals, security fences, and rail tracks was erected in the New Mexico desert. This realistic evaluation site operated for several months before our crew and US government personnel began their assignments inside Russia. It was fascinating for me to witness a practice run of the planned procedures at that mockup's delivery portal: a pseudo "Russian" IRBM loaded onto a "USSR" flatbed railroad car, marked with the infamous Red Star, and with "Soviet" troopers standing guard! It was very serious and important work, but it felt like we were all acting in a Hollywood film shoot for an adventure movie. Lights! Camera! Action!

54

CAREER ADVANCEMENT AND CUSTOMER BONDING

IN 1971, AFTER many years assigned to technical management of the AWG-9/Phoenix program, I was promoted to division manager, directing all company aspects of that program—it was the largest Hughes business endeavor at the time. The program was about to begin production. We were meeting or exceeding all of our contract obligations, and we even were beginning to deliver substantial profits to the company. In 1973, initial deployment of two *Tomcat* squadrons aboard the USS *Enterprise* went very well, and the sale of seventy aircraft to Iran soon followed.

The upcoming radar competition for the F/A-18 *Hornet*'s radar began in 1975, and I was asked to lead the proposal effort as an assistant group executive of the Radar Systems Group. My two excellent assistants, Freeman Nelson for technical and Jim Drake for business, greatly eased the strain of this challenging responsibility during the proposal, and while we performed on the contract. During the next few years, managing this fast-moving project to a technical success and the largest revenue business in Hughes history was personally invigorating and very educational. For the first time in my experience, the customer was another defense contractor rather than the government. McDonnell Douglas had great depth in the technical skills needed to monitor our design, and had a considerable self-interest in overseeing financial and contractual matters. This meant less flexibility in decision-making but a greater mutual understanding of the optimum methods for problem solving.

A harrowing event took place during the proposal period regarding the detailed design requirements. The specifications defined an antenna pointing accuracy that was virtually unattainable. Freeman and I traveled to the St. Louis headquarters of McDonnell Douglas and in a large meeting explained our inability to meet the rigid numbers; then pointed out that they had reserved all the acceptable error margin for the radome. The final proposal was due in a week. I stated that unless the requirement was relaxed, we would not submit an offer for the program! A daring gambit, but I would not sign up for the impossible. Fortunately, McDonnell-Douglas relented and we celebrated that great win a month later.

Then, in 1983, the unfortunate early death of President John Richardson resulted in Dr. Malcolm Currie's moving to corporate as a senior executive. (Mal had led the Research Laboratories for Hughes, spent a year in Washington, D.C., as deputy secretary of defense, and became Hughes CEO in 1988. After his retirement in 1992, he became a very effective chairman of the board of trustees for USC.) Allen Puckett chose me to replace Mal as Missile Systems Group president. This Group was responsible for six weapon product lines being manufactured and twenty projects in development. Although a tremendous challenge, I considered (and still do) this to be the ideal and most exalted position in the entire company. Lucky me!

I faced a big hurdle to gain acceptance by the 14,000 Group employees located in Canoga Park, California; Tucson, Arizona; Eufaula, Alabama; and La Grange, Georgia. Imagine surviving my first meeting with thirty senior managers (I already knew them all personally because of my long involvement with the Phoenix missile) and being greeted by one most able but crusty old timer, who stated, "We don't need some slick operator from downtown coming here to tell us what to do. We're doing just fine already!" After a moment of shocked silence, all I could think to say was, "Well, I'll give it my best shot." In retrospect, I should have suggested that he personally pass on his viewpoint to Allen Puckett. My usual behavior was to quickly forgive and forget, but that public rejection took a long time for me to accept—the comment was in such great contrast to the traditional Hughes family relationship! The subsequent five years in that position were very stressful, but did not seem to include any rejection by key members of this remarkable team.

Education by Our Customers

In addition to many interactions with the combat aviator community described in Part Four, I learned a lot from visits to diverse areas of active military operations on the surface or undersea. In my years as a Hughes executive, I tallied visits to fifteen Naval Air Stations, twenty-two Marine bases, twenty-five Air Force sites, and twenty-nine Army bases. Apart from journeys on destroyers and cruisers (one trip was to witness a surface-to-air missile launch against a drone) plus a day's cruise aboard a nuclear submarine, I sailed in or flew onto eleven different aircraft carriers: *Bon Homme Richard* (CV-31), *Constellation* (CV-64), *Enterprise* (CVN-65), *Hornet* (CVS-12), *John F. Kennedy* (CV-67), *Kitty Hawk* (CV-63), *Midway* (CVB-41), *Nimitz* (CVN-68), *Oriskany* (CV-34), *Ranger* (CV-61), and *Yorktown* (CV-10). On the USS *Kennedy* I was privileged to occupy the Admiral's quarters, since he was not present. I enjoyed many more exciting military surface adventures and transport flights as part of my military mixing.

USS *Enterprise* Aircraft Carrier
(courtesy of the National Naval Aviation Museum)

Most meaningful was a week aboard the USS *Kitty Hawk* while it was executing strike missions against North Vietnam from "Yankee Station" in the northern Gulf of Tonkin.

Vice Adm. Malcolm Cagle, Commander Seventh Fleet, and William Colby of the CIA were both there. Having dinners nightly with them was most enlightening (although there were zero words about the CIA).

Hughes teammate Ralph Shapiro (later president of Support Systems Group) and I photographed and made detailed observations of combat operation sequences, aircraft battle damage, electronic maintenance, weapon stowage, and aircraft and missile deck handling. Upon returning home, we reported a summary of our findings to 3,000 Hughes employees working on the electronics and primary missile slated for the *Tomcat*.

That trip was an eye-opener for a civilian: attempting to sleep while in a bunk directly beneath a catapult as it flung aircraft aloft, talking to the men who were working extended hours every day, seeing the hazardous activities on the windy flight deck, and hearing of losses in some strike missions. Ralph and I had been flown from Cubi Point Naval Air Station in the Philippines in a C-2 *Greyhound* (known as a COD, carrier onboard delivery) aircraft. Seated facing backward, with no side windows to peer from, the three-and-a-half-hour trip and the jolt of the tail-hook arrested landing on the USS *Kitty Hawk* required a lot of faith!

Our return was delayed due to repair problems on all the aircraft carrier transport aircraft at Cubi Point. For the next twenty-four hours, we were required to check at two-hour intervals to see whether a *Greyhound* had arrived to fetch us back to Cubi. One finally arrived, but an engine failed on the approach to the carrier. Twelve hours later, we were told to quickly board the aircraft; a repair crew had worked continuously to fix the engine. There had been no time to verify that repair by running the engine: scheduled strike aircraft required the deck space. An officer shouted to me, "We've got to get rid of that 'xxxx' COD. As soon as the engines start, we'll launch!" The return flight to the Philippines was uneventful, but the very next week that same *Greyhound* went down at sea, losing nine Navy personnel, including two of captain rank. The hand of fate had surely helped Ralph's and my return from Yankee Station.

My trip in a "Boomer" strategic nuclear submarine from Bangor, Washington, was exciting–watching undersea navigation, observing simulated SLBM launches, and riding upward at a 45-degree angle in an emergency breach as the huge vessel literally jumped like a whale out of the sea. It was also amusing: the captain never acknowledged my presence but continuously catered to the CEO of a large forestry and lumber mill. I guess that that man's importance to the crew's families' living environment was far greater than that of an executive of the company that had designed, built, and supported over half of that submarine's exotic electronic equipment!

A special visit to the Marine Base at Camp Pendleton, California, was a double thrill. A practice assault on the beach reminded me of World War II landings in the Pacific islands, but with more modern and much more effective equipment. Landing craft were faster and more able to climb ashore, naval artillery was very accurate, and air cover by helicopters and strike fighters seemed extremely effective. (In 1992, I visited Guadalcanal, and visualized what a blessing today's hardware would have been to our Marines fifty years earlier.)

Author Visits Marines at Camp Pendleton, California
(personal files)

The second part of the visit was far inland: practice shots of the anti-tank TOW missile. The weapon launcher was atop an armored personnel carrier, with a moving target one-half mile distant. One attempt was very scary: when the Marine gunner squeezed the trigger nothing happened, a "hang-fire" apparently caused by a mechanical failure to start the rocket motor. Personal safety was at stake, since it was not known if the warhead fuse had somehow been prematurely armed. A very cautious withdrawal by the gunner, followed by appropriate deactivation procedures resulted in no injuries.

The Army's Fort Sill in Oklahoma is the center for artillery training. It was here that Apache chief Geronimo was held captive in 1886. An Indian legend tells that previously he had evaded capture here by leaping with his horse from a high ridge into the nearby river! It was a thrill to see the historic parts of this famous fort. Fort Sill gives civilians an opportunity annually to watch mobile artillery battery emplacements in the field, observe fire zones, and witness live shots of a Copperhead projectile (a cannon round guided to its target by its internal seeker tracking a laser spot projected by a forward trooper). The historic finale performance is quite emotional. Accompanied by bugle calls and drums, horse-drawn howitzer units appear from behind a ridge; guns are placed, hand loaded, and fired. Suddenly, it is 1863: the equipment and uniforms are a recreation of those of a Union Army artillery unit in the Civil War. That day provided an astonishing demonstration of the sharp contrast between inaccurate mass-fire barrages of the old days and the precise guided projectiles today.

Huntsville, Alabama, is the site of the Army proving ground for most explosive weapons. In 1984, I had the opportunity to launch a TOW 2 antitank missile. Still in evaluation before production approval, this new configuration designed by Hughes was a considerable improvement over its predecessor TOW, with longer range, a larger warhead, and earlier fusing to enhance armor penetration. My test shot was against a moving simulated tank at about a half-mile range. I placed the crosshairs on the target and pulled the trigger. A big whoosh! Tracking the target became quite difficult, since the rocket motor exhaust plume caused considerable obscuration. If only there had been a crossing wind to clear that smoke! Nonetheless, I was able to hold the launcher optics without jitter, although seeing the target only intermittently, for the flight duration of several seconds. The missile's bright tracking beacon could be seen clearly in the launcher optics in spite of the smoke. Since the missile travels only a few feet off the ground, the most common error by novice gunners is to let the crosshairs droop, causing the weapon to strike the ground before target impact. But this green operator still managed to achieve a direct hit! The experience not only improved my bonding with Army field commanders, but also increased my acceptance by the Hughes

Hughes Annual Trophy for Best Air Force Fighter Squadron
(personal files)

Missile Systems Group professional staff.

Eglin Air Force base in Florida is both an operational aircraft site and the principal facility for evaluation of new equipment. Once I had the thrill of entering an enclosure housing a B-1 *Lancer* bomber exposed to -55°F! Even with a lot of surface protection over me, only cautious breathing helped avoid my mouth and lungs freezing! On another occasion I was privileged to present the Hughes Trophy to the 58th Tactical Fighter Wing—an annual award for that year's best Air Force fighter unit, begun in 1953.

This F-15 *Eagle* squadron had achieved sixteen Iraqi aircraft kills in 1991's Operation Desert Storm, the highest score of any Air Force unit. It was a real honor to meet and shake hands with these pilots. At the formal dining celebration that night, my wife Connie was seated next to Gen. Charles Horner, who had commanded Air Force operations in that conflict. He introduced himself to her saying, "I'm General Horner—just call me 'Chucky'." A great way to foster relaxed conversation. The trophy is now on display at the National Museum of the US Air Force at Wright Field, Ohio.

All these encounters and many more contributed to a deep and meaningful understanding of our military customers. Marketing, developing, testing, manufacturing, training operators for use, and long-term support were more correctly done because of the knowledge gained from these experiences. I did my best to pass along the information and customer feelings I acquired to all employees, and I encouraged them to also witness operations in the field.

Personal Aviating

Hughes Aircraft Company's roots and heritage were strongly aviation oriented. While I had done a lot of military visitor-flying, I judged that my professional career would be further enhanced by hands-on aviating. Private piloting know-how would also greatly increase bonding with military customers. Personally experiencing their operating problems and safety demands, and being able to communicate in their own special language, made brotherhood easier. Knowing and understanding very different military professions and organizations becomes simpler if one can somewhat appear as a military facsimile. A desire to jump into the cockpit was already deep in my psyche, so getting to it was only a matter of time and adequate money.

When I was appointed Missile Systems Group president in 1983, its headquarters were in Canoga Park and my daily commute was only twenty minutes each way, although there were frequent trips to Washington, D.C., and Arizona. My two sons, Bruce and Jeff, were off to college and Connie was surrounded by and active with many close friends.

In this situation, I felt comfortable in starting private flying lessons. Although the company workload was at a high level and very demanding, and weekend time taken up with the lessons was somewhat burdensome to Connie, at least we could both look forward to the promise of exciting airborne adventures together.

Camarillo Airport was only twenty minutes from home, and had an excellent flight school using Cessna 152 and 172 airplanes. Two to three hours per week there, plus study time at home, permitted solo flight in a short time. It was a great treat to endure the traditional achievement celebration for first solo flight: the instructor scissors a large rear section of the student's shirt and signs it as a memento for surviving this vital milestone! This achievement was followed by journeys with my flight instructor to distant places for more hours of flying seasoning. One Channel Islands trip was across twenty miles of Pacific waters, with a scary landing strip in a canyon with breezy crosswinds. The gravel surface inclined steeply uphill for landing and downhill for departure, regardless of wind direction. My instructor made the touchdown, but this student was able to execute a wobbly but reasonably safe takeoff. My FAA license-qualifying test was fairly routine, even with the required "stall recovery"—until the examiner caused a "failure" of the flaps: stuck full down for maximum drag. Thinking up the solution took a bit longer than it should have, but the sensible idea to add power and avoid altitude loss flashed into my mind. Just in time to pass the test flight. License earned!

Rental aircraft allowed many fun trips to remote airports in Southern California: the deserts of the Palm Springs region, the mountains near Lake Arrowhead and the High Sierras, the Channel Islands including Catalina, and small towns in the central San Joaquin Valley. Passengers usually included family members or friends vacationing from other states. One was a young Japanese woman who had never before been to the United States with its wide range of mountain and desert vistas. We went to an old-time airport near Mojave where the airstrip, hangars, lunchroom, and surrounding landscape all looked like a Western cowboy movie from 1930. (It has been used in filming many Hollywood movies). Yasuko felt she had been treated royally in an imaginary dream world!

In a single day, I qualified for seaplane flying, but with very little confidence after only four hours of "stick time" at the controls. The setting was the Salton Sea, a giant lake created many years ago by a human error in an attempt to control the Colorado River. Its salt content was extreme, and periodically an increase in the salt proportion caused by excess evaporation would practically exterminate the large fish population. That day, the beaches were carpeted with a continuous strip 15 feet wide, composed of stinking dead fish that we waded through to board the seaplane. Landing the machine successfully was very difficult: seldom can a pilot accurately perceive the aircraft's distance above a glassy water surface to touch down smoothly. My final landing was in a narrow canal dredged for commercial shrimp cultivation. A stiff crosswind had developed, so I needed a lot of hands-on instructor help to avoid striking the side banks. I surely did not want to try that day's adventure again!

Private flying expanded to travels from Camarillo to Sunriver, Oregon, a favorite escape from the stress of professional work. About eight hundred crow-flight miles north, it has an enjoyable high desert climate with sweeping views of the snow-capped Cascade Mountain range. To get there in a short time, allowing us weekend trips without interfering with work responsibilities, I purchased a high-speed Mooney 201, replaced five years later with a faster Mooney TLS.

These craft were capable of flight at 24,000 feet and speeds near 250 miles per hour, making mincemeat of those eight hundred miles. Monthly visits to Sunriver became easy. Once, coming home, because of stiff tail winds we made the journey in only one-and-a-half hours.

The next training step was qualification for instrument flight, a far more tedious and difficult learning experience. My excellent but demanding instructor was Steve Kuehle, a transport pilot for Hughes, who was willing to do the lengthy instruction during weekends. Many flights were made in "socked-in" conditions, where neither the ground nor lateral views were possible while at altitude. A typical flight was one hundred miles to the field at Ontario, California. After a long delay at the field, one return flight was through very unstable clouds and updrafts; control of altitude and roll attitude was very difficult. Steve emphasized the virtue of logical and calm self-control in such a hazardous situation. Several times he would bat me on the hands, shouting, "Why are you doing it that way?" After I qualified for this license, his lessons in reasoning were invaluable in my flights in inclement weather.

Executive transport around the many facilities in the Los Angeles area was by Bell helicopters with a single pilot. Sitting in the left-side copilot's seat offered a chance to try the controls, if there was a willing pilot. After the craft reached cruise altitude, the first duty, requiring a lot of practice, was to simultaneously maintain altitude, speed, course, and stability. Most novices cannot stop a "cat's cradle" motion; instead of steady flight the aircraft repeatedly does small rhythmic pendulum rolls. A sensitive but steady hand is needed to avoid over-control, which

Mooney TLS Recreational Aircraft
(personal files)

worsens the cycle. This student did quite well with that problem, but never attempted the very tricky takeoff and landing maneuvers. During these transitional movements, there is a requisite reversal of rudder control movements, so casual or inept attempts do not work! Once, one of the helicopter pilots was most adept at saving the aircraft from crashing at Culver City. As he approached the landing area, the engine failed. Helicopters have a very steep glide path when power to spin the rotor is off, and, in this case, it was necessary to pass over the jet-blast fence at the end of the runway. When the failure occurred, the aircraft was critically short of altitude, but with the pilot's expert touch, it skimmed over by inches and was safely set down hard. Luckily, no passengers were aboard. And even more fortunately for me, there were no distressful moments during my many trips around Los Angeles.

Surviving Calamity

My 1,000 hours of personal flying included some near crashes. The first was a flat spin in my early training, resulting from a practice stall recovery. After three full rotations and a scary view of the rapidly approaching rocky ridgeline, I recalled the instruction to pull power to idle, which quickly allowed controlled return to safe flight. Several other potential disasters happened in very bad weather because icing caused huge weight increases and the loss of wing lift. These events can happen suddenly and are very alarming, as there is a rapid loss of altitude. Hopefully, the warmer air at lower levels causes enough ice to melt from the wings, as occurred in one icing incident over Fresno.

Another of my errors was to enter a surprisingly dense cloud formation over the Sierra Nevada. Although qualified for "blind flying," my transition to the instrument panel was slow and poor. Instead of keeping the Mooney in level flight, there was a startling and rapid loss of altitude. I recovered, luckily not having hit any invisible craggy peaks, and obtained instrument flight routing approval from the ground controller at Reno, Nevada. Arrival home in California became a celebration.

In all these hazardous cases, there were no passengers with me. However, twice with my wife aboard, I had to land in blinding and gusty rains. It was extremely difficult to see the runway on final approach. In both cases, it happened after four hours of tiring flight, and with alternative airports also "socked in." Sheer necessity inspired success. One of those followed a trip from Camarillo to our favorite resort in Oregon. About fifty miles from the airport, cruising on instruments in dense clouds above sharp mountain ridges, the engine suddenly stopped! I tried every technique I could think of to relight; nothing worked. Descending rapidly in a glide, we broke under the clouds to discover the rugged peaks only 200 feet below! At that instant, the engine coughed and restarted. I assume icing had blocked the engine's air intake, and residual engine heat had melted the bad stuff. Since Sunriver had no instrument landing facilities, I altered course to nearby Bend and made a very difficult landing in heavy rain. Quite an "accelerated aging" experience!

My personal piloting came to a decisive conclusion with the 1993 crash of my Mooney TLS in northern California. That year I suffered the tragic loss of my beloved wife Connie, who had been treated for lymphoma for many years; my early retirement in 1991 had been taken to extend our time together. After her passing, I tried many diversions, including a lot of long-range flying. In late summer, I was off for several weeks to Colorado, Wyoming, Montana, and British Columbia. On the way back home, to add to my list of California airport landings (I already had checked off 154 of the 300 airports), I successfully added three more. Samoa Airport in Eureka became airfield number 158 and simultaneously turned into "number one memorable crash" for this pilot. There was a stiff 30 miles per hour crosswind, beyond the aircraft's safety rating, but there was no air traffic controller on the ground to relay this information. My high-speed touchdown started halfway along the short runway with insufficient distance to stop. Full power and partial retraction of the landing gear were not enough to clear the brush-covered sand dunes beyond the paved strip. The crunch was horrible, breaking the airplane fuselage in half and stopping the engine as the propeller impacted the ground. I was severely injured and unconscious, while electrical power still pumped fuel out the severed fuel transfer lines.

That strip was used in World War II for submarine-search blimps and is almost abandoned now. Fortunately, there was a Sunday automobile drag race nearby, with a fire-truck ambulance stationed in case of an auto accident. The rescuers had me out in only a few minutes, pinching off two cut arteries in my left leg and right arm, preventing my death through loss of blood. Recovery from seven life-threatening injuries took eight weeks, much of which was in intensive care. Such an example of incompetent flying, after accumulating 1,000 hours solo, was enough to make me turn away from piloting small craft! What lessons should budding pilots take from this account? Stick to good weather flying conditions in daylight, continually maintain proficiency, and always practice caution.

Crash! Eureka, California 1993
(courtesy of *Times-Standard*, Eureka, California)

PART NINE

FINALE

THE UNITED STATES defense business was at the peak of its golden era in 1986 as the push of President Reagan for military modernization and the initiation of the Strategic Defense Initiative sparked further government funding increases. At the same time, hostile relations with the USSR were relaxing dramatically. The Soviet philosophy changed radically when Mikhail Gorbachev took office and in 1985 adopted *glasnost* (government openness, or as the Russians said themselves, "tipping a vase to let someone see into it, but not see its bottom") and *perestroika* (economic reform) in 1987.

The Cold War between the United States and the USSR finally ended, in large part due to the superior weaponry in the US arsenal—and its reliability and readiness—all assembled in a dispersed massive inventory. Forty-four years of excessive investment of its national resources in self-destructive strategies eventually crippled the USSR and set up its formal dissolution in 1991. It simply could no longer sustain the formidable economic strain. The existence of many Hughes systems forced part of that excessive investment.

Further chaos came from the inept governance of Boris Yeltsin and Russia's inexperienced attempts to become a capitalist-based economy. (In 2007, I was told by a knowledgeable woman in Russia that Yeltsin was drunk most of the time, even when she formally interviewed him for a national TV broadcast!) Activists and immoral businessmen were very destructive, outrageously enriching a few and increasing poverty for many others. Elsewhere, hard-line policies mellowed and a move from communism toward pseudo-capitalism came to the People's Republic of China after the infamous Tiananmen Square protests in 1989.

These "sea changes," especially the improved relations with Eastern Europe, should have reduced the US defense budget, with a decline in business for contractors like Hughes, and this did begin to occur in

1990—but another national concern arose.

The US focus on world troubles shifted to the Middle East. Extreme unrest in the oil producing Gulf States led to an Iraqi invasion of Kuwait and destruction of its oil fields in 1990. Perceiving a meaningful threat to US oil sources, and gaining UN support, President Bush initiated Operation Desert Storm, assembling a large coalition force to free Kuwait. Restoring regional balance by invading Iraq to decimate its military power was also a goal. The effort was successful. Absolute command of the air was achieved quickly; vital targets in the capital city, Baghdad, were precisely struck, causing little civilian damage; ground combat operations were conducted both day and night with minimal friendly-force losses against an opposing force double our size and equipped with a Soviet-made arsenal. Eighty-eight different combat systems made by Hughes played a significant role. In addition, the company's satellites gave complete real-time surveillance of Iraqi activities and flawlessly linked command and control of all coalition forces with the Pentagon (details are still classified).

The United States removed its troops from Iraq after one hundred days, reducing the expenditure of our resources as well as avoiding further damage to political relations with many other Middle East nations. But just replacing the equipment expended in the conflict increased the US defense budget for resupply.

The fate of Hughes was affected by these world events, but, more crucially, it was altered forever by the unfortunate actions of non-DoD portions of the US government.

55

A CONVERSION
OF OUR SOUL

Dᴜʀɪɴɢ Hᴜɢʜᴇꜱ Aɪʀᴄʀᴀꜰᴛ Company's growing and prosperous years we enjoyed an almost magical inner sense of enterprise and individual freedom. John Mendel, former president of the Industrial Electronics Group, expressed this feeling in part when he told me in 2008, "I enjoyed the free-form we had at Hughes. Many other companies are too rigid and regimented. The biggest reason for our success was to use internal R&D funds to the maximum. We often could not stop a marginal project, but this sometimes resulted in a surprise technical discovery." This feeling is well expressed in *Outliers: The Story of Success*, by Malcolm Gladwell, which states that innovative people are highly motivated by three work characteristics: autonomy, complexity, and awareness of the benefits from hard effort. That was the Hughes way! The creative spirit and dedication to our mission to enhance US battle readiness and push into space symbolized our soul. These feelings had not been affected by Mr. Hughes's gift of the corporation to the Howard Hughes Medical Institute in 1953. Perhaps that soul was even a bit more stable and stronger because of our greater separation from the indecision, interference, and lack of oversight of our founder. However, after his death in 1976 the government applied heavy pressure on HHMI to divest itself of its exclusive ownership of Hughes Aircraft Company. After that divestiture, we became another publicly owned enterprise, with onerous demands for short-term flashy results and a higher priority on profit. The opportunities to remain at the front edge of worldwide electronics technology using R&D investment also began to fade. Much of the inner soul and spirit to leap forward was lost. A national treasure was seriously damaged by its major beneficiary, the US government.

A lasting foundation supporting the Hughes Aircraft Company soul was the heritage of sustaining and expanding the work of the Howard Hughes Medical Institute by supplying its principal financial support for thirty-two years.

56

HOWARD'S EMPIRE

By THE LATE 1960s, the Howard Hughes empire was colossal. Gathered into a conglomerate called the Summa Corporation, the collection of assets reporting to Mr. Hughes had many unrelated components. Modest segments were the Hughes AirWest passenger airline and a small holding of Atlas Mining. (In 1968 Howard had sold his 78 percent ownership of TWA for $546 million, the largest cash transaction in the United States up to that date). The empire's giant was Hughes Tool Company in Texas, with five major subsidiaries and vast real estate holdings in Nevada, California, Arizona, and the Bahamas. (The oil-drilling tool segment bearing the name Hughes Tool Company was sold for $150 million in 1972, and the conglomerate holding firm was renamed Summa Corporation.) The empire held 25,000 acres of land, 2,500 mining claims, 6 hotels, and 2 TV stations in Las Vegas and Reno; its annual gaming revenues were 13 percent of Nevada's total. Thousands of acres of undeveloped land were assessed at $100 million. Most of the California and Arizona property was leased to Hughes Aircraft Company. The HHMI reported to Mr. Hughes as its only trustee, and its assets were well documented as the endowment of a legitimate "charitable trust;" profits from the donated Aircraft Company were the only source of income to support that Institute. By 1970, the total number of employees in the entire empire was 67,400, and the rapidly growing staff at Hughes Aircraft Company had topped 26,000. (In the following fifteen years that staff grew to 85,000). The most inventive part of the empire had focused on electronics, carrying the Hughes name, although he had stated his own dream as, "I want to be remembered for only one thing—my contribution to aviation."

57

HHMI SELLS HUGHES

THE TRANSFER OF ownership from Mr. Hughes to HHMI was thought by many in the government to be a tax avoidance maneuver. The position of the Internal Revenue Service was that HHMI, as a charitable trust, could not exclusively own Hughes Aircraft Company and use its income as the principal source of HHMI's operational funding. After eight years of legal preparation, the IRS challenge reached a judicial decision: on April 4, 1984. Federal Judge Grover C. Brown in the Chancery Court of Delaware appointed a new managing board of directors for HHMI, replacing the internal group that had functioned since the 1976 death of Mr. Hughes. Judge Brown directed them to plan a significant change in ownership of the aircraft company. These new directors included lawyer Irving Shapiro, who had designed the wartime resource-rationing plan for the Roosevelt administration, and who in 1981 had retired as CEO of DuPont. He was instrumental in strategizing and managing the court's required sale of Hughes. Another board member was William Lummis, a Texas lawyer who had solved the complicated scramble for inheritance of the estate of Mr. Hughes, who died intestate. Mr. Lummis, Howard's second cousin, bore an amazing physical resemblance to his famous relative, including a matching speaking voice and intonation. (When I asked him how this resemblance could be possible, he responded, "I don't have any idea, I only met him once!") Hughes Aircraft Company owed much of its subsequent stability to both Mr. Shapiro and Mr. Lummis. They saw the merit of our creative organization and ensured its survival as a unified entity.

In January 1985, the board hired the investment management firm Morgan Stanley to arrange the sale of Hughes as an undivided asset. The board also directed HHMI in reinvesting the resulting funds in a diversified portfolio. HHMI's endowment reached $14.8 billion by 2010. The reader is encouraged to read the Appendix to learn of the astounding achievements of HHMI as told by its President Emeritus Purnell Choppin.

In a short time, the many bidders for Hughes were narrowed to five front-runners: Allied Signal, the Boeing Company, Ford Aerospace and Communications Corporation, General Motors Company, and Honeywell International.

Howard Hughes Medical Institute Headquarters, Chevy Chase, Maryland, 1997
(courtesy of HHMI)

These finalists were already in similar businesses and had the ability to meet the likely price. Each company was coded with a bogus name to mask its identity until its top people entered the conference room (as silly as identifying each corporation with the name of a professional football team in its headquarters city and leaving the individual visitors nameless!) As the CEO and president of each firm separately toured the Hughes facilities and were briefed by our key executives, their guises were laughable because they all were well-known public figures.

During our intensive briefings to each bidder about our business status—I detailed the status of the Missile Systems Group in a three-hour session for each one—we needed to be accurate and thorough about every product line and financial condition. I found the briefings and questions very difficult, since revealing such details to a competitor could be ruinous to our future. On the other hand, avoiding questions or fibbing would be unethical and possibly illegal. I asked myself if this particular set of folks in the briefing room was going to be our owner—in which case I would be happy to reveal everything—or if they would remain a voracious competitor—then I would try to tell 'em nothin'! Government security classifications also prevented complete candor. Tough decisions!

58

SALUTING
GENERAL MOTORS

O<small>N</small> J<small>UNE</small> 5, 1985, General Motors won the auction for a price of $5.2 billion, comprising $2.7 billion in cash and 50 million shares of a new stock named GM class H. This stock entitled its owners to share earnings through dividend distributions, but to have no rights to under-lying capital assets (traditionally called a tracking stock).

Hughesnews HUGHES
SPECIAL

Hughes Aircraft Company, El Segundo, Calif.   June 7, 1985

General Motors wins bid for Hughes
New era opens

Roger B. Smith

**GM history
a lesson
in innovation**

Allen E. Puckett

**Financial
record shows
solid growth**

Hughes Aircraft Co. was no-tified Wednesday by the Howard Hughes Medical In-stitute that General Motors Corporation will be its new owner.

The Howard Hughes Medi-cal Institute, sole owner of Hughes Aircraft Co. since in-corporation in 1953, an-nounced that GM will acquire Hughes for $2.7 billion in cash and 50 million shares of a new General Motors Class H Com-mon Stock. The transaction is valued in excess of $5 billion.

The medical institute, which has been re-evaluating its ownership of Hughes Aircraft Co., has been investigating an outright sale of the company for the past six months.

Under the agreement, tion process," he continued.

"The linking of these two highly successful companies—each a leader in its field—will provide great opportunities for growth and development.

"The extensive resources and expertise accumulated by General Motors through 76 years of achievement will en-able Hughes to continue its growth at the leading edge of technology and General Motors will be strengthened in those areas in which Hughes has long excelled."

Commenting on the purchase, General Motors Chairman Roger B. Smith said, "The acquisition of Hughes Aircraft Co. represents the combination of two of the world's premiere industrial by maintaining Hughes intact as a separate and independent enterprise with the current management having discretion and full authority to run their business.

"At the same time, GM's ex-pertise in electronic and me-chanical sciences and high volume manufacturing would further increase the com-petitiveness of Hughes Aircraft in defense and space busi-nesses."

Excerpts from a press release distributed by GM explain that the acquisition is contingent, among other things, upon the authorization by holders of GM's $1 2/3 Common Stock and Class E Common Stock of the creation of a new Class H Common Stock.

GM Buys Hughes Aircraft Company
(courtesy of UNLV)

421

Roger Smith, CEO of GM, announced to the press after the purchase:

"We are mindful of Hughes Aircraft's stature as a critical national resource, one which has contributed immeasurably to the defense needs of the nation . . . Hughes is one of the few organizations that has extensive experience in systems engineering . . . which will be applied to GM's manufacturing needs at our 152 plants nationwide."

General Motors management merged Hughes Aircraft Company and Delco Electronics Corporation, the existing internal supplier of automotive electronics, and jointly named the new organization Hughes Electronics Corporation, a subsidiary of General Motors, with GM-H stock certificates.

GM-H Logo
(courtesy of Bob Parke)

I believe the $5.2 billion was the largest transaction of this type in US history. Hughes had risen from a company whose physical asset value was close to zero in 1954 (almost all of the land and facilities were rented from Hughes Tool or the government) to this enormous value. We started with nothing but innovative zeal, enthusiastic professional talent, and a vital mission; sound fiscal management and reinvested earnings resulted in this enormous expansion in only thirty years. There had been no financial support or transfers from Mr. Hughes during that time span; our only growth had to arise from healthy self-generated earnings. Pat Hyland often expressed his corporate philosophy about the meaning of earnings: "Long-term profit is one real-life way to measure our efforts on the one hand; the other way is to watch our growth."

Kudos must be given to the Hughes team led by Tom Keene in the control and investment of the retirement funds set aside for long-term employees. These funds were aggregated by withholding a small percentage of an employee's salary, with another half of that amount added by the company. Hughes had the obligation, and made a commitment, to pay generous retirement benefits to participating retirees. Normal pension time was at age 65, but a popular option was to allow early retirement starting at 55 by summing a candidate's age and service years until the "magic 75" was reached. As you can imagine, the obligations of this important fund grew to large figures as the staff aged. For many years, these funds were adroitly invested in stocks, bonds, and other commercial papers. At the time of the GM purchase, the pension funds were substantially larger than the company's payment obligations—in sharp contrast to most other firms, whose accounting books showed a substantial shortfall between funds available and pension obligations. Such deficits caused Congress to pass more stringent regulations demanding more liquid assets committed to their pension obligations. This act caused many firms, including GM, to sell subsidiaries and other assets in order to attain the liquidity level mandated by the government. Why didn't GM put Tom Keene in charge of their fund management?

Operating Changes

Hughes's entry into GM was quite orderly and placid. Senior GM executive Donald Atwood (later appointed Assistant Secretary of Defense) became the center of Hughes operations oversight, with Allen Puckett remaining as Hughes CEO. The company structure with seven product line Groups was left intact, as was that of its GM-H sister organization Delco, with no company segment reassigned to other GM units. Highly rated technical and managerial staff members were encouraged to remain with GM-H by means of a financial reward called the LTIP (long term incentive plan). Specific award amounts were set for staff members chosen by the senior executives. Each LTIP award was paid in three equal annual installments, starting at the end of one year of continued employment after the GM purchase—an effective technique to assure staff retention for at least three years. The new GM-H stock also provided a better way to reward Hughes personnel: for the first time, personal gain from company success became possible either by employees directly buying stock or by management awarding stock options, which allowed stock purchases within the next three years at the award date's price. If the stock's market price had increased during that time, the employee would enjoy an immediate capital gain, with any such gains subject to IRS tax only when the employee sold the stock. If the market value was lower when the option was due, the employee could elect not to purchase, thus suffering no loss. Such a financial incentive was highly motivational for all our staff, although the new importance of profit had the potential for managers (looking for future personal gain) to overly limit the traditional internal R&D reinvestment that had stimulated our inventive spirit for so many years.

General Motors did little to replace or interchange Hughes and GM senior or middle management, except for appointing Michael Smith as vice president of corporate finance (he became Hughes CEO in 1993) and John Higgins as head of the corporate legal staff. Don Atwood was stalwart in trying to allow Hughes to operate in its traditional innovative free-will spirit, and GM did not impose specific financial goals on Hughes. However, demands of the GM-H public marketplace and imposition of plodding procedural rules by the ancient automotive giant constrained that free spirit. The Hughes staff had long been blessed (and spoiled) by an agile senior management, who previously had been unencumbered by rigorous operating rules other than those imposed by the government. Short-term profits now began to be more important than R&D investment. Ouch!

Did these changes harm Hughes's performance? That's difficult to answer. By 1986, Hughes had more than 82,000 employees, racked up $6.7 billion annual sales with a $10.7 billion backlog, and had only $100 million of long-term debt. All this was backed by a very comfortable product diversity: no single program was more than 6 percent of annual sales and the top ten added up to only 40 percent of the total. Business volume flattened the next year, however, and began to decline, for two reasons. First, at the time of GM's acquisition, competitors in the marketplace had greatly increased their design and manufacturing capabilities in all the disciplines that Hughes had excelled in for thirty-five years. Many electronic firms could offer adequate solutions previously available only from Hughes, and frequently they offered lower prices. Second, the arms race with the Soviets was slackening, lessening DoD funding and motivation. Continuing the glorious "Golden Era" business growth was considerably more difficult. (It should be noted that for several years profits by Hughes more than offset GM's losses in its primary automotive business, so Wall Street could clearly see that GM did indeed benefit from the 1985 acquisition.)

The great fear of our senior executives was that lethargy might seep in to the psyche of our creative professionals, diminishing their inspirational leaps. The growing demand for short-term financial results was both good and bad: our staff had been too pampered with little pressure on cost control; new management disciplines gave positive operating benefits. But the displacement of R&D from its lofty perch as the first priority could become a "real downer," felt by everyone. Our ability to endure losses to achieve long-term technology triumphs might no longer seem acceptable. However, during the first five years after Hughes became GM-H, IR&D funding as a percentage of total sales did not decline significantly; the climate became cooler in the mid-1990s as the guiding philosophy of top corporate executives changed.

Our engineers also experienced a disappointment. As publicly stated by Roger Smith, GM's objective in acquiring Hughes had two aspects, one of which was to incorporate systems engineering techniques into its many lethargic manufacturing plants. Our CEO Mal Currie made repeated attempts to transfer our system engineering understanding and practices, with little success. There seemed to be no desire to accept new ideas, and the old-time attitudes prevailed. Efforts by GM to incorporate the computer system skills of its other acquired subsidiary, EDS (Electronic Data Systems) led by CEO Ross Perot, were also slow moving. After acquiring Hughes and EDS, GM had become the largest corporation in the world, so one might think that anything could be done with skill and speed; however, both energetic electronics subsidiaries were continually frustrated by the conservative and protective tribal groups within GM who repeatedly foiled any suggestions for changing their operating methods. Those powerful duchies also somehow managed to oust GM's CEO Roger Smith, who strongly supported the new technical and operational approaches. The gigantic corporation was bogged down by a glacial speed in decision-making and an entrenched tribal management structure.

The other GM goal was to incorporate a new style of electronic design into its principal automotive product lines. There were numerous opportunities to exploit Hughes's well-established capabilities: nighttime vision, radar safety sensors, cruise control, liquid crystal instrument imaging, navigational computation and display, single-wire multiplexed data transfer, efficient electrical primary drive power, and digital microelectronic devices for many functions. Many projects were begun, showing very attractive results, but few were quickly incorporated. Delco's concern that enthusiastic cooperation with Hughes might endanger its authoritative business position within GM was part of the problem; it understandably wanted to remain the sole developer and producer of any new electronic devices for GM automobiles.

More acute was the aforementioned ultraconservative decision-making practiced by the entrenched GM hierarchy. A new device had to be well proven, evaluated for market attractiveness, and methodically inserted into the automobile configuration, with emphasis on minimal disruption of the steadily marching production lines. Although these credos minimized financial risks, they were large handicaps in what had become a very competitive market. In those days, GM usually took five years to insert a clever new design into production, while the Japanese took half that time. By 1990, GM had reduced that lag to three years, but the agile Japanese competitors had already gotten down to only eighteen months. This awful molasses drag dismayed and discouraged the many "break-the-rules" engineers at Hughes, who had consistently introduced a new device into production in only twelve months! The public knows what GM's turtle-like response time did to its stature in the world automobile market: sadly, falling from number one to just one of many.

As the 1980s proceeded, Hughes continued to perform well in its many established product fields, adapting to the sharp changes in our markets and trying to be an effective team contributor to our new owners. There were many more spectacular technical and business advances, with only a few minor difficulties along the way.

Management Moves

Bud Wheelon became Hughes CEO in 1987, and during the next year made a number of significant changes in the senior executive staff. In 1988, he invited me to become corporate executive vice president for operations, responsible for keeping our dynamic group executives (who were well capable of managing their 14,000-person organizations) co-ordinated with executive office goals and operating standards. This selection was indeed an honor for me. Missile Systems Group problems were well in hand: production was now stable after the 1984 quality problems, exciting new development contracts had been won, and our difficult super-project AMRAAM was on track. However, because of my wife's continuing battle with lymphoma, I had been seriously planning to retire early that year. After much discussion at home, with Connie gracefully not wanting to hamper my career, I accepted the promotion, but proposed a limit of two years of service.

Things went well in this position of high-level responsibility; we all still felt part of a huge well-knit family. As you have seen, the company was a most exciting place as viewed from the top: hundreds of product lines in every field of electronics, a dynamic and talented staff, exposure to new inventions on a daily basis, and much potential growth that lay ahead in integrating with GM. Except for a defense industry downturn in 1989, as always seems to happen in that business sector before an unanticipated major conflict (Operation Desert Storm was coming in 1991), the Hughes enterprise was stable and eminently successful. We did have to reduce staff because of the market decline, but we did this by offering very attractive extra benefit packages (nicknamed by some the "silver seatbelt!") to encourage early retirement by a large number of selected senior (and highly paid) staff members. Those who accepted were delighted with their packages and the company quickly regained that financial investment by accruing meaningful reductions in total operating expenses.

A year later, President Donald White retired, and Bud asked me to take that position. I did so (subsequently reporting to Mal Currie when he became CEO after Bud retired), somewhat extending my two-year obligation. In August of 1991, I finally took early retirement and was able to capture almost two more years with Connie.

In my years in management positions with Hughes, it was clear that the fortunes of executives are often critically affected by the skills of a vital teammate nearby, their secretary or executive assistant. Those professionals set the style and operating personality of the office, and are responsible for important data management and communication links. For many years I greatly benefited from the dedicated help of several of these professionals; two were particularly significant. Eileen Jennette Zinn was most effective in organizing and prioritizing daily tasks. She had an enthusiastic "Boston Irish" personality, spoke up strongly when she felt I was in error, and did a fine job of heading off unnecessary office intrusions. Eileen even watched my health: she once let me know I was downing twenty-seven cups of coffee each day, and forcefully recommended a switch to a decaffeinated variety. A most beneficial rescue! She also collected many samples of the doodle sketches that I habitually made during long meetings and presented them as framed art works at a staff party for my twenty-fifth anniversary of service with the company. Unfortunately, she was unable to commute to the far-away Missile Systems Group in Canoga Park when I was assigned there. When I moved to corporate headquarters, I was rewarded with the appearance of Carol Harris, who had formerly teamed with Pat Hyland when he was CEO Emeritus. She was from South Dakota, possessed an elegant appearance, and was most efficient and well organized. Her background, dedication, and wisdom made it much easier for me to enter the senior executive level. She set our office demeanor as friendly and open, backed by responsibility, integrity, and personal stature.

What a marvelous working life I enjoyed! I was the beneficiary of much great luck and good timing (being in the right place at the right time), and progressed well in those forty years. My boyhood dreams of direct involvement in the excitement and advancement of aviation were fulfilled, partly because of dedicated personal effort, but mostly from being part of the unique, almost exotic, Hughes Aircraft Company throughout its golden era.

59

CONTACT WITH FAMOUS AVIATORS AND OTHER DIGNITARIES

I ENJOYED MANY PRIVILEGES in my positions with Hughes. Mixing with all elements of the military was fun and educational, and the excitement of many flights in combat aircraft was irreplaceable.

It was also inspiring to meet and casually chat with three US Presidents: Gerald Ford, Ronald Reagan, and George Bush, Sr. (I missed Jimmy Carter because of timing difficulties.) Seeing Howard Hughes striding down the stairs at Culver City was a real thrill, but even better was to actually shake hands with many distinguished aviators who had achieved historic fame. Here are a few of those men and women whom I met:

- "Jimmy" Doolittle, air racing veteran of the 1930s, a key player in perfecting instrument flying, and famed for planning and commanding the dramatic 1942 B-25 raid on Tokyo. (Those land-based bombers were launched from the USS *Hornet* aircraft carrier in dangerously rough Pacific seas with only enough fuel to reach the friendly part of China to attempt landing.)
- Paul Tibbets, who in August 1945 flew the B-29 *Enola Gay* from Tinian Island to Hiroshima and delivered "Little Boy," the world's first combat atomic bomb, which quickly brought about Japan's surrender (thereby probably saving 2 million Allied lives, and five times that many Japanese, by avoiding the planned invasion of Honshu).
- Chuck Yeager, who reputedly had the best US fighter pilot eyesight in World War II (spotting hostile fighters forty miles away!), and who, in the Bell X-1 on 1 October 1947, became the first person to sustain level flight at speeds beyond the sound barrier.

- Scotty Lamoreaux, with his F-4 records of highest altitude and fastest cross-country speed.
- Buzz Aldrin, who followed Neil Armstrong to become the second human to walk on the lunar surface in the 1969 "One small step for man, one giant leap for mankind" mission to and from the Moon.
- Randy "Duke" Cunningham and his RIO (radar intercept officer) Willy "Irish" Driscoll, who were the top Navy fighter aces in Vietnam. In one sortie they scored three victories, including taking down the best North Vietnamese fighter pilot! Unfortunately, the Cunningham I met became Cunningham the Congressman, who was convicted of accepting bribes from a defense contractor seeking project awards from the Pentagon.
- Steve Ritchie, the Air Force's number one Vietnam ace.
- "Chappie" James, a fighter pilot with the Tuskegee airmen in WW II, Korea, and Vietnam, who later became the first African-American to achieve the rank of 4-star general in the US Air Force.
- Bob Hoover, North American Aviation test pilot, who performed aerobatics with a twin-engine *Shrike* transport aircraft, and earned the reputation of being the steadiest hand on the controls (with onboard television showing ground observers a full water glass atop the instrument panel that did not quiver or spill a drop while the aircraft completed a vertical loop or a full barrel-roll).
- Dick Rutan and Jeanna Yeager (no relation to Chuck Yeager), who in 1986 teamed to fly, in the Model 76 *Voyager* (designed by his brother Burt Rutan), the first nonstop flight around the world without refueling.

Hearing these pilots' expressive and enthusiastic tales about their colorful backgrounds was a long-lasting inspiration; there was always hope that some of that skill might rub off on me with that handshake!

In another—but very different—encounter with a group of notable people, about three years after becoming part of the GM family, I was personally outraged by an obvious insult to the reputation of Howard Hughes, which I felt honor-bound to rectify. As our company's official representative, I was invited to attend the black-tie grand opening of the spectacular San Diego aerospace museum. It is well located: much of aviation history is connected with the area around this city. The new and spiffy entry gallery featured photos and bronze plaques lauding the many famous achievers in the evolution of manned flight. Viewing the numerous tributes, I was shocked to note that there was no mention of Howard Hughes. After asking several museum board members about this omission, I was tartly informed that a long-standing dislike of Mr. Hughes by many senior citizens of San Diego had forced the board to veto him as an honoree in the gallery. This hostility had flamed when Mr. Hughes caused extended delays in the design approval of locally-based Convair's 660 and 880 commercial airliners. Mr. Hughes was the first 660 buyer, and the purchase contract gave him design approval rights, which he fully exercised. Because his arbitrary objections delayed the new aircraft's entry into service by at least a year, the aircraft failed to match competitive offerings by Boeing and Douglas, even though the resulting 660s and 880s were better performing aircraft. Their belated availability meant significant losses in market share and consequently a drastic reduction of the Convair workforce, which in turn caused venomous resentment throughout the city (Convair was the largest local employer), as well as the ire of stockholders worldwide.

This unfortunate set of events was certainly ample reason for a permanent distaste for the man, but like him or not, Howard Hughes had contributed far more to the progress of aviation than most of those cited in the museum. I sent the board a letter promising no future contributions from our company (we had already given large sums for the museum's initial establishment). A new portrait and bronze plaque soon appeared in the entry gallery. Amazing what it takes to influence important people!

60

PARADISE LOST

Debilitating pressures on GM in the 1990s came from two sources: the new government regulations requiring that liquid assets be maintained on the company's financial books at a much higher percentage of its employee retirement obligations and the necessity to fight harder for automobile market share. Huge amounts of new cash were needed, so GM's board decided to divest itself of several subsidiaries in saleable fragments, including Electronic Data Systems and Hughes Electronics.

Thus began the tragic dismemberment of our unique collection of creative talents. We were a family: sharing skills, spurring innovation, feeling a dedication to vital national missions, and harvesting the yield of an excellent business base. We were virtually a modern-day Camelot, with many Merlin magicians, fading into mere legend. The company had already been sold once, with few negative results; but we had emerged as an integral unit. This time the family would be dissolved and its members farmed out to other firms with very different objectives and management styles. Perhaps selling the segments separately resulted in more money for GM, but it was most unfortunate that this fragmentation occurred. Even the renowned Hughes name with its mystical aura would vanish. In many other mergers and acquisitions the titles of brand-name corporations were preserved: Chance Vought, Lockheed Martin, McDonnell Douglas, McKesson-Robbins, Northrop Grumman, Sears Roebuck. Why this was not done with at least the largest part of Hughes is an unknown.

61

WHAT COULD HAVE BEEN

Other difficulties for Hughes emerged in the 1990s in addition to an owner obsessed with selling the company: a defense market substantially in decline and many more competitors with the ability to create very advanced electronics. The question arises whether or not Hughes could have done better in coping with this altered market situation. Should or could the senior technology experts within the company have been more intuitive and assertive with their bosses to steer the firm along a path more appropriate than that which actually occurred? At least five years were available for progress along a different strategic and tactical route.

Milt Radant, the corporate vice president for technology in the first half of the 1990s, reminisced in 2010 on why the company reached such a dismal end. Perhaps these thoughts will help leaders of other high-technology companies facing radical changes that challenge their future existence.

"As the Cold War came to a close and defense budgets were slashed, we, like other companies, faced the issues of downsizing, merging with other companies, or somehow being favorably acquired. I became involved in many high-level studies of our company, its organizations, technology strengths, possible weaknesses, and what we should consider for the unpredictable future. We initiated a number of creative diversification projects; most were driven by our technological strengths.

"To provide focus, a new diversification office was established. Working with them, I helped plan the corporate expenditures to form new product bases; there were continual reviews and improvements of the many suggested projects. It soon appeared that our long list had to be cut back, with much higher funding levels placed on just a handful. The current CEO, Mal Currie, was very near retirement and suggested that the 'new guy' should make those choices.

"Our thinking about diversification was strictly technology driven, as it had always been at Hughes, and may not have been the best method to use as we approached a completely different business environment. The high-technology motivation was quite natural for us when we dealt with the government, but other than in satellites and a few industrial electronics products, the company lacked experience in successful commercial ventures. We usually considered the public consumer not an appropriate customer and several new tries in the consumer market ended unsuccessfully.

"While GM owned Hughes, it put some effort into fulfilling its public statements justifying the Hughes purchase: to extract technology for the automobile business. Several projects were started, and Hughes brains were picked to learn in depth our unmatched technology-driven system engineering expertise. This could have led to new commercial businesses for Hughes, but visionary leadership was lacking. The corporate heads were focused on financial control and restructuring issues. (Author's note: it is very likely that an unstated constraining directive by the GM Board was to defer any risks to avoid difficulties in a potential piecemeal divestment of its GM-H subsidiary.)

"One example is the power-converter chain for the EV-1 electric car. It did enjoy limited success, and I don't know how much of this technology has carried into the current GM electric car. This could have been a major consumer product for Hughes, building on one of our core technological strengths. Some products of GM's former subsidiary Delphi are traceable to our firm: the head-up display, radar collision avoidance sensor, infrared night imaging sensor, and OnStar navigation, but none of these led to new Hughes product lines, as they were not assigned to Hughes to manufacture.

"In 1992, a new CEO began to push a different agenda: to cut back, sell pieces, and merge segments with other companies. The guiding messages for the future were financial restraint and a focus on the commercial customer in only a few areas. There was little interest in exploiting our technology strengths and how to shape them to meet the future business situation. This surely did not feel like the old Hughes spirit! DirecTV seemed to be the one bright spot getting attention from the top; could other possibilities have benefited from high-level management attention? A good example of a lost opportunity was the development of a new landing-aid radar for the Boeing 777. Hughes corporate executives withdrew our active participation in this proposal even though it was known that Boeing considered us the top contender for this competition. The Hughes design approach was distinctly more elegant and higher performing than the others offered. Was this fine program really not suitable for the new GM goals for Hughes?

"In trying to continue our traditional technology-driven approach, I suggested several new thrusts which needed significant corporate funding. As a result, I was directed to spend the money first on a market study to determine what the potential new customers actually might want and to develop a business plan. In retrospect, this was a better approach; a change in emphasis to guide our investments into formerly unexplored markets. This thinking was quite different from going after government projects, where advanced technology was king. Unfortunately, there were no experienced helmsmen to help steer our way into this new marketplace with its multiplicity of customers.

"Nonetheless, I thought it was vital to thoroughly understand our core competencies that might best apply to these new markets. To this end, a large group of us focused on defining those skills: external experts gave us help, we visited similar electronics firms to find contrasts, and wrote descriptive papers. This effort was intended to find the best paths to move our company forward into the new world and still continue as a vibrant technology jewel. One of the best and shortest descriptions of our core competency was: 'We design, develop, and manufacture sophisticated electronic systems that contain advanced sensors, extensive information processing, and effective man-machine interaction devices.' A comprehensive list of competencies defined our many strengths.

"Surprisingly, the GM-directed senior corporate executives completely ignored this powerful tool! Perhaps there was a way to have pushed them harder to listen and take action, but regrettably, we old timers didn't succeed; Hughes might have effectively used this information base to reshape the company focus. We could have set up new business units, taken responsibility for high-tech subsystems for other firms' new products, or profitably licensed our technologies. It is unfortunate for the United States that GM allowed what happened: taking us apart instead of finding ways to salvage more of the company and progress into a new Hughes era.

"The lesson for today's corporations is how to sufficiently recognize a threatening change in its marketplace and quickly reshape the organization to match the future. We didn't really do this, and probably it was a functional failure by the entire cadre of experienced Hughes senior management. This history certainly speaks to a need for visionary leadership during critical times in the life of a corporation."

The really tragic loss to the company in the mid-1990s was that of management's ability to sustain the innate operating character of Hughes. Jim Uphold, a senior program manager in the Radar Systems Group, describes this fundamental character in this way:

"The Hughes Aircraft Company I knew was a large association of technical experts whose collective knowledge spanned everything in the physical sciences. They could analyze everything, design anything, and build the most complex systems that demonstrated superb performance. The best virtue of this aggregation, in my view, was the willingness of individuals to share what they knew and cooperate with one another to solve problems. Some observers characterize this behavior as being like that of a family; I think it is better stated as being team-like.

"There were very few situations when Hughes people weren't already experts in a needed technology because it was either too new or too classified. That is when a special team was formed to unravel the new challenge and reduce it to common practice. These were often the most attractive assignments of all because the team members became new technology pioneers. This was certainly the case for the development of stealthy radars for stealthy aircraft.

"Finally, we did our work as well as we could to keep our

promises to our customers. Hughes Aircraft Company was characterized by technical superiority, cooperative work practices, and technical and business integrity. Hughes was the best at what it did during its life and times and there hasn't been an equal since."

The author of this book adds to Milt's and Jim's wisdom: "I hope GM is listening!" I retired from Hughes before the dismemberment began, but I surely hope the automotive company has learned ways to improve its internal operations. It is also regrettable that a group of entrepreneurial Hughes senior staffers did not break away and start a new company, as Ramo and Wooldridge had done in 1953. In that case, they received unlimited financial backing by the US government to manage the emerging ICBM programs. Unfortunately, no such critical emergency demand appeared on the US horizon in the 1990s to spark another successful management revolt. Too bad!

62

DOOMSDAY
AND REMEMBRANCE

In 1997, OUR most formidable competitor, Raytheon, purchased the defense-related segments of Hughes from GM for $9.3 billion, this sector representing 70 percent of the Aircraft Company's annual revenue. In 2000, Boeing bought the spacecraft design and manufacturing unit for $3.7 billion, followed in 2003 by the commercial service DirecTV being sold to News Corporation for $6.6 billion.

It takes complex mathematical accounting to properly determine the financial benefits to GM from acquiring Hughes Aircraft Company, but the following is a reasonable guess of the capital growth rate of the $2.7 billion cash investment. The segment divested in 1997 had compounded at 14.5 percent annually; the 2000 portion had grown at 16 percent yearly; and the 2003 segment had compounded at 17 percent for eighteen years. Of course, this capital value growth was in addition to an aggregate of more than $15 billion in earnings. That was a pretty substantial reward for winning the auction in 1985!

The only remnant of Hughes Aircraft Company, originally chartered as an independent company subsidiary, is Hughes Network Systems, a provider of ground-based equipment to inter-tie satellite networks. For the moment, there is still a "Hughes" name on an electronics firm.

What a dismal ending to a golden life! Seldom has there been such a cluster of excellence. Fortunately, in the last few years there have been several other collections of uninhibited creative talent in the United States, such as Apple, Hewlett Packard, Intel, Microsoft, Texas Instruments, and Google, who continue to achieve breakthroughs in technology and high performance equipment and software. (It is quite likely that our purchasers Raytheon and Boeing now reflect the passion our firm once had. Due to security and proprietary regulations, I have not had an opportunity to examine their technology breakthroughs of the last twenty years, nor the agility with which any advances were done. In any case, I am most grateful to those corporations for providing historic data for the preparation of this book.) Most of the discoveries exploited in the new Information Age began in the closing part of aerospace's Golden Era. Perhaps the innovative Hughes philosophy has helped others reach beyond the state of the art in new fields to meet the world's changing needs. Hopefully, the Hughes soul has somehow been passed on to another generation that will push for rapid progress in making a better world.

1992 Brochure
(courtesy of UNLV)

63

PIONEERING
TECHNICAL ACHIEVEMENTS

AT THIS POINT in the story, it seems appropriate to reflect on the numerous technology achievements of the company. A number of these qualify as worldwide "first-time-ever" breakthroughs, but to avoid debate—like the one that still surrounds whether or not Alexander Graham Bell was the first inventor of the telephone—this listing omits such claims.

For many years the company carried more than 4,000 active patents; picking the highlights is difficult. In every case listed below, however, the company led the way in bringing the idea to practicality and became the principal supplier to almost all customers. The listing ignores chronology; rather, items are grouped into categories already familiar to readers of this book; the subjects, arranged alphabetically, include identifiable products, hardware and software components, fabrication processes, and examples of spectacular behavior of complex systems. All were made possible by the immense collection of skills within the Hughes family: analysts, circuit and hardware designers, software developers, technicians, testing experts, system engineers, program managers, and manufacturing professionals.

1. Computer Networking
    •   Command and control air defense networks with massive amounts of software designed for entire nations and navies, and with unlimited targeting capacity at extended ranges
    •   Real-time position locations of all troops and combat assets for field commanders
2. Computing and Signal Processing
    •   Airborne digital computers giving increasingly greater operating

speed and versatility

- Internal digital computers for submarine-launched ballistic missiles, performing navigation, targeting, and warhead control
- Digital signal processing for detailed analysis of signals from laser, infrared, and radar receivers
- Programmable signal processors with functions and performance easily modified with software, used in many types of military and civilian systems

3. Consumer Electronics
   - Digital watches, giving precise time information shown on a liquid crystal display
   - DirecTV system network providing direct satellite broadcast of TV signals to home subscribers
   - Hands-free cell phones using voice recognition technology
   - Automotive head-up display projecting speed and other instrument data overlaying the windshield, minimizing eye and head movement
   - Automotive radars to assist in speed control and collision avoidance
   - Infrared imaging sensors in automobiles, giving nighttime viewing on a look-through display overlaying the forward scene
   - OnStar navigation and emergency services for General Motors and other automobile manufacturers

4. Lasers and Optics
   - Operational lasers of numerous types, now used worldwide for military and civilian tasks
   - Q-switch technology for lasers, providing operational control and insertion of masses of digital information for communication
   - Laser rangefinders enabling accurate weapon attacks against hostile targets
   - Extremely precise and adaptive optics for visible and infrared sensors operating in the rigors of space, military combat equipment, and high-energy laser devices
   - Transmission of radar signals over optical fibers to permit new lightweight radar designs

5. Microelectronics
   - Thin-film process for fabricating multiple layers of dense high-speed interconnections for completion of microelectronic chips
   - Submicron lithography for shaping minute circuits in microelectronic chip sub-layers
   - Silicon-sapphire semiconductor circuits enabling resistance to nuclear radiation

- Ion-beam implantation to create microelectronic circuit elements by doping semiconductor alloys; the changed material characteristics yielded higher performance, reduction in size, and lower cost of the many elements embedded in the chips
- Self-aligned gate design permitting many more transistors on a microelectronic chip
- Complementary metal-oxide-semiconductor (CMOS) transistors for low power circuits
- Gallium arsenide (GaAs) alloys enabling fabrication of high speed, low noise transistors for RF power amplification, efficient solar cells, and charge-coupled devices
- Mercury-cadmium-telluride (HgCdTe) materials for making high sensitivity, long wavelength infrared detectors

6. Missile Guidance
- Proportional navigation control equations for missile steering that overcame the previous overcorrection of directional errors which had caused wobbling flight
- Antitank missile guidance by command-wire dispensed from spools within the flying missile
- Active radar within the missile for precise terminal guidance in air-to-air missiles
- Air-to-ground missiles with accurate guidance from a TV or infrared imaging system
- Multiple guided missiles simultaneously in flight after launch from a single fighter against as many as six widely spaced targets
- World's longest-range air-to-air missile shot, resulting in a direct hit from 120 miles away
- Torpedoes with wire-guided command, as well as semiactive midcourse and active terminal homing using sonar

7. Night Vision
- Infrared sensor arrays with many thousands of detector elements generating high-resolution imagery
- Serial-scan processing of infrared detector strings to greatly improve image formation
- Hand-held infrared imaging devices for police, firemen, miners, and building-insulation contractors

8. Operator Displays
- Multiple purpose storage display tubes for improved viewing in fighter aircraft
- Head-up display allowing pilots to view instrument data on a transparent screen superimposed on the real outside scene

- Sensor and weapon pointing by the pilot using crosshairs projected onto a transparent disc mounted to his helmet
- Liquid crystal light valve arrays for large display screens

9. Radars
- Lightweight traveling-wave tubes providing high transmitting power with precise frequency control and wide frequency bandwidth, now used in many devices for all forms of electronic communication, whether on land, at sea, in the air, or in space
- Frequency-scan and phase-scan radar antennas, providing beam positioning without physical movement of the hardware
- All-digital radars, yielding high performance and flexible operating mode selection
- Pulse-Doppler radars, providing velocity measurement and separation of target returns from unwanted background clutter
- Track-while-scan radars with the ability to continue search of broad areas while maintaining track of numerous dynamic targets
- Stealth radars virtually undetectable by hostile search radars or sniffer detection receivers
- High power radio frequency modules with precise phase control for advanced active-array antenna transmit/receive elements
- Machine tooling to rapidly fabricate precise microwave passageways in large radar planar arrays

10. Satellites and Spacecraft
- Geosynchronous orbiting satellites that appear at a fixed position in the sky when viewed from Earth
- International and national communication networks via geostationary satellites
- Spin-stabilization for effective and low cost satellite attitude control
- Sun sensors with unique processing for a satellite aspect control reference device
- Despun cores to enable very large satellites to remain spin-stabilized without tumbling
- Ion engines for spacecraft thrusters using electrical power from solar cells
- Soft-landing on the Moon with TV and scientific measurements of the soil transmitted to Earth
- Satellite relay transponders with multiplexed throughputs many times the capacity of previous systems, providing unlimited global communications in all electromagnetic frequency bands
- The Thematic Mapper and Multispectral Scanner instruments that made it possible to gather facts about the natural resources of the Earth from space

11. Strategic Defense
    - Comprehensive infrared surveillance from space of enormous land areas to detect any ICBM launch
    - IR detection and tracking from great distances of ICBM mid-course and terminal vehicles
    - Destructive intercept of ICBM terminal vehicles with a small, agile, and accurate IR-guided missile without using a warhead
    - High-energy laser weapon destruction of satellites, aircraft, helicopters, and in-flight missiles
12. Surface Weapon Fire Control
    - Artillery projectile detecting and tracking with computations allowing rapid and accurate counter-fire against a hostile battery
    - Tank weapon fire control functioning under any weather condition day or night, operating accurately even with the tank moving at 30 mph over rough terrain
13. Surveillance
    - High-resolution ground maps from aircraft covering large areas with real-time radar imagery
    - Long-range ship and aircraft surveillance systems using sophisticated electronic phased array antennas and Doppler signal processing
    - Multispectral scanning used in space to simultaneously provide comparative and interpretive images from visible, TV, laser, infrared, and microwave radars
    - Long-range undersea surveillance, location, and identification of submarines

64

NOSTALGIA NURTURED

Some of the nostalgia for the dramatic saga surrounding Howard Hughes and the Hughes Aircraft Company can still be savored. Although surrounded by newly constructed office and residential buildings, remains of the most important structures of the old Culver City facilities

Spruce Goose nest to become offices

Site where Hughes'
seaplane was built
is to be renovated

Roger Vincent

The decaying former headquarters of aviation giant Howard Hughes will be turned into an office campus for creative tenants as part of a $50-million makeover of the famous operation at Playa Vista.

The complex includes the enormous hangar where Hughes built his infamous Spruce Goose airplane but is now used mostly as a soundstage for movie and television production. The seven-story structure will be upgraded to contain multiple sound stages that could be used simultaneously, new owner Wayne Ratkovich said.

Ratkovich, a Los Angeles developer who specializes in renovating historic buildings, expects to complete a $32.4-million purchase of the former Hughes property Friday. His company, Ratkovich Co., and his fi-

WOODEN AIRPLANE: Howard Hughes' massive Spruce Goose is shown under construction in the Playa Vista hangar in the 1940s.

AEROSPACE

Plant's legacy extends across the globe, beyond

Hercules Campus Development Announcement, 2010
(courtesy of *Los Angeles Times*)

444

Hughes complex gets a $50-million redo

[Playa Vista, from B1] closure from a consortium of lenders led by KeyBank.

The property is occupied by 8 buildings, including the hangar, most of them from the years around World War II when Hughes operated his Hughes Aircraft Co. in the area south of what is now Marina del Rey. It was there that Hughes set out to build a seaplane capable of carrying 750 soldiers nonstop from Honolulu to Tokyo.

Among his many challenges was the fact that no plane that big had ever been built, and he couldn't use materials considered crucial to the war effort, such as aluminum. He decided to use wood and settled on birch, which made the popular nickname "Spruce Goose" irksome to him.

The plane, officially dubbed Hercules, had a 220-foot wingspan, weighed 200 tons and flew only once — for about one minute — in 1947.

The plane has been gone since then and now resides in a McMinnville, Ore., museum. But the vast redwood hangar where it was built is still in demand as a sound-stage and generates about $1.3 million a year in rent from filmmakers, Ratkovich said. Much of director James Cameron's 3-D epic "Avatar" was shot there.

In a nod to Hughes' storied seaplane, Ratkovich will call his new development the Hercules Campus. He plans to divide it into three smaller complexes connected by landscaping. Targeted tenants include media, entertainment and

'Wayne Ratkovich is well-known for his sensitive restoration of historic buildings … and we welcome him to the community.'

PATTI SINCLAIR,
Playa Vista co-president

Crews will immediately start cleaning up the site, Ratkovich said, and put new roofs on every building but the Spruce Goose hangar to make sure they are water-proof. Engineers will be tasked with making the buildings energy efficient.

"We hope to use fuel-cell technology and solar technology with the long-term goal that entire complex will be off the grid someday," Ratkovich said. "This site makes you want to reach, and we are going to reach."

The makeover will take up to three years to complete, he said, but may happen sooner if demand for the 225,000 square feet of office space is strong. Except for periodic use by film crews, the buildings are empty.

Offices at Playa Vista have periodically experienced high vacancy since the first new office building after the Hughes era was completed in 2002. Last

who represents Ratkovich.

"These [buildings] are unlike anything else on the market," he said. "They will have a low-rise campus feel with a historic preservation aspect."

The former Hughes properties are in roughly the middle of Playa Vista, a 464-acre planned community. The first phase of more than 3,200 homes is virtually complete, and the community has more than 6,500 residents, along with shops, parks, a fire station, a library and an elementary school under construction. Playa Vista has more than 1 million square feet of office space and has room for an additional 2.2 million square feet.

Other historic properties renovated by Ratkovich include the Oviatt and Fine Arts buildings and Wiltern Theater in Los Angeles and the Alex Theatre in Glendale. He also has made over the former C.F. Braun & Co. office campus in Alhambra and, most recently, a 30-story high-rise at 5900 Wilshire Blvd.

"We have become good students of some of the best engineering and construction techniques in restoring these buildings," he said.

"Wayne Ratkovich is well-known for his sensitive restoration of historic buildings in Los Angeles, and we welcome him to the community," said Patti Sinclair, co-president of Playa Vista.

Also expected to close Friday is the sale of 10 acres of Playa Vista to Dallas-based Lincoln Property Co.

HISTORIC SITE: The Playa Vista hangar where the Spruce Goose was built, as seen from one of several buildings in the former Hughes Aircraft Co. complex.

At Sela · Los Angeles Times

Plant at heart of aerospace empire

[Hughes, from B1] dream up technologies and then go on to develop them. We fed on one another," said D. Kenneth Richardson, a former Hughes president who is writing a book about the company, "Hughes After Howard."

The key to Hughes' success was attracting some of the nation's most talented young engineers and scientists. Richardson said. It was a tradition that was started in the early 1950s when the

force of 3,000 before co-founding a rival company in 1953 that would later become TRW Inc., which in 2002 was acquired by Century City-based Northrop Grumman Corp.

Hughes grew rapidly with the onset of the Korean War and then the Vietnam War. At the height of the Cold War, Hughes had more than 80,000 employees, most of them in California, making it the state's largest industrial employer.

longer manufacturing facilities in Southern California that bear the Hughes name, dozens of buildings are vestiges of the company's past. Boeing Co.'s sprawling 1-million-square-foot satellite manufacturing facility and Raytheon Co.'s 17-million-square-foot electronics enclave, both in El Segundo, were once pieces of the Hughes defense empire.

"It's a tragedy that the name of the company has been lost to history," said

Legacy's Global Reach
(courtesy of *Los Angeles Times*)

have been preserved and designated as a California State Historic Site.

Raleigh Studios now uses the huge "cargo building" hangar as a movie-making facility, but the unique wooden structure with its artistic redwood support columns and arches is still visible; its conference rooms are spiced with photographs of the flying boat being assembled and of Mr. Hughes at several historic moments. The cafeteria, fire station, flight test offices, and medical clinic remain on site. Most exciting are Buildings 1 and 2, separated by stately rows of sycamore trees, which are also protected by Historic Site rules. Senior administration and Air Force offices occupied these structures. The insides have been partially stripped, except for the Building 1 entry and the office used by Howard Hughes. Plans are underway by the Ratkovich Company of Los Angeles to preserve the historic exteriors while restoring and modernizing the interiors in most of the buildings, re-landscaping the surroundings, and leasing the space as office facilities. The campus will become a collective center of entertainment and creative arts activities. This revitalization, to be called the Hercules Campus, will ensure a most appropriate future to this legendary site. The Ratkovich Company has a fine reputation for bringing alive historic properties, with seven notable projects already completed in the Los Angeles region. President Wayne Ratkovich meaningfully explained the company's policy of blending the new with the old, ensuring and enriching a legendary heritage. Here is an excerpt from his 2011 speech at a Hercules Campus open house sponsored by the Los Angeles Conservancy: "We celebrate the remarkable achievements of the people of Hughes Aircraft Company. They were truly gifted and dedicated people whose stunning accomplishments protected our nation and changed our world for the better. We have every intention of sharing this remarkable history with the future occupants of our development to be known as the Hercules Campus. We will join them in celebrating the vision, the ambition, the daring, the inventiveness, the determination and the creativity that precedes all of us on this historic site and in the eleven buildings that comprise the Hercules Campus."

While wandering around the grounds today, one can visualize being welcomed by the effervescent receptionist Junior Strahl, proceeding to the second floor, and entering the mahogany-paneled office of Mr. Hughes, in which Air Force Secretary Talbot demanded that he be an active president or find someone else to do the job. That ultimatum resulted in HHMI and the freedom for the Aircraft Company to excel. (In 2010, the author was interviewed by Bill Hennigan of the *Los Angeles Times* in connection with a story about the planned redevelopment of the historic site. We sat on portable chairs surrounded by the remains of those same mahogany walls; that setting stirred memories of many meaningful past events!)

At the other end of Building 1, one can visualize Mr. Hyland vigorously protesting when an Air Force general demanded that he construct a much larger, more pretentious office in order to be considered a genuine top executive. (What nonsense!). Pat complied to keep our primary customer happy.

Most of the Hughes historic documents and artifacts are contained in the files of Raytheon, Boeing, and News Corporation (the current owners of major segments of the business), as well as some residuals at GM. These are not normally accessible to the public. Some company documents are resident in the Lied Library at the University of Nevada Las Vegas. These do convey a sense of wonder to those previously unfamiliar with our accomplishments. The director of the library, Peter Michel, stated in 2009:

> "This collection provides unique and comprehensive internal documentation of one of the United States' most influential engineering firms for half a century . . . with the greatest long-term impact on electronics engineering accom-

plishments. Remarkable developments in military electronics and worldwide communications networks still hold a primary place in American industrial and commercial progress. These archives form a significant historical record of the legacy of American icon Howard Hughes."

Building 1, 2010
(personal files)

Other records of Hughes Aircraft Company, including oral interviews of key company participants, form a portion of an extensive project sponsored by the Huntington Library in San Marino, California, and USC. This ongoing effort, led by Peter Westwick, will provide a meaningful and personalized archive of the aerospace industries that blossomed in California over the last one hundred years.

Building 1 Reception Lobby, 2011
(personal files)

Cafeteria Building, 2010
(personal files)

Cargo (Hangar) Building, 2010
(personal files)

Cargo Building with H-4 Wing, 1943
(courtesy of UNLV)

65

SUMMING UP

THE PUBLIC TODAY is familiar with the unusual life of Howard Hughes (most of it colored by sensational but inaccurate folklore), but most people have never heard of Hughes Aircraft Company and all it accomplished after Mr. Hughes faded away in the 1950s. Much of the work for the Department of Defense, CIA, and National Reconnaissance Office was shrouded in secrecy and still cannot be revealed after many years of active deployment. Many other products were housed within combat vehicles, such as fighter aircraft, ships, and tanks, with superb battlefield performance. Their brand-name manufacturers were publicly honored, with little recognition that Hughes systems were a major reason for the vehicles' combat excellence (providing the eyes, the ears, the brains, and the punch of the primary weapons). And millions of people benefit from the worldwide telephone and television communications that synchronous satellites provide, with no awareness of a connection to an Aircraft Company that didn't make airplanes, but had a spectacular history nevertheless.

Our family accomplished many miracles, bringing to the world increased security and a better quality of life. Yes, there was a Hughes after Howard—one that made an indelible imprint on world history. In spite of our undeserved demise, we should be remembered as an unusual enterprise with a noble mission that redefined many technology frontiers. The dynamic team that made all this possible should be mighty proud of what it did.

Figure 9.1. Hughes Aircraft Company Timeline

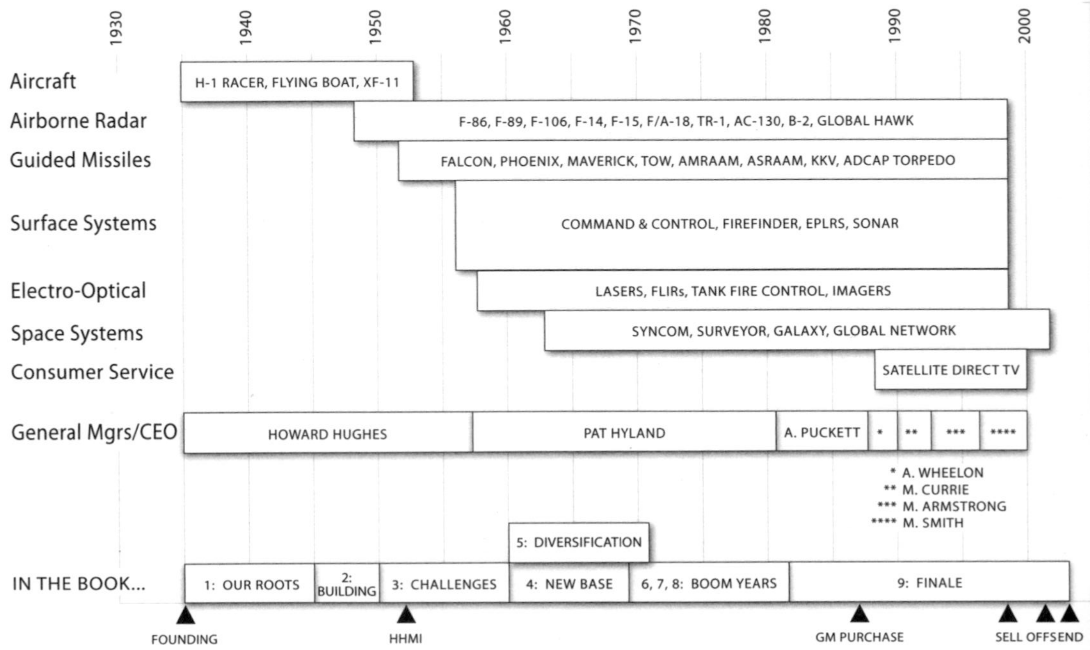

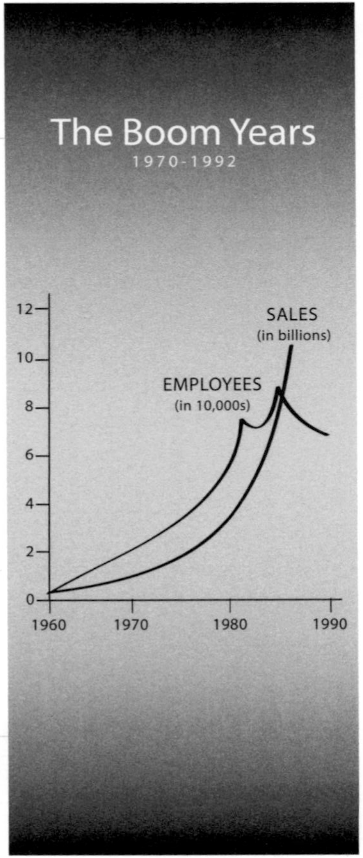

| Year labels | 1930 1940 1950 1960 1970 1980 1990 2000 |

Aircraft — H-1 RACER, FLYING BOAT, XF-11

Airborne Radar — F-86, F-89, F-106, F-14, F-15, F/A-18, TR-1, AC-130, B-2, GLOBAL HAWK

Guided Missiles — FALCON, PHOENIX, MAVERICK, TOW, AMRAAM, ASRAAM, KKV, ADCAP TORPEDO

Surface Systems — COMMAND & CONTROL, FIREFINDER, EPLRS, SONAR

Electro-Optical — LASERS, FLIRs, TANK FIRE CONTROL, IMAGERS

Space Systems — SYNCOM, SURVEYOR, GALAXY, GLOBAL NETWORK

Consumer Service — SATELLITE DIRECT TV

General Mgrs/CEO — HOWARD HUGHES | PAT HYLAND | A. PUCKETT | * | ** | *** | ****

* A. WHEELON
** M. CURRIE
*** M. ARMSTRONG
**** M. SMITH

IN THE BOOK...

FOUNDING ▶
1: OUR ROOTS
2: BUILDING
HHMI ▶
3: CHALLENGES
4: NEW BASE
5: DIVERSIFICATION
6, 7, 8: BOOM YEARS
GM PURCHASE ▶
9: FINALE
SELL OFFSEND ▶▶▶

The Boom Years
1970-1992

EMPLOYEES
(in 10,000s)

SALES
(in billions)

0 2 4 6 8 10 12

1960 1970 1980 1990

APPENDIX

THE HOWARD HUGHES
MEDICAL INSTITUTE

In 1926, Howard R. Hughes Jr. wrote a letter declaring that a large share of his assets should go to a corporation to be known as the Howard R. Hughes Medical Research Laboratory, whose objective was to be the prosecution of scientific research. Hughes was only twenty-one years old then, and such a letter was most unusual for such a young man.

His mother died when he was fifteen and his father when he was eighteen. However, he definitely was not typical. At the age of eighteen, he took control of the Hughes Tool Company after the death of his parents. His father had founded the firm, based on his invention and patenting of a unique drill bit, which was the first bit able to drill through hard rock—a revolutionary breakthrough for the oil industry that made possible the expansion of oil fields in Texas and worldwide and made Howard R. Hughes Sr. very wealthy.

What eventually flowed from the Tool Company, particularly the Hughes Aircraft Company, has been the topic of this book. But Howard Hughes Jr. had far-ranging ambitions beyond Tool Company affairs. By the time he was twenty, he had left Houston, Texas, for Hollywood to be involved in movie-making and aviation. His first major movie was *Hell's Angels,* a World War I based film in which Jean Harlow made her debut. Other films included *Scarface*, *The Front Page*, and *The Outlaw.*

His contributions to aviation were enormous: breaking new ground in aircraft design and setting short-course, transcontinental, and around-the-world speed records. The first two records were set in a plane that Hughes designed and built, the H-1.

It was his interest in aviation that indirectly rekindled his interest in medical research. In 1946, he was test flying the XF-11 photoreconnaissance prototype and a mechanical failure caused an almost fatal crash landing. His severe injuries required a long stay in the hospital. During his convalescence he and his physician, Dr. Verne Mason, a Professor at the University of Southern California Medical School, spoke often about medical research, leading to Howard's lifetime interest and support.

He began funding a number of outstanding young physician/research scientists from his personal bank account. In 1953, the Hughes Aircraft Company was spun off from the Tool Company conglomerate and given in toto to the newly-founded Howard Hughes Medical Institute (HHMI). Distinguished individuals setting up the Institute included, in addition to Dr. Mason, Drs. George Thorn from Harvard, Hugh Morgan from Vanderbilt, and Alan Gregg from the Rockefeller Foundation. The charter of HHMI reads: "The primary purpose and objective of the. . . . Institute shall be the promotion of human knowledge within the field of the basic sciences (principally the field of medical research and medical education) and the effective application thereof for the benefit of mankind." It is important to note that the words 'basic research' were inserted by Howard Hughes himself. He said he wanted the Institute to do fundamental research and "to probe the genesis of life itself." He thought that well-supported basic research would yield big dividends, even if not always immediately spectacular.

Although HHMI is a tax exempt private philanthropy, it is not a foundation; it is a medical research organization (MRO), which is governed by a special set of Internal Revenue Service (IRS) regulations. As an MRO, it must carry out research directly, with scientists (called investigators), who are not grantees but become employees of the Institute; they may also be members of the faculty of the institutions where they are based.

For the first three decades, the activities of HHMI were important but relatively modest in comparison to what was to come. HHMI's revenues were derived solely from dividends from the Hughes Aircraft Company. The Institute supported excellent research by outstanding scientists, but they were limited to investigators in relatively few medical schools and hospitals in the US. During most of this period HHMI pursued three areas of medical research: Genetics, Immunology, and Metabolic Regulation (now termed Cell Biology). In 1983, Neuroscience was added.

The modern history of HHMI began in 1984, when a new set of outstanding Trustees were appointed: Helen Copley, Chair of The Copley Press; Frank Gay of Summa Corporation; Dr. Donald Fredrickson, Director of the National Institutes of Health; James Gilliam Jr., Senior Vice President and General Counsel of Beneficial Corporation; Hanna Gray, President of the University of Chicago; William Lummis, Chairman of The Howard Hughes Corporation; Frank Petito, former Chairman of Morgan Stanley; Irving Shapiro, former Chairman of DuPont, and Dr. George Thorn, who was elected as chairman of the Board. Since then, other notables have served as Trustees, including former Secretary of State James Baker; Charlene Barshefsky, Senior International Partner, WilmerHale; Dr. Joseph Goldstein, Professor and Chairman, Department of Medical Genetics, University of Texas Southwestern Medical Center at Dallas; Garnett Keith, Chairman, SeaBridge Investment Advisors; Fred Lummis, Platform Partners, LLC; Paul Nurse, President, The Rockefeller University, President, Royal Society, London; Dame Alison Richard, former Vice Chancellor, the University of Cambridge; Clayton Rose, Professor of Management Practice, Harvard Business School; Kurt Schmoke, Dean of the Howard University Law School and former Mayor of Baltimore, and Anne Tatlock former Chairman and CEO, Fiduciary Trust Company International.

In 1984, the trustees were determined that HHMI should fulfill its potential as a great biomedical research organization. However, they faced a dilemma: all of the Institute's assets were in the Hughes Aircraft Company and the dividends from that source were insufficient for the expanded tasks. They made the historic and extraordinarily wise decision to sell the company. The company's purchase by General Motors in 1985, described earlier in this book, occurred most fortunately when the defense industry market was at its peak value. The resulting approximate $5 billion endowment, to be invested in a very diverse portfolio, now made HHMI the then largest private philanthropy in the United States. The Trustees then recruited an experienced and impressive team to lead HHMI in its expansion. Participants included Donald Fredrickson as president, Purnell Choppin Chief Scientific Officer (followed by his serving as president from 1987 through 1999; he was succeeded as Chief Scientific Officer in 1987 by Maxwell Cowan, formerly Provost of Washington University in St. Louis); George Cahill, former Professor of Medicine at Harvard Medical School as Vice President for Scientific Training and Development; Graham Harrison, former head of the United States Steel Pension Fund as Vice President and Chief Investment Officer; Robert White, former Assistant Treasurer of Ford Motor Company as Chief Financial Officer, and William T. Quillen, former Judge of the Chancery Court of Delaware as Vice President and General Counsel.

The rate of expansion was truly remarkable. In 1984, there were 54 HHMI investigators in eighteen institutions, and the annual budget was $36 million. By 1986 there were 132 investigators with an annual $230 million budget, of which $116 million was for construction of new research laboratories. Those funds allocated just to facility construction exceeded the Institute's total outlay for biomedical research in the preceding twenty-five years. By 2000, the number of investigators had grown to

330 located at more than seventy institutions, and the annual budget had reached $609 million; the endowment had grown to $13.4 billion. In 2010 there were 384 investigators at seventy-two institutions, an annual budget of $889 million, and the endowment was $14.8 billion.

An important decision in 1986 was to alter the method of selecting investigators. Previously, they were appointed only at a few chosen medical schools or hospitals that were allotted a limited number of slots to fill. The new procedure was to identify the most talented and productive researchers regardless of where they were located. Beginning in 1988, the selection of investigators was made through a series of nationwide competitions. The guiding principle of HHMI was, and still is, to support people rather than projects by finding the most talented and creative people showing the best potential to make important contributions. Those chosen are given the freedom and resources to follow their scientific noses.

In 1987, HHMI reached an historic agreement with the IRS to alter the scope of an MRO to allow expenditures beyond the then-current limitations, which constrained expenditures only to those performed by employees of the Institute at locations in conjunction with a hospital. The new ruling was that after HHMI had spent at least 3.5 percent of its endowment valuation in a given year on that class of investigators, it could make additional expenditures on other tasks related to biomedical research. Also, the relationship with a hospital could be scientific, rather than just geographic. In addition, after the Institute had expended at least 3.5 percent of its endowment annually in support of investigators who were employees, funds could be expended for other purposes related to biomedical research through a grants program, including science education, which had been included in its original charter. Dr. Joseph Perpich became the first leader for grants and special programs. Programs were created at every level of science education: elementary school, high school, college, graduate school, and postdoctoral fellowship. A large component in the college program was for outreach to high school students including those from minority groups. HHMI also supported precollege science education at natural history museums, aquariums, zoos, botanical gardens, and medical schools. The college undergraduate segment spent $30 million annually, and the total grant program reached $100 million. HHMI's programs for science education became the largest of any philanthropic institution.

Starting in Canada and Mexico, an international research scholar program was created to support outstanding scientists abroad, selected through a competitive grant process. This program rapidly expanded so that, by 1999, 177 researchers in nineteen countries had received grants. Meetings of these international schools have been held in Prague, Warsaw, Buenos Aires, Budapest, Rio de Janeiro, Moscow, Tallinn, and Lisbon.

In 1993, a new and beautiful headquarters complex and conference center was completed on 22 acres in Chevy Chase, Maryland. *The Architectural Digest* featured the complex in one of its issues and the *Washington Post* called it an "architectural miracle."

By 1999, six research areas were supported: Cell biology, Computational Biology, Genetics, Immunology, Neuroscience, and Structural Biology. Nobel Prize winner Dr. Thomas Cech succeeded Purnell Choppin as president in 2000, and HHMI continued to thrive and expand. Others in key roles during this period were Peter Bruns, David Clayton, Gerald Rubin, and Jack Dixon.

In the science education area a new program of HHMI Professors was established in which professors were appointed who were not only distinguished scientists but had a deep and active interest in undergraduate teaching. Their charge was to "take a fresh look at undergraduate science education and then share their best practices with each other and the broader community." Also a Gilliam Fellows program was created for minority college students, named for James H. Gilliam, one of the original Trustees who died in 2003.

Another spectacular venture began that year: the Janelia Farm Research Campus occupying 291 acres on the Potomac River in Virginia. In this $500 million, superbly equipped research center, in the words of Tom Cech, "physicists, computer scientists, chemists, and engineers can work side by side with the biologists and define the problems to be tackled." Highly functional laboratories, a large conference center, and housing facilities permit visiting guest scientists to work with the permanent HHMI investigators and staff. Dr. Gerald Rubin became its director, and in 2006, the breathtaking complex opened. Rubin stated a major challenge: "How does the brain process information? What new scientific tasks, including imaging technologies and computational methods, will be needed for image analysis?" The Janelia Farm Research Campus has flourished, with currently forty-five outstanding laboratory groups and an annual budget of $103 million.

The Institute has long supported research in infectious diseases, and in 2009 HHMI and the University of Kwazulu in Natal, South Africa, jointly established a comprehensive research center in Durban, constructing a $20 million building dedicated to research on HIV and tuberculosis. South Africa has the largest number of cases of HIV of any nation and one of the highest rates of tuberculosis in the world.

HHMI has committed $60 million in grants to sustain this important groundbreaking project.

In 2009, Robert Tjian became president, and the Institute embarked on another phase of its history which will no doubt be as exciting and productive as its past. By any standard, HHMI through its investigators and grants has been enormously successful in making great and highly original advances in basic and clinical biomedical research and education. To cite only one measure of these contributions, eighteen HHMI investigators have won the Nobel Prize. They and others have made major contributions to expanding human knowledge and improving human health that are too numerous to summarize. To learn more, visit the Institute's website at www.hhmi.org.

This brief account began with the indication that the initial revenue that made the HHMI possible was the invention of a three-headed bit for drilling oil wells. It seems fitting that an institution dedicated to exploration and innovation, and to creating revolutionary advances in biology, medicine, and science education, owes its foundation to a revolutionary invention.

Purnell W. Choppin
President Emeritus,
The Howard Hughes Medical Institute
March 2011

NOMENCLATURE

THROUGHOUT THIS BOOK many designators were used in descriptions of products, organizations, or design thrusts. Those chosen were the nomenclatures traditionally employed within the government and the aerospace industry; all are shown below for the reader's reference.

There are many ways to organize lists of aircraft, weapons, spacecraft, and types of technology. The many acronyms and familiar names are herein alphabetically sequenced within their particular subject category. The most commonly used designator is shown first, whether it is a name (example: Phalanx, Syncom, FreScan) or an official symbol (F-108, GEADGE, 407L).

AIRCRAFT

United States military aircraft are designated with one or two letters followed by numbers. The letters indicate primary mission and development status. Most commonly used are:

A = attack
B = bomber
C = cargo
E = electronic
F = fighter
H = helicopter
K = tanker
P = photo or pursuit
R = reconnaissance
S = surveillance
T = trainer
U = utility
X = experimental
Y = prototype

A-4 *Skyhawk* (Navy); Douglas

A-6 *Intruder* (Navy); Grumman

A6M *Zero* (Japan); Mitsubishi

A-10 *Thunderbolt II* "Warthog" (Air Force); Fairchild-Republic

A-26 *Invader* (Army); Douglas

AC-47 *Spooky*/"Puff the Magic Dragon" (Air Force); Douglas

AC-130 *Spectre/Spooky* (Air Force); Lockheed, Boeing

AH-1 *Cobra* helicopter (Army); Bell

AH-56 *Cheyenne* helicopter (Army); Bell

AN-225 transport aircraft (Soviet); Antonov

AV-8 *Harrier* (RAF, USMC); Hawker Siddely, McDonnell Douglas

B-1 *Lancer* (Air Force); North American

B-2 *Spirit* (Air Force;) Northrop-Grumman

B-17 *Flying Fortress* (Army); Boeing

B-25 *Mitchell* (Army); North American

B-26 *Marauder* (Army); Martin

B-29 *Superfortress* (Army); Boeing

B-47 *Stratojet* (Air Force); Boeing

B-52 *Stratofortress* (Air Force); Boeing

B-58 *Hustler* (Air Force); Convair

B-66 *Destroyer* (Air Force); Douglas

Blenheim bomber, first night fighter (RAF); Bristol

C-2 *Greyhound* (Navy); Grumman

E-3A *Sentry* AWACS (Air Force); Boeing

F3D *Skyknight* (Navy); Douglas

F3H-2 *Demon* (Navy); McDonnell

F-4 *Phantom* (Navy, Air Force); McDonnell

F-5 *Freedom Fighter* (Air Force); Northrop

F-8 *Crusader* (Navy); Chance-Vought

F-14 *Tomcat* (Navy); Grumman

F-15 *Eagle* (Air Force); McDonnell-Douglas

F-16 *Fighting Falcon* (Air Force); Lockheed

F/A-18 *Hornet* (Navy); McDonnell-Douglas

F-22 *Raptor* (Air Force); Lockheed-Martin

F-35 *Lightning II* (Air Force): Lockheed-Martin, Boeing

F-86 *Sabre* (Air Force); North American

F-89 *Scorpion* (Air Force); Northrop

F-94 *Starfighter* (Air Force); Lockheed

F-101 *Voodoo* (Air Force); McDonnell

F-102 *Delta Dagger* (Air Force); Convair

F-106 *Delta Dart* (Air Force); Convair

F-108 *Rapier* (Air Force); North American

F-111B *"Flying Edsel"* (Navy); General Dynamics

F-117 *Nighthawk* (Air Force); Lockheed

Fw 190 fighter (Luftwaffe); Focke-Wulf

H-1 *Racer* (Private); Hughes

H-4 *Hercules* (Army); Hughes

HK-4 (initial designator for the H-4)

JB-1 *Bat* flying wing bomber (Air Force); Northrop

KC-135 *Stratotanker* (Air Force); Boeing

L-18 *Lodestar* (Commercial); Lockheed

M-138 *China Clipper* flying boat (Commercial); Martin

MH-60R multimission helicopter (Navy); Sikorsky

MiG-15, 16, 21 fighters (Soviet); Mikoyan & Gurevicj

Model 76 *Voyager* (Private); Rutan Aircraft

MQ-1 *Predator* surveillance drone (Air Force); General Atomics

P-2 *Neptune* submarine search (Navy); Lockheed

P-3 *Orion* submarine search (Navy); Lockheed

P-47 *Thunderbolt* (Army); Republic

PBY *Catalina* seaplane (Navy): Consolidated

RQ-4 *Global Hawk* drone (Air Force); Northrop-Grumman

660 & 880 airliners (Commercial); Convair

S-7N *Viggen* fighter (Sweden); Saab

SR-71 *Blackbird* (Air Force); Lockheed

Su-27, 29 fighters (Soviet); Sukkhpi

TA-3 *Skywarrior* (Navy); Douglas

TA-4 *Skyhawk* (Navy); Douglas

TLS private aircraft (Commercial); Mooney

TR-1 radar reconnaissance version of U-2 (Air Force); Lockheed

Tu-95 *Bear* bomber (Soviet); Tupolev

201 private aircraft (Commercial); Mooney

U-2 *Dragon Lady* (Air Force); Lockheed

UH-1 *Iroquois/Huey* (Army); Bell

XF-11 photo-reconnaissance (Army); Hughes

XH-17 *Sky Crane* helicopter (Army); Hughes

YF-12 interceptor version of SR-71 (Air Force); Lockheed

AIRBORNE SYSTEMS

AI = First air intercept radar - British 1940

ALFS = airborne low frequency sonar

AOA = airborne optical adjunct

APG = piloted aircraft radar fire control

APG-33, 36, 37, 40, 51 = Hughes fighter radars of the 1950s

APG-63 & -70 = F-15 radars

APG-65 & -71 = F/A-18 radars

ARBS = angle rate bombing system (ASB-19)

ASARS = advanced synthetic aperture radar system

ASG = airborne special guidance

ASG-18 = F-108 and YF-12 fire control system

AWACS = airborne early warning system

AWG = piloted aircraft armament fire control system

AWG-9 = F-14 weapon control system

C-NITE = Optical, IR, laser target sight for helicopters

E-1 through E-10 = Hughes fighter radars later designated with APG numbers

FLAMMR = forward looking advanced multimode radar

FLIR = forward looking infrared

HMS = helmet mounted sight

INFANT = *Iroquois* night fighting night tracker

IRSTS = infrared search and track system

JSTARS = joint surveillance and target radar system

LASR = low altitude Soviet radar

MA-1 = fire control system for F-102 & F-106

MMRDSP = multimode radar digital signal processor

MG = missile guidance

MG-3, 10, 12, 13 = radars for several fighters in the late 1950s

M-65 = TOW launchers for helicopters

PINE = passive infrared night equipment

SAR = synthetic aperture radar

TARAN = radar for Swiss *Mirage* fighter

TRAM = target recognition and attack multisensor

TRIM = target recognition infrared multisensor

TSU = telescopic sight unit for helicopters

WEAPONS

AA-11 = Soviet short-range IR missile

AAM-A-2 = air to air missile (original designator for Falcon)

ADCAP = advanced capability torpedo

Agile = experimental IR air-to-air missile

AGM = air-to-ground missile

AGM-62 = Walleye guided bomb

AGM-65 = Maverick air-to-ground missile

AGM-130 = stealth cruise missile

AIM = air intercept missile

AIM-4 = Falcon air-to-air missile

AIM-7 = Sparrow air-to-air missile

AIM-9 = Sidewinder air-to-air missile

AIM-47 = Super Falcon air-to-air missile

AIM-54 = Phoenix air-to-air missile

AIM-120 = AMRAAM (advanced medium range air-to-air missile)

ASRAAM = advanced short range air-to-air missile

BQM = aerial target drones

Copperhead = laser guided cannon projectile (M-712)

Exocet = French antiship cruise missile

GAR = guided air-to-air rocket

GAR-1, 2, 4 = series of Falcon air-to-air missiles

GAR-9 = Super Falcon air-to-air missile

GAR-11 = nuclear warhead version of GAR-9

GBU = guided bomb unit

GBU-15 = TV guided bomb

Hawk = surface-to-air missile (MIM-23)

Hellfire = laser guided antitank weapon

ICBM = intercontinental ballistic missile

IRBM = intermediate range ballistic missile

JB-3 = Tiamat radar guided missile

KKV = kinetic kill vehicle

M-67 = Davy Crockett tactical nuclear weapon

Mk-46, 50 = lightweight torpedoes

Mk-48 = heavy torpedo (later upgraded to ADCAP)

Nike = surface-to-air missile

RAM = rolling airframe missile for ship defense

Redeye = surface-to-air IR missile (FIM-43)

Sea Sparrow = shipboard version of AIM-7

SLBM = submarine launched ballistic missile

SM-62 Snark = early cruise missile

SRM = British short range IR air-to-air missile

Standard Missile = shipboard air defense weapon (SM-3)

Tartar = Navy air defense missile

THAAD = terminal high altitude area defense anti-ICBM missile

Tomahawk = cruise missile (R/UGM-109)

TOW = Tube-launched Optically tracked Wire-guided antitank missile (BGM-71)

UGM = underwater-launched guided missile

UGM-27 = Polaris SLBM

UGM-73 = Poseidon SLBM
UGM-96, 96A = Trident I & II SLBMs
V-1 buzz bomb (German) = air-surface weapon

SURFACE AND SEA SYSTEMS

AAS (US) = advanced automation system for air traffic control
ACDS = advanced combat direction system
ADGE (multinational) = air defense ground environment
Aegis (Navy) = task force combat system
AEGIS (NATO) = airborne early warning environment integration
   system
ALFS (Navy) = airborne low frequency sonar
Alpha Class (Soviet) = advanced nuclear-powered submarine
ATC (multinational) = air traffic control networks
AWSHORAD (Army) = all weather short range air defense system
BQH-4 (Navy) = experimental submarine sonar towed array
BQQ-5, -6 (Navy) = submarine sonar towed array
CAATS (Canada) = air traffic control system
CVA (Navy) = designator for aircraft carrier
CWS (Navy) = close-in weapon system for ship defense (see Phalanx)
DD-297 *Fuller* (Navy) = destroyer in 1923
EPLRS (Army) = enhanced PLRS
FLORIDA (Switzerland) = air defense and management system
FLORAKO (Switzerland) = replacement for FLORIDA
407L (Air Force) = mobile air defense network
GEADGE (Germany) = air defense ground environment
GLLD (Army) = ground laser location designator
Guardian (Commercial) = modular ATC system
HADR (Army) = Hughes air defense radar
H-3118 = first of a series of Hughes computers for command- and-
   control systems and display consoles
IADS (Iceland) air defense system
IPD (Navy) = improved point defense radar for ships
JBADGE (Japan) = basic air defense ground environment
JTIDS (Air Force) = joint tactical information distribution system
LASR (Air Force) = low altitude surveillance radar
LFA (Navy) = low frequency active sonar transmitter
LHA (Navy) = amphibious aircraft carrier, mostly with helicopters
Link-11 (Navy) = communication link for NTDS
LTD (Army) = laser target designator
M1A1 (Army) = *Abrams* tank

M2/M3 (Army) = *Bradley Fighting Vehicle*
M27 (Army) = *Patton I* tank
M60A3 (Army) = *Patton II* tank
MIRACL (DoD) = mid-infrared advanced chemical laser
Mk-23 (Navy) = target acquisition system for IPD
MOPMS (Army) = modular pack mine system
MPQ-64 Sentinel (Army) air search radar
MPS (Army, Navy) = mission planning station
MSG-4 (Army) = mobile missile monitor air defense
NADGE (NATO) = air defense ground environment
NECCCIS = Northern Europe command communication control
    information system
NODLR (Army) = night observation device long range
NTDS (Navy) = naval tactical data system
OJ-452 (Navy) = one of a family of acoustic data display consoles
PEWS (Kuwait) = preliminary early warning system
Phalanx (Navy) = close-in ship defense gun (see CWS)
PLRS (Army) = position locating reporting system
PRC-104 (Army) = ManPack portable radio
ProScan (Commercial) = hand-held infrared imager
RealScene (Multinational) = 3-D computer images from surveillance
    photographs
SEALITE (Navy) = experimental high energy laser
SID (Navy) = standard information display
SLQ-32 (Navy) = electronic warfare suite
SPS (Navy) = surfaces ship radar search
SRS (Commercial) = stereo retrieval system
SSN-688 (Navy) = *Los Angeles* class submarine
SURTASS (Navy) = surveillance towed-array sensor system (UQQ-2)
SWATH (Navy) = small water plane area twin-hull ship
TAS (Navy) = target acquisition system
TPQ-36, 37 (Marines & Army) = FireFinder ground transportable
    radar anti-artillery systems
TSQ-51 (Army) = mobile missile monitor
TUBA (Navy) = submersible sonar towed array
UYQ-21 (Navy) = standard surface display system

SPACECRAFT AND SPACE SYSTEMS

AML = amplitude modulated link for cable TV
Apollo (NASA) = vehicle for human transit to Moon
Anik (Canada) = communications satellite system

DirecTV (Commercial) = satellite TV network serving consumers' homes

Early Bird (Comsat) = communication satellite follow-on to Syncom

Galaxy (Commercial) = fully integrated satellite communication network

Galileo (NASA) = orbiter and probe explored Jupiter

GMS (Japan) = geostationary meteorological satellite

GOES (NOAA) = geostationary operational environmental satellite

GPS = global positioning system

HS-367 (Commercial) = spin stabilized satellite with de-spun core

HS-601 (Commercial) = three-axis stabilized satellite

Hubble (NASA) = satellite-borne telescope

Intelsat = owner and service provider of global communication satellites

LEASAT (Navy) = communications satellite network operated under lease

MSC-46 (Army) = ground terminal for satellite communications net

MSS (NASA) = device for multispectral scanning of Earth resources

OnStar (Commercial) = automobile navigation system

OSO (NASA) = orbiting solar observatory

Palapa (Indonesia) = communications satellite network

Pioneer Venus (NASA) = orbiter and multiprobe explorer

Surveyor (NASA) = Moon probe that made first soft landing

Syncom (NASA) = first geosynchronous satellite

TACSAT (Air Force) = experimental reconnaissance satellite

Thematic Mapper (NASA) = satellite for observations of Earth

TECHNOLOGY TERMS

AESA = active electronic-scanned antenna

AM = amplitude modulation

Analog = measurement of varying signals by their magnitude and timing

Bandwidth = segment of electromagnetic frequencies

Bit = binary digit

Byte = eight bits

CIP = common integrated processor for radar signals

CORDS = coherent on receive detection system experiment

CRT = cathode ray tube

DBS = Doppler beam sharpening

DDSP = digital Doppler signal processing

Digital = numerical translation of signal characteristics

DIP = dual in-line microelectronic package

Doppler shift = signal frequency change due to relative speed of object and observer

DRS = IR detection and ranging system

DYCOMS = dynamic coherent measurement system for radar cross sections

ECCM = electronic counter-countermeasures

ENIAC = electronic numerical integrator and computer

EW = electronic warfare

FCS = fire control system

FPA = focal plane array (usually pertains to IR)

FM = frequency modulation

FreScan = frequency scanning antenna system

Geostationary = satellite orbiting at same rate as rotation of Earth

Geosynchronous = satellite orbits directly over the same spot on Earth

gHz = giga-Hertz: a frequency of 1 billion cycles per second

GPS = global positioning system

HF = high frequency radio waves

HgCdTe = mercury cadmium telluride IR detector material

HMS = helmet mounted sight

HUD = head-up display

Hz = Hertz; frequency in cycles per second

IFF = identification, friend or foe

IR = infrared

kHz = 1,000 cycles per second

kW = kilowatt; 1,000 watts of power

Laser = light amplification by stimulated emission of radiation

LCLV = liquid crystal light valve

LLTV = low light television

LO = low observable by radar and other sensors

LPIR = low probability of intercept radar

LSI = large scale integration of electronic circuit elements

Mach = measure of sound speed in air

MIMs = miniature inline modules for antennas

mHz = mega-Hertz; 1 million cycles per second

MMIC = monolithic microwave integrated circuit

MOPA = master oscillator power amplifier

MOPS = 1 million operations per second

MTI = moving target indicator

Multiplexing = many differing groups of information simultaneously carried in a single stream of data transmissions

Orbit = path traversed by an object rotating around a large mass

Pixel = singular spot on a display image; their quantity in a given area defines resolution

PPI = plan position indicator; a display format method

PRF = pulse repetition frequency

Pulse Doppler = radar pulses with frequency control for Doppler shift measurement

QEO = quadratic electrooptic effect for pulsing lasers

Radar = radio detection and ranging

RAM = radar absorptive material for coating surfaces

RATSCAT = radar target scatter test site

RCS = radar cross-section; a measure of the reflection of impinging radar beams

Sniffer = receiver to detect any electromagnetic radiation

Sonar = sound navigation and ranging

SRS = stereo retrieval system

TadIl-J = electronic communication coding format (Navy)

TDI = time delay integration

Thermal imaging = creating visual pictures from infrared emissions

TSU = telescopic sight unit

TWS = thermal weapon sight

TWS = track-while-scan radar processing

TWT = traveling wave tube amplifier

UHF = ultrahigh frequency radio waves

VHF = very high frequency radio waves

VLO = very low observables by radar

NATIONAL, MILITARY ORGANIZATIONS, AND OTHER TERMS

ACLU = American Civil Liberties Union

ADC = Air Defense Command (Air Force)

AEC = Atomic Energy Commission

Ames Research Center, Moffett Field, California; NASA scientific management

Area 51 = see Dreamland

Black = high security classification program

BMD = Ballistic missile defense

BMDA = Ballistic Missile Defense Agency (Army)

C&C = command and control

C3 = command, control, and communication

C4 = command, control, communication, and computers

C4ISR = command, control, communication, computers, intelligence, surveillance, and reconnaissance

Caltech = California Institute of Technology

Cargo building = double hangar in Hughes Culver City plant where H-4 *Hercules* was built

CEO = chief executive officer

CIA = Central Intelligence Agency

Comsat = government sponsored agency for US space communication

COD = carrier onboard delivery aircraft (Navy)

COO = chief operating officer

COTS = commercial off-the-shelf

CPFF = cost-plus-fixed-fee method of contracting

DARPA = Defense Advanced Research Projects Agency, a segment of DoD

Delco = electronics subsidiary of GM

DoD = Department of Defense

Dreamland = high security test area in Nevada

EDS = Electronic Data Systems, subsidiary of GM

FAA = Federal Aviation Agency

FAD = fleet air defense (Navy)

FBI = Federal Bureau of Investigation

FCC = Federal Communications Commission

FFP = firm-fixed-price method of contracting

GIB = guy-in-back; rear seat crew in fighters (Air Force)

GE = General Electric Company

GM = General Motors Corporation

GM-E = EDS common stock

GM-H = Hughes common stock

HAC = Hughes Aircraft Company

HHMI = Howard Hughes Medical Institute

Hughes Tool Company = Texas corporation controlling most of Howard Hughes industrial assets

Huntsville, Alabama = Army technology development center

Intelsat = consortium of companies for global satellite communication networks

IPG = international planning group (Europe)

IR&D = (internally funded) research and development

IRS = Internal Revenue Service

ITSO = International Telecommunications Satellite Organization

Johnsville Center, Pennsylvania = manages electronics programs (Navy)

JPL = Jet Propulsion Laboratories, Pasadena, California

JTF = Joint Task Force: cooperative effort by several military services to

achieve a single mission
KGB = Soviet intelligence agency
LAX = Los Angeles International airport
LTIP = long-term incentive compensation plan (Hughes)
MIT = Massachusetts Institute of Technology
NAS = Naval Air Station
NASA = National Aeronautics and Space Administration
NATO = North Atlantic Treaty Organization
NavAir = center for managing air programs (Navy)
NOAA = National Oceanic and Atmospheric Administration
NORAD = North American Air Defense
NRO = National Reconnaissance Organization
PanAmSat = pan-American satellite organization
R&D = research and development projects
RFP = request for proposal
RIO = radar intercept officer in fighters (Navy)
SAC = Strategic Air Command (Air Force)
SALT = Strategic Arms Limitation Talks
SAR = special access required; a national security classification
SBS = Satellite Business Systems
SDI = Strategic Defense Initiative
SDIO = Strategic Defense Initiative Office
SEI = Software Engineering Institute (US)
SEATO = Southeast Asia Treaty Organization
Skunk Works = Lockheed special projects facilities
TAC = Tactical Air Command (Air Force)
TI = Texas Instruments Corporation
ToolCo = Hughes Tool Company
TWA = Trans World Airlines
UCLA = University of California, Los Angeles
UN = United Nations organization
UNLV = University of Nevada, Las Vegas
US = United States of America
USA = US Army
USAF = US Air Force
USC = University of Southern California
USSR = Union of Soviet Socialist Republics
VP = vice president
Warsaw Pact = assembly of Eastern Block nations dominated by Soviets
WCO = weapon control officer in fighters (Navy)
WSO = weapon system operator in fighters (Navy)
Wright Field, Dayton, Ohio; manages air technology (Air Force)

BIBLIOGRAPHY

Bɪᴛꜱ ᴏꜰ ɪɴꜰᴏʀᴍᴀᴛɪᴏɴ were gleaned from some of the following publications, and have been cited where they were used. The contents of others listed below provide expanded details of many issues and events relevant to the topics of this book.

Aviation Week & Space Technology Magazine. Several issues, especially in the years between 1970 and 1985.

Barlett, Donald L. and James B. Steele. *Howard Hughes: His Life and Madness.* New York: W.W. Norton, 2004.

Berlin, Irving. *Annie Get Your Gun.* 1946.

Berry, F. Clifton Jr. *Inventing the Future: How Science and Technology Transform Our World.* New York: Brassey's/Macmillan, 1993.

Clausewitz, Carl von. *On War.* Berlin: Dümmler Verlag, 1832.

Collier, Peter and David Horowitz. *The Fords: An American Epic.* New York: Summit Books, 1987.

Fortune Magazine. April 1968 issue cover.

Gavaghan, Helen. *Something New Under the Sun: Satellites and the Beginning of Space.* New York: Springer-Verlag, 1998.

Gladwell, Malcolm. *Outliers: The Story of Success.* New York: Little, Brown and Company, 2008.

Grier, William H. and Price M. Cobbs. *Black Rage.* Eugene, OR: Wipf and Stock, 2000.

Gugliatta, Guy, "Spin Doctors," *Air and Space* Magazine, September 2009.

Hughes Aircraft Company. *At the Forefront of Technology.* Culver City, CA, 1986.

———. *Hughes Space & Communications, A Perspective.* Los Angeles: Hughes Aircraft Company,1982.

———. *The Chairman's Program,* Culver City, CA, 1990.

———. *This Is Hughes.* Culver City, CA, 1985.

HughesNews. Hughes Aircraft Company: Culver City CA. Various issues.

Hyland, L.A. (edited by W. A. Schoneberger). *Call Me Pat: The Autobiography of the Man Howard Hughes Chose to Lead Hughes Aircraft Company*. Virginia Beach, VA: The Donning Company, 1993.

Isaacson, Walter. *Einstein, His Life and Universe*. New York: Simon and Schuster, 2007.

Los Angeles Times articles by Ralph Vartabedian, 1981; Roger Vincent, 2010; and W. J. Hennigan, 2010.

Marrett, George J. *Tasting Death: Hughes Aircraft Test Pilots and Cold War Weaponry*. Westport, CT: Praeger Security International, 2006.

McVey, Bruce. *Airborne Weapon Control Systems History*. Culver City, CA: Hughes Aircraft Company, 1978.

Pond, Norman H. *The Tube Guys*. West Plains, MO: Russ Cochran Publishing, 2008.

Potocnic, Herman. *The Problem of Space Travel, The Rocket Motor*. Berlin: Richard Carl Schmidt & Company, 1929.

Ramo, Simon. *The Business of Science: Winning and Losing in the High-Tech Age*. New York: Hill & Wang, 1988.

Real, Jack G. with Bill Yenne. *The Asylum of Howard Hughes*. Bloomington, IN: Xlibris, 2003.

Rich, Ben R. and Leo Janos. *Skunk Works*. New York: Little Brown & Co., 1994.

Richelson, Jeffrey T. *Wizards of Langley*. Boulder, CO: Westview Press, 2001.

Smith, G. F. "The Early Laser Years at Hughes Aircraft Company." In *IEEE Journal of Quantum Electronics*, Vol. 20, No. 6, June 1984.

Stimson, G. W. *Introduction to Airborne Radar*. Culver City, CA: Hughes Aircraft Company, 1983.

Time Magazine, April 29, 1957 issue cover.

Walker, Scott. *As I Remember: A Walk Through My Days at Hughes Aircraft 1961-1997*. Carmel, IN: Hawthorne Publishing, 2010.

Wikipedia Internet-based encyclopedia.

ABOUT THE AUTHOR

Ken Richardson, raised in Hawaii, began at Hughes Aircraft Company as a radar design engineer, and in forty years of service, rose to become president of its Missile Systems Group and then corporate president and chief operating officer. This team of more than 80,000 employees created products at the forefront in every field of electronics technologies.

Ken received degrees with honors in engineering and business administration from Tufts University, USC, and UCLA. In the early 1990s, each of these institutions, as well as the Los Angeles Unified School District, selected him for its annual award for leadership excellence. He has served as trustee on the boards of six large nonprofit organizations.

An active life included raising two sons, sailing, scuba diving, golfing, backpacking, earning a private pilot license, hands-on flights in many military aircraft, and visits to one hundred nations. After retiring in 1991, he now resides with his wife, Charlotte, in Santa Barbara, California, and enjoys activities with four grandchildren.